Content Evaluation of Textual CD-ROM and Web Databases

Database Searching Series

Carol Tenopir, Series Editor

Cases in Online Search Strategy. By Bruce Shuman.

Online Retrieval: A Dialogue of Theory and Practice. Second edition. By Geraldene Walker and Joseph Janes.

Content Evaluation of Textual CD-ROM and Web Databases. By Péter Jacsó.

Content Evaluation of Textual CD-ROM and Web Databases

Péter Jacsó

Chair of the Library and Information Science Program of the Information and
Computer Sciences Department, University of Hawaii

Editor: Carol Tenopir

2001
Libraries Unlimited
A Division of Greenwood Publishing Group, Inc.
Englewood, Colorado

Dedicated to my sons, Daniel and Adam, who make me a proud father.

LIBRARIES UNLIMITED
A Division of Greenwood Publishing Group, Inc.
P.O. Box 6633
Englewood, CO 80155-6633
1-800-237-6124
www.lu.com

Library of Congress Cataloging-in-Publication Data

Jacsó, Péter
    Content evaluation of textual CD-ROM and Web databases / Péter Jacsó ; editor, Carol Tenopir.
      p. cm. -- (Database searching series)
    Includes bibliographical references and index.
    ISBN 1-56308-737-5
      1. Databases--Evaluation. 2. Web databases--Evaluation. I. Tenopir, Carol. II. Title.
III. Database searching series (Unnumbered)

ZA4450 .J34 2001
005.74--dc21

                                                   2001038299

Contents

Illustrations

Acknowledgments

I am grateful to Carol Tenopir, who not only encouraged me to write this book, but once again was also willing to edit my writing. She has provided many important comments and suggestions, and her support and nudging throughout the project that dragged on for three years was very valuable.

Rich Lane is thanked for relentlessly shepherding this book through the editing process, and Joan Torkildson for copyediting the manuscript and saving me from inaccuracies and inconsistencies that I criticize in databases. Susan Johnson's help in fact checking was invaluable. Any errors that may have remained are solely my responsibility.

I much appreciate the support of Tom Hogan, president of *Information Today*, who put me on the map by providing me regular space to write columns in his newspaper and magazines, and to offer workshops dealing with database quality at the National Online Meeting since 1990. I much respect him for not even trying to censor me, even when I criticized repeatedly a database that he acquired. He is not only an astute businessman, but is also a much respected gentleman.

I also thank all the former and current editors of my columns in *Information Today*, *Computers in Libraries*, *Database*, *Online & CD-ROM Review*, and *Online Information Review*, especially those who took the lion's share of editing most of my columns: Paula Hane, Marydee Ojala, David Hoffman, and John Eichorn. The Gale Group is thanked for offering me Web space and editorial support for my monthly reviews of digital reference resources. These writings helped me to stay focused on these important issues.

While writing the book, I thought with great pleasure of the best of my students, especially those who shared my interest in database evaluation: Lois Kiehl, Susan Johnson, Rich Gazan, Pam Cahn, Jennifer Winter, Marcia Kemble, Kimberley Scott, Justin Goo, Beth Tillinghast, Jennifer Jackson, Jessica Gehle, Nancy Kleban, Ellen Peterson, Evangeline Alexander, and Marilyn Reppun. They kept me on my toes through their smart and thought-provoking questions and comments, and were inspirationally active in my courses, workshops, and brown-bag seminars, discussing database quality and evaluation issues.

Don Hawkins, editor-in-chief of, and former senior technical editor to Information Science Abstracts (ISA) is acknowledged. His numerous editorials on the Web site of ISA, and his writings in traditional publications about the perceptions and misperceptions about a specific database, motivated me in writing this book. His position about quality issues from the file producer's perspective often differ from — and thus complement — my opinion from the user's side.

Thanks simply don't do justice when it comes to giving credit for the extraordinary support of my wife, Judit Tiszai. She has been an awesome partner in every phase of this project, from doing online and offline research, to making illustrations based on the analysis of the results, and to the more mundane tasks of managing the manuscript and compiling the bibliography. More important, she remained an awesome partner in the rest of our lives in spite of all the trials and tribulations that come with such a project.

Introduction

Database has become a household term in the past decade. In the United States and other highly developed countries, homemakers and homebodies, cashiers and car mechanics, music teachers and psychologists, high school dropouts and homeless people use databases. Every university and college student and most elementary and high school students use several databases during the course of their studies. Employees in many businesses are expected to be familiar with some databases. Others are required to explore new databases that can help them and their co-workers to be more efficient.

Of course, all of this is made possible by the Internet and the many high-quality free databases on the Web. Excellent and poor databases alike appear on the Web like mushrooms after rain because of the relative ease of publishing on the Web. Proportionally, however, there have been as many poor products among the traditional fee-based online and CD-ROM databases as there are among those that were born on the Web. (I refer here to the hundreds of searchable Web-born databases, not the mere Web sites.)

An exploding number of end-users (library patrons, researchers, and home users) need to know the limitations, strengths, and weaknesses of the databases they use. This book is primarily for those who advise end-users in selecting the databases most appropriate for them: librarians and information specialists in school, college, public, and special libraries; and those who critique and review databases, or compile database guides and directories for end-users (or do all of these things).

Libraries remain the center of guidance for information, even if not of the information collections themselves. Librarians and information specialists remain the most trustworthy and competent sources for finding the most appropriate information to satisfy the information needs of end-users, whether using a fee-based or a free service.

These days you will find database "reviews" in all kinds of magazines, from *Better Homes and Gardens* to *Horses and Hounds* to *PC Magazine*. Often, these are merely rephrased quotes from publishers' blurbs. Many Web users feel the urge to compile and publish top lists of databases without knowing the basics of database evaluation. Some librarians and information specialists, who have never published reviews of reference sources before, feel compelled to share their less than insightful opinions about Web-born databases.

It is no accident that the best reviews come from persons who have learned their trade in the printed world. Jim Rettig, Cheryl LaGuardia, Mary Ellen Bates, Reva Basch, Marydee Ojala, Barbara Quint, Ken Kister, and Ken Black are a few of the best reviewers. There is a reason that library and information science periodicals, such as *Database, Online, Information Today, Choice, Reference Book Bulletin,* and *Library Journal* are the best sources for database reviews. It is not surprising that librarians helped create the most useful Web directories and guides, such as SignPost, Librarian's Index and the Internet, BUBL, and INFOMINE, which stand out in the crowd.

This book is intended for librarians, information specialists, and database reviewers to provide a systematic approach to the set of criteria that can be used for evaluating the content of databases. The software and hardware aspects of database access are not covered here, although they certainly play an important role in how efficiently one can find information.

The content characteristics of databases are described and explained. Positive and negative examples are used to illustrate the major traits of databases. Databases used by information specialists were an obvious choice for illustrations. Many of the other databases chosen for illustration are widely popular and offer themselves for examples that can be understood by people without special training in the subject field. Some of the databases were chosen because they illustrate the deficiencies extraordinarily well. This sample group represents various categories of databases (directories, indexing, abstracting, and full-text databases). The following databases are used the most often. Others may be mentioned only once or twice, when they illustrate a particular criterion very well.

Database	Content Provider
Library and Information Science Abstracts (LISA)	G. K. Saur
Information Science Abstracts (ISA)	Information Today
Library Literature (LibLit)	H. W. Wilson
Internet & Personal Computing Abstracts (IPCA)	Information Today
Social Science Search (Social SciSearch)	Institute for Scientific Information
Psychological Abstracts (PsycINFO)	American Psychological Association
Mental Health Abstracts (MHA)	IFI/Plenum
Ulrich's International Periodicals Directory (Ulrich's)	R. R. Bowker
The Serials Directory (TSD)	EBSCO
ISSN Online International Serials	Data System
Gale's Directory of Databases	Gale Corporation
World Databases	G. K. Saur
Bowker's Complete Video Directory (BCVD)	R. R. Bowker

Names of companies and databases keep changing. Just in the course of writing this book, UMI dropped the spelled-out version of its name (University Microfilm International), put up the name of its parent company with a qualifier Bell & Howell Learning and Information, then as the book went to press, changed to ProQuest, after the name of its powerful information retrieval system.

Mergers, acquisitions, and joint publications also cause headaches. The R. R. Bowker company that was acquired by Elsevier before I started to write the book had several ready-reference databases under its own imprint, then published databases jointly with G. K. Saur under the Bowker-Saur imprint, then parted from the German company as I was finishing the book, and by the time you read this, the company, or at least many of its digital assets, may be sold by Elsevier to one or more buyers.

The names of some of the file producers, databases, and companies will have changed by the time this book is published. Following are the most important changes that I am aware of:

From	To
University Microfilm International (UMI)	Bell & Howell Information and Learning*
Information Access Company (IAC)	(part of the) Gale Group
Library Literature & Information Science Full Text (LibLit)	Library Literature

---

*In June 2001 again changed its name to ProQuest, using the name of its popular software.

Information systems identify a database by a variety of database (file) numbers or acronyms. In such situations, an explanatory description, such as "the DIALOG version of Ulrich's" or "Bowker's CD-ROM version of Ulrich's," is used instead of file 480, or Ulrich's Plus on Disc. In other cases, when only one version of a database is used for illustration throughout the book, the name as it appears on the online system is used, such as Social SciSearch for the DIALOG version of the ISI citation database. Graphs may have shorter acronyms for space reasons (such as SocSCI), but the related narrative text will use the preferred longer name format. In the case of search screen shots, the names or codes used by the host system will appear, such as file 7 for Social SciSearch. Again, the surrounding text will provide adequate clues.

Many of the tests for evaluating database content characteristics are software-dependent. DIALOG provides the most and by far the best possibilities for testing and is used the most often in this book. It is also the most widely used service by schools of library and information studies. However, examples are shown also from other implementations of the databases, including the online and CD-ROM search software of Ovid, SilverPlatter, Bell & Howell Information and Learning, H. W. Wilson, and several others (mostly designed for Web implementations) that are uniquely developed for a particular database by the original content provider, such as Barnes & Noble, Amazon.com, or the All Movie Guide. (Only the URL of free Web databases will be given in the text, and only when a specific example may make it necessary for the reader to consult the site or a specific page of the site. The sites are easy to find by their names cited here, using the various Web directories.)

You may not have the time, resources, or interest to evaluate databases by all the criteria discussed in this book. Some criteria may not apply to the database in which you are interested. Nevertheless, these criteria will be helpful in creating a checklist of questions to ask the database publishers, especially in the case of the fee-based services, when you are entitled to get detailed answers to such questions as the pattern of coverage of purportedly core journals, the time lag between the publishing of primary documents and the availability of their records in a database, or the availability of specific data elements, such as document type or LC classification number across the entire database.

The content of databases keeps changing, mostly for the better, although there are exceptions. Information Science Abstracts was taken over in 1998 by Information Today. Although it has been improving in some respects, it does not come close in quality (as was expected) to Internet & Personal Computing Abstracts (IPCA), formerly known as Microcomputer Abstracts, the flagship database of Information Today.

Although records added since 1998 are of better quality (certainly the ones "handed down" by IPCA), the database added half as many records a year as before and dropped essential information science journals or reduced their coverage to a bare minimum, as illustrated in chapters 4 and 5 about database dimensions and database source coverage. Other database publishers may have solved some of the problems discussed in this book. In your evaluation you will need to examine the then-current version of the databases. Unless noted otherwise, the tests for this book were done between July 1999 and November 2000, with some of them being run again in July 2001 when reading the galley proofs of the book.

I have provided consulting services for several of the companies mentioned in this book, and I am a columnist for *Information Today,* and the Gale Group, which are, in turn, producers of files and in some cases also publishers of databases. I made all efforts to not let this fact influence my judgment about the quality of their databases.

Database Products, Producers, and Publishers

It is helpful to start this book with explaining terms that are used throughout the text. Some of them are in common use, but readers may have different interpretations of them. Others may have special meaning and require definition and explanation to remove ambiguity. It is also important to see clearly the distinction between the methods and the media of database delivery.

A *database* is the result of a chain of intellectual and technical processes. Various organizations and individuals are involved in these processes. Occasionally, a database is the result of an enthusiastic and competent individual (as was the case with the splendid Encyclopaedia of the Orient), or of a small group of people (as was the case with the masterpiece product, the Internet Movie Database). Often, databases may be bought out by larger corporations that adapt and integrate the databases in their stable. From the perspective of this book, the best way to define the most essential terms related to databases is to follow through the process and introduce the agents and the products from the initial to the interim to the final phases.

The process starts with the production of a computer-readable file, which is called the *datafile*. For decades the datafile has been the source that allows the computer to generate a printed version of indexing and abstracting publications, full-text journals and newspapers, and dictionaries and encyclopedias. The datafile is usually on magnetic tape. To make a database from the datafile, index files must be generated, the datafile may need to be restructured, and search software must be added to the datafile. Typically, datafile producers license the datafile for third parties to make a database of the datafile's contents; hence, the common name *content providers*. In the literature, datafile producers are also known as *database producers*.

The licensees process the datafiles for publishing on CD-ROM or online. They become the publishers of the database. The database publishers may develop their own indexing and search software or license it from a software developer.

Some database publishers (also known as *online vendors* or *online service providers*), such as DIALOG, license content from hundreds of content providers. Some datafiles, such as Pediatric Renal Diseases, are licensed to a single database publisher; others, such as MEDLINE, are licensed to dozens of database publishers. Increasingly, the file producers also publish databases from their own datafile(s). H. W. Wilson and Bell & Howell are examples of companies that widely license their datafiles for third parties and also publish them on their own Web sites.

DATAFILES AND THEIR PRODUCERS

The datafile producers select, collect, organize, and record information about books, articles, conference papers, dissertations, companies, people, products, services, and so on. The datafile producers arrange the recorded data in some structure and usually add information that is not available directly from the source. This information enhances the value of the datafile by adding elements such as classification codes, subject headings, abstracts, or a combination of these. In our sample group, the American Psychological Association (APA), used to be only a datafile producer that provided the content for third parties to publish various versions of *Psychological Abstracts,* the classic printed abstracting and indexing source. (In 1999 the APA also became a database publisher, creating its own database version, PsycINFO Direct, which has a free subset for demonstration purposes at *http://www.psycinfo.com/demo.) Content provider* is a narrower term than *file producer,* as the content provider may not produce a computer-readable file but just licenses the content, such as a print guidebook, "as is" to third parties.

From the other side of the table, some of the datafile producers get the license to process and convert existing printed sources of others into a datafile. For example, Microsoft licensed the content of the *Zagat Restaurant Guide* and created a database of it on its Sidewalk site (*http://www.sidewalk.com*) that it sold later to Ticketmaster which folded it into Citysearch. Zagat was the content provider, or file producer (if it provided the content to Microsoft as a file), and Microsoft was the database publisher. Zagat later also became a database publisher after publishing its own content on the Web, available at *http://www.zagat.com.*

In the context of this book, a datafile always refers to an information collection in computer-readable format. The datafile may be purely textual (such as a bibliographic datafile), textual-numeric (such as a company directory that has descriptive and financial information), or predominantly numeric (such as a statistical datafile). The datafile may include graphics, still and moving images, and sound and video clips in addition to text, as is the case with all of the general interest multimedia encyclopedias. The datafile may be a facsimile collection of original documents, such as the set of forms used by the Internal Revenue Service (IRS). The facsimile content can be significantly enhanced in the database creation process, as in the International Women's Periodicals file or in the entire ProQuest database family, by creating index entries for the entire text.

Datafile producers offer for licensing the entire content or a subset of it. For example, the National Library of Medicine offers licenses to different subsets of the MEDLINE file. Subsets may be created by language, time period, or type of sources. For example, the core MEDLINE database includes only records from the journals that appeared on the Brandon-Hill list of most essential medical journals. The list is available at *http://www.nnlm.nlm.nih.gov/psr/outreach/branhill.html.* EBSCO has an English MEDLINE that includes only the English language subset of the source base. Others may license only the past few years of MEDLINE, not the entire database, which goes back to 1966.

In another example, the Education Resources Information Center (ERIC) datafile is licensed by some in its entirety, including records for both the journal and the report subsets along with the full text of ERIC Digests. Others may license only the journal subset. The ClinPsyc subset of the Psychological Abstracts datafile includes only records for articles that discuss clinical practice. Bowker licenses the Books in Print records with or without reviews. A third version includes only records for books that are out of print. The name of the database as implemented may not reflect these differences. DIALOG, for example, uses the name Books in Print, even though its version includes almost a million records for books out of print and tens of thousands of book reviews.

More and more datafile producers choose also to publish their own content on the Web. These are often the best implementations, as the file producers know their content best, and using the appropriate software can bring out the best of the file. Online service providers need to implement databases with a view to consistent interface, search template, and output formats that would work with dozens and occasionally hundreds of databases. File producers who publish only a few databases on the Web can custom-make them without the constraints of conforming to an existing design framework that a large online information service must impose on its databases.

For example, Responsive Database Services (RDS) has the best implementation of its four datafiles that have been licensed to a number of database publishers and information service providers. The free ERIC version produced by the Assessment and Evaluation Clearinghouse of ERIC (*http://www.ericae. net*) is incomparably better than the fee-based CARL version of ERIC. Zagat's own version of its Restaurant Guide database (*http://www.zagat.com*) runs circles around the interface, search, and output options offered by the former Microsoft's Sidewalk site (*http://national.sidewalk.citysearch.com*), even though Microsoft really knows how to design databases and undoubtedly has the software tools and the personnel to do so.

DATABASE CREATION AND RETRIEVAL SOFTWARE AND THEIR PRODUCERS

Making a database from a datafile requires a set of programs. Two major, distinct software components are used in this process. One component is the *buildware* for restructuring, converting the data elements in the datafile, and creating various indexes. Once the datafile is processed by the buildware, the result is the *dataware*, a modified version of the original content. Unlike the datafile, which is in a standard file format (tagged, comma and quote delimited, MARC [Machine Readable Catalog format], and so on) that can be processed by various programs, the dataware is in a proprietary format that can be read only by the *searchware* component. It cannot be used by another software. The searchware includes the interface, the navigation system, the help file, the command interpreter, and the search engine. The dataware and searchware together make the database. It is their integration that creates a database from a datafile for users, but there is a third component: the buildware.

Those who search the database do not have to know about the buildware—the dataware creation software. Still, it has an important impact on how one can use a database. The buildware determines which data elements are selected from the datafile (which ones are made browsable), how the indexes are created, how the record is segmented, which data elements are searchable, and so on.

The buildware and searchware software components are usually developed by independent software developers who license the software to those who want to make databases from datafiles. This is especially true for CD-ROM databases and Web databases published directly by the file producers. For CD-ROM databases, for example, the *OptiWare* software of Online Computer Systems has been very popular. It was licensed, among others, by R. R. Bowker for its entire database family, by many national libraries for the CD-ROM version of their national catalogs, and by Public Affairs Information Services for its PAIS database. The *CD-Answer* software of Dataware Technologies has been the most widely used for CD-ROM databases.

For Web database publishing, there are a number of options (Jacsó 1998d). Many of them are add-ons for existing database management software. One of the least expensive and simplest Web database publishing software is *Reference WebPoster* from Research Information Services. *Reference WebPoster* can take any database created by ProCite, Reference Manager, or EndNote and convert it into a decently searchable Web database. On the high end, there is Inmagic's *Web Publisher* software, which converts databases created by DB/Textworks into a sophisticated Web database. CGI offers a low-cost, complete software, *Biblioscape*, that is not a piggyback program. It provides full service not only to create a database from a datafile but also to create the datafile itself. It is a very competently designed labor of love by Paul Chen, who updates and enhances the software at a rate that major software development companies could envy. This kind of individual accomplishment is made possible by the opportunities offered by the Web.

Online information services typically develop and maintain their own buildware and searchware in-house. They use these programs to process the datafiles licensed from content providers. That kind of software is usually not licensed out to others. DIALOG, Lexis-Nexis, Bell & Howell, and Ovid keep their buildware software to themselves, though some may provide the searchware component for local mounting of the dataware by universities and corporations. SilverPlatter has a rather unique scenario, as its

WebSPIRS software is licensed to H. W. Wilson, one of its competitors in the Web database publishing arena. OCLC licenses its spiffy SiteSearch buildware and searchware for local implementation of any datafiles.

DATABASE PUBLISHERS

Those who integrate dataware and searchware, as well as provide user documentation and support, are the database publishers. Many of the database publishers, such as DIALOG, Ovid, and SilverPlatter, don't produce their own content (except for utility files such as DIALOG's Finder databases); instead they license content from third parties. Other database publishers publish their own content only. This is the case with H. W. Wilson and was the case with Bell & Howell until 1998 when the latter began licensing some datafiles from H. W. Wilson. Some publishers mix their own content with that of third parties. EBSCO Publishing and OCLC are the best examples of this variation. EBSCO has its own abstracting and indexing, full-text, and directory databases and publishes them along with content provided by third parties. OCLC publishes its own union catalog, among others, and many databases for which they license the datafile from third parties.

An increasing number of datafile producers and content providers have become publishers themselves, at least on the Web platform. They continue to license their products to database publishers but also mount their own versions. This approach has tradition. Bell & Howell, Information Access Company (now part of the Gale Group), H. W. Wilson, and Gale have been both widely popular content providers and database publishers. It is the extent of this approach that is novel. Producers of a single file or of a few files have now also hopped on the bandwagon. Sociological Abstracts is an example of this. Their indexing and abstracting file was licensed to at least a dozen online and CD-ROM publishers, and in 1998 the company (now part of Cambridge Scientific Abstracts) added its own version on the Web. It is rather unusual for a file producer to withdraw the file from database publishers upon launching its own version. It is even more unusual that in doing so it offers only a free version, but that is what the American Society of Civil Engineers did with its nifty ASCE database (Jacsó 1997d).

Until the early 1990s, licensing of content for CD-ROM databases was usually exclusive. SilverPlatter had the largest user base with exclusive access to many of the most popular bibliographic databases, such as PsycLit and Sociofile. After the exclusive deals expired, CD-ROM licensing followed the pattern of nonexclusive licensing. By the year 2000, the licensing strategies were as liberal as they could get, and they created a users' market. Bell & Howell and H. W. Wilson serve as the best examples for this variety of cross-licensing. Bell & Howell publishes different versions of its flagship ABI/INFORM, Dissertation Abstracts, Periodical Abstracts, and Magazine Express databases in online and/or CD-ROM formats and licenses these to many database publishers. It also licenses some of H. W. Wilson's full-text files, publishing them on both its Web site and/or CD-ROM. It offers abstracting and indexing, full-text, page-image, and full-text-plus-images versions of its files on CD-ROM and on its Web site using its own software, ProQuest. In addition, it has a CD-ROM version of INSPEC, as well as CD-ROM and online versions of some of H. W. Wilson's indexing and abstracting files, including the Applied Science &Technology database.

H. W. Wilson provides its datafiles to many of the largest online services, including Ovid, DIALOG, OCLC, SilverPlatter, and Bell & Howell. The latter two also publish H. W. Wilson's files on CD-ROM. H. W. Wilson has CD-ROM and online versions of the entire run of its indexing, abstracting, and full-text databases. The CD-ROM software is an in-house development; the Web software, however, is an adapted version of the WebSPIRS software. This polygamous relationship among file producers, software developers, and database publishers is very advantageous for customers, as they can choose whatever format they prefer with the software that is most familiar to their end-uses.

DATABASE DELIVERY OPTIONS

Corporations and colleges have several options to make databases available to their employees and students. They also have the opportunity to test the efficiency of the options because licensing contracts are usually for a year or two. Databases can be offered online or on CD-ROM.

Traditional Databases

The CD-ROM alternative was very popular from the late 1980s to the mid-1990s. It represented a breakthrough for many libraries that could not afford and control the use of the traditional transaction-based online services that charged a fee for online connect time and for items displayed and printed. These online services were accessible through a dial-up telephone connection or leased lines, which added to the cost of searching. These database services were used by trained search intermediaries, not end-users, to keep tabs on costs.

The CD-ROM alternative offered access to databases from one or more computers at a fixed subscription rate. Simultaneous access by several users required a networked version of the database—typically at a significant surcharge. Such access also often resulted in the deterioration of response time and needed manual scheduling of the use of the databases. Networking required significant installation and maintenance efforts from the library. The CD-ROM databases were also restricted to local use. The relatively slow access precluded remote log-in to such databases, although there were sporadic efforts to use CD-ROM databases from remote computers. Within these constraints they remain efficient for very large databases, such as the ProQuest databases with hundreds of CDs that contain the full text of millions of documents, many of them in text and graphics and in page-image formats.

However, with the dramatic increase in the capacity of hard drives, along with the equally dramatic decrease in the price of such storage devices, the CD-ROM versions of databases have given way to online versions. The process has been accelerated by the widespread availability of fast Internet connection. With the return to the online model, most information services started to offer fixed-rate subscription plans. The rate usually depends on the number of simultaneous users—monitored automatically—that are allowed access, or on the total number of employees in a corporation or students in a college. Access may be based on a password or on an IP address that authenticates the Internet protocol address of the originating computer that requires access.

The online version may be a locally mounted version of the datafile licensed by the corporation, college, or school. The high-end Online Public Access Catalogs (OPAC) programs have been endowed with features that make it possible to build a database and offer options that have not been part of online public access catalog software, such as search operators to specify distance and sequence requirements of words in the query to distinguish, for example, *information industry* from *industry information* or *library school* from *school library*. Such options are necessary in databases that have long and substantial abstracts, and especially in databases that have full-text records. Customization of the buildware and searchware is done locally to reflect local preferences and features. Alternatively, an institute may choose the option of subscribing to a remote online database (or group of databases) hosted by one of the online information service providers. The responsibility of maintaining and running the system rests with the information service provider in this scenario.

Until the early 1990s, most of the online services that offered access through the Internet relied on the limited Telnet software, which did not allow graphical interface and was mostly limited to purely textual information—a step back from the CD-ROM versions. Since the mid-1990s, access to online databases through Web browsers has become predominant, as it offers graphical interface and graphic content alike.

Tenopir and Neufang (1995) have been following the change of preferences in the database delivery options at several college libraries. From the content evaluation point of view, these delivery options come into play when considering the cost and efficiency of providing access to a variety of content.

Web-Borne Versus Web-Born Databases

There is quite some confusion about the term *Web databases*. Many believe that it implies that Web databases are free. Nothing could be further from the truth. Actually, there are more fee-based databases on the Web than free Web databases. It does not help to clarify the issue when DIALOG's former CEO, Dan Wagner, hyped it by claiming that DIALOG has more information than the entire Web. As DIALOG itself is on the Web, the claim is definitely faulty. Perhaps the DIALOG claim means that it has more information than the rest of the Web. Wrong again. If you just look at Lexis-Nexis, which is also available on the Web, and a few of the largest fee-based database services on the Web, the math certainly would not prove the point.

When the issue is whether an information source is available on the Web, it is appropriate to refer to it as a Web database—whether or not it is free or fee-based. When an existing database is ported from the proprietary dial-up system of the publisher (as most professional databases were), it is referred to in this book as the *Web-borne* version of the database. This applies to most of the online databases discussed in this book. On the other hand, when a database was published first on the Web, it is referred to in this book as a *Web-born* database. For example, the Books in Print database, which DIALOG, Ovid, OCLC, Silver-Platter, and other traditional online services ported to the Web, is a Web-borne database. Barnes & Noble, Amazon.com, and the Fatbrain databases, on the other hand, are Web-born databases.

Database Content Evaluation Criteria

Databases can be evaluated by numerous criteria. A database is perceived first through its interface and search engine. Not even the most informative, reliable, and accurate database can be successful if its software component is not intuitive and user-friendly. The informativeness of the help file, as well as the quality of the user guides, may also play a role in evaluating databases. Another set of criteria relates to the performance evaluation of the database, such as its average response time.

This book does not deal with these software issues, although they undoubtedly have an impact on how the database content is judged. For example, the index-browsing capabilities of the search software may improve users' impressions of a database. If a database has unusual, inconsistent, or misspelled subject terms, but Service A allows users to browse the index and Service B does not, then the database on Service A will likely get a better evaluation grade because misspelled terms are recognizable to users while browsing the index. It is less frustrating to see how many misspellings there are for the descriptor *psychopharmacology* in the Mental Health Abstracts (MHA) database (figure 2.1) than it is to miss important records or try to guess all the possible misspellings in a field that is supposed to be under strict authority control in every database. Without the capability of viewing the index, finding all misspellings is like trying to find a black ring in a dark tunnel on a moonless night. If the software also allows users to pick several terms at a time from an index, at least users may feel comfortable that they can select at one fell swoop all of the variant and incorrect formats of country names that appear in Information Science Abstracts (ISA) (figure 2.2). The poor users of the DOS version of ISA remain uninformed about the many inaccuracies and inconsistencies in the country and language fields of this database because these indexes are not browsable.

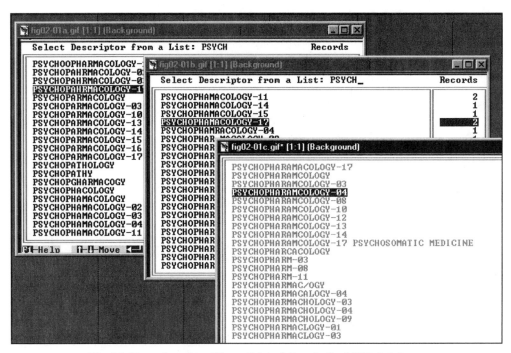

Fig. 2.1. Excessive misspellings of descriptors in the MHA database.

Fig. 2.2. Selecting multiple index entries at one time in Information Science Abstracts.

Some errors in a database can be compensated for by search features such as truncating the search term to allow the retrieval of variants or misspelled formats with different endings. Inconsistent spelling formats of the patent assignee names in ISA (figure 2.3) are relatively easy to retrieve in one fell swoop by truncating at the last common character, such as PA=MITSUBISHI?. This truncation, of course, does not help to retrieve records that have a misspelling in the beginning part of a word, such as *Mistibushi, Misubishi* or *Mitshubishi* for this company in this database.

DATABASE EVALUATION PROCESS

This book focuses on the qualitative and quantitative aspects of database content. The systematic evaluation of the content of databases is one of the core activities of database quality assessment. Although one may get some impressions about a database just by casual use, a sound decision for choosing one database over another or one implementation over another must be based on facts and tangible data that the file producer or the database publisher may not volunteer.

```
DIALOGWEB.          C      📰    🌱   $    🚫   ?
Command Search           new search  databases  alerts  cost  logoff  help

                         Dialog Response

        Ref    Items   Index-term
        E1        1    PA=MISTUBISHI
        E2        1    PA=MISTUBISHI DENKI (JP)
        E3        1    *PA=MISUBISHI
        E4        1    PA=MISUBISHI DENKI K K (JP)
        E5        3    PA=MIT
        E6        1    PA=MIT TECH CORP.
        E7        6    PA=MITA
        E8        1    PA=MITA INDUST. CO. (JP)
        E9        4    PA=MITA INDUSTRIAL CO. LTD. (JP)
        E10       1    PA=MITA INDUSTRIAL CO., LTD., JP
        E11       1    PA=MITECH
        E12       1    PA=MITECH CORP.
        E13       1    PA=MITEL
        E14       1    PA=MITEL CORP (CA)
        E15       3    PA=MITRE
        E16       3    PA=MITRE CORP.
        E17       2    PA=MITSHUBISHI
        E18       1    PA=MITSHUBISHI DENKI (JP)
        E19       1    PA=MITSHUBISHI DENKI K K (JP)
        E20     246    PA=MITSUBISHI
        E21       1    PA=MITSUBISHI CHEMICAL CORP. (JP)
        E22       1    PA=MITSUBISHI CHEMICAL INDUSTRIES LTD. (JP)
        E23       1    PA=MITSUBISHI CORP. (JP)
        E24       2    PA=MITSUBISHI DENK K K (JP)
        E25       3    PA=MITSUBISHI DENKI
        E26       9    PA=MITSUBISHI DENKI (JP)
        E27     190    PA=MITSUBISHI DENKI K K (JP)
        E28       1    PA=MITSUBISHI DENKI K K(JP)
        E29       1    PA=MITSUBISHI DENKI K.K.
        E30       3    PA=MITSUBISHI DENKI K.K. (JP)
        E31       1    PA=MITSUBISHI DENKI KABUSHIKI (JP)
        E32       1    PA=MITSUBISHI DENKI KAIBUSHIKIK KAISHA (JP)
        E33       1    PA=MITSUBISHI DENKI KK
        E34      12    PA=MITSUBISHI DENKI KK (JP)
        E35       4    PA=MITSUBISHI DENKI KK, JP
        E36       1    PA=MITSUBISHI DENKI, JAPAN
        E37       1    PA=MITSUBISHI DENKI, KK, JP
        E38       1    PA=MITSUBISHI ELEC. INFO. CENTER AMERICA, INC.
        E39       1    PA=MITSUBISHI ELEC. INFO. TECH. CNT. AMERICA, INC
        E40       1    PA=MITSUBISHI ELECTRIC CO. LTD. (JP)
        E41       1    PA=MITSUBISHI ELECTRIC CORP.
        E42       1    PA=MITSUBISHI ELECTRIC CORP. (JP)
        E43       1    PA=MITSUBISHI JUKOGYO K K (JP)
        E44       1    PA=MITSUBISHI K K (JP)
        E45       1    PA=MITSUBISHI KK (JP)
        E46       1    PA=MITSUBISHI LTD. (JP)
        E47       1    PA=MITSUBISHI SEMICONDUCTOR AMERICA INC.
        E48       1    PA=MITSUBISHI SEMICONDUCTOR AMERICA, INC.
        E49       1    PA=MITSUBISHI, D. K K (JP)
        E50       1    PA=MITSUBISHI, DENKI, JAPAN
```

Fig. 2.3. Excerpt from Patent Assignee Index of ISA.

The content evaluation of databases requires a battery of tests, experiments, analyses, and other research procedures and methods. These help to corroborate the loosely presented claims of the file producers and publishers as to the scope, composition, coverage, time span, and currency of the database, as well as the accuracy, consistency, and completeness of the data elements of the records that make up the database.

Content evaluation starts at the point where the publishers of source documents provide presumably proofread, error-free information to the abstracting and indexing service or—in the case of full-text databases—directly to the database publisher. It ends where the intermediary or end-users consult the search results. Between these two points are many potential problem areas that warrant evaluation. Williams (1990) points out that the quality of data can be affected anywhere in the chain from information generation to database use. She warns that although value is added along the chain from author or originator to end-user, there is also the potential for introducing error through commission, omission, rearrangement, or emphasis.

It is discouraging to see the cavalier attitude that file producers and publishers have toward database content quality as they hide behind the shield of legal disclaimers. Tenopir (1995, 122), after studying online services' terms and conditions of use that include disclaimers, concludes that their language "suggests that no-one is responsible" for content quality. Indeed, the disclaimer from a Dun & Bradstreet database on DIALOG (figure 2.4) sounds like the scripts that captive soldiers have to recite in front of television cameras in PR-hungry rogue countries. Many file producers and database publishers pledge their dedication to quality and vigorously promise actions that are never delivered, but their products and disclaimers do not reinforce these pledges. To some extent this is understandable, as file producers and database publishers can easily get away with negligence and misleading claims that would bring charges of malpractice or false advertising in many other professions.

---

6. You will not knowingly provide Information to a customer located in South Africa.

C. Terms Which Apply to Both End Users and Information Professionals

1. YOU ACKNOWLEDGE THAT THE AMOUNT YOU PAY TO The Dialog Corporation FOR THE INFORMATION RECEIVED FROM D&B WILL IN MOST INSTANCES REPRESENT A SMALL PORTION OF YOUR OVERALL COST OF THE PROJECT, TASK OR FUNCTION FOR WHICH THE INFORMATION WILL BE USED. YOU ALSO ACKNOWLEDGE THAT THE TYPE OF INFORMATION TO BE PROVIDED BY D&B TO The Dialog Corporation AND FURNISH TO YOU WILL CONTAIN A DEGREE OF ERROR. FINALLY, YOU ACKNOWLEDGE THAT THE PRICES WHICH D&B CHARGES The Dialog Corporation FOR INFORMATION ARE BASED, IN PART, UPON D&B'S EXPECTATION THAT THE RISK OF ANY LOSS OR INJURY WHICH MIGHT BE INCURRED BY YOU (AND/OR YOUR CUSTOMER IN THE CASE OF AN INFORMATION PROFESSIONAL) IN RELIANCE UPON THE INFORMATION WILL BE BORNE BY YOU (AND/OR YOUR CUSTOMER IN THE CASE OF AN INFORMATION PROFESSIONAL) . FOR THESE REASONS, YOU AGREE THAT YOU ARE RESPONSIBLE FOR DETERMINING THAT ALL INFORMATION PROVIDED BY D&B TO The Dialog Corporation AND FURNISHED TO YOU IS SUFFICIENTLY ACCURATE FOR YOUR PURPOSES. NEITHER D&B NOR The Dialog Corporation MAKES ANY REPRESENTATIONS OR WARRANTIES OF ANY KIND WITH RESPECT TO THE INFORMATION, INCLUDING, BUT NOT LIMITED TO, ITS CORRECTNESS, COMPLETENESS, CURRENTNESS, MERCHANTABILITY OR FITNESS FOR A PARTICULAR PURPOSE OR WITH RESPECT TO THE MEDIA ON WHICH THE INFORMATION IS PROVIDED AND NEITHER D&B NOR The Dialog Corporation SHALL BE LIABLE FOR ANY LOSS OR INJURY ARISING OUT OF OR CAUSED, IN WHOLE OR IN PART, BY D&B'S OR The Dialog Corporation's NEGLIGENT ACTS OR OMISSIONS IN REPORTING, COMMUNICATING OR DELIVERING THE INFORMATION, DIRECTLY OR INDIRECTLY, TO YOU.

2. YOU AGREE THAT NEITHER D&B NOR The Dialog Corporation's WILL BE LIABLE FOR CONSEQUENTIAL DAMAGES, EVEN IF ADVISED OF THE POSSIBILITY OF SUCH DAMAGES.

Fig. 2.4. Disclaimer from a Dun & Bradstreet database.

It is quite telling, on the other hand, that many Web-born databases carry a prominent request for users to let the database publisher know about errors found in the database (figure 2.5), and many even provide a hotlink for the users to directly contact them. This is what Mintz (1990) suggested in 1990 when she made a plea for database publishers to institute a "Fixit" command that would directly work from the search process. NewsNet was the only—now regretfully defunct—online service that implemented it. This author's recommendation for implementing a database label similar to the one required by the Food and Drug Administration (Jacsó 1993a) has not yet been publicly implemented by any traditional file producer or database publisher. Interestingly, Web-born databases, such as the Internet Movie Database, the All-Movie Guide, and the Computer Science Bibliography, offer statistical information similar to the proposed label (figure 2.6).

Quint (1995) points out that intermediaries and professional searchers are the database industry's final control team. Equally important, they are the ones who advise fellow professional searchers through their reports about serious deficiencies in databases, as Pagell (1987), Orenstein (1989, 1993), and Mintz (1995) have been doing in memorable feature articles, and as Basch, Bates, Ojala, Quint, Tenopir—and this author—have been doing in regular editorials and columns. Although these database reviews, commentaries, and picks and pans do not reach casual end-users, they provide some feedback to file producers and database publishers. They, in turn, occasionally heed recommendations and either improve their products (as was the case with Economic Literature Index), remove the offending database from their offerings (as DIALOG removed the clinically dead Political Science database), or terminate the contract with the original file producer (as was the case with IFI/Plenum Data Corporation, which formerly produced the ISA database for Documentation Abstracts, Inc. that terminated its contract with IFI/Plenum after receiving the database evaluation report of this author).

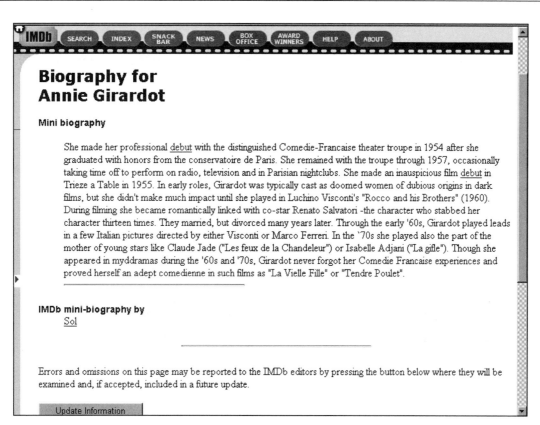

Fig. 2.5. Hotlink for error notification from the Internet Movie Database.

Subject Area	Number of references with		
	Abstracts	Keyword Fields	URLs
Others/Unclassifieds	19913	79288	23464
Theory/Foundations of CS	2303	32805	4914
Mathematics	1736	37299	7771
Artificial Intelligence	2947	11068	2966
Parallel Processing	11206	40224	4055
Computer Graphics	2434	40473	5077
Technical Reports	35060	5345	19680
Compiler	6013	25718	6411
Softw.Eng./Formal Methods	4713	5157	4391
Distributed Systems	2321	18603	5058
Databases	5452	9394	1170
Neural Networks	1051	1023	486
Human-Comp. Interaction	16680	5965	4709
Operating Systems	2236	3073	1198
Typesetting	1175	4363	423
Logic Programming	380	1566	97
Object-Oriented	596	3485	394
Wavelets	537	646	279
Total	116753	325495	92543

Fig. 2.6. Database statistics in the Computer Science Bibliography database (excerpt).

HISTORY AND LITERATURE OF CONTENT EVALUATION

With the Web becoming the largest vanity press in the world, there is a surge in interest, if not in database content evaluations, in counseling users about the dangers of using Web-born databases. Many breathlessly warn about the dangers of unreliable, inaccurate, obsolete, and incomplete information circulating on the Web. Few seem to know that these dangers have been lurking in professional databases and in their predecessors—the printed abstracting and indexing publications and directories—for decades. Even fewer seem to know who published what in academic journals, trade magazines, books, and conference proceedings about the evaluations of these sources. Most merely regurgitate the cliché warnings; at best, they are spiced with some anecdotal evidence. Occasionally, an author may even explicitly claim the absence of prior literature even if there is an abundance of articles discussing the problem. Hurst (1999) claims in her book that the "biggest discovery we found [*sic*], one not discussed to our knowledge in any information science or library publication, is that there are frequent years-long gaps in coverage."

In Chapter 5, about journal coverage in this book, you will find many references to articles and book chapters that discuss exactly this issue, including those by Pagell (1987), Orenstein (1993), Grzeszkiewicz and Hawbaker (1996), Tenopir (1995), and Jacsó (1995, 1997a). In an article mostly excerpted from her 1999 book but which removed the "to our knowledge" clause, Hurst (2000) strengthened and broadened her claim by purporting that "no one has loudly protested the inconsistent journal names, the gaps in years indexed, nor the fact that often only key articles from a journal are indexed, not the entire issue." Loudness is, of course, in the ears of the beholder, but inconsistent journal names alone have been harshly criticized for a long time by information professionals such as Williams and Lannom as early as 1981, Tenopir (1997), LaGuardia (1991) about Philosopher's Index, Jacsó (1998b, 1999b) about Economic Literature Index and PASCAL, Johnson (1999), and Jacsó (1999c) in a variety of library and information science publications.

In reality, much has been published about database content evaluation. It was not merely the honorable duty of this author (1997a) in the *Annual Review of Information Science & Technology* to give credit to those who pioneered such research. It was also to serve as background for anyone interested in learning the milestones and most important areas of this research area. It is particularly important at least to give credit to those whose theoretical and practical contributions from the era of printed abstracting and indexing publications, and from the pioneer days of the online and CD-ROM databases, have paved the way and served as the model for the competent evaluations done during the 1980s and 1990s.

Most of the database content evaluation activities that we see today originate from the evaluation of their forerunners in print form. Goldberg (1992) emphasizes that "whether it be a printed or automated index, many practices and standards remain the same, and the evaluative criteria for printed indexes should be equally applied to CD-ROMs." This may be extended to the guidelines for evaluating library collections, abstracting and indexing journals, or various printed encyclopedias (discussed in the classic textbooks of Katz 1987, Lancaster 1979, and Kister 1986) that can be easily adapted to database collections of an online service, and to individual databases. These works have more current editions, but the original editions are cited to indicate how far content evaluation goes back even in monographs.

Martyn and Slater's (1964) article on testing abstracting journals, and the seminal article of Lancaster (1971) about the evaluation of indexes and abstract journals, remain valid and applicable to the electronic versions of secondary information services even today. The first large-scale analysis of spelling errors done by Bourne in 1977 defies obsolescence. In an in-depth review of citation studies, the warning by Smith (1981) that incorrect citations may influence the conclusions drawn from citation studies rings even more true today than it did 15 years ago. Williams and Lannom (1981) could publish today their 20-year-old paper about the lack of standardization of the journal names in databases, updating only their statistics but not their message.

One of the classic comprehensive studies evaluating indexing and abstracting services was conducted by Pauline Atherton Cochrane using Physics Abstracts, and then written with Stella Keenan in 1964 (Atherton Cochrane and Keenan, 1965) and can serve as a model for competent and professional evaluation today. This applies to many of her other lucid and illuminating writings that played a major role in my choosing librarianship as a profession in the late 1970s, and database evaluation from the late 1980s. The story of this research is recalled by Atherton Cochrane at *http://www.libsci.sc.edu/bob/ISP/cochrane2.htm*.

The data collection for the study of the relationship between time lag and place of publication in Library and Information Science Abstracts (LISA) and Library Literature by Turtle and Robinson (1974) was not assisted by computers, but their methodology, succinct and clear evaluation, and criticism are exemplary for anyone doing database quality research on timeliness today. The same can be said about the research of Tenopir (1982) regarding the bibliography and subject profile methods of evaluating database coverage.

The study of Japanese information network and bibliographic control of scientific and technical literature by Gibson and Kunkel in 1980 sparked interest in exploring the coverage of Japanese journals, conference papers, and patents for many years to come. Ewbank (1982), in his guide to selecting—primarily factographic—databases provided standards that appear in today's evaluation checklists as criteria such as scope, completeness, source coverage, precision, accessibility, report formats, and technical support. The overall problem of dirty data was signaled by Norton (1981) and Pemberton (1983) at the beginning of the 1980s.

While the databases in general, and the library and information science databases in particular, leave much to be desired even today, evaluations of them in the period 1960–1990 provide exemplary models for comprehensiveness, methodology, and reasoning.

The articles of Gilchrist (1966), Goldstein (1973), Edwards (1976), Gilchrist and Presanis (1971), Dansey (1973), Bottle and Efthimiadis (1984), LaBorie, Halperin, and White (1985), and Stieg and Atkinson (1988) were the most comprehensive studies about the content of databases and their print format predecessors. Many had novel methodologies for measuring criteria and/or presenting findings.

There have been relatively few studies that used a large number of test searches, large sets of sample records, or parallel evaluation methodology. One of the most comprehensive studies was done in the early 1980s by faculty members of the College of Information Studies at Drexel University to evaluate MEDLINE's coverage and indexing of the medical behavioral sciences literature (Griffith et al. 1986). This study served as a model for many later studies on a much smaller scale. Sparck Jones and Van Rijsbergen (1976) pointed that the inconclusive nature of many retrieval tests may be attributable to the inadequacy of the test collections used, primarily to the lack of adequate file size for retrieval experiments. Pao (1989) examined 48 data sets used in tests and found that 41 sets contained less than 5,000 items, of which 17 had fewer than 500 items. Regrettably, few studies used the parallel method of subject profile and bibliography approach for database evaluation that Tenopir (1982) tested and compared using GeoRef and GeoArchive as target databases.

The availability of many databases in CD-ROM format opened yet a new horizon for content evaluation for two reasons. The unchangeable content of CD-ROM databases allows researchers to reproduce previous searches to verify the results, or to run different tests on an identical database, changing one variable at a time. The unlimited, nonmetered use of the database for a fixed license fee allows researchers to reproduce previous searches for verifying results, and to extend their analysis to the entire database—a possibility that is rarely feasible with online systems (Jacsó 1992a). The problem of small, nonrepresentative samples has been somewhat overcome by the availability of computer software that processes appropriately large and well-selected samples. Despite these possibilities, census analysis of the entire population of records in a database (as was done splendidly by Hood and Wilson [1994] with the CD-ROM version of LISA) is still atypical.

The increased interest in database quality is partly due to the fact that computer-readable databases offer convenient targets of evaluation, and the bundled search software itself can often be a powerful tool of evaluation. These significantly decrease the tedium of analyzing large samples. The introduction of CD-ROM technology kindled this interest even more. CD-ROM license agreements are usually not of the "till-death-do-us-part" nature, but rather short-term commitments in the form of subscriptions. This makes librarians and information specialists more inclined to learn more about these electronic information sources and to reconsider their choices based on the evaluation of the content of the databases.

Free Web databases could offer excellent opportunities for searchers to explore the content of those databases. However, their software and data structure may not make them as amenable for evaluative searches as the traditional online and CD-ROM information resources. For example, Web-born databases often don't have browsable, field-specific indexes that help explore the accuracy and consistency of data elements, and there is usually no data element that would indicate when records were added to the database, as there are for most of the database records on DIALOG, Ovid, and SilverPlatter. The software may not offer such features that help to determine, for example, the total number of records in a database. In spite of these limitations, there are better and more efficient possibilities for evaluating content than were available with print publications that involved an enormous amount of "grunt" work.

Database Subject Scope

In the broadest sense, the scope of the database defines the coverage. *Scope* includes such aspects as its subject area, size, composition, currency, extent of coverage of source documents or objects (journals, companies, and music recordings), and the coverage by language and geographic origin. In the strictest sense, the scope of a database defines its topical coverage. Some of the criteria, such as the subject area, the size of a database, and the extent of source coverage, are interrelated and must be considered in context.

How good the scope of a database is can be a subjective issue. It should satisfy the interest of an individual user or the user population of a library or an institution. One of the most attractive features of Web-born databases is that they can offer deep and broad coverage of a highly specific topic that is of prime interest to only a relatively small number of people. The Climbing Database (*http://www.btinternet. com/~suckalemon/classic-rock.html*) and the excellent Biographies of Women Mathematicians database with biographical essays of about 100 scientists (*http://www.agnesscott.edu/lriddle/women/women.htm*) are good examples of this.

Somewhat broader is the subject scope of the 4000 Years of Women in Science biographical database (*http://crux.astr.ua.edu/ 4000WS/4000WS.html*). It has slightly more entries (about 140 at the end of 1999), but a narrower time span, covering mostly pre–twentieth century women scientists. The archINFORM database (figure 3.1) has information about 8,000 architectural projects of the twentieth century and illustrates that small is beautiful indeed (*http://www.archINFORM. de*). Such a database would not have been feasible for the large commercial online and CD-ROM publishers because of its limited scope and small target group. Even if a database is small, it may be feasible on the Web, and it is appreciated when the scope statements are clear and straightforward, and thus orient the user fairly. For example, the AIAA Meetings Papers searchable citations database (figure 3.2) makes its scope clear at the home page (*http://www2.aiaa.org/Research*). So does the Pennsylvania Flora Project Database (*http://www.upenn.edu/pafloral dbsearch.html*).

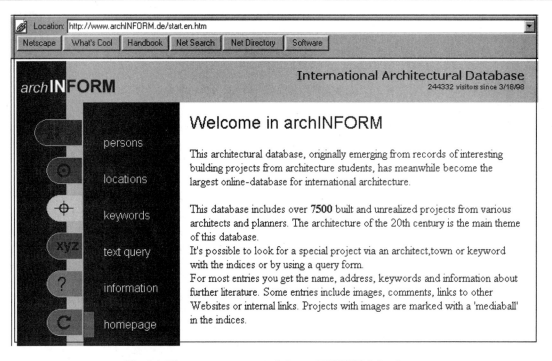

Fig. 3.1. The scope statement of the archINFORM database.

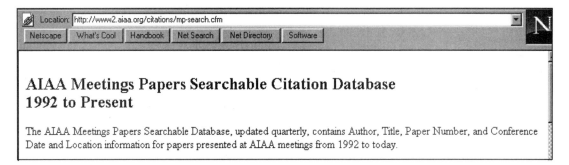

Fig. 3.2. AIAA's explanation of its database scope.

The name or acronym of the database often alludes to its topical scope. For example, Library Literature, Library and Information Science Abstracts, and Mental Health Abstracts clearly identify the subject area of the database. PsycINFO and PsycLIT allude to it, too. Sometimes the name of a database by itself may not be sufficiently informative. Information Science Abstracts covers a number of library science and information technology journals, as the scope notes of its every implementation make clear (figure 3.3).

Only test searches can really reveal what's in a name or behind a name. Statements of coverage displayed optionally by request (such as clicking on the *i* symbol in Ovid or typing *?file 202* in DIALOG) can also provide orientation to the scope of a database. Be forewarned that, along with publicity blurbs on the file producers' or database publishers' home page, these statements often need to be taken with a grain of salt (actually, with much more than a grain).

Chapter 5 illustrates a case when a statement by the editor of the Information Science Abstracts database restricts the scope of ISA by claiming that it covers information science as opposed to other databases that it was compared to, such as Library Literature and Library and Information Science Abstracts that cover library and information science. This may confuse users who read in the file description section of the bluesheet of DIALOG that "Information Science Abstracts provides references and abstracts in the fields of information science and library science" (*http://library.dialog.com/bluesheets/html/bl0202.html*). On the other hand, there are databases whose publicity claims perfectly match the reality. This is consistently the case with the H. W. Wilson family of databases (figure 3.4).

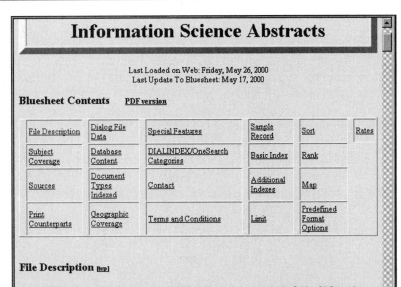

Fig. 3.3. The scope notes of the Information Science Abstracts database.

Fig. 3.4. Scope note of a Wilson database.

The case of the Scirus directory published by Elsevier clearly illustrates that neither the name recognition, nor the claims of a publisher about the scope of a database can be taken literally. Elsevier displays a logo prominently on every screen, heralding "Scirus, for scientific information only." A search by this author for some scientific information about reference sources on comparative religion brought up as top hits some sites that included words in the title page that are considered to be the most vulgar. A follow-up search for four-letter words yielded 38,000 hits. A visit to some of the sites confirmed that this directory is not exactly for scientific information only (*http://www2.hawaii.edu/~jacso/extra/infotoday/scirus/scirus.html*).

The word *comprehensive* pops up quite often in scope statements by file producers, but the meaning of the word is obviously interpreted differently. The World Databases of Bowker-Saur, featuring about 10,000 records, calls itself comprehensive in its publicity blurb. Gale's Directory of Databases also bills itself as comprehensive, and with 15,000 database records, the claim seems to be much more justified. If we add to this the fact that World Databases has a record for each and every implementation of a database, while Gale creates a single record by media type (i.e., one record for online versions of MEDLINE and one record for its CD-ROM versions), the comprehensiveness claim of World Databases becomes far more unrealistic. Test searches for the databases mentioned in this section confirm the impression that the Bowker-Saur database is far from comprehensive.

There were no records for such databases as Library Literature or Library and Information Science Abstracts, even though the latter is not only a British database but also one maintained by—you guessed correctly—Bowker-Saur. The query for entries with the words *library* and *literature* finds only a single record, Information Science Abstracts, because it says that it covers library literature (figure 3.5a). The query for entries in which the word *microcomputer* is adjacent to *abstracts* finds only the record for Computer Abstracts and there is no record for Microcomputer Abstracts (figure 3.5b). (The search was done before the database changed its name to Internet and Personal Computing Abstracts.) Not surprisingly, this World Databases directory does not have an entry for World Databases itself. Nor was it ever updated.

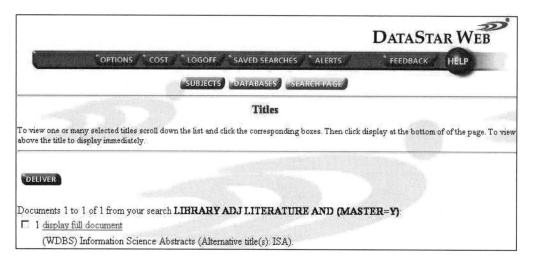

Fig. 3.5a. No record for Library Literature database.

The Gale Database of Publications and Broadcast Media claims to be "a comprehensive file containing detailed information on 61,000 newspapers, magazines, journals, periodicals, directories, newsletters, and radio, television and cable stations and systems." Deducting the records about the broadcast stations and systems, the rest accounts for about 50,000 periodical publications. Such filtering makes viable the comparison with Ulrich's Periodical Database and Serials Database of EBSCO, both also boasting comprehensive coverage—and information on about 210,000 and 155,000 periodicals, respectively.

Then again, the comprehensiveness of The Serials Directory (TSD) and Ulrich's Periodical Database takes on a different meaning in light of the facts that the ISSN Database has 850,000 records, and the Library of Congress Serials subset has nearly 900,000 records. None of the smaller databases mentions any restriction in its scope, but there must be many, and some may justify the apparently narrower scope. For example, limiting the scope of a database by language of the documents and by country of publication is reasonable, and may explain the smaller size and narrower scope.

Documents 1 to 1 of 1 from your search **MICROCOMPUTER ADJ ABSTRACTS AND (MASTER=Y)**:

☐ 1 display full document

(WDBS) Computer **Abstracts.**

Fig. 3.5b. No record for Microcomputer Abstracts database.

There might be far less obvious reasons, too, for the smaller size and the perceived scope of a database. For example, the policy of successive entry cataloging (when following a title change, a new record is created by EBSCO and the record of the former title is also retained in the database) yields an advantage to EBSCO over Ulrich's by the sheer number of titles because Ulrich's has been applying the latest entry cataloging principle. Under this policy, the record created for the successor title incorporates information about the former title, and the record for the former title is eliminated.

For this difference in approach, EBSCO has a record each for *Laserdisk Professional, CD-ROM Professional,* and *E Media Professional* (figure 3.6), plus an additional record for *E Media Professional* (without an ISSN for no reason) and a record for *CD-ROM News Extra,* which was an ill-conceived and short-lived supplement of *CD-ROM Professional.* Ulrich's has a single entry under the current title only and includes the two former titles in that record (figure 3.7). Considering the excessive rate of title changes of periodicals, this can cause quite a significant difference in comparing the purported scope of the databases by doing test searches by title words, publishers, descriptors, country names, language, and so on.

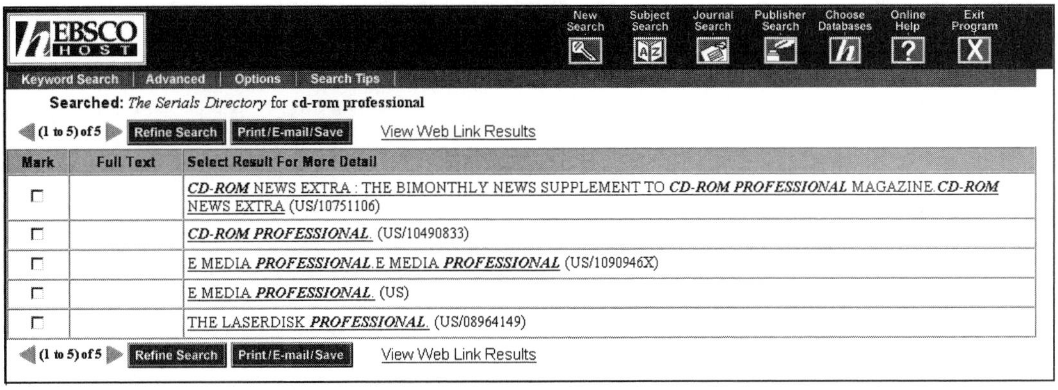

Fig. 3.6. Separate records for the current and previous titles of a journal in EBSCO.

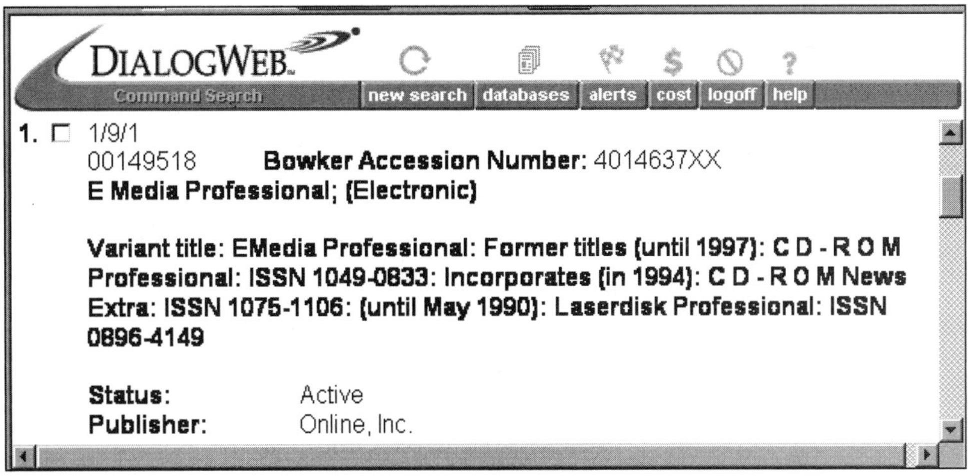

3.7. A single record for the current and previous titles of a journal in Ulrich's.

Another way to gauge the scope of the databases is to conduct test searches. Making test searches in the title field index for a word (*bibliometrics)* or a compound term (*artificial intelligence)* is a quick and easy way to get a feel for the coverage of a database on a few topics. The results of a few simple searches may make the user feel skeptical or confident about the claim of the datafile producer or publisher about covering topics, especially the ones that are prominently mentioned in the publicity materials. The results of title searches alone are not conclusive (except in extreme cases discussed next). They should be evaluated along with the results of testing the database's composition, currency, retrospectivity, and journal base, as well as the policy that governs the selection of the items to be included in the database. The query may be combined with a publication year range to limit the search result to the most current two to three years to test the freshest part of the database. Such a query looks like this:

S supercomput?/ti AND PY=1998:2000 (on DIALOG)

F supercomput* in ti AND PY=1998-2000 (on WebSPIRS)

Sometimes a test in the target database alone would raise doubt about the scope of the database. The previous search in the ISA database in November 2000 yielded zero hits. Although obviously not all the articles or conference papers that discuss supercomputers would have that word in the title, it is inconceivable that none of them would in a database that lists supercomputers as one of its 22 major subjects specifically mentioned on the database bluesheet that was updated twice in 2000. A search without the title field limitation (i.e., in the title, abstract, and descriptor fields) yielded a single record for the most current three years; not exactly vigorous coverage.

Single database searches may shed enough light on the reality of claims made in statements of scope, but multiple database testing can put things into more appropriate perspective. Searching the title index alone provides a somewhat level playing field by eliminating differences caused by differences in abstracting and indexing practices. Obviously, the database that includes the query term as a descriptor would have a larger number of hits than the database that uses a synonym or a narrower term for a descriptor.

For absolute fairness in this test, the search should be limited to the same time period and the same language(s) that are purportedly covered in all the databases. If possible, the search should be limited to the same document types, such as journal articles or conference papers, to eliminate differences because of the differences in document type coverage. This is hard to do because databases may not use a document type field or may use it very inconsistently.

LISA, for example, does not use such a field, so articles, conference papers, and reviews can't be distinguished unambiguously. ISA does use the document type field, but it is not reliable. For example, records about conference papers appear as "monographic chapter" in one year, "monographic" in another year, and, since 1999, as "journal articles." It is to be understood that diversity in language and document type coverage, as well as the retrospectivity of the coverage, may be important assets for some of the users, and these should be tested when the composition and time span of the database are tested.

Beyond these considerations, it must also be borne in mind that some less obvious processing features may distort the comparative results, such as the difference between the ways that the indexes are built. In making comparisons based on title word searches, it is important to verify that the title indexes are built from the same field(s) in all the databases tested. If one database builds the title index from the title and subtitle fields, this may distort the results. If a third database also uses the title enhancement field or subfield, the differences may appear more substantial than they really are. (Title enhancements are very useful because they add information for fluffy titles and help in searching and scanning result lists. H. W. Wilson, for example, provides very informative title enhancements, as discussed in Chapter 6.) In the case of serials directories, depending on the implementations of the datafile, the title index may include only the title proper and key title in one database, while the other also includes terms from the former, successor, alternate, parallel, spine, or variant titles.

Similar reasons might explain the enormous differences in the results of test searches by artists in music directories or catalogs. A search of legendary musician Mark Knopfler yields 14 hits in Amazon.com (figure 3.8) and 112 in Borders.com (figure 3.9). The reason for the whopping number of albums in Borders.com is that it finds all the albums on which Mark Knopfler is a guest artist because its artist index is created also from the liner note data field that includes such information. Abstracting and indexing and full-text databases are usually not problematic in this regard, although as mentioned earlier, databases that use enhanced titles, such as the H. W. Wilson databases, would certainly have an advantage in comparisons based on title word searches.

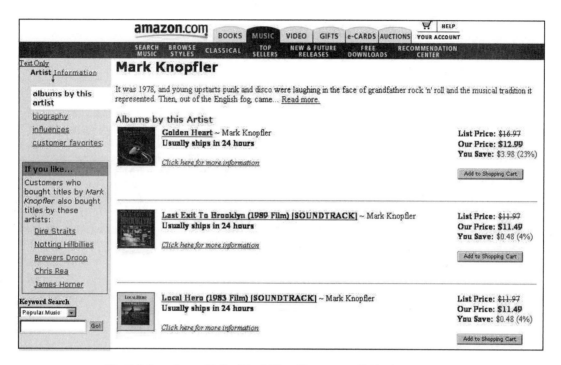

Fig. 3.8. Search results for Mark Knopfler as an artist in Amazon.com.

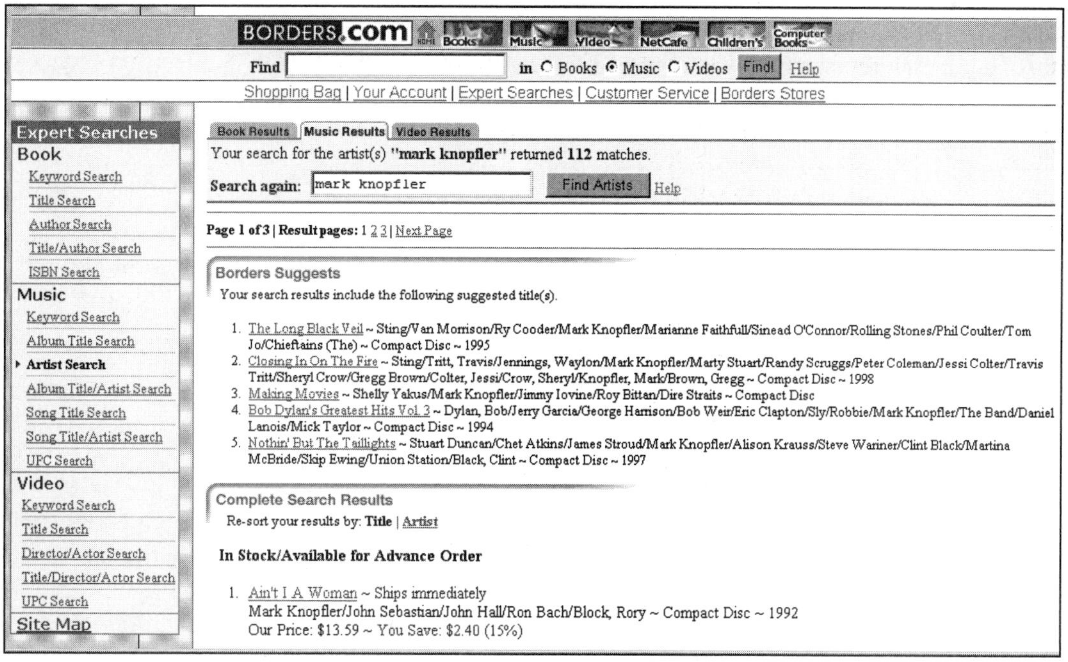

Fig. 3.9. Search results for Mark Knopfler as an artist in Borders.com.

Database publishers sometimes provide information about the particularly strong aspects of their database coverage. These may not be accurate, however. IFI/Plenum, the former producer of Information Science Abstracts, listed on its home page (and also on the DIALOG bluesheet and its publicity pamphlet) 27 topics for which "ISA is your primary reference source" (figure 3.10). Even at first blush, the claim seems very unlikely and unrealistic. It is as if Haworth Press would brag in its catalog that it is your primary source for books about dynamic object models or persistent Web connectivity.

The list, now revised, was flush with buzzwords that are thrown around at COMDEX press parties. The database was not. A search for such buzzwords as *firewall* and *listserver* (also searched as two words and in the plural format) turned up two and three records in the entire database. Library Literature and LISA also had merely two records, but their producers never claimed that for listservers and firewalls, their respective databases are "your primary reference source." Although the new management of the database has replaced this absurd subject coverage list with a more reasonable one, it is not free of misleading claims, as the earlier supercomputing example illustrates, and some further examples will illustrate. The term was changed from *supercomputing* to *supercomputers* in one of the three revisions since the takeover, but only a lonesome record was added to the database about this topic, as proven by a follow-up query that searched the title, abstract, and descriptor indexes.

It is easy to call such extreme bluffs by performing a quick and simple search in the target database. It requires more work when topical searches yield a large number of records. The largeness of the set must be put into perspective by performing test searches in comparable databases, comparable indexes, and comparable time frames. To provide a level playing field, *comparable* is an important word here. A keyword search—or in DIALOG's parlance, a Basic Index search—in a full-text database could yield an order of magnitude larger number of hits than in an abstracting/indexing (A/I) database. An A/I database stands a much better chance of retrieving far more records that include the search term(s) than an indexing-only database.

Searching in the descriptor field could also distort the results of comparison searches. It would favor disproportionately the database that uses the search term as a descriptor over the other databases that use a broader, narrower, or synonymous term or a different spelling instead of the word used in

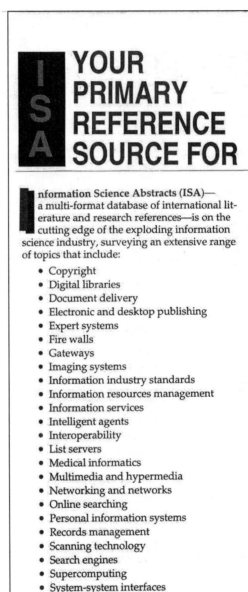

Fig. 3.10. ISA buzzword page.

the test query. This is the case, for example, when one database uses the descriptor *CD-ROM* and the other uses *optical disk,* as the ERIC database does. Value added information elements such as abstracts and the use of most specific terms can be very important, of course, but should be evaluated in their own right, under the quality of indexing criteria, discussed in Chapter 10.

For some topics, even searches such as these may not be perfect. American authors primarily use the term *postpartum depression*. European authors and authors from the Commonwealth often prefer the term *puerperal depression*. Consequently, using the former term would give advantage to MEDLINE over EMBASE (which has a wider European source base), and the latter term would do the opposite. Indeed, making a search in the basic index without any field or data restriction confirms this. The term *puerperal depression* finds 352 records in EMBASE and only 22 in MEDLINE. The term *postpartum depression* retrieves 149 records from EMBASE and 218 records from MEDLINE.

For similar reasons, using the British term *issue system* or *loan system* but not the American *circulation system* would favor LISA (372 records) versus ISA (87 records). Limiting the search to the title field would yield an even larger discrepancy: 74 records for LISA and 13 records for ISA. Of course, indirectly this sheds some light on the geographic source coverage of databases, but there are other approaches for that purpose. A good compromise could be achieved by searching for both the American and the British terms and their variant formats.

To gauge the purported subject coverage in topics where ISA claimed that it "is on the cutting edge," the DIALINDEX database was used to check 10 databases. DIALINDEX has the index files from all the databases but not the master records. It is an exceptionally useful database to find the most promising databases about any topic that can be described with a few keywords. DIALINDEX identifies the databases by their file numbers as used by DIALOG: INSPEC (2), COMPENDEX (8), ABI/INFORM (15), LISA (61), PASCAL (144), Trade & Industry Database (148), ISA (202), Microcomputer Abstracts (233), Computer Database (275), and Library Literature (438).

DIALOG assigns rank numbers to the databases for each query. Number 1 is assigned to the database with the largest number of postings for the query, number 2 for the second largest, and so on. If there is a tie between databases, DIALOG ranks them in increasing file number order. For example, if LISA and ISA have an equal number of hits and they would tie for rank number 6, LISA (file 61) is assigned number 6 and ISA (file 202) gets number 7. This may slightly distort the rank, so the evaluator is advised to overrule the automatic rank if this occurs, and give the same rank for databases that yield the same number of hits.

The buzzwords on the ISA subject list were modified only minimally in the query to include singular and plural formats, hyphenated and single-term variants, and the most likely spelling variations. Every second term was selected from the list. The higher the rank number, the worse the relative position of the database. The compound rank numbers were calculated by totaling the rank values for each query. Figure 3.11 shows that ISA (file 202) never reached number 1, number 2, or number 4 rank; reached number 3, number 5, number 6, and number 7 once; reached number 8 twice; and reached number 9 and number 10 three times. It ranked at the very bottom of the list in this comparison where it had the absolute home-court advantage.

One may wonder how this database fares in subject areas that are not its specialties. Such anomalies would naturally make the evaluator also wonder if presenting baseless claims may run in the (database) family. It seems so, based on test searches made in the Mental Health Abstracts (MHA) database of IFI/Plenum.

DIALINDEX RANK ORDER										
	File Number									
	2	8	15	61	144	148	202	233	275	438
/ti										
digital libraries	2	6	8	3	1	5	7	10	9	4
electronic and desktop publishing	3	10	6	5	8	2	9	4	1	7
fire wall	5	6	3	8	7	1	9	4	2	10
imaging systems	1	3	6	10	4	2	8	7	5	9
information resources management	5	9	7	4	8	1	3	10	2	6
intelligent agents	1	5	6	8	3	2	9	7	4	10
list servers	4	10	5	8	9	2	6	3	1	7
multimedia and hypermedia	3	5	6	8	7	1	10	4	2	9
online searching	5	7	9	2	6	5	3	8	10	1
record management	3	9	1	4	8	2	5	10	7	6
search engines	5	9	3	6	8	1	10	4	2	7
virtual reality	2	4	6	9	5	1	8	7	3	10
world wide web	3	7	4	5	8	1	10	6	2	9
Total title score*	41	90	70	80	82	26	97	84	50	95
Compound rank order	**2**	**8**	**4**	**5**	**6**	**1**	**10**	**7**	**3**	**9**

* The lower the better!

Fig. 3.11. Buzzword result matrix.

The "competing" databases were PsycINFO, EMBASE, and MEDLINE. Again, the home page of the file producer mentions specific subject areas where "MHA is noted for its excellent coverage" (figure 3.12).

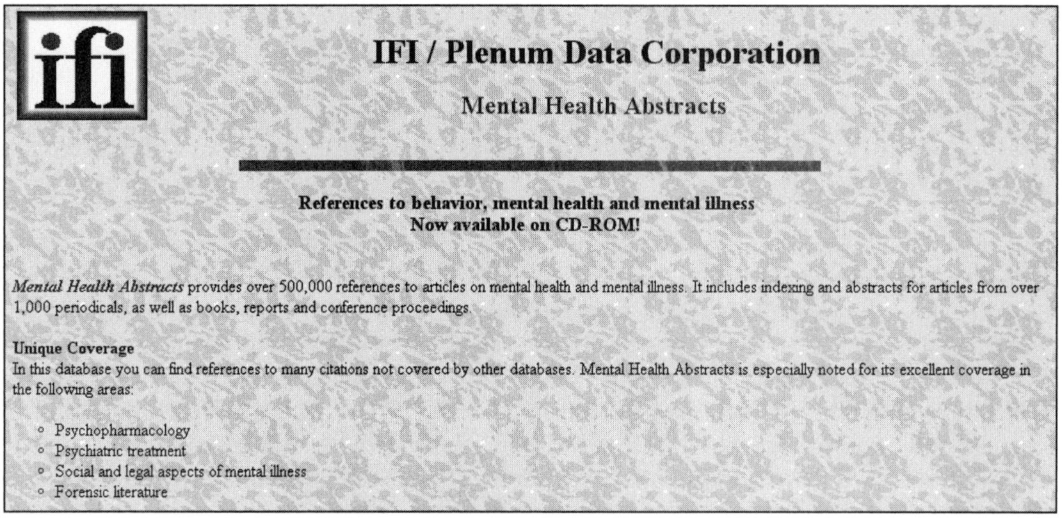

IFI / Plenum Data Corporation

Mental Health Abstracts

References to behavior, mental health and mental illness
Now available on CD-ROM!

Mental Health Abstracts provides over 500,000 references to articles on mental health and mental illness. It includes indexing and abstracts for articles from over 1,000 periodicals, as well as books, reports and conference proceedings.

Unique Coverage
In this database you can find references to many citations not covered by other databases. Mental Health Abstracts is especially noted for its excellent coverage in the following areas:

- Psychopharmacology
- Psychiatric treatment
- Social and legal aspects of mental illness
- Forensic literature

Fig. 3.12. Claims of subject scope of Mental Health Abstracts.

The subject terms were slightly modified to allow for variant word endings, such as *psychopharmacolog?* to retrieve *psychopharmacology, psychopharmacologist(s), psychopharmacological*, and so on. MHA landed in the last position for three of the four areas, even though it could put its best foot forward. Results of searches for two of MHA's purported top subjects are illustrated in figure 3.13. MHA's postings were strikingly low, considering that its coverage goes back to 1967—significantly longer than that of the EMBASE database. When the search was limited to the past 10 years, MHA's performance became even more disappointing.

Although the topic of cost is discussed in Chapter 12, it must be mentioned here that MHA used to have a 150 percent higher connect time rate than PsycINFO, and the very well-performing MEDLINE database was already available free of charge (although not on DIALOG). Once again, the old adage that you get what you pay for is often not valid with databases. Neither may mean much the name recognition of the file producer in another business. The parent company of IFI/Plenum, for example, has been a respected publisher. Similarly, Elsevier is the largest publisher of science journals, but its Scirus directory claims on every page "for scientific information only" to link the user to tens of thousands of sophomoric and utterly vulgar sites as illustrated at *http://www2.hawaii.edu/~jacso/extra/*.

At that site of this author, you can also find a link to an illustrated guide to the nonsense data in the expensive Population Demographics database of Claritas. The statistics about nearly 6,000 communities with zero population yield weird statistical measures, to say the least.

Such tests can also be run on a set of topics of primary interest to the target population. This would give an impression of the subject scope of databases pertinent for a specific user or user group—regardless of the purported subject coverage of the databases tested. The test searches may easily be limited by time period, by country of publication, or by language when one knows the preference of the user population for the specific discipline.

For example, researchers in the humanities are known to have a greater preference than computer scientists for books published 10 to15 years ago; therefore, the test methods must be customized for the discipline and the need of the target user groups. This is illustrated in the sections about the dimension of databases and their coverage of source documents in terms of countries and language of publications in Chapter 5.

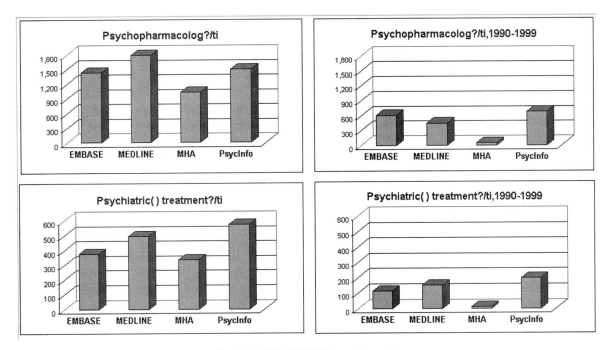

Fig. 3.13. DIALINDEX search results.

This type of testing is easiest on DIALOG, DataStar, and WebSPIRS, as they have special commands and databases for searching only the indexes of databases. DIALOG calls it DIALINDEX, DataStar calls it CROS, and WebSPIRS has a special function (Find Database) to run such searches (figure 3.14).

Fig. 3.14. The Find Database function in WebSPIRS.

The search may be done in a series of databases, even without this cross-index search, but it takes longer, of course, and costs more. DIALOG facilitates such multi-file searches by classifying its nearly 500 databases into one or more topical groups. These groups have names such as PSYCHOLOGY and LIBRARY AND INFORMATION SCIENCE. The abbreviated version of the group names (PSYCH and INFOSCI in our example) can be used in both DIALINDEX and OneSearch searches. The latter performs the search in the real databases identified within the group.

Users are warned not to rely exclusively on the predefined topical database groups of DIALOG, however, because they often include nearly irrelevant databases and omit highly relevant databases. For the subject of psychology, for example, the DIALOG PSYCH database group lists the British Education Index, the National Technical Information Services (NTIS) database, and A-V Online—not exactly the databases that spring to one's mind about psychology.

On the other hand, DIALOG omits from this group the highly relevant databases MEDLINE and EMBASE (figure 3.15). When one exercises common sense in selecting databases and formulating queries, such test searches provide a good starting point for proceeding with the evaluation and exploration of other features of the databases, such as their size and composition, source coverage, and currency.

```
1: ERIC                                                 ▼
1: ERIC
6: NTIS - National Technical Information Service
7: Social SciSearch®
11: PsycINFO®
34: SciSearch® - a Cited Reference Science Database - 1990-
35: Dissertation Abstracts Online
37: Sociological Abstracts
46: A-V Online
65: Inside Conferences
86: Mental Health Abstracts
88: IAC(SM) Business A.R.T.S. (SM)
94: JICST-EPlus - Japanese Science & Technology
98: General Science Abstracts/Fulltext
121: British Education Index
142: Wilson Social Sciences Abstracts
144: PASCAL
149: Health & Wellness Database(SM)
163: AgeLine
434: SciSearch® - a Cited Reference Science Database - 1974-1989
```

Fig. 3.15. The ill-defined PSYCH database group of DIALOG.

Database Dimensions

The first impression that we get of a database is not unlike the first impression we get of a person. Just as we notice immediately how tall, how big, and how old a person is, we learn from the first publicity blurb how large the database is and how far back it goes. Just as the first impression about a person based on a short encounter may be wrong, so can the first impression about a database. These characteristics can be important, but only if one understands their implications, how the measurement data proudly reported in glossy brochures were calculated, and what is behind those numbers that are meant to depict a database.

SIZE AND COMPOSITION

Radio and television commercials, printed ads, and the *Guinness Book of World Records* may have conditioned many people to believe that bigger is better. It is no accident that database publicity materials prominently position their claim regarding the size of the database. Common sense, however, warns you that largest is not equal to best. Russia may have the largest fleet of commercial airplanes in Europe, but its airline ranks among the worst in safety, comfort, service quality, and timeliness. The largest seafood restaurant does not necessarily serve the best calamari, oysters, shrimp, and crab. Much depends, of course, on the individual preferences of what makes a seafood buffet the best; yet, the size of the restaurant is not necessarily a prerequisite. The same applies to databases.

The largest medical database that does not cover journals of East Asia to an adequate extent may not be the best for someone looking for developments in or clinical reports from that region. The largest company directory may be of little value for a corporation that does most of its business with Eastern European countries if the database does not list companies in Poland, Hungary, Slovakia, the Czech Republic, and Romania.

It is quite telling about the obsession with database size that Barnes & Noble threatened Amazon.com with a lawsuit over the claim of the latter that it offers the largest bookstore on the Web. No matter what, Amazon.com certainly won over many Web users by its pioneering venture, top-notch software, and splendid services long before

27

Barnes & Noble even thought of coming to the Web, although it may now flank the exclusive tag line "the world's largest bookseller online." As soon as Barnes & Noble started to divert money from its legal team and started to pay money for good programming and attention to issues other than size, it improved its database content functionality tremendously. All the while, Amazon.com spread itself thin over many areas from toys to kitchen utensils, and the size of its book database could not save its stock from plummeting.

It is also quite telling about the obsession with size that a search on the Northern Light search engine found 11,153 Web pages that carry the phrase *largest database*. According to the first page of the result list, the sites include the largest database of 1) restaurant listings, 2) preaching and teaching videos, 3) lenders in Oregon, 4) eligible bachelors, 5) Thai real estate, 6) personal ads, and 7) parasailing information. The word *largest* itself occurs in over 4.6 million pages—according to this, well, largest search engine.

The size of the database can still be a useful indicator if interpreted correctly and in context. This information is usually easy to get from the publisher or from the database itself. It is always better to derive the data from the database than from the possibly outdated documentation. In most of the DIALOG databases, the (intended) update date is added to the records; therefore, a fully truncated search (S UD=?) will tell you the current size of the database. In databases using the SilverPlatter software, there is no full truncation possibility, but the FIND UD>Ø command will provide the total number of records. Figure 4.1 shows the results of the search to determine the size of Information Science Abstracts (file 202), Library and Information Science Abstracts (file 61), and Library Literature (file 438), using the S UD=? statement. The results reflect the size of these three databases as of the last week of 1999.

Gauging the size of the relevant subset of a multidisciplinary database is also possible if there is a data element that clearly identifies the subset. This is the case in the Social SciSearch database (file 7) and the Trade & Industry Database (file 148). Figure 4.2 shows that the size of the information and library science subset of these databases is comparable to the previous three databases. Bell & Howell also has good coverage of information and library science literature in the ABI/INFORM and the Periodical Abstracts PlusText databases, but neither identifies the category to which a record belongs; hence, it is not possible to determine the size of the information and library science subsets in these databases.

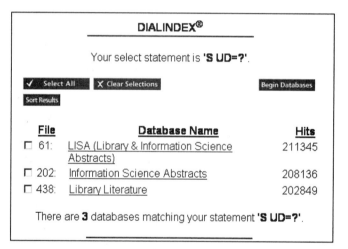

Fig. 4.1. Size of three library and information science databases.

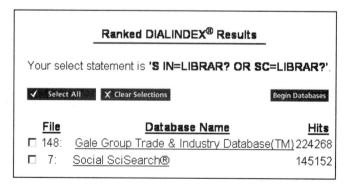

Fig. 4.2. Determining the size of the information and library science subset in Social SciSearch and the Trade & Industry databases.

In databases that don't have update fields in a particular implementation, other techniques may be applied. Usually, there are a few data elements in most databases that are very likely to be available in every record and have a limited range of values. In the software used by Bowker in its own implementation of the Bowker's directories, there is no update field, but there are other data fields that can be assumed to be present in every record. For example, in the Ulrich's database (Ulrich's International Periodicals Directory), the status of a periodical can be active, ceased, or unverified; therefore, the search SS=$ will likely result in the total number of records. In the Who's Who directories of Bowker, the postings in gender index can be a good search criterion to determine the size of the database. With the safe assumption that biographees are either male or female, every record has status and gender information, even if the value of that data element is "unverified" or "undetermined." Users are warned that in many databases, tens of thousands of records do not have an assumed data element, as discussed in the section on record completeness in Chapter 9.

This full truncation would also work on such fields that are practically always present, such as the title field, but it may take a long time to execute a search such as TI=$ in Bowker's own CD-ROM implementations, because the number of unique entries can be millions in a mega-database. It can certainly be done, however, and was done by this author on a fast computer and with a fast CD-ROM drive in the Windows version of the software, as illustrated in Chapter 9. Be forewarned that in the DOS version, the screen may get disabled after a specified amount of inactive time; thus, the search may end while the searcher is away.

In several databases, there are fields with binary values, such as English or non-English language, or Private or Public company type, or the population in a psychology database Human or Animal. If these are assigned consistently in every record, then the size can be determined by executing a simple *or* search statement for that field: s LA=(English or Non-English). CD-ROM databases that use the software of Dataware Technologies (such as Historical Abstracts) typically can use the search terms *none* and *all* for a field to determine the size of the database. The buildware component of the software generates these two special index entries for every field that is indexed.

If in a record, say, the publication year is present, the number of postings for the pseudo index entry of the publication year index *all* is increased by one. If the field is absent, then the posting of the pseudo index entry *none* is increased by one. The same happens for these pseudo index entries of all the fields being indexed. As these index entries are generated when the database is created, the search takes only a second when doing the *all* then *none* searches, even for the title field.

Most of the search software developed directly for the Web (instead of ported from traditional online versions) doesn't offer the possibility to determine the size of the database using one of the previous methods. Although the publication year can be searched, it usually cannot be used on its own, but only as a limit field in addition to a subject or author search. For example, we have to take at face value the size of the databases as claimed by Amazon.com and Barnes & Noble.

Although the Publisher/Date search template in Amazon.com allows searching for books published before, during, or after a year specified, when the option *before 2001* is chosen alone, it returns a message that a publisher name or a keyword must also be specified. Similarly, Barnes & Noble offers searching by three price categories, as well as by type of medium (paperback, hardcover, large print, or audiobook), which could be perfect candidates for determining the size of the database. Unfortunately, these search criteria can be used only as qualifiers with a title, author, or subject search.

Learning the size of a database is not sufficient in itself. That figure must be put in the context of the database composition. To judge the meaningful size of the database, it is essential to know what the units are for which a record is created. The World Databases directory of G. K. Saur (WDBS) creates a record for each and every implementation of a database—plus a master record. This inflates the number of records in the World Databases. Gale, in its Directory of Databases, creates a record for each medium in which a database is incarnated (i.e., there is one record for the magnetic tape version(s), one for the CD-ROM version(s), and one for the online version(s) of a database, but not for each and every CD-ROM and online implementations).

For the Mental Health Abstracts database there is a record for the online variety of this database and another for the CD-ROM version in the Gale directory (figure 4.3). WDBS has a record for the CompuServe, WestLaw, and DIALOG versions of the online database—one for each, plus a master record (figure 4.4). This highly dilutes the size of the database, especially because both CompuServe and WestLaw connect to DIALOG to serve up this database. WDBS, by the way, is not aware of the existence of the CD-ROM version of the MHA database.

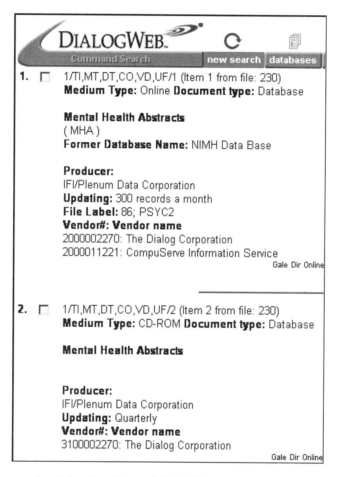

Fig. 4.3. One record each for the online and CD-ROM versions of MHA in Gale's directory.

The other serious and more important implication is that it is far more expensive to search the G. K. Saur database, where the display of each and every record costs four dollars and the free hit-list format does not provide any clue as to which record is for which incarnation (figure 4.4). It is a guessing game if you display the records for the DIALOG, WestLaw, or CompuServe variations of the MHA database.

It adds insult to injury when you find out how incredibly inaccurate the information in the World Databases is and that much of the same nonsense information is carried over from one record to the other, with a charge of four dollars for each. This is the case even when minimal editorial care or competence would have sufficed to spot glaring errors, as in the case of a subset edition of a database. Quite often, the only differences between records are the name of the file and the name of the vendor.

WDBS claims in all four records about MHA that it adds 18,000 records per update. The number in itself is absurd, and it is propagated by carrying it from one record to the others that describe the MHA database (figure 4.5). The correct number is about 300 per update, as reported by the Gale directory and proven by browsing the update index of MHA.

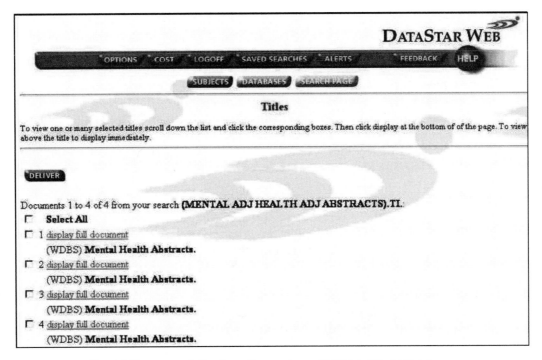

Fig. 4.4. Four records for the online versions of MHA in World Databases.

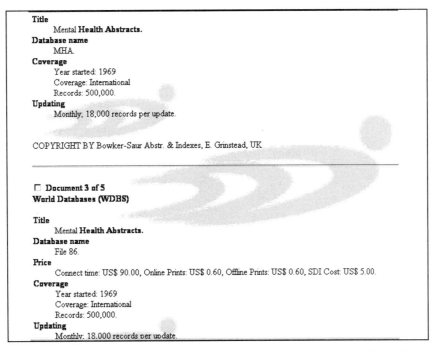

Fig. 4.5. Absurd information is carried over from one record to another in the World Database.

More reasonable and more traditional decisions for the unit of description may also lead to significant differences in database size. As illustrated in the previous chapter, in the Ulrich's database, Bowker uses the latest entry principle for creating a record for each serial. This means that if a serial changed title, the record for the former title is eliminated and the relevant elements (title and ISSN) are incorporated into a new record. In contrast, EBSCO uses the successive entry principle and creates a separate record for each serial that changed title and retains the record for the former title.

There is a significant difference in how databases handle review articles that include critiques of a number of works. For example, every "Péter's Picks and Pans" column in *EContent* (formerly known as *Database*) reviews three or four databases. This column is covered by several databases, including ABI/INFORM, Trade & Industry Database, Periodical Abstracts PlusText, Social SciSearch, and ISA. Until 1997 most of the databases created a single record for the entire review article.

Since 1997, however, Social SciSearch has started to create separate records for each work reviewed, and many other file producers switched to this system (ABI/INFORM, Trade & Industry Database, and Periodical Abstracts). By 1999 ABI/INFORM had switched back to the one-record-per-article principle. Trade & Industry Database in 1999 created three records for the three reviews in the first column published in 1999, but only one record for the second column. Others, such as ISA and LibLit, remained at the one-record-per-article principle, which puts them at a disadvantage in size comparison, particularly when the depth of coverage of journals is compared.

This is especially true for the Wilson databases that have a large number of review records with a single record per article, not a different record for every work reviewed in the article. Readers' Guide Abstracts, for example, had more than 220,000 records for book review articles. Many of the reviews critiqued more than one book, but since H. W. Wilson did not dilute its database size to make one record for each book reviewed, users don't pay in time and especially in per item display and print fees to retrieve each record.

The different and inconsistent treatment of review articles explains the oddities in the search results in figure 4.6. LibLit (file 438) and ISA (file 202) processed the first two articles in 1999 as a single record each. Trade & Industry Database (file 148) created three records for the first article and one for the other. LISA (file 61) did not process any of the review articles or any of the articles in the 1999 issue of *Database* magazine up to July 1999 (the last issue under this journal name). ABI/INFORM (file 15) created one record for each of the three 1999 review articles. Social SciSearch (file 7) created a total of nine records, one for each of the three reviews in all three articles. This is a minor issue in databases of hundreds of thousand of records, but when coverage is compared on the author or journal level, the differences can be significant.

Search History
Database Details

Set	Term Searched	Items	File	
S1	AU=JACSO? AND JN=DATABASE? AND PY=1999	20		Display
S1	AU=JACSO? AND JN=DATABASE? AND PY=1999	2	438	Display
S1	AU=JACSO? AND JN=DATABASE? AND PY=1999	2	202	Display
S1	AU=JACSO? AND JN=DATABASE? AND PY=1999	4	148	Display
S1	AU=JACSO? AND JN=DATABASE? AND PY=1999	0	61	Display
S1	AU=JACSO? AND JN=DATABASE? AND PY=1999	3	15	Display
S1	AU=JACSO? AND JN=DATABASE? AND PY=1999	9	7	Display

Fig. 4.6. The effect of differences in processing review articles.

The total number of records in Bowker's Complete Video Directory can be misleading without realizing that there are numerous records for the very same movie (figure 4.7). Beyond the obvious omissions and inconsistencies in some records (such as MPAA ratings or Gene Wilder as the primary contributor identified in the hit list), and the differences in price and recording format (VHS versus Betamax) in some of the triplicate and quadruplicate records, the only difference among the half dozen other records for the same movie is in obscure details. These details may be of interest only to video dealers, but not to the patron in an audiovisual library where this database is often used. Even if the differences might be important (as in the recording format), it would be better to create a single record that can accommodate the different particulars of the various editions. The $0.00 price is very attractive but not true.

This approach may not comply with the Anglo-American Cataloging Rules (AACR2), but directory databases don't have to follow those rules, which are meant as access tools for the actual holdings of libraries. Laudably, Bowker started to embrace this union record concept in its own CD-ROM version of *Books in Print* (BIP), where different editions and bindings are listed within a single record. Although this reduced the size of the database, it was for the benefit of users, and again, AACR2 rules don't apply for directory entries. The collocation of information in a single record simplified the search process. Unfortunately, not all the publishers of the online versions of BIP followed this policy, to the detriment of those using transaction-based pricing. They have to pay for each and every record even if the substantial information (title, author, publisher, etc.) is essentially the same.

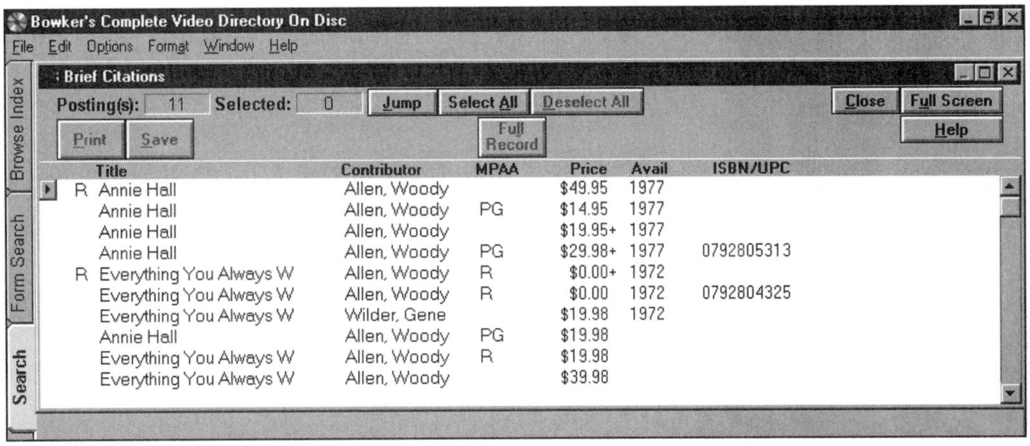

Fig. 4.7. Multiple records for the same movies in Bowker's Complete Video Directory.

The Internet Movie Database shows the most elegant and fair solution for handling multiple versions of the same movie. There is one record retrieved for *Annie Hall* (figure 4.8), and among the dozens of fields of value added information, there is a hotlinked subrecord that is displayed when choosing that option about the DVD-specific release of the movie (figure 4.9).

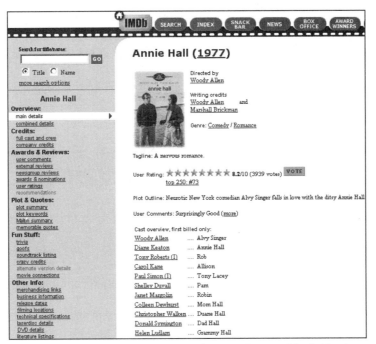

Fig. 4.8. The master record for *Annie Hall* in the Internet Movie Database.

Fig. 4.9. The satellite record for the DVD-specific information of *Annie Hall*.

Although the inflation of database size may be based on ill-conceived or at least arguable concepts, excessive numbers of duplicate records is a sign of careless or incompetent management (or both) in building the database, and suggests disregard for the user. Among the CD-ROM movie directories, *Cinemania* has been by far the best by virtue of its excellent content, especially the coveted reviews of Roger Ebert, Leonard Maltin, and Pauline Kael. Microsoft did not inflate its database size by creating separate records for each review. These were hyperlinked to a single master record of the movie itself.

Corel, in its inferior movie directory, proudly advertises 90,000 records, failing to mention that a very large number of records are duplicates and triplicates with widely different information about cast lists, duration, and other data elements. In addition, the movie ratings and reviews seemed to have been done by reviewers recruited by those annoying "Do you want to earn $300 a day watching movies?" ads at bus stops. This low-quality database can be chalked up to Corel's lack of experience in creating a database; after a few years, Corel abandoned it.

It is especially frustrating for the user to find out that the size of an abstracting and indexing database is grossly inflated by duplicate and triplicate records, where not even the possible excuses of the directories apply. It was more disappointing when a supposedly professional datafile producer (e.g., IFI/Plenum) produced a file, Information Science Abstracts, meant for librarians and other information professionals, that was ridden with duplicates and triplicates. In a critique of this database, Jacsó (1997e) estimated—based on test searches—that there were about 12,000 duplicate pairs in this database (and also in the print version).

Although there are duplicates in other databases as well, this proportion was unprecedented in a database of fewer than 200,000 records. It was of deep concern that the producer of the file was not aware of the extent of duplicates. The vice president of the company, who has also been the long-time editor of the database, asserted that "since IFI took over the production and added a sophisticated duplicate detection system in 1987, the occurrence of duplicates or triplicates has ended" (Allcock 1997).

Did it? A relatively simple check (figure 4.10) using DIALOG's IDO (Identify Duplicates Only) command showed that this statement must not have been based on facts or reality. Of the 67 articles from the 1990 issues of *ASLIB Proceedings*, 30 (half of the 60 duplicate pairs) records were duplicates. In 1991, out of the 76 records, there were also 30 duplicate records and 1 triplicate record.

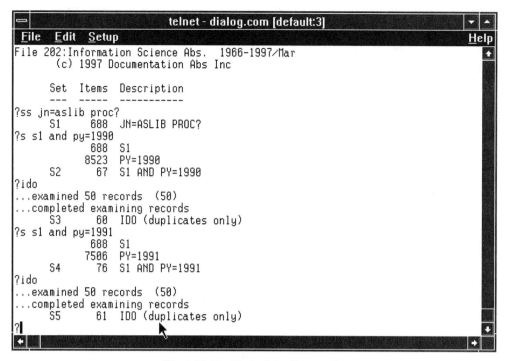

Fig. 4.10. Duplicate detection results.

DIALOG's duplicate detection algorithm is very good, but it is not perfect, and its findings should not be taken at face value. It checks only the author and the title fields. A consequence of this method is that items of a regular column with a common title but without a distinguishing subtitle (such as Savvy Searching, for example) will be identified as duplicates. Records for book reviews often simply carry the title "Book review." Reviews by the same author will be identified as duplicates even though they are not. To the human eye, this is obvious, as the volume, issue, or pagination number clearly distinguishes one review from the other, but DIALOG's duplicate detection algorithm does not check these data elements. It may also be that the same author published the same article in different journals, which is not prudent, but it is accurate to enter a record for both.

On the other hand, genuine duplicates may be missed if the title is not transcribed in the same way in two records for the same article. British and American spelling differences are handled well by the algorithm, as are minor differences in punctuation, but not all bases are covered to identify real duplicates. Probably the most efficient method for the evaluator doing duplicate detection searches is to use a few select journals for testing.

Beyond visually checking each purported duplicate, there is another method to control the reliability of duplicate reports: doing the duplicate detection in one or more other databases that cover the test journal(s) comprehensively. For example, in the case of the test journal *ASLIB Proceedings*, INSPEC, Library and Information Science Abstracts, and Social SciSearch make the best control group for ISA. The assumption is that if the DIALOG software falsely identifies duplicates for any of the previously mentioned reasons, these should show up in all the databases covering the same journal. Figure 4.11 clearly shows that this is not the case. In the control group, only Social SciSearch has duplicates and merely a single pair of duplicates. ISA has 156 duplicate pairs out of the 224 records.

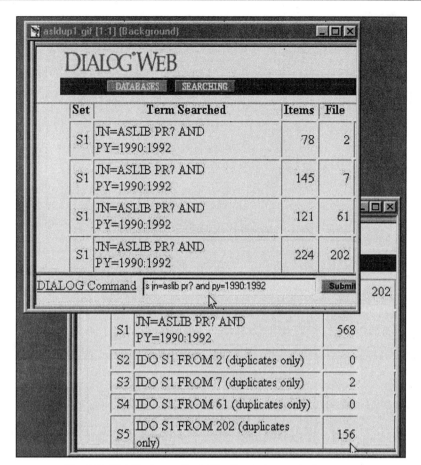

Fig. 4.11. Duplicate result verification using control groups.

The excerpts shown from the WinSPIRS version of ISA for its tighter output (figure 4.12) make it clear that these are indeed records entered into ISA twice—or even three times, as in the case of the article about Key Technologies with misspelled subtitles. The analysis of the year of data entry, in thousands of records, also indicated that a large percentage of the duplicates were entered after 1987, which was contended by the editor as the year when the adding of duplicates was eliminated. Maybe the duplicate detection sysem was not that sophisticated after all. The typical pattern for this journal, and for most of the duplicates, is that duplicates were added three years after the first record. Without these duplicates, the database would not have shown an enviably consistent and round number of 800 records in most update batches in 1995.

The new file producer gave priority to eliminating the duplicates and triplicates, but there were still enough left at the end of 2000 to illustrate the case from the DIALOG online version of ISA (figure 4.13).

ISA Document Number in Printed Publication: 9503375
The corporate information management function.

Journal: ASLIB Proceedings
Source: Vol. 44 Issue 3 p. 107-114 Mar 1992

Information Science Abs. (Dialog® File 202): (c) Information Today, Inc.

ISA Document Number in Printed Publication: 9205890
The corporate information management function.

Journal: ASLIB Proceedings
Source: Vol. 44 Issue 3 p. 107-114 Mar 1992

Information Science Abs. (Dialog® File 202): (c) Information Today, Inc.

ISA Document Number in Printed Publication: 9502938
The difficulties and problems encountered in establishing a computer network in Poland. CRT-POLKOM.

Journal: ASLIB Proceedings
Source: Vol. 44 Issue 4 p. 151-155 Apr 1992

Information Science Abs. (Dialog® File 202): (c) Information Today, Inc.

ISA Document Number in Printed Publication: 9205734
The difficulties and problems encountered in establishing a computer network in Poland CRT--POLKOM.

Fig. 4.12. Excerpt from the duplicate list in ISA.

DIALOGWEB.

Command Search | new search | databases | alerts | cost | logoff | help

1. ☐ 2/AU,TI,JN,SO,BN,DE,SC/1
   ISA Document Number in Printed Publication: 9503515
   Collaboration in the '90s. The IMA Compatibility Project.

   Author (Affiliation): Dodds, P.V.W.
   Journal: CD-ROM Professional
   Source: Vol. 5 Issue 1 p. 88, 90-91 Jan 1992
   Descriptors: INTERACTIVE SYSTEMS; MULTIMEDIA SYSTEMS; ORGANIZATIONS
   Subject Class Header (Number): Information Science and Documentation, Professional and Organizational Aspects (01.03)
   Information Science Abs. (Dialog® File 202): (c) Information Today, Inc. All rights reserved.

2. ☐ 2/AU,TI,JN,SO,BN,DE,SC/2
   ISA Document Number in Printed Publication: 9301180
   Collaboration in the '90s--the IMA compatability project.

   Author (Affiliation): Dodds, P. V. W.
   Journal: CD-ROM Professional
   Source: Vol. 5 Issue 1 p. 88-90 Jan 1992
   Descriptors: DATA FILES; FUTURE; MULTIMEDIA SYSTEMS; OBJECT-ORIENTED SYSTEMS; PUBLISHING ; SOFTWARE; USERS; VENDORS
   Subject Class Header (Number): Information Processing and Control, General Aspects (05.00)
   Information Science Abs. (Dialog® File 202): (c) Information Today, Inc. All rights reserved.

Fig. 4.13. Duplicates still left in ISA.

Other online and CD-ROM search programs don't offer duplicate detection (except for Ovid, which added this feature in 1999), but those that download records into a bibliographic information management software (such as Reference Manager or ProCite) can use the customizable duplicate detection feature of those programs. In the now-defunct consumer-oriented Search-by-Search version of ISA on the Web, the cost of displaying and printing duplicate and triplicate records could hit hard the casual users who typically pay out of their own pockets. No wonder that the service went south in a short time.

In the CD-ROM versions of databases, duplicates don't incur out-of-pocket expenses but do involve extra work to remove the duplicates from the final result list. Of course, they also serve as an indicator for the quality of a database. After 15 years of producing this database, Documentation Abstracts, Inc. terminated its contract in 1998 with IFI/Plenum, and production was taken over from IFI/Plenum by Information Today.

Unfortunately, new duplicates are still being entered into the system, as shown in figure 4.14. This reality questions the effectiveness of duplicate detection. Duplicates are a burden on users in terms of both time and money. Note also that not only the descriptors, but even the broad subject classifications, are different in the duplicate pairs. In the print version that lists the records arranged by broad subject classification, the duplicates did not show up under the same category, so users may not have had the feeling of déjà vu. Online and CD-ROM users certainly would.

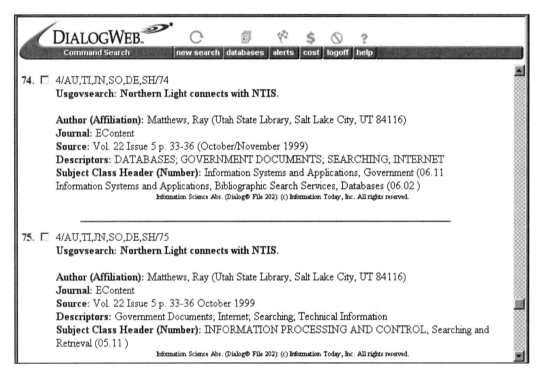

Fig. 4.14. Newly added duplicates.

There are other more important considerations that may influence one's perception of the appropriateness of a database, such as the type and language of the documents covered, the types of articles included, the extent of coverage of core journals, and the balance of record distribution across time. These considerations are of interest in their own right and are discussed in the following sections.

TIME SPAN

Databases differ significantly in their retrospective coverage. In itself, there is nothing wrong with a short time span of a database. Neither is a very long time span necessarily a virtue. It depends on the preferences of the users and the nature of the database. In several online systems, the default time span for searching is set to cover the current year and the previous two years. This suggests that most users are interested in articles not older than two to three years. In 1998, UMI (now Bell & Howell) introduced its Newsstand database with a start year of 1998. Although it has unusually short retrospective coverage among the abstracting and full-text databases, the purpose of the database—as its name alludes—is to be an electronic newsstand. It is still far more retrospective than the real newsstands that carry only the current issues of journals, magazines, and newspapers. Launching the DIALOG database version of *Newsweek* in February 2000 without any back file, nevertheless, is too extreme for a single source database.

The *Computer Select* CD-ROM database of Ziff-Davis had a similarly short time span—one year—for good reason. *PC Magazine Plus*, another CD-ROM product, follows the same principle of including the issues of only the past 12 months in every new edition, bumping off the one from the 13th month. This unusual type of coverage is also known as *rolling coverage*. Computer literature becomes obsolete in the shortest time, especially those articles that report about or evaluate new computer hardware and software. Yesterday's news is history in computer technology.

This does not apply equally to research papers in computer science, although it is remarkable that in the sciences subset of the Journal Citation Reports of the Institute for Scientific Information (ISI), the computer science journals have the shortest cited half-life. Cited half-life measures how many years backward from the year of publication it takes to accumulate 50 percent of the citations in a given journal. These are very useful data to judge the adequacy of the retrospective coverage of a database in a given discipline.

Although individual preferences certainly vary in terms of need for retrospectivity in a literature search, and they may vary for different projects of the same individual, the obsolescence of a given field of study is a good measure against which to compare the time span of databases.

In library and information science, the cited half-life is calculated for 21 of the 56 journals monitored by ISI (figure 4.15). It is calculated only for journals that received 100 or more citations. The cited half-life was more than 10 years for two journals and ranged from 1.2 years to 8.8 years for the rest. (ISI does not calculate the exact cited half-life in cases in which it is larger than 10 years.) This half-life data puts into perspective the retrospective coverage of the LIS databases and databases with substantial LIS coverage, as shown in figure 4.16. It suggests that a 15- to 20-year time span would be more than appropriate for most of the searches. If the searcher is interested in the widely used professional journals in library and information science instead of the academic journals, even a much shorter time span would suffice. That puts into perspective the importance of retrospective coverage of databases.

Journal Citation Reports - 1997 Social Sciences Edition

File Edit View Calculations Options Help

Journal Rankings

Mark	Rank	Journal Abbreviation	ISSN	1997 Total Cites	Impact Factor	Immediacy Index	1997 Articles	Cited Half-life
	2	J DOC	0022-0418	284	1.250	0.120	25	8.8
	2	MIS QUART	0276-7783	1091	1.620	0.267	15	8.8
	4	ANNU REV INFORM SCI	0066-4200	133	1.000			8.3
	5	COLL RES LIBR	0010-0870	318	0.785	0.171	35	6.4
	5	J AM SOC INFORM SCI	0002-8231	903	1.260	0.313	96	6.4
	7	RQ	0033-7072	117	0.298	0.111	9	6.2
	8	INFORM MANAGE	0019-9966	508	0.697	0.024	42	6.1
	8	LIBR QUART	0024-2519	122	1.360	0.250	12	6.1
	10	SCIENTOMETRICS	0138-9130	463	0.691	0.088	57	6.0
	11	INFORM PROCESS MANAG	0306-4573	367	0.578	0.000	51	5.9
	11	J INFORM SCI	0165-5515	193	0.427	0.154	39	5.9
	13	INT J GEOGR INF SCI	1365-8816	365	1.093	0.100	40	5.0
	13	J ACAD LIBR	0099-1333	122	0.208	0.000	39	5.0
	15	B MED LIBR ASSOC	0025-7338	306	0.565	0.104	48	4.6
	15	LIBR TRENDS	0024-2594	117	0.391	0.000	35	4.6
	17	LIBR J	0363-0277	184	0.248	0.212	99	4.3

Sort: Cited Half-life   Filter: INFORMATION   56 Journals   0 marked

Fig. 4.15. Cited half-life of library and information science journals.

Databases / Years	65	66	67	68	69	70	71	72	73	74	75	76	77	78	79	80	81	82	83	84	85	86	87	88	89	90	91	92	93	94	95	96	97	98	99
ISA																																			
LISA																																			
ISI																																			
Trade & Industry																																			
LibLit																																			

Fig. 4.16. Retrospective coverage of LIS-related databases.

Similarly, the cited half-life of psychiatry journals monitored by ISI is a good indicator of the value of retrospectivity in PsycINFO and Mental Health Abstracts. Although the former deals with the broader discipline of psychology, the focus of Mental Health Abstracts is psychiatry (according to the database blurb), so the psychiatry subset of 80 journals in the ISI database may be more relevant as the basis for this comparison. ISI uses the notation "10 years" for journals whose citation half-life is more than 10 years. Discounting these from the subset of 63 journals that have cited half-life measures (out of the entire psychiatry subset of journals), the range is from 2.6 years to 9.6 years (figure 4.17). The cited half-life is not necessarily a perfect measure. Those who publish in academic journals must cite others. Many may do so even without doing manual searches and reading the cited articles, and rely only on the abstracts in databases. This, in turn, has an impact on the cited half-life.

Journal Citation Reports - 1997 Social Sciences Edition

File   Edit   View   Calculations   Options   Help

Journal Rankings

Mark	Rank	Journal Abbreviation	ISSN	1997 Total Cites	Impact Factor	Immediacy Index	1997 Articles	Cited Half-life
	1	ACAD PSYCHIATR	1042-9670	77	0.420	0.045	22	
	2	ACTA PSYCHIAT SCAND	0001-690X	6245	1.588	0.136	169	8.5
	3	AM J GERIAT PSYCHIAT	1064-7481	274	0.670	0.432	37	3.0
	4	AM J ORTHOPSYCHIAT	0002-9432	1862	1.718	0.689	61	> 10.0
	5	AM J PSYCHIAT	0002-953X	22478	6.501	0.943	283	7.3
	6	ANXIETY	1070-9797	113	1.512			2.7
	7	ANXIETY STRESS COPIN	1061-5806	81	0.583	0.000	18	
	8	ARCH GEN PSYCHIAT	0003-990X	23238	10.751	1.798	104	9.4
	9	ARCH PSYCHIAT NURS	0883-9417	207	0.439	0.000	38	5.4
	10	AUST NZ J PSYCHIAT	0004-8674	839	0.574	0.340	100	7.0
	11	B AM ACAD PSYCH LAW	0091-634X	408	0.469		0	7.8
	12	B MENNINGER CLIN	0025-9284	272	0.321	0.077	26	8.7
	13	BEHAV MED	0896-4289	219	0.622	0.105	19	6.6
	14	BRIT J MED PSYCHOL	0007-1129	981	0.667	0.167	30	> 10.0
	15	BRIT J PSYCHIAT	0007-1250	13851	3.265	0.744	195	8.3
	16	CAN J PSYCHIAT	0706-7437	1511	1.151	0.520	102	7.1

Sort: Journal Abbreviation   Filter: PSYCHIATRY   80 Journals   0 marked

Fig. 4.17. Cited half-life of journals in psychiatry.

One would think that the original time span of the PsycINFO database, going back to 1966, would be more than sufficient in light of the cited half-life. In an interesting and unusual development, the American Psychological Association added to its database a substantial amount of records for 300,000 documents from carefully and systematically selected pre-1966 publications.

On the other end of the spectrum are disciplines of the humanities, where books, treatises, and articles published in past centuries are often used by current researchers. For many social scientists, material that is a quarter-century old is current. In this regard, the difference in retrospective coverage of the Arts and Humanities Search database of ISI (20 years) and Wilson's Humanities Abstracts (16 years) may be significant.

Beyond the database level time span, attention must be paid to idiosyncrasies in the coverage of core journals and other important journals of a discipline. The idiosyncrasies include late start of coverage, early termination of coverage, uneven coverage, and gaps in coverage. Related to these symptoms are the shallowness and tardiness of coverage, but these are discussed in the sections about the depth of coverage, and the currency and update patterns later in this chapter. Most of the examples for problems in time period coverage will be illustrated on the ISA database that offers the largest variety of extreme idiosyncrasies for many journals.

The start date of coverage of a database typically indicates the earliest year of *some* of the publications covered by the service, and by no means suggests that *all* the sources are covered from that date onward. This is obvious if a title started publication later than the start period of the database. For example, the earliest possible date of coverage for the journal *Internet Reference Services* is 1997—when it started—regardless of the start year of coverage of the database. Many databases, however, don't pick up a journal immediately. When the journal is picked up, it may be covered only from that year onward or given retrospective coverage from the first year of publication. The latter is a better approach within reasonable limits, assuming that none of the really core journals of a field have been missed by the database.

Late pickup of titles can be most easily spotted by comparing competing databases, as illustrated in figure 4.18. The most efficient way to profile the characteristics of the period coverage of a database is to expand and display the publication year index. On the journal level, the time period coverage can be quickly gauged by using the RANK feature of DIALOG. It extracts values in the field specified by the user, such as the publication year in this case, and ranks the values by occurrence or alphabetically. There is a limit for the size of the result set that can be ranked. Currently, it is 10,000 records.

After selecting the most important journals and creating a set for each of them, the sets should be ranked displaying the number of records for each year in chronological order (figure 4.19). What strikes the eye in the ISA database is not the time span of the coverage of the excellent British library automation journal *Program,* but the depth of it, or rather the lack of depth. It's hard to decide whether to consider this a gap (as in 1972, 1975–1976, 1978–1979, and for almost a decade between 1988 and1996), an early termination of coverage, a temporary termination, or just a pathetic noncoverage. The single item from 1977 is barely enough for a life sign.

RQ 1960	Database start year	RQ records from	Late start in years
LISA	1969	1973	4
Social SciSearch	1972	1975	3
ISA	1966	1970	4
LibLit	1984	1984	0

Fig. 4.18. Late pickup of core journals.

Some datafile producers provide a journal list that clearly indicates from which year they cover a particular journal and in which year they stopped its coverage. (Terminating coverage may be justified for many reasons. The natural one is when the journal ceases publication or changes title; hence, the coverage under that title also ceases.) EBSCO, Bell & Howell, and H. W. Wilson indicate both the start and end years of coverage and make the journal lists available on the Web. A sample of some of the journal lists is available at *http://www2.hawaii.edu/~jacso/extra/journalbase/.*

Some allow the customization of the content of the journal list output by the user. Bell & Howell, for example, lets the user choose the following fields to be included: Title, Journal Code, ISSN, Abstract Dates, Full-Text Dates, and Image Dates. LISA published a journal list on the Web in 2000, but it was outdated at the time of posting. It does not include the journals that changed titles in 1999, such as *Database* to *EContent* or *Library Software Review* to *Library Computing*. They are listed only under their former names (*Database* and *Library Software Review*, respectively).

The content of the LISA journal list is the simplest that one can imagine: merely the journal name appears. ISA is even less informative about its journals. The new editorial team immediately stopped publishing the core journal list. Undoubtedly, it turned out to be an inconvenient evidence for the negligent treatment of serials by the previous file producer that ignored entire issues, volumes, and runs of volumes of core journals that were supposed to be indexed in their entirety (Jacsó 1997e). Instead, an editorial listed the new journals that are to be covered (http://www2.hawaii.edu/jacso/extra/savvy/journalbase/journalbase.html).

```
RANKING SET BY PY (JOURNAL: PROGRAM)
------------------------------------
RANK: S1/1-230    Field: PY=  File(s): 202
(Rank fields found in 230 records -- 20 u

RANK No.   Items   Term
--------   -----   ----
    15       6     1966
    11       8     1967
     9      13     1968
    13       7     1969
    10       9     1970
    16       6     1971
     8      15     1973
    18       3     1974
    20       1     1977
    12       8     1980
     5      18     1981
    14       7     1982
     4      19     1983
     1      25     1984
    19       3     1985
     6      18     1986
    17       5     1987
     2      23     1997
     3      20     1998
     7      16     1999
         ---end of results---
```

Fig. 4.19. Ranking a journal title set by publication year in chronological order.

Some of the titles listed ceased publication well before the announcement; others were not covered in the following year, yet others produced merely one or two records in 1998, 1999, and 2000, including two of them that the editors urged users to pay special attention to. (figure 4.20).

Database publishers (as opposed to file producers) usually do not make available such time period coverage information, although it would be easy to make it an appendix to the help file in the online and CD-ROM versions of a database.

The start coverage of journals listed by the file producers should not be taken at face value. Some file producers claim coverage of journals that are barely covered in the first few years of the time span of the database. Magazine Article Summaries (MAS), the first indexing and abstracting database of EBSCO, professed coverage from 1984 for most titles. In fact, it merely sprinkled the database with a few records (even for undoubtedly core journals of general interest) from 1984 (and often later) issues of journals (figure 4.21a).

1998 items	1999 items	2000 items	Journals	1998 items	1999 items	2000 items	Journals
5	0	0	AI Magazine	5	0	0	Booklist
16	0	0	Bottom Line: Managing Library Finances	18	16	0	Bulletin of the Japan Special Libr. Association
1	0	0	Byte	2	0	0	Computer Life
10	4	0	Computerworld	1	0	0	DBMS
0	0	0	Digital Publishing Strategies	0	0	0	Fee for Service
1	1	1	Forbes	2	0	0	Fortune
1	0	0	Home Office Computing	4	2	0	Imaging
134	114	0	Information Today	2	1	0	InfoWorld
0	0	0	Inside the Internet	3	2	0	International Journal of Information Sciences and for Decision Making
44	15	0	Internet World (was Webweek)	8	3	0	IntraNet Professional
2	0	0	LAN Times	18	24	0	Link-Up
5	6	0	Multimedia Schools	3	1	0	Network
2	0	0	New Media (NewMedia)	29	0	0	PC Magazine
9	6	0	PC Week	2	2	0	PC World
8	0	0	Proceedings of the Geoscience Information Society	27	0	0	Proceedings of the Off-Campus Library Service Conference
6	0	0	School Libraries Worldwide	6	0	0	Software Magazine
1	0	0	WebWeek (now Internet World)	2	0	0	Windows Magazine

Fig. 4.20. New journals promised to be covered by ISA and their actual coverage.

This is obvious at a quick glance and is in sharp contrast to the characteristically substantial and balanced coverage of journals in H. W. Wilson databases, as shown in figure 4.21b. (A sudden surge in coverage may be justified if a journal's publication frequency increases or if, for other reasons, the number of articles published in a year increases. This was the case when *CD-ROM Professional* became a monthly magazine from one issued six times a year.)

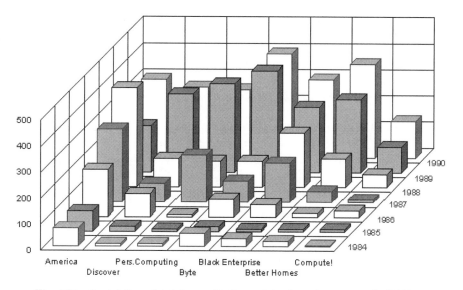

Number of records from journals (MAS)

Fig. 4.21a. Sprinkling of database with few entries from top sources in MAS.

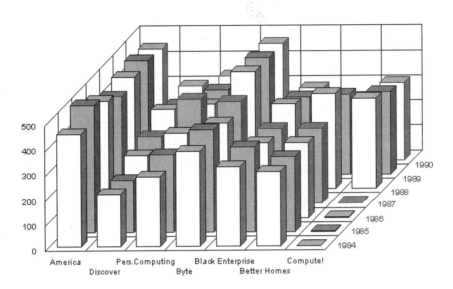

Fig. 4.21b. Well-balanced coverage of top sources in Readers' Guide Abstracts.

DEPTH

Exploring and understanding the depth of coverage of journals covered by a database is essential in evaluating the appropriateness of that database. The mere presence of journal titles in a database does not guarantee substantial coverage for those titles. Studies of journal coverage in the 1960s and early 1970s often were restricted to determine if a set of journals had been covered by one or more printed indexing and abstracting sources and what the overlap was at the journal level among them. These studies were mostly based on the cumulative indexes of the I/A sources, but even so, it required tedious work. The comprehensive studies of Gilchrist (1966), Goldstein (1973), and Edwards (1976) were limited to journal title level comparisons and did not discuss the depth of coverage of the journals. Even so, they paved the way for later studies that compared the depth of coverage of selected journals in databases.

This is important to know, not only for casual users who may not realize how many articles of an important journal are absent from a database, but also for researchers who do bibliometric and scientometric studies. These studies examine publishing patterns and citation behavior to rank authors, institutions, journals, and even countries based on database searches. They explore research fronts and trends in disciplines where journal publications are the dominant sources to signal productivity. Publication productivity is a key consideration in tenure, grant, and certain job applications. Gaps and heavy fluctuations in coverage, as well as shallow, inconsistent, tardy, and prematurely terminated coverage of journals, can seriously distort the results of bibliometric and scientometric studies, and may mislead any users who assume that what they found in a database is all that was written about the subject in prestigious journals that are claimed to be covered in a database.

Savvy users know that they have to search two or three databases to achieve an adequately comprehensive retrieval. Even experienced users, however, may fall victim to claims of coverage presented in cliché-ridden publicity materials that promise comprehensiveness. As we saw in Chapter 3 about the subject coverage, the most absurd public relations claims can be easily verified by simple title word searches across a few databases. Claims about the depth or exhaustivity of journal coverage are more difficult to verify.

The great variety in journal name abbreviations, punctuation, and spellings within some databases and among different databases requires defensive search strategies that predict, explore, and accommodate possible variations. When the journal name field is only phrase-indexed (as in most DIALOG databases), formulating a query is a rather cumbersome procedure. If the journal name field is both word- and phrase-indexed, the query can be formulated more flexibly, as is the case in the Ovid and OCLC implementations of most of the databases.

Printed guides and journal lists may include the first and last year of coverage of each journal in a database. These may be useful to orient users who consult these lists, but do not guarantee the exhaustive coverage of the journals in the specified period. As seen in the previous chapter, proud announcement of coverage of new journals is not a guarantee, either. It is also quite common that the first year of the initial period of a journal's coverage is rather shallow. This may apply to the entire database, as was illustrated through the example of comparing the first few years of coverage of seven journals in Readers' Guide Abstracts and Magazine Article Summaries. The landscape of the coverage visualized by figures 4.21a and 4.21b spoke for itself.

The designation of journals as core titles should not be taken at face value in every database. Such a designation implies the most exhaustive (usually cover-to-cover) coverage of the journal. Omitting certain types of documents from an issue of a core journal (such as obituaries or announcements) may be acceptable (especially if this is made clear in the documentation or the help file, and if the rule is applied consistently). Omitting feature articles is not acceptable. Omitting entire issues and volumes of purportedly core journals is the equivalent of malpractice in other professions. Among the databases with LIS coverage, only ISA and INSPEC designate journals with core journal status, and ISA stopped the practice, as discussed previously. By definition, all the journals in the ISI databases are core journals without special designation, as every journal in the ISI databases is said to be given cover-to-cover coverage.

Excuses referring to the difficulty of receiving the core journals (Allcock 1997) may not seem reasonable considering that all the core journals in ISA are U.S., British, or Canadian titles. Neither is the reference to the high prices of journals. It comes with the turf and does not justify omission of entire volumes (Jacsó 1997e). Such claims may not trigger sympathy from users who are paying premium prices for the database and who know that most of the purportedly core journals in a LIS database have a yearly subscription price of below $100.

Beyond looking at the depth of coverage of individual journals in a single database, a better perspective can be gained by having some benchmark against which the depth of coverage can be measured.

The time span of coverage in a database cannot be separated from the depth of coverage. Depth cannot be easily determined, as it is a moving target. Depth of coverage—that is, the amount of records created for a journal during its coverage in the database—varies from year to year, independent of the possible change in volume of the number of articles published in a journal. This was shown earlier in figure 4.19, a pathetic coverage pattern for *Program*, a highly respected British journal in library automation in the ISA database.

Widely uneven, roller-coaster coverage is unnerving for journals that are mainstream publications for the discipline, and it is unacceptable for purportedly core journals. *Library Quarterly* certainly would deserve the inclusion of all the articles in a volume, but it is obviously not the case in ISA (figure 4.22). The same applies to another respected journal, *Library Trends*. Even without looking at their coverage in other databases, it is quite obvious that this capricious coverage has nothing to do with the number of articles published in these two journals.

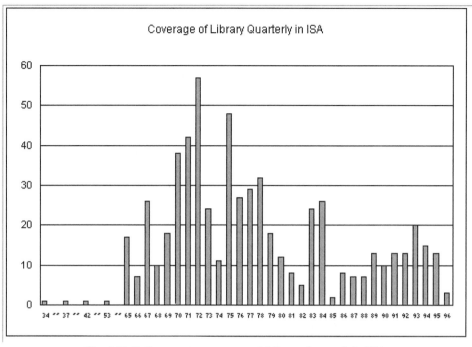

Fig. 4.22. Roller-coaster coverage of *Library Quarterly* in ISA.

When a similar pattern appears with purportedly core journals of ISA, such as *Government Information Quarterly*, *Journal of Documentation*, *RQ* (now *Reference & User Services Quarterly*), or *Information Technology and Libraries* (figure 4.23), one may find it difficult to believe that "core journals are covered in their entirety" as the ISA User Guide claims.

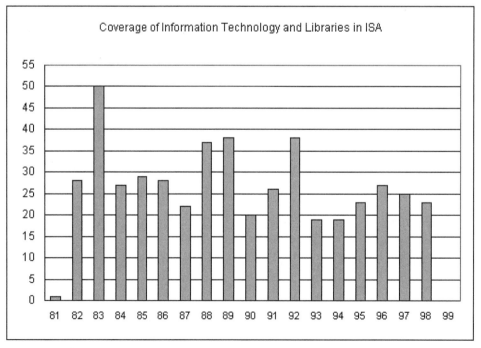

Fig. 4.23. Roller-coaster coverage of *Information Technology and Libraries* in ISA.

The extreme case of roller-coaster downslope is the gap that occurs when there are no records for a journal for an entire volume or a run of volumes. Although one may empathize with the database editor's problems of missing an issue or two occasionally, as shared by the former database editor of ISA (Allcock 1997), in the case of the ISA database, it has been a recurring problem unprecedented in any other database. It is a big problem in the case of prestigious journals even if they are not considered core journals by the datafile producer, as is the case with the journal *Program* (figure 4.24), and an even bigger problem for purportedly core journals of the database, such as *Scientometrics* (figure 4.25).

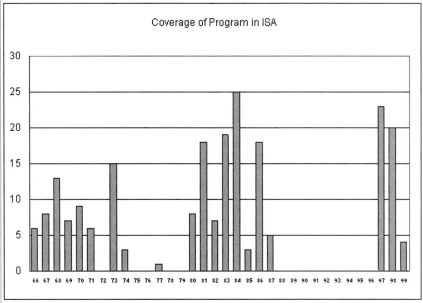

Fig. 4.24. Gaps in coverage of the prestigious *Program* in ISA.

A gap (a temporary suspension) can turn into early termination of the coverage of an important journal. Sometimes it's difficult to determine in which state of coverage a journal is. After a few years of total suspension of coverage, some of the clinically dead titles (from the perspective of the file producer, that is) show some minimal vital signs. This was the case with *RQ*, one of the top-ranked library journals that remained on the list of core journals of the printed edition of ISA throughout 1994 and 1995, even though in those years there was not even a single record from *RQ*. It then resurfaced in ISA with a meager four records in 1996. It is certainly a unique treatment for purportedly core journals. In a twist to the plight of coverage of this excellent journal, in mid-1997 it indeed ceased publication under its former title, *RQ*. It was not picked up for coverage by ISA under its new title, *Reference & User Services Quarterly,* until later in 1998.

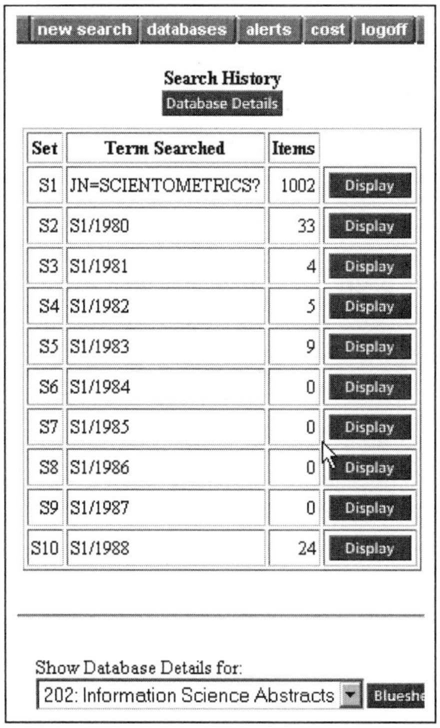

It is difficult to understand when a file producer stops covering a journal that is considered to be key for its subject area. This happened in LISA when it stopped covering *Online* magazine. At the end of 2000, there were still no records for items published in the 1999 and 2000 issues of this journal (figure 4.26). One cannot decide

Fig. 4.25. Gaps in coverage of *Scientometrics*, a purportedly core journal, in ISA.

whether it is suspension or termination of coverage. In either case, it is a blunder. The same may happen to *EContent* in LISA. After 36 records for items from 1999, no records were added for articles published in the journal's 2000 issues. After presenting these findings at a conference, the author was advised that LISA will make an effort to fill the gaps and resume the coverage of these two important journals. Indeed, as this book went to press, the June 28, 2001 update of LISA added the missing records. It is better late than never.

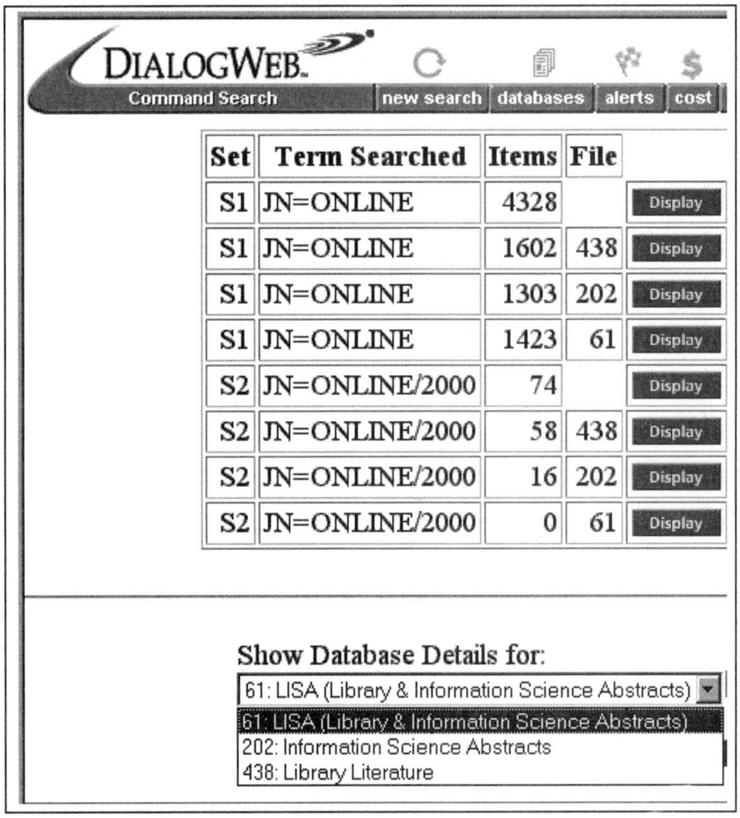

Set	Term Searched	Items	File	
S1	JN=ONLINE	4328		Display
S1	JN=ONLINE	1602	438	Display
S1	JN=ONLINE	1303	202	Display
S1	JN=ONLINE	1423	61	Display
S2	JN=ONLINE/2000	74		Display
S2	JN=ONLINE/2000	58	438	Display
S2	JN=ONLINE/2000	16	202	Display
S2	JN=ONLINE/2000	0	61	Display

Show Database Details for:

61: LISA (Library & Information Science Abstracts)
61: LISA (Library & Information Science Abstracts)
202: Information Science Abstracts
438: Library Literature

Fig. 4.26. Suspension or termination of coverage of *Online* in LISA.

The new producer of the ISA database is trying to patch up those gaps, which were reported first in an unpublished document made available to the board of directors of ISA by this author, then published in an article in *Library and Information Science Research* (Jacsó 1998a). These retroactive completion efforts were badly needed, but had an impact on the processing of current issues of important journals, as discussed in the section on currency in this chapter. The filling of the gaps was intended from 1990 onward (a reasonable target), but fell short in the case of several titles that are essential for the subject areas of the database.

Retrospective time coverage in directory databases is a more complex issue. In certain directories, such as company directories and who's who–type databases, retrospective coverage is not that relevant because users are mostly interested in current company data, such as current name, address, e-mail and fax number of companies, and prominent individuals. In the case of book directories, the situation is different, as usually a record is created for every edition, and records for former editions are kept. The same applies to movie and music directories, too. In such cases, it is important to know how far back the coverage of the database goes. The REMARC database of the Library of Congress is one of the book catalogs with the longest retrospective coverage and is of particular importance for researchers to track down a book published in the fifteenth century. This cannot be done in *Books in Print*, *British Books in Print*, Amazon.com, Barnes & Noble, or even in *Books Out of Print*.

As with bibliographic and full-text databases, the earliest stated start year of coverage of directories should not be taken at face value. Often, there are only a few records for that period. On the other hand, both bibliographic and directory databases may go back further, with a substantial number of records than the start year displayed on the database labels, or the publicity blurbs may suggest. ISA, for example, has notable coverage for articles published before 1966, the stated start year of coverage. Ovid lists on its home page the time span of AGRICOLA as starting in 1979, but the publication year index shows substantial coverage from the mid-1970s (figure 4.27).

Plotting the time period coverage can reveal extremely substantial differences among databases. While PsycINFO shows a substantial growth in coverage across years that is in perfect harmony with the growth of publications of the discipline, Mental Health Abstracts shows an unparalleled decline since it was taken over by IFI/Plenum in 1983 (figure 4.28). The yearly volume of updates shrunk by an order of magnitude. The two databases that were competing neck-to-neck until the early 1980s diverged in an opposite direction. MHA's nosedive makes it a product that is of little use for students and practitioners of psychiatry and psychology, because of the dramatic shrinkage of its source coverage, journal base, and depth of coverage, as discussed in this chapter and in Chapter 5.

MHA shows similar problems of journal coverage, as discussed earlier about ISA. Although it never distinguished core journals from regularly and occasionally covered journals, the early termination of coverage of many of the essential journals in the areas where MHA is touted to be especially useful, such as psychopharmacology or psychiatric treatment, had debilitating effects on this database (although some subscribing universities fail to notice it and keep paying for the MHA database).

O V I D	Year of Publication Index Display

(Perform Search) | A-Z | Back in Index | | Main Search Page | Forward in Index |

Choose from among the following index entries:

Select	Year of Publication	# of Citations
☑	1975.yr.	7042
☑	1976.yr.	8367
☑	1977.yr.	17963
☑	1978.yr.	86354
☐	1979.yr.	176817
☐	197?.yr.	67
☐	197u.yr.	607
☐	1980.yr.	173997
☐	1981.yr.	159271

Fig. 4.27. AGRICOLA starts substantial coverage earlier than suggested.

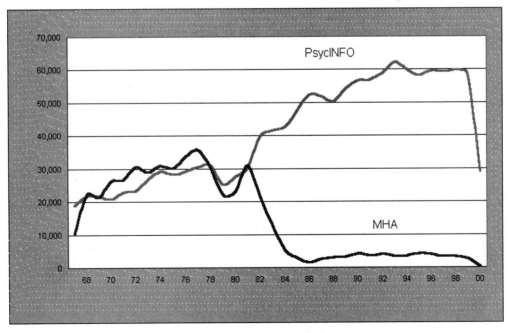

Fig. 4.28. Coverage in PsycINFO and MHA across years.

Profiling the time period coverage of databases is easy. In most systems, the publication year index can be displayed and downloaded into a file from which a chart can be generated. If this option is not available, a series of searches by publication years can be made and the resulting search log saved in a file for importing into a spreadsheet. Although data collection is quick and easy, it always warrants a careful approach. As discussed in Chapter 9 on record completeness, the publication year in many databases has not been assigned to records in the first several years of building the database. In others, the publication year field includes some other data. If it happens on a large scale, it may distort the time period coverage profile of a database.

Wrong data are difficult to spot, except when they are obviously wrong to the naked eye. Before you would believe that AGRICOLA has thousands of records for documents published before Gutenberg was born (figure 4.29), think about its feasibility and realize that these are typos (for example, 1078 instead of 1978) or other erroneous numbers typed in the publication year field. Before you plot the publication years beyond 2000, realize that these are also likely to be typos. Such a publication year value is not absolutely impossible in a database in 1999, but it is feasible only in a database such as EVENTSLINE, which has records for events scheduled for up to the year 2005, or *Books in Print*, which includes records for the forthcoming titles print subset.

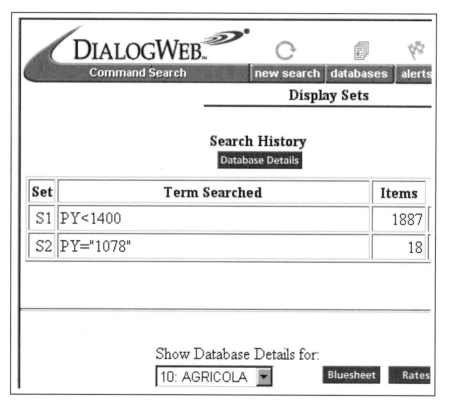

Fig. 4.29. Infeasible publication years in AGRICOLA.

Equally absurd are the PY=200 values in the Information Science Abstracts database for the records added in the first update of 2000. Beyond the fact that it was a bad start for the new millennium (if you subscribe to the notion that it started in 2000), it deprived users who limited the search to the current year of potentially relevant and timely records. Although this erroneous publication year appears in only 71 records, they represent 100 percent of the items added to the database in the first update for year 2000 issues of journals. It is ironic to see the mistake in the record about an article that mentions the survival of the Y2K bug—obviously a bit prematurely (figure 4.30). Later in the year, ISA corrected the publication year in these records.

Record 1 of 2 in ISA 1966-2000/03
TI: On the Net in 2000.
AU: Notess,-Greg-R.
SO: Online Vol. 24, Issue 1, p. 71-73, January 200.
PY: **200**
AB: As the world plunges forward into 2000, with the dreaded Y2K transition behind it, the Internet marches onward, growing, mutating, and affecting all sorts of interactions between businesses, consumers, family, and friends. The pace of Internet change was dizzying in 1999, and there is great excitement for the future of intranets, extranets, and cost-cutting through Web-based consumer service. Forecasts some changes that may be in store for 2000 and beyond by overviewing some of the major trends of 1999 with respect to electronic commerce, vertical portals, shopping search engines, domain name registration, and mergers and acquisitions in the information industry.
AN: 9904021

Fig. 4.30. The Y2K bug in one of the ISA records.

When the production of a file is taken over by a new company, it is always worth it to revisit and re-evaluate the quality of the database, including its depth of coverage. This happened in 1998 when Information Today acquired the ISA database and hired its former technical advisor. Although the new producer eliminated the list of core journals, the revised subject coverage statement of the database (figure 4.31) provides some starting points for checking much-needed changes in the depth of coverage of topics that are considered the primary areas of the database. The 30 months that have passed since the takeover of the ISA database while this book was being completed provided a sufficient time frame to see if positive changes have been implemented.

DIALOG 202

Information Science Abstracts

FILE DESCRIPTION

Information Science Abstracts provides references and abstracts in the fields of information science and library science. International in scope, the database indexes and abstracts articles from over 300 journals, as well as from books, research reports, conference proceedings, and patents. Each record includes the bibliographic citation and abstract as well as descriptors drawn from a controlled vocabulary. The Information Science Abstracts database corresponds to the printed publication of the same name, which is published by Information Today, Inc.

SUBJECT COVERAGE

Subjects indexed include:

- Abstracting and Indexing
- Artificial Intelligence
- Bibliometrics
- Cataloging, Classification, and Indexing
- CD-ROM Technology
- Computer Science
- Decision Support
- Document Delivery
- Educational Technology
- Electronic Publishing
- Information Management
- Information Theory
- Library Administration
- Management Information Systems
- Medical Informatics
- Multimedia Systems
- Online Information Retrieval
- Optical and Laser Technology
- Standards
- Supercomputers
- Telecommunications

DIALOG FILE DATA

Inclusive Dates: 1966 to the present
Update Frequency: 9 times per year
File Size:
More than 208,000 records as of December 1999

CONTACT

Information Science Abstracts is produced b Information Today, Inc.. Questions concerning f content should be directed to:
Information Today, Inc.
Department ISA
143 Old Marlton pike

Medford, NJ 08055-8570
Phone: 609-654-6266
Toll Free: 800-300-9868
Fax: 609-654-4309

Donald T. Hawkins
Editor-in-Chief

Phone: 908-647-4754
Fax: 908-647-4754

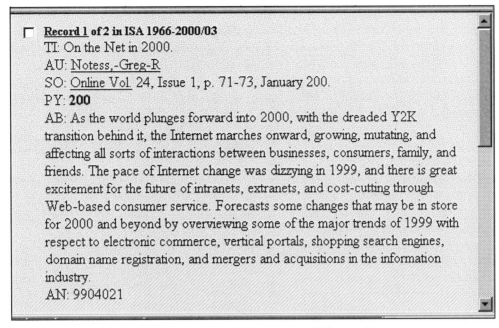

Fig. 4.31. The revised subject coverage statement of the ISA database.

Unfortunately, the problems with the depth of coverage of purportedly prime areas of the database (as well as the problems of currency) remained under the new management in the ISA database. A quick look at the result of the publication year search reveals a sharp decline in the number of records added to the database in the past three years under the new management (figure 4.32).

The actual numbers contradict the promising statement in the October 1998 editorial (figure 4.33), which claimed that "the next few issues of ISA will contain more abstracts than usual." Just the opposite happened. This trend makes it very unlikely that the depth of coverage of the designated prime subject areas of the database will improve.

The number of journals covered did not change considerably until 2000 (figure 4.34), which implies that if much fewer records were added in the most current 30 months, it just made the coverage of journals (and topics) even more shallow. Since 1999, the titles of conference proceedings have been entered in the journal name field, and the conference papers have been assigned the document type "article" (yet another document type after flip-flopping between "monographic" and "monographic chapter" for conference papers). This increases both the number of "journals" and the number of "articles" covered in these two years, so the picture is somewhat worse than it appears.

DIALOGWEB.		
Command Search		**new search** **databases**
E1	8352	PY=1985
E2	9419	PY=1986
E3	9404	*PY=1987
E4	9623	PY=1988
E5	8625	PY=1989
E6	8421	PY=1990
E7	7529	PY=1991
E8	8348	PY=1992
E9	7856	PY=1993
E10	8064	PY=1994
E11	8921	PY=1995
E12	9327	PY=1996
E13	6449	PY=1997
E14	4655	PY=1998
E15	3618	PY=1999
E16	71	PY=200
E17	1102	PY=2000

Command

Fig. 4.32. Sharp decline in the number of records added to ISA in the most current years.

Information Science Abstracts

Donald T. Hawkins
Editor-in-Chief

Lynn A. Murray
Editor

Editorial • *October 1998*

• About the Editors •

Currency is a major concern to publishers of abstract databases, and we at Information Today are no exception. We are pleased to note that *Information Science Abstracts (ISA)* has no backlog. As soon as journals are received from the publishers, relevant articles are selected from them, and they are then sent to our dedicated and hard-working abstractors. The abstracts are usually returned to us within 10 days or less, and they then appear in the next issue of ISA.

In the light of the above statements, readers of *ISA* may wonder why this issue contains some abstracts dating back as far as 1990. These are part of the *ISA* quality improvement program that was mentioned in an earlier Editorial. Using current technology, we have conducted a detailed field-by-field scan of the *ISA* backfile, with the goal of repairing many of the errors that have crept in over its prior 30 years of existence. This process revealed some gaps in the coverage of several journals. We expect to add the abstracts of these older articles to forthcoming issues of *ISA*, so that the coverage of the database will be as complete as possible back to 1990. Because we will also be maintaining currency, the next few issues of *ISA* will contain more abstracts than usual.

After the quality improvement program is complete, we expect to turn our attention to significantly expanding the list of journals covered by *ISA*. Suggestions for new titles to add are therefore solicited.

Fig. 4.33. Some promising statements from an early ISA editorial.

In light of an essay by the editors of the database published by DIALOG (*http://library.Dialog.com/products/f202.html*), which claims that there is no backlog in the database, the fact that by September 2000 there were only 114 primary sources (including proceedings) suggests a significant decline not only in the number of records but also in the number of sources to be covered in 2000 (figure 4.34).

The very same editorial shown in figure 4.33 contemplated the plan of "significantly expanding the list of journals covered by ISA." This obviously did not happen. While the numbers in figure 4.32 are somewhat inflated by the inconsistent, inaccurate, and hence different spellings of the journal names, this applies equally to the period under the old and the new management and does not distort the picture.

Publication year	# of "journals"	# of "journal" records	Total # of records	Depth factor
1995	224	6,421	8,921	28.67
1996	234	6,838	9,327	29.22
1997	228	5,653	6,449	24.79
1998	278	4,645	4,655	16.71
1999	234	3,618	3,618	15.46
2000	117	1,173	1,173	10.03

Fig. 4.34. Declining depth factor between 1995 and September 2000.

The depth of coverage at the individual journal level has also been suffering. The pattern in the current three years shows the same shallow, or roller-coaster, coverage and gaps that crippled the pre-1998 segment of the database. Although the list of core journals is not published anymore, the sources sampled for depth of coverage represent the most important journals in the subject areas that are purportedly in the focus of ISA.

For example, *MIS Quarterly* (also searched under the fully spelled-out name also used in ISA, *Management Information Systems Quarterly*) is on a steep downward roll (figure 4.35) in spite having been the top-ranked journal in the library and information science category by the Journal Citation Reports issued in 1999. The same declining trend is true for *Library Administration and Management*, another prominently mentioned subject on the ISA bluesheet and a highly ranked journal in Journal Citation Reports (figure 4.36).

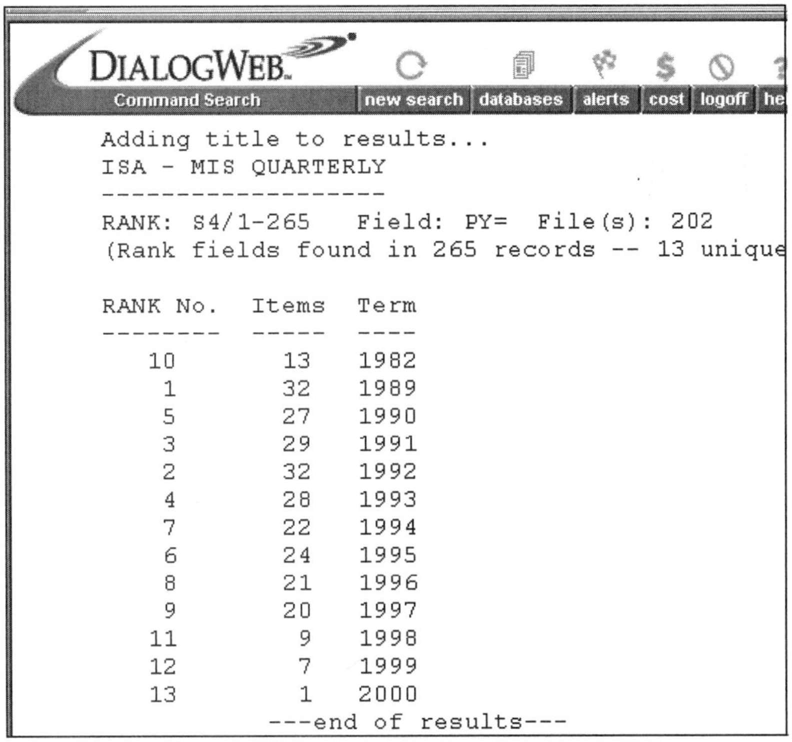

Fig. 4.35. *MIS Quarterly* coverage on a steep downward roll.

```
DIALOGWEB.          C      🗐    ❦    $    ⊘   ?
Command Search           new search databases alerts cost logoff he

ISA - LIBRARY ADMINISTRATION & MANAGEMENT
-------------------------------------------
RANK: S17/1-248    Field: PY=   File(s): 202
(Rank fields found in 248 records -- 13 unique

RANK No.  Items  Term
--------  -----  ----
     9      12   1988
    10      12   1989
    11      10   1990
     5      22   1991
     8      17   1992
     7      20   1993
     4      24   1994
     1      38   1995
     2      36   1996
     3      26   1997
     6      21   1998
    12       5   1999
    13       5   2000
          ---end of results---
```

Fig. 4.36. Declining coverage of *Library Administration and Management* in ISA.

The *NFAIS Newsletter,* which is dedicated to the topic of abstracting and indexing, listed as the first item in the subject coverage section of the ISA bluesheet, was totally ignored in 1999, then rebounded in 2000, as shown in figure 4.37.

Set	Term Searched	Items
S1	JN="NFAIS NEWSLETTER"	199
S2	S1/2000	33
S3	S1/1999	0
S4	S1/1998	17
S5	S1/1997	34
S6	S1/1996	36

Show Database Details for:
202: Information Science Abstracts ▼ Bluesheet

Fig. 4.37. Entire 1999 year missing from NFAIS coverage in ISA.

Beyond the poor coverage of important journals, there is also the question of journals that are not covered by a database at all, even though they clearly represent the best sources for the subject that the database claims to cover. These issues are discussed in Chapter 5 about the journal base.

CURRENCY

One of the most often cited advantages of online databases over their printed equivalents is their timeliness. The currency of databases indicates how fast a record becomes available in a CD-ROM or online database after the publication of the primary document. Evaluating this measure has been reported extensively since the 1960s in studies by Gilchrist (1966), Gilchrist and Presanis (1971), Dansey (1973), Edwards (1976), and Turtle and Robinson (1974) for the printed indexing and abstracting services in library and information science. Bottle and Efthimiadis (1984), Ernest, Lange, and Herring (1988) and Jacsó (1992a) extended the time lag studies to electronic products and beyond the field of library and information science. Jacsó (1992a) demonstrated various techniques to measure time lag on a large scale. Some of these techniques were used by Lawrence and Lenti (1995) in testing the currency of the International Aerospace Abstracts database against some of its peer databases.

Comparison across databases with similar coverage is particularly informative. Hightower and Schwarzwalder (1991) measured the currency of 24 databases with materials science coverage. The time lag differences were stunning. While a few databases managed to enter nearly 67 percent of the records in the same year the original document was published, in the Soviet Science & Technology database there was not a single such record. This may explain why, without the "*Sputnik* pressure," NTIS produced a disappointingly low 5 percent of records available in the same year when the document was published.

By 1998 this ratio improved: 18 percent of the records added to the database were for documents published in the same year. In 1999 this same-year ratio increased to 24 percent but at the expense of volume. Although in 1998 a total of 72,143 records were added to the database, in 1999 only 45,430 were added.

Soremark (1990) found that for records that appeared both in MEDLINE and EMBASE, the former lagged behind two to four months on the average. By 1999, MEDLINE's timeliness was superior to that of EMBASE—at least on the PubMed site that introduced the PreMEDLINE records. These records—added daily—provide basic citation information and abstracts but no MeSH descriptors. When these records are completed, they become full-fledged MEDLINE records. This update is done daily on the PubMed system. Considering that this is a free database, it is a big asset for those who want to get the scoop about upcoming publications. In another test for currency, a search on December 23, 1999, for the terms *medical* and *publication year 2000* PY=2000 yielded 186 records from EMBASE on DIALOG and 443 from PubMed.

Jaguszewski and Kempf (1995) compared the currency of four current awareness services in the fields of chemistry and mathematics. They found that Uncover was the most current, followed by Inside Information, ContentsFirst, and Current Contents on Diskette, although ContentsFirst was more current than Inside Information in chemistry.

Web databases hosted directly by file producers will dramatically improve the timeliness of databases as the intermediary, the third-party database publisher, is eliminated. At this early stage, such direct posting on the Web by the content provider is typically done to add yet another channel to existing ones to publish a database. In the long run, this trend may threaten the online services that publish the content of third parties. As through the Web everyone can be reached, online publishers of third parties' content will have to work hard to justify the added cost and unavoidable delay of their intermediation. This is especially true for the small online services.

The appeal of one-stop shopping, cross-database searching, duplicate removal, and sophisticated and powerful search engines will remain good reasons for offering databases through database "supermarkets" in addition to the self-publishing of databases by the content providers. Users, however, should compare the timeliness of data on different hosts.

In such comparisons, you have to consider if all the hosts have the same source file. Some hosts, for example, may not use the non–English language subset of MEDLINE, which could dramatically improve its timeliness, considering the delay in getting foreign language primary documents.

In comparing the currency of different databases, you have to be particularly careful to compare apples with apples. Databases on weekly update schedules obviously would be more current than the monthly updated ones, which are, in turn, more current than the quarterly updated databases. However, such factors may justify the use of one database over another comparable one. (Doing the test on the day when one database has just been updated and the other was just about to be updated can distort the results unfairly.)

In comparing the currency of newspaper databases, you have to realize that the full-text version is likely to be directly fed to the online service before the presses start rolling at the printer. Databases that add substantial index terms to newspaper article records, such as the National Newspaper Index, are delayed simply because the indexing process takes time. The databases that also offer abstracts (such as Bell & Howell's Newspaper Abstracts Daily) are likely to have the longest time lag. It is no accident that on the day following the funeral of King Hussein of Jordan, the full-text digital newspapers with direct feed into the database version had the most records about the funeral, and most of the indexing and abstracting databases did not even know about the passing away of the king.

Newswires are supposed to be the most current among databases, but a test on July 15, 1999, showed that not all of the newswires were up-to-the-minute, and the Canada Newswire database—which promises multiple updates each day—was 10 days late on DIALOG (figure 4.38). Note that online database services get the information after a specified moratorium (usually a few hours) expires. A 10-day delay is way beyond any moratorium. AP News, U.S. Newswire, AFP English Wire, and AFP International French Wire were one day behind, and PR Newswire was two days behind. Only Japan Economic Newswire and Canada Newswire were significantly behind schedule.

Newspapers, by definition, are daily, but it does not mean that they are literally up-to-date on the online service of a third party. A quick look at the banners of the Papers category of DIALOG databases gives a first impression how current the databases are. Unfortunately, the banners do not always reliably reflect the update date. They should, because it is an automatic process to add the update date to the banner. The most reliable check for newspaper database updatedness is to run a search specifying the current day (or the current day and the previous one or two days for mercy).

Such a search on December 23, 1999, showed that most of the newspaper databases really were up to date, and only a few were delayed by one or more days. The *San Jose Mercury News* seemed to

```
                    DIALINDEX®
         _____

    File   Name
    ----   -------------
     258:  AP News Jul_1984-1999/Jul 14
     261:  UPI News_1999-1999/Jul 15
     605:  U.S. Newswire_1999-1999/Jul 14
     606:  Africa News_1999-1999/Jul 15
     607:  ITAR/TASS News_1999-1999/Jul 15
     609:  Bridge World Markets News_1989-1999/Jul 15
     610:  Business Wire_1999-1999/Jul 15
     612:  Japan Economic Newswire(TM)_1984-1999/Jul 09
     613:  PR Newswire_1999-1999/Jul 13
     614:  AFP English Wire_1991--1999/Jul 14
     615:  AFP Intl French Wire_1991--1999/Jul 14
     616:  Canada NewsWire_1999-1999/Jul 05
     618:  Xinhua News_1999-1999/Jul 15
     649:  NEWSWIRE ASAP(TM)_1999/Jul 15
```

Fig. 4.38. List of newswire databases with update banner.

have been the most belated. The banner indicated its last update as of December 18, 1999. The searches for the update fields for UD=19991223, UD=19991222, and UD=19991221 proved that it was updated last on December 21, 1999 (figure 4.39)—not too good for a newspaper from the Silicon Valley, but not as bad as the banner suggests. In my experience, banner dates are correct for about 80 percent of the databases on DIALOG, including all the databases with library and information science coverage.

Users of the Ovid system know at log-in time how current the databases are because the list of databases with the date banner are automatically displayed (figure 4.40). (Ovid also sends e-mail messages, if you wish, about database updates.) SilverPlatter and H. W. Wilson have a similar start-up screen that advises users of the update status of databases (figures 4.41 and 4.42). In DIALOG the database and banner listing are not automatic and must be initiated by the user by selecting the databases and using the SHOW FILES command (figure 4.43).

```
                      Dialog Response

File 146:WASHINGTON POST ONLINE 1983-1999/DEC 23
          (c) 1999 WASHINGTON POST
File 471:NEW YORK TIMES FULLTEXT-90 DAY 1999/DEC 22
          (c) 1999 THE NEW YORK TIMES
File 489:THE NEWS-SENTINEL 1991-1999/Dec 22
          (c) 1999 FT. WAYNE NEWSPAPERS, INC
File 490:TALLAHASSEE DEMOCRAT 1993- 1999/Dec 22
          (c) 1999 TALLAHASSEE DEMOCRAT
File 492:ARIZONA REPUB/PHOENIX GAZ 1986-1999/Dec 22
          (c) 1999 PHOENIX NEWSPAPERS
File 494:ST LOUISPOST-DISPATCH 1988-1999/Dec 21
          (c) 1999 ST LOUIS POST-DISPATCH
File 496:THE SACRAMENTO BEE 1988-1999/Dec 21
          (c) 1999 SACRAMENTO BEE
File 498:DETROIT FREE PRESS 1987-1999/Dec 21
          (c) 1999 DETROIT FREE PRESS INC.
File 630:LOS ANGELES TIMES 1993-1999/DEC 22
          (c) 1999 LOS ANGELES TIMES
File 631:BOSTON GLOBE 1980-1999/Dec 22
          (c) 1999 BOSTON GLOBE
File 633:PHIL.INQUIRER 1983-1999/Dec 21
          (c) 1999 PHILADELPHIA NEWSPAPERS INC
File 634:San Jose Mercury  Jun 1985-1999/Dec 18
          (c) 1999 San Jose Mercury News
File 638:NEWSDAY/NEW YORK NEWSDAY 1987-1999/Dec 22
          (c) 1999 NEWSDAY INC.
```

Fig. 4.39. Checking for current day coverage in newspaper databases.

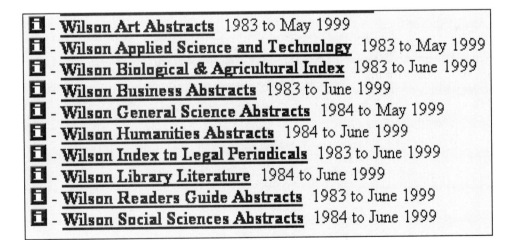

Fig. 4.40. Excerpt from Ovid's database list with date banners.

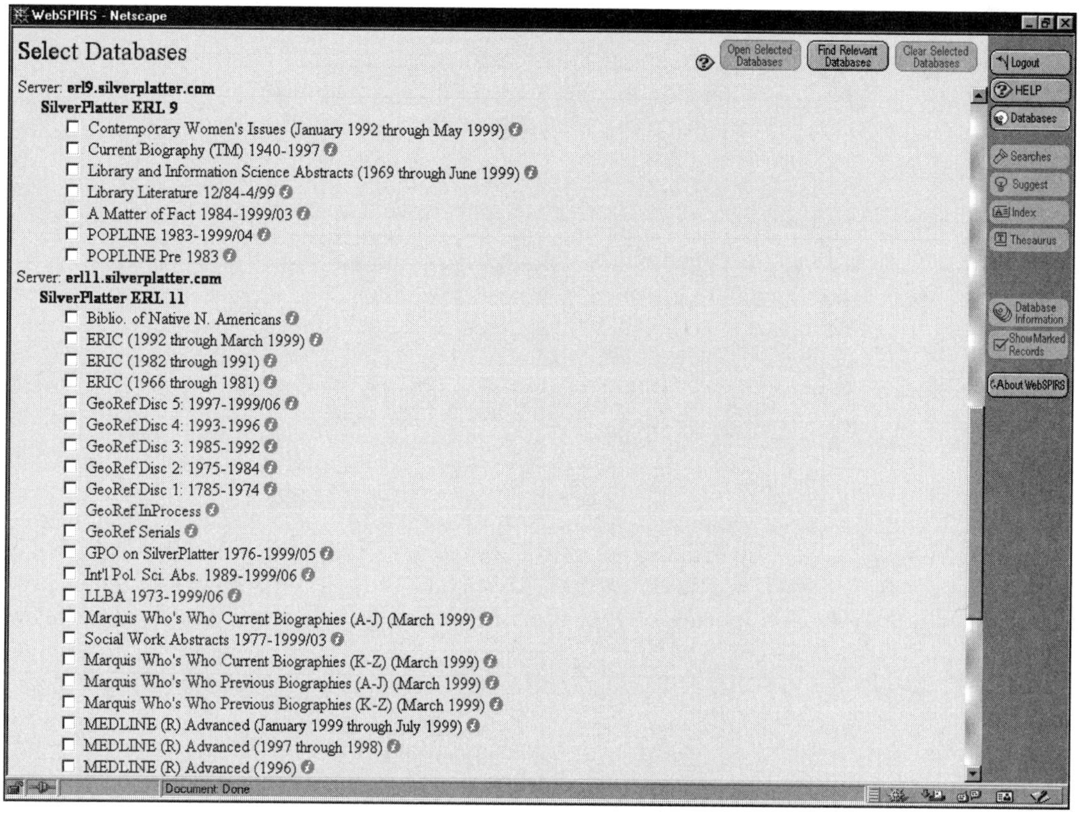

Fig. 4.41. Excerpt from SilverPlatter database list with date banners.

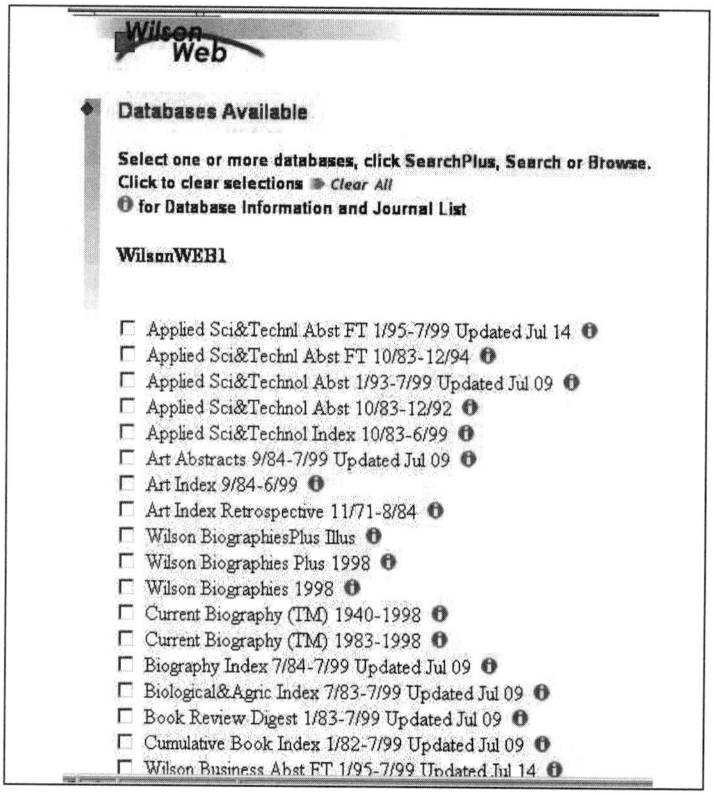

Fig. 4.42. Excerpt from H. W. Wilson database list with date banners.

The previous screen shots also illustrate the difference in delays of updating databases on different hosts. It is no surprise that the file producer's versions were the most current for H. W. Wilson's Biological & Agricultural Index, Art Abstracts, and Applied Science & Technology, as well as for Business Abstracts. In Business Abstracts, Biological & Agricultural Index, and Humanities Abstracts, Ovid and DIALOG were identical. Ovid was better than DIALOG with Readers' Guide Abstracts, and DIALOG was better than Ovid with the rest of the files, sporting June 1999 updates.

A consistent pattern of updating a database is a prerequisite for timely availability of records, of course. Looking at the update index sheds some light on the pattern but does not tell the whole story. The value in the UD (update) field indicates the year and the week, month or quarter, or just the sequence number of the intended update date of the set of records added. Sometimes this coincides with the actual update dates; sometimes it does not. Even so, displaying the UD index may show unexpected gaps.

This is the case of the ISA database, which, although it was promised to be updated 11 times a year, was updated only 8 times in 1999 (figure 4.44). In early 2000, ISA announced that the database update will be reduced from the nominal 11 times a year to 9 times a year; about six weeks apart each. It turned out to be wishful thinking. The database update was even more haphazard in 2000 than before, and users were left without updates for months in a row. As of November, 2000, ISA was updated six times and certainly not evenly distributed.

LISA (figure 4.45) and Library Literature (figure 4.46) were updated 12 times in 1999, and the updates were very regular in both databases. However, LISA showed serious gaps in 1998. It had no updates according to the UD field in 1998 for January, February, April, May, June, and November, and the March update was minimal (figure 4.45). Library Literature was updated on schedule in both 1998 and 1999 (figure 4.46).

```
                DIALINDEX®
        _____

File   Name
____   _____
  98:  General Sci Abs/Full-Text_1984-1999/Jun
  99:  Wilson Appl. Sci & Tech Abs_1983-1999/Jun
 141:  Readers Guide_1983-1999/May
 142:  Social Sciences Abstracts_1983-1999/Jun
 143:  Biol. & Agric. Index_1983-1999/Jun
 435:  Art Abstracts_1984-1999/Jun
 436:  Humanities Abs Full Text_1984-1999/Jun
 437:  Education Abstracts_1983-1999/Jun
 438:  Library Literature_1984-1999/Jun
 553:  Wilson Bus. Abs. FullText_1982-1999/Jun
```

Fig. 4.43. Excerpt from the DIALOG database list with date banners.

Set	Term Searched	Items
S1	UD=199901	609
S2	UD=199902	469
S3	UD=199903	433
S4	UD=199904	495
S5	UD=199905	0
S6	UD=199906	452
S7	UD=199907	0
S8	UD=199908	422
S9	UD=199909	0
S10	UD=199910	385
S11	UD=199911	917
S12	UD=199912	0

Show Database Details for:
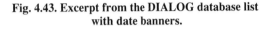
202: Information Science Abstracts Bluesheet

Fig. 4.44. Update pattern in ISA in 1999.

Set	Term Searched	Items
S1	UD=199901	1328
S2	UD=199902	826
S3	UD=199903	1201
S4	UD=199904	888
S5	UD=199905	1051
S6	UD=199906	1092
S7	UD=199907	1318
S8	UD=199908	1163
S9	UD=199909	1201
S10	UD=199910	997
S11	UD=199911	1708
S12	UD=199912	1152

Show Database Details for:

61: LISA (Library & Information Science Abstracts) Blu

Fig. 4.45. Update pattern in LISA in 1999.

Set	Term Searched	Items
S1	UD=199901	1088
S2	UD=199902	1442
S3	UD=199903	2268
S4	UD=199904	3076
S5	UD=199905	1448
S6	UD=199906	1632
S7	UD=199907	1444
S8	UD=199908	1678
S9	UD=199909	1851
S10	UD=199910	1215
S11	UD=199911	1616
S12	UD=199912	1311

Show Database Details for:

438: Library Literature   Bluesheet   Rates

Fig. 4.46. Update pattern in Library Literature in 1999.

For those who were updating their databases regularly, the UD index was a reliable indicator for the update pattern. However, some file producers skipped one or more months of update, then submitted several months of updates to catch up. The records were added with the UD field set to the month when the database was meant to be updated. After the fact, users could not tell if the update pattern was really like it appears to have been. This is akin to a baby-sitter who skips the five or six meals a day a baby is supposed to have on schedule, and then rams all the meals down the baby's throat once at 10:00 P.M., before the parents come home. She got all the meals for the day in, did she not?

Following a debate on the pages of *Database* magazine between Allcock (1997) and Jacsó (1997c), DIALOG introduced the ZD field for several databases. It is automatically generated when the database is actually updated. It reflects the accurate date and the number of records added. Comparing the entries in the UD index and the ZD index pinpoints the differences clearly (figure 4.47). In the case of ISA, the update due in January was added on April 9, the February update on May 20, the March update on June 7, and so on. The update for May was skipped, and the one for July must have been the off month. It could have been used to catch up somewhat with the backlog and bone up on the volume of new records, which was barely more than 50 percent of the previous years.

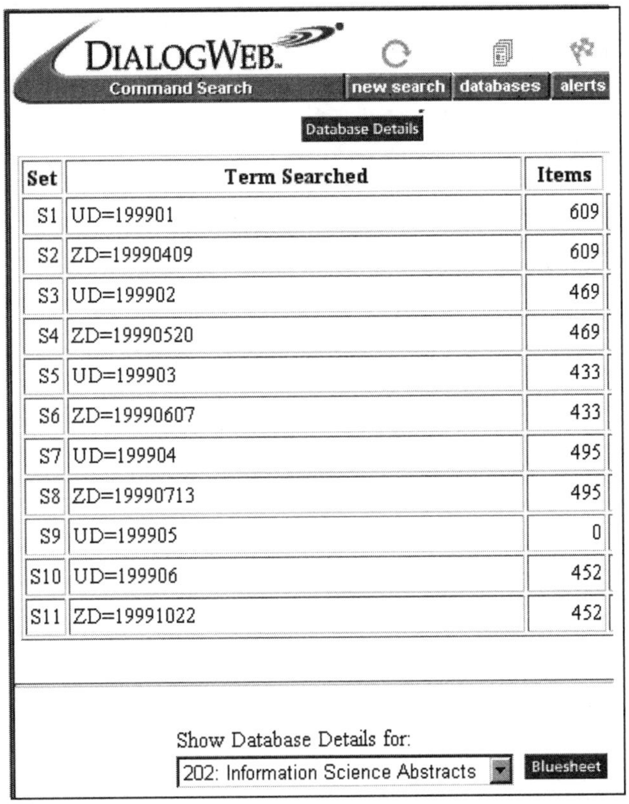

Set	Term Searched	Items
S1	UD=199901	609
S2	ZD=19990409	609
S3	UD=199902	469
S4	ZD=19990520	469
S5	UD=199903	433
S6	ZD=19990607	433
S7	UD=199904	495
S8	ZD=19990713	495
S9	UD=199905	0
S10	UD=199906	452
S11	ZD=19991022	452

Show Database Details for:
202: Information Science Abstracts

Fig. 4.47. Comparing UD and ZD index values for actual update pattern in ISA.

Even a "squeaky clean" update pattern does not guarantee current information. The second or third update run in a given year may not carry any records for publications of that year in some databases, even if they are updated monthly. On the other hand, for other monthly updated databases, even the first update may have records for articles published in the current year. Figures 4.48 and 4.49 illustrate the composition of the total update sets of 1999 from the three library and information science databases, and from the library and information science subsets of Social SciSearch and Trade & Industry databases, respectively. The charts show what percentage of the records are for documents of the current year, the previous year, two years before, and older. The meager volume of records added to ISA deserves special attention, as it is about 30 percent of the updates of previous years.

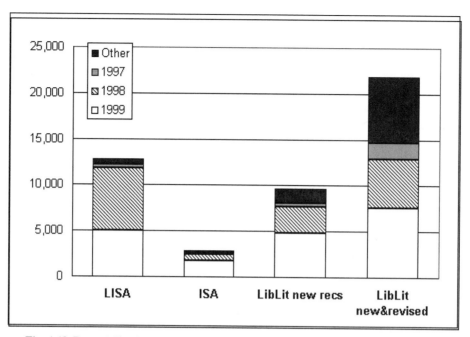

Fig. 4.48. Record distribution by publication years in 1999 updates in LIS databases.

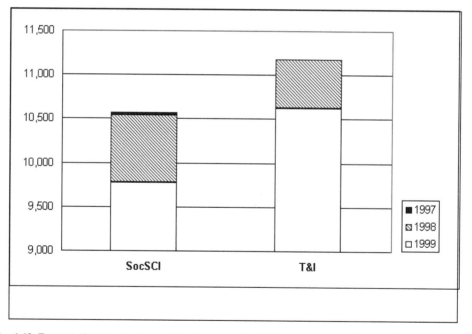

Fig. 4.49. Record distribution by publication years in 1999 updates in databases with LIS coverage.

Another way of measuring the time lag on an adequately large scale is to select several thousands or even tens of thousands of records of a given publication year and determine what the distribution of the update years was for those records—that is, how many of them were added in the same year as the publication year, the next year, two years, three years, or even more years later. Figures 4.50 and 4.51 illustrate the results of this technique comparing ISA and LibLit. LISA could not be used for this test because several batches of updates between November 1997 and June 1998 were aggregated into one large entry (UD=199711-199806) in the UD index, containing 7,905 records. This means that there is no way to tell the difference between a November 1997 and a June 1998 update, or any other dates in between.

You always must check such idiosyncrasies, which can seriously distort the results. In the case of the LibLit database, only the records that had the ST=NEW RECORD field value were analyzed, as H. W. Wilson did a massive record revision operation (but not at the expense of current entry). A few, small-volume correction batches do not have an impact on the results.

```
DISTRIBUTION OF UPDATE YEARS FOR PY=1990 PUBLICATIONS IN ISA
-----------------------------------------------------------------
RANK: S1/1-8421   Field: BN=   File(s): 202
(Rank fields found in 8421 records -- 10 unique terms)

RANK No.   Items   %Ranked   Term
--------   -----   -------   ----
      2    3132     37.2%    90
      1    4111     48.8%    91
      3     716     08.5%    92
      4     301     03.6%    93
      9      13     00.2%    94
      6      38      00.5%    95
      8      19     00.2%    96
     10       2     00.0%    97
      5      69     00.8%    98
      7      20     00.2%    99
           ---end of results---
```

Fig. 4.50. Test query to determine delay of update from the publication year in ISA.

```
DISTRIBUTION OF UPDATE YEARS FOR PY=1990 PUBLICATIONS IN LIBLIT
-----------------------------------------------------------------
RANK: S1/1-15301   Field: AA=   File(s): 438
(Rank fields found in 15301 records -- 5 unique terms)

RANK No.   Items   %Ranked   Term
--------   -----   -------   ----
      1    7199     47.0%    BLIB90
      2    6727     44.0%    BLIB91
      3    1034     06.8%    BLIB92
      4     328     02.1%    BLIB93
      5      13     00.1%    BLIB94
           ---end of results---
```

Fig. 4.51. Delay of updates from the publication year in LibLit.

It is true that a next year update means quite another thing for a publication that was published in December and added to the database the following January, and for a publication that appeared in February of 1997 and was added to the database in November of the next year. If you work with large numbers of records, these extremes will even out.

The appeal of such techniques is that it is very easy to refine the set and repeat the search. It takes only a few minutes when you want to check, for example, if there is any difference in the time lag pattern of conference paper versus journal article records, or English language and foreign language publication records.

It is worth it to make such distinctions because an international database, such as LISA, covers many journals from developing and less-developed countries. In these cases, much of the delay can be attributed to the lateness of the source publications (that is, a January issue is published only in April). Mailing delays of the journals can also be significant. Of course, publication of U.S. journals, especially the scholarly ones, including library and information science journals, is also often delayed. Sometimes the delay is so bad that the publisher combines two issues (saving on postage costs, but wreaking havoc in serials control).

Care must also be taken to eliminate correction records that may appear in a database several months later than the original record. This is possible if the correction records are identified by a special symbol after the update date, such as in UD=9902C, or by using a special field as H. W. Wilson does by offering the ST=NEW RECORD and the ST=REVISION OR CORRECTION RECORD index entries.

Yet another possibility for determining time lag on the journal level is to use the digits of the data element that identify the year of creating or adding the records. Such a data element is not available in every database, but in many it is. In Information Science Abstracts, for example, the first two digits of the BN data element identify the year of the print issue of the database, so it is quite easy to reconstruct how belatedly records were added for the journals that IFI/Plenum claimed to be core journals.

Ranking the result set of *RQ* records by update year to show the update pattern (figure 4.52) does not give the impression that it enjoyed core journal treatment. It was covered only from 1990 (when it was added to the database, much belatedly with a meager six records), then nothing in 1994, and again a meager four records in 1996. In evaluating the major features of the ISA database, Jacsó (1998a) used *RQ* as the journal that epitomizes the utterly unprofessional treatment of even such purportedly core journals. Records for *RQ* (and some other core journals) were added to ISA in 1997, 1998, and 1999—belatedly, so now there is a good coverage across publication years (figure 4.53).

The belated addition explains why there are so many records added to *RQ* these years, even though the journal ceased publication under that title in mid-1997. The hasty filling of the gaps did not improve the currency of the database, however. There were no new records added for many journals. The number of yearly volume of records plummeted and reached an all-time low in 1999.

The update year and publication year pattern of *RQ* in LibLit shows a far more favorable currency (figure 4.54). Ideally, the bars representing the volume by update year and publication year should be almost identical to each year. The same asynchrony that we saw with *RQ* is characteristic of many of the other "core" journals in ISA, including *CD-ROM Professional*, which also ceased publication under this title in 1996. As shown in figure 4.55, more records were added to ISA in 1997 and 1998 (the two years after the journal ceased publication under that title) than in the previous six years together. Although this is certainly a late awakening, it is better late than never.

```
                        Dialog Response
                    ────────────────────────

    Adding title to results...
    RQ UPDATES IN ISA FOR 1990-1997 BY UD YEAR NUMBER
    ------------------------------------------------------

    RANK: S6/1-284    Field: BN=  File(s): 202
    (Rank fields found in 284 records -- 9 unique terms)


    RANK No.   Items   Term
    --------   -----   ----
        8         6    90
        5        30    91
        4        31    92
        7        23    93
        3        33    95
        9         4    96
        1        78    97
        2        53    98
        6        26    99
                 ---end of results---
```

Fig. 4.52. Update year pattern of *RQ* in ISA.

```
Adding title to results...
RECORDS OF RQ BY PUBLICATION YEAR
---------------------------------
RANK: S1/1-710    Field: PY=  File(s): 202
(Rank fields found in 710 records -- 28 unique terms)

RANK No.   Items   Term
--------   -----   ----
   27         7    1970
   24        13    1971
   16        24    1972
   22        19    1973
   26        12    1974
   23        15    1975
   17        21    1976
   28         5    1977
   25        13    1978
   18        21    1979
   10        27    1980
   12        26    1981
    6        35    1982
   20        20    1983
   11        27    1984
   15        25    1985
   13        26    1986
    8        30    1987
    7        32    1988
    9        28    1989
   14        26    1990
   19        21    1991
    1        56    1992
    3        40    1993
    5        36    1994
    4        37    1995
    2        48    1996
   21        20    1997
         ---end of results---
```

Fig. 4.53. Publication year pattern of *RQ* in ISA.

```
rqinliblit.gif [1:1] [Background]                    rqupdliblit.gif [1:1] [Background]

                                                                        Dialog R

Adding title to results.              Adding title to results...
RQ RECORDS BY PUBLICATIC              RQ RECORDS ADDED TO LIBLIT - RA
------------------------              ------------------------------
RANK: S2/1-1354    Field:             RANK: S2/1-1354    Field: AA=  F
(Rank fields found in 13              (Rank fields found in 1354 reco

RANK No.   Items   Term              RANK No.   Items   Term
--------   -----   ----              --------   -----   ----
   13        56    1984                  1       146    BLIB85
    1       126    1985                  4       118    BLIB86
    3       114    1986                  9        89    BLIB87
    5       112    1987                  2       145    BLIB88
    4       113    1988                  5       114    BLIB89
    2       118    1989                  6       113    BLIB90
    6       112    1990                  7       100    BLIB91
    9       100    1991                 11        80    BLIB92
    7       110    1992                  3       144    BLIB93
    8       107    1993                  8        94    BLIB94
   10        88    1994                 13        51    BLIB95
   11        85    1995                 10        85    BLIB96
   12        79    1996                 12        75    BLIB97
   14        34    1997                      ---end of results---
         ---end of res
```

Fig. 4.54. Actual update year and publication year pattern of *RQ* in LibLit.

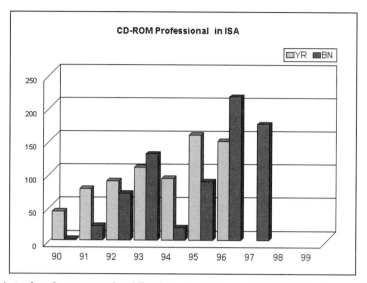

Fig. 4.55. Actual update year and publication year pattern of *CD-ROM Professional* **in ISA.**

Currency of databases is more critical than retrospectivity, as for most users current information is more important than historical information. Very often users are willing to pay more for current information. This is clearly illustrated by the price of transcription services that charge far more for transcripts of current television and radio programs than for one-week-old or one-month-old transcripts. Sometimes a retrospective subset of a database covering, say, 1966 to 1982 is much less expensive than the 1983–1999 segment.

In directories, encyclopedias, or biographical databases, the best way to test currency is to check to see if fairly current information about a person, company, country, or journal is available in the database. For example, in the case of the major CD-ROM encyclopedias that were published in late summer of 1999, the obvious checks for currency testing included such things as the inclusion of the 1998 Academy Award–winning movies (announced in March 1999), the 1999 Pulitzer Prize winners in drama and poetry (announced in mid-April 1999), and the 1999 NBA championship (decided by the game on June 25, 1999).

Of the three general interest encyclopedias, none included information about the 1999 Pulitzer Prizes. *Compton's* proved to be the most current in the other two tests (figures 4.56 and 4.57). *Microsoft Encarta* was the second best, and as with *Compton's,* the fresh data made it into the appealingly designed table graphs (figure 4.58). Surprisingly, the otherwise-very-good *Grolier Encyclopedia* fared badly on all three of the tests. Its Academy Awards headline promises listings for 1990 to Present, but it ends with the 1997 winners (announced in March 1998). Its poorly designed table is another matter, but it was also disappointing (figure 4.59).

1991	'The Silence of the Lambs'	Anthony Hopkins ('The Silence of the Lambs')	Jodie Foster ('The Silence of the Lambs')	Jonathan Demme ('The Silence of the Lambs')
1992	'Unforgiven'	Al Pacino ('Scent of a Woman')	Emma Thompson ('Howards End')	Clint Eastwood ('Unforgiven')
1993	'Schindler's List'	Tom Hanks ('Philadelphia')	Holly Hunter ('The Piano')	Steven Spielberg ('Schindler's List')
1994	'Forrest Gump'	Tom Hanks ('Forrest Gump')	Jessica Lange ('Blue Sky')	Robert Zemeckis ('Forrest Gump')
1995	'Braveheart'	Nicolas Cage ('Leaving Las Vegas')	Susan Sarandon ('Dead Man Walking')	Mel Gibson ('Braveheart')
1996	'The English Patient'	Geoffrey Rush ('Shine')	Francis McDormand ('Fargo')	Anthony Minghella ('The English Patient')
1997	'Titanic'	Jack Nicholson ('As Good as It Gets')	Helen Hunt ('As Good as It Gets')	James Cameron ('Titanic')
1998	'Shakespeare in Love'	Roberto Benigni ('Life is Beautiful')	Gwyneth Paltrow ('Shakespeare in Love')	Steven Spielberg ('Saving Private Ryan')

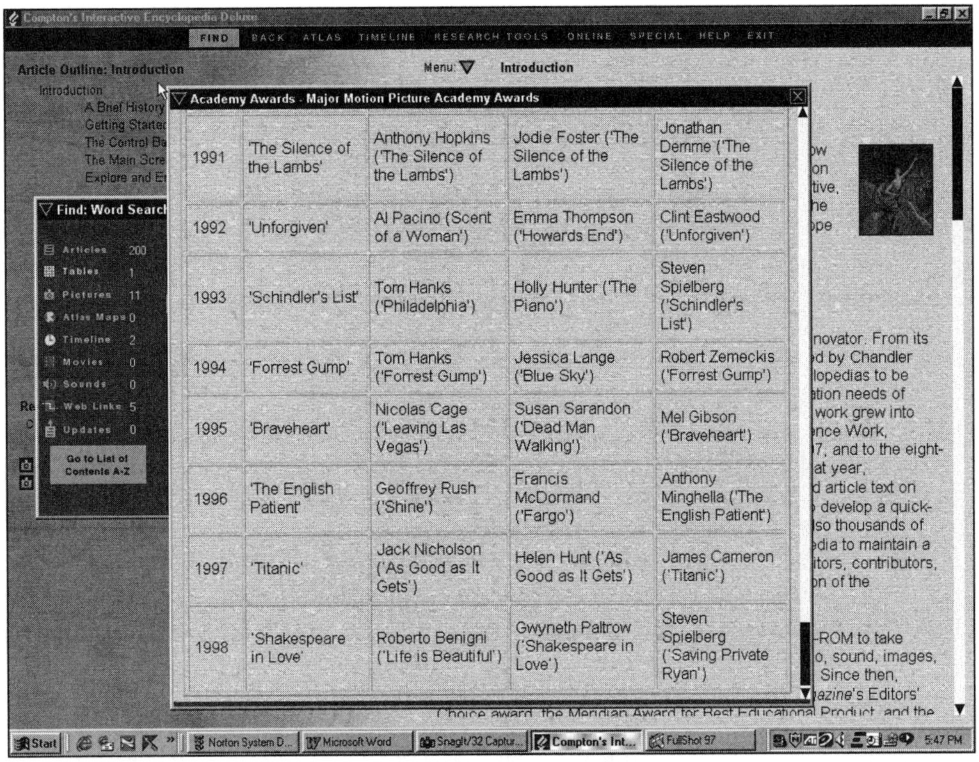

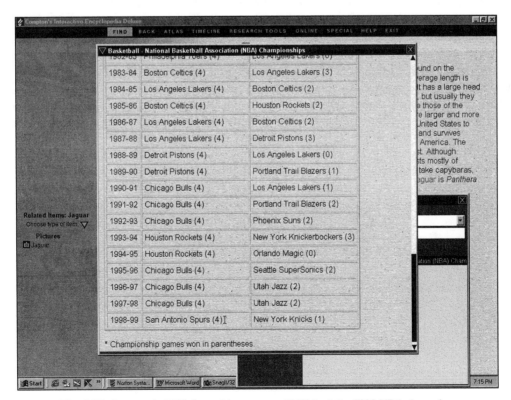

Fig. 4.56. *Compton's 2000* (issued in summer 1999) had the 1998 Academy Award–winning movies (announced in March 1999).

1983-84	Boston Celtics (4)	Los Angeles Lakers (3)
1984-85	Los Angeles Lakers (4)	Boston Celtics (2)
1985-86	Boston Celtics (4)	Houston Rockets (2)
1986-87	Los Angeles Lakers (4)	Boston Celtics (2)
1987-88	Los Angeles Lakers (4)	Detroit Pistons (3)
1988-89	Detroit Pistons (4)	Los Angeles Lakers (0)
1989-90	Detroit Pistons (4)	Portland Trail Blazers (1)
1990-91	Chicago Bulls (4)	Los Angeles Lakers (1)
1991-92	Chicago Bulls (4)	Portland Trail Blazers (2)
1992-93	Chicago Bulls (4)	Phoenix Suns (2)
1993-94	Houston Rockets (4)	New York Knickerbockers (3)
1994-95	Houston Rockets (4)	Orlando Magic (0)
1995-96	Chicago Bulls (4)	Seattle SuperSonics (2)
1996-97	Chicago Bulls (4)	Utah Jazz (2)
1997-98	Chicago Bulls (4)	Utah Jazz (2)
1998-99	San Antonio Spurs (4)	New York Knicks (1)

* Championship games won in parentheses.

Fig. 4.57. *Compton's 2000* (issued in summer 1999) had the 1999 NBA champion.

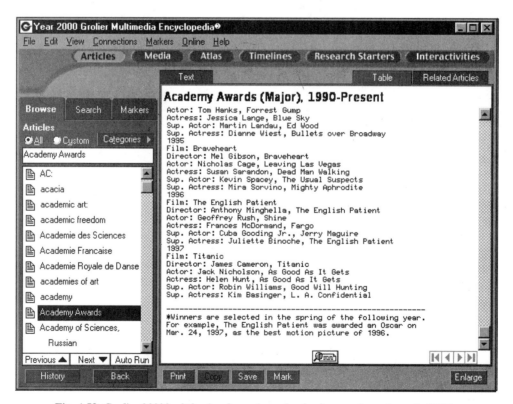

Fig. 4.58. *Microsoft Encarta 2000* had the 1998 Academy Award–winning movies.

Fig. 4.59. *Grolier 2000* had the Academy Award–winning movies only up to 1997.

Online databases and online encyclopedias are at an advantage, as they can be updated continually, and, quite often, they are. Checking the entries about King Hussein of Jordan three months after his passing and then in every subsequent month is one of the tests I used for checking currency. It is particularly disappointing that the A&E Biography database (*http://www.biography.com*) still had not updated his entry ten months after his death (figure 4.60), nor was it aware of the deaths of five of the six former Nobel laureates who passed away in 1999.

Fig. 4.60. Outdated biography of King Hussein at the end of 1999.

Everything is relative, of course. The Electric Library's version of the *Columbia Encyclopedia,* third edition, also has King Hussein ruling, Frank Sinatra singing, and Sir Georg (not George) Solti conducting in September 2000. The fifth edition, which was replaced by the sixth edition in March 2000, also available free through the Information Please Web site (*http://www.infoplease com*), had current information for all the tests. Most users just see the moniker "Columbia Encyclopedia" and probably don't know about the currency differences (and other differences) between the two versions. Many may be out of luck for good because typing the word *encyclopedia* by itself as a URL (even without the *www* prefix and the *com* suffix) would take the user to the Electric Library version of the encyclopedia, which was also upgraded in 2001 and offers the unabridged 6th edition of the *Columbia Encyclopedia.*

Database Source Coverage

The coverage of a database refers to the type, genre, language, and geographic origin of the primary sources processed by the file producer. Journal coverage is of special importance, as every area has its own core journals that are the most widely circulating, the most prestigious in the profession, or the most acknowledged in academia. The criterion of "most widely circulating" must be approached, of course, with a grain of salt, as tabloids are among the highest circulating rags, but they are not too relevant in any profession except perhaps the entertainment industry. Then again, some of the overrated refereed journals that circulate in 300 to 400 copies and that often lack relevant content would have a far lower circulation figure had they not been part of association membership but sold for subscription.

TYPES OF SOURCES

The types of sources covered may be an important distinguishing factor among databases with similar subject coverage, or among different implementations of the "same" database. Interestingly, such important distinguishing factors may remain hidden from the typical user if the database publisher does not make a point of emphasizing them. The sources covered by documentary (i.e., indexing, abstracting, and full-text) databases are usually easy to determine. Evaluating source coverage in directories is more problematic because of the greater variety and ambiguity in determining what qualifies as a source document, a subject, or an object.

Directory Databases

Few users would realize that DIALOG's implementation of the Bowker database includes not only records from the *Books In Print* volumes (along with *Forthcoming Books*) but also *Books Out of Print* records. Bowker has been publishing separate print volumes under separate titles for these two categories of books. It also offers separate CD-ROM volumes based on the status of the book. Most online and CD-ROM publishers offer only the records for books with the in-print and forthcoming status. Expanding and searching on the status index in the DIALOG version makes it clear that in mid-1999, there were nearly 900,000 records in this database that would really deserve the moniker BIP/BOP (figure 5.1) and then some.

Furthermore, there are also more than 220,000 records with reviews from well known and time-honored sources of book reviews (figure 5.2). Again, in the CD-ROM arena, there is a more expensive version of *Books In Print with Book Reviews;* therefore, this extra feature in the DIALOG implementation would deserve some mention in the title, such as "BIP/BOP with Reviews." It could be a selling point in the fierce competition with Amazon.com, Barnes & Noble, and Borders. Oddly, in spite of these two important and substantial sources, the DIALOG version is less expensive than some of the other versions of BIP that do not have reviews or records for the out-of-print books. (There was a free version of *Books Out of Print* made available by Bowker for any users who registered, but it became a fee-based service late in 1999.)

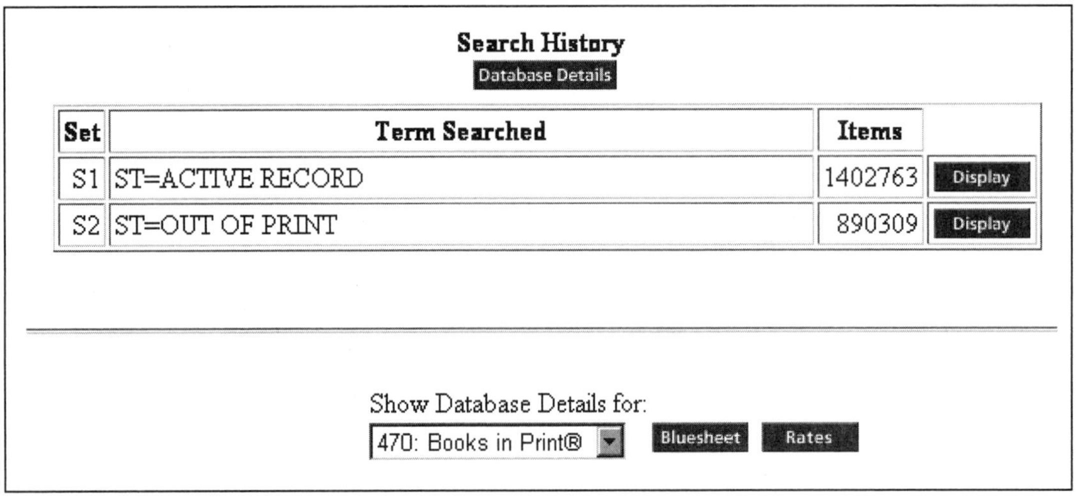

Search History

Database Details

Set	Term Searched	Items	
S1	ST=ACTIVE RECORD	1402763	Display
S2	ST=OUT OF PRINT	890309	Display

Show Database Details for:

470: Books in Print® Bluesheet Rates

Fig. 5.1. Records for books out of print in the DIALOG version titled Books in Print.

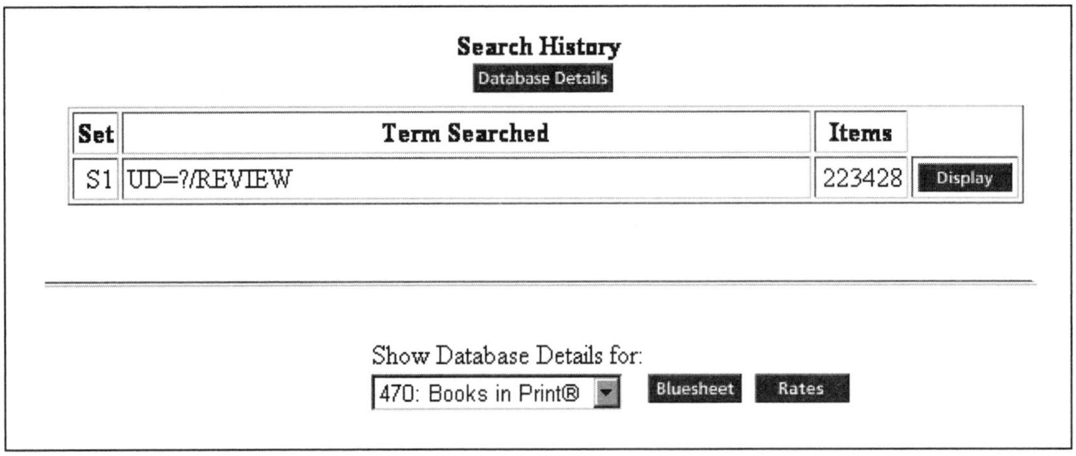

Search History

Database Details

Set	Term Searched	Items	
S1	UD=?/REVIEW	223428	Display

Show Database Details for:

470: Books in Print® Bluesheet Rates

Fig. 5.2. Records with reviews in DIALOG's Books in Print database.

Beyond the substantially different geographic coverage between Ulrich's International Periodicals Directory and The Serials Directory (TSD) of EBSCO, the types of serials covered is another important differentiator. Ulrich's seems to cover far more in-house publications and internal organs than TSD. This is not necessarily relevant for the typical user, but may be for the serials librarian who is the last resort in the hunt for an obscure periodical. The status of the serial is the filtering factor for PubList, a very substantial and free subset of Ulrich's. PubList covers only active titles. This limit is not a serious disadvantage for most users, but is not mentioned in the extensive online help file, which merely refers to 150,000 serials and 8,000 newspapers.

The lack of information about the status of the serials covered by PubList may be confusing when searching for a journal that recently changed its title (i.e., ceased publication under that title). For example, *Database* magazine became *EContent*. The user who is not aware of the title change would be surprised not to find the journal using the title search because the former title field is not indexed in the title index. While PubList's hands are tied in a sense by Ulrich's, it has freedom to decide how to index the datafile and what information it should provide in the FAQ file. (There are other differences in record content as well, as discussed in Chapter 6.)

Without sounding blasphemous, it is worth mentioning that in the remarkably poor implementation of the Merriam-Webster Biographical Dictionary by Zane Publishing, there is no mention of the special "status" filter. Only dead famous people are included. It adds further to the confusion that many of the famous people who were alive when the print edition came out more than a decade ago have since passed away, so the user is likely to remain clueless about the "source" coverage in this database.

In company directory databases, the private or public nature of the companies covered is often an essential criterion, and might make the source coverage of some company directories unacceptable. Another reason for the substantial difference among company directory databases is that companies may need to have a net sale or number of employees (or both) beyond a minimum level to qualify for inclusion. These differences in source coverage explain why Moody's 5,000 Plus has about 40 percent fewer company records than Standard & Poor's, and less than half as many as Disclosure (about 12,000).

Again, for many searchers who search for the largest companies within an industry, the differences in source coverage are not relevant, as all the databases include records for the top players. On the other hand, the very high selectivity of these databases in sources covered becomes apparent in light of the entire population of U.S. businesses (estimated to be around 15 million). Even the largest company directory databases, the American Business Information Directory and Dun's Market Identifiers, include information only for less than 70 percent of them (Lavin 1998).

The difference in the source coverage of movie directories makes it difficult to compare them. *Cinemania*, which was discontinued on CD-ROM in 1997, then online in 1998, included only feature movies, whereas *Bowker's Complete Video Directory* also has records for thousands of vocational films.

In comparing database directories, Nicholls (1998) points out that neither the Gale Directory of Databases nor the World Databases of Bowker-Saur provides extensive coverage of CD-ROM databases. This is evident from the comparison with Gale's own CD-ROMs in Print database and Waterlow New Media Information's Multimedia and CD-ROM Directory (figure 5.3). Beyond the type of medium, the genre of the databases is also a factor in the source coverage in the Gale Directory of Databases and the World Databases directories.

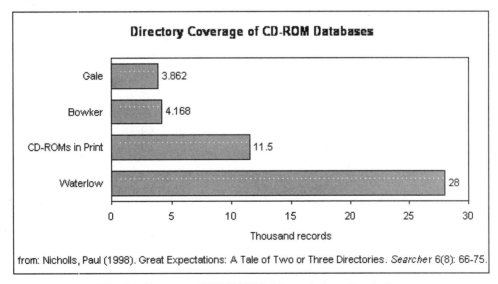

Fig. 5.3. Coverage of CD-ROM databases in four directories.

Documentary Databases

The types of sources in documentary databases are relatively easy to define: journals, magazines, newspapers, monographs, book chapters, conference papers, and dissertations are the most common types. Except for coverage of core journals from a subject field, there are no mandatory rules or universal expectations for source coverage. These are determined by the preferences of individual users and by the overall preferences of the user community.

Preferences may vary even for the same searcher, depending on the purpose of the search. In preparing for a doctoral dissertation proposal, the candidate is likely to prefer a database with as comprehensive source coverage as possible, including doctoral and master's theses. Among many other reasons, this would rule out the use of Mental Health Abstracts in the field of psychology, which does not include dissertations. On the other hand, PsycINFO has significant coverage of such documents, but this still may not mean comprehensiveness. (*PsycLIT*, the CD-ROM version, does not have records about dissertations at all.) Weston and Lauderdale (1988) found that PsycINFO did not include one-third of the psychology dissertations available in Dissertation Abstracts. A simple search in mid-1999 confirmed this finding (figure 5.4). For the sake of simplicity and comparability, the search was limited to the root word *psycholog* in the title field, as it was not known whether PsycINFO takes dissertations from Dissertation Abstracts that are classified under psychology only or also from related areas. The time frame was set to 1990–1999.

Search History

Database Details

Set	Term Searched	Items	
S1	PSYCHOLOG?/TI,1990:1999 AND DT=DISSERTATION? FROM 11	2496	Display
S2	PSYCHOLOG?/TI,1990:1999 FROM 35	3644	Display

Fig. 5.4. Comparing coverage of PsycINFO and Dissertation Abstracts using a title search.

The more comprehensive nature of Dissertation Abstracts proved relative when compared with the WorldCat database of OCLC, which has about twice as many dissertations overall as Perry and Salisbury (1995) found. This has to do with the fact that OCLC also has tens of thousands of records for bachelor's theses from its member libraries. On the other hand, it may miss many relevant master's and doctoral dissertations submitted in prestigious schools whose libraries are not OCLC members. A responsible searcher must consider these facts when looking at the numbers.

The mere claim that a database covers dissertations should not be taken at face value. LibLit (which has the most consistent source coverage and in every regard delivers what it promises) does not back up its claim to cover library and information science theses. It has only a few dozen thesis records. Information Science Abstracts had the same idea and never followed through with it. It added 47 records in 1985; 475 in 1986; and 245 in 1987, then stopped the practice (figure 5.5).

Newsletters can be crucial for many searchers, and building a database exclusively on this type of source document was a successful venture for NewsNet until 1997 when the Web-based newsletter services forced NewsNet to go out of business.

Conference papers are essential for those who need to keep up with the latest developments in sciences and social sciences. Most of the scholarly journals have such a massive backlog of manuscripts that for many researchers, conferences are the preferred publishing venue for hot topics. Based on an approximation search, LISA and ISA seem to have much stronger—although not consistent—coverage of conference proceedings than LibLit (figure 5.6). It must be emphasized that in LISA and ISA, you cannot search by the document type "conference proceeding" or "conference paper," and in LibLit the document type "speech" may be ambiguous. MHA again cannot qualify for those who need information about conference papers, while PsycINFO has solid coverage of this type of document.

Set	Term Searched	Items
S1	JN="DISSERTATION ABSTRACTS INTERNATIONAL"	767
S2	S1/1985	47
S3	S1/1986	475
S4	S1/1987	245
S5	S1-S3	767

Show Database Details for:

202: Information Science Abstracts ▼ Bluesheet

Fig. 5.5. Dissertation records in ISA.

Search History
Database Details

Set	Term Searched	Items	File	
S1	SO=(PROCEEDINGS OR PAPERS OR MEETING OR CONFERENCE)	29158		Display
S1	SO=(PROCEEDINGS OR PAPERS OR MEETING OR CONFERENCE)	1246	438	Display
S1	SO=(PROCEEDINGS OR PAPERS OR MEETING OR CONFERENCE)	16496	202	Display
S1	SO=(PROCEEDINGS OR PAPERS OR MEETING OR CONFERENCE)	11416	61	Display
S2	DT=SPEECH	8660		Display
S2	DT=SPEECH	8660	438	Display
S2	DT=SPEECH	0	202	Display
S2	DT=SPEECH	0	61	Display
S3	S1 OR S2	37347		Display
S3	S1 OR S2	9435	438	Display
S3	S1 OR S2	16496	202	Display
S3	S1 OR S2	11416	61	Display

Fig. 5.6. Conference papers in ISA, LibLit, and ISA.

Research reports are potentially relevant for many searches, but their often troublesome availability may make them less appealing. National Technical Information Services (NTIS) built a database originally dedicated to reports. The ERIC database has a subset, the RIE (Resources in Education) collection, which offers records to nearly a million research reports, conference papers, and instructional materials. LISA added a research subset in the early 1990s, featuring records about ongoing research projects, including reports.

Researchers as well as university and college students and faculty in the humanities are known to have much stronger preferences for books than scientists. Social scientists are in the middle in this regard, and individual preferences may vary, of course. LibLit (and the H. W. Wilson database family) have very many book reviews, LISA has none, and ISA has practically none. The short bibliographic citations to book reviews (and other review articles) in the Wilson databases are less informative than the ones in the other databases that often provide an indication if the review is positive, negative, or neutral. This information is sometimes difficult to determine from the review, so this feature is not always present in the records of these databases, but the file producers deserve credit for trying. "Abstracts," however, are a different story, as discussed in Chapter 11.

Closely related to this is another document type: the analytic level book record created for individual chapters of a book. This is perhaps one of the most important recent developments in both PsycINFO and PsycLIT. Adding to their value is that, in most of the online and CD-ROM implementations, the monographic and analytic records are hyperlinked. This is a software issue but is a typical case for software bringing the most out of the data content. It deserves special mention because very often the online and CD-ROM implementations of a database differ in exactly this respect, namely in the inclusion or omission of certain document types.

Sociofile, the CD-ROM version of Sociological Abstracts, for example, did not include book review records until 1997. The CD-ROM version of Biological Abstracts does not have records for either book reviews or conferences, let alone for conference papers. For many users of the online version, the inclusion of exactly those sources of information makes a big difference, and results in the largest number of unique records when doing multiple database searches (Snow 1998).

The presence of records for editorials in a database is not necessarily an asset. It depends on the type of editorials. In scholarly journals and in the highest quality general interest periodicals such as *Newsweek*, *Time,* and *U.S. News & World Report*, the editorials are often more substantial than some of the feature articles. In trade journals, the editorials are usually mini-introductions to the feature articles, not unlike the courtesy notes of conference chairs to introduce the next speaker. There are exceptions, however. For example, in *Database* (now *EContent*) and *Online*, the editorials are typically mini-articles in their own right.

Some of the harshest critiques for the lack of quality in databases appear as editorials and guest editorials. To some extent, the same applies to letters to the editor (not included in most databases). They may present important assents and dissents to previously published articles, and could be and should be hyperlinked to those. Of course, many are just generic accolades to the editors or authors without topical substance. They are the equivalent of air kisses and don't deserve a record in a database. H. W. Wilson's policy is a remarkably good one for solving the dilemma: letters to the editor are included if they are from prominent persons. ISA does not have such document types and cuts the Gordian knot by assigning the document type "article" to a letter to the editor.

Browsing the document type indexes doesn't always reveal the presence of these document types. They may be lumped under the generic document type "article." In other databases, there is a separate index, often called "article type," which makes the distinction. (This is true in all the H. W. Wilson and many of the Gale/IAC databases.) The LISA database avoids possible problems by simply not including document or article type information (except for research reports). Sometimes the document type nomenclature is obscure either because of coding or because of terminology, which may be a software implementation issue. H. W. Wilson's own version of LibLit (figure 5.7a), as well as the versions of SilverPlatter (figure 5.7b) and Ovid (figure 5.7c), spell out the article types instead of using cryptic codes. This a much better solution than the one used in the DOS versions of LibLit or the one in the current DIALOG version of the ERIC database, which still uses numeric codes for document types.

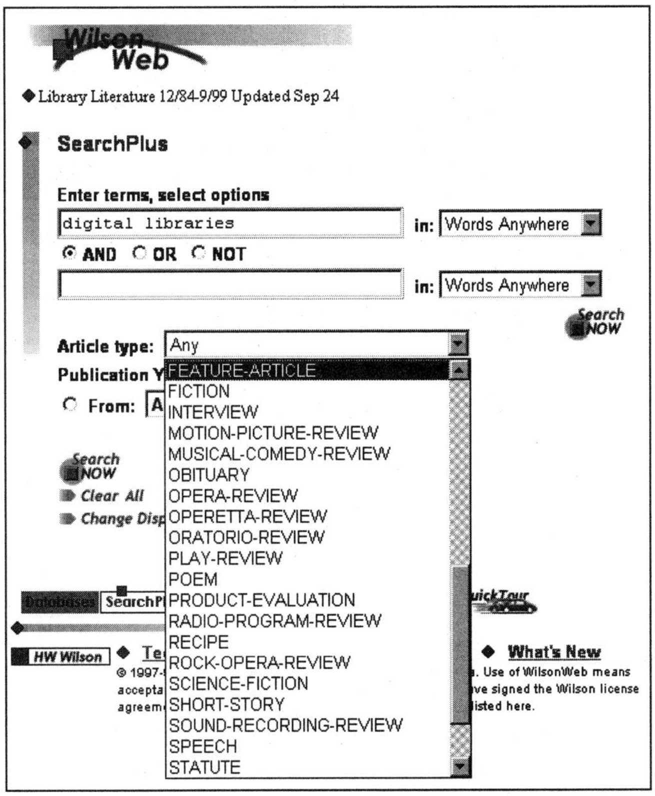

Fig. 5.7a. H. W. Wilson's version of LibLit.

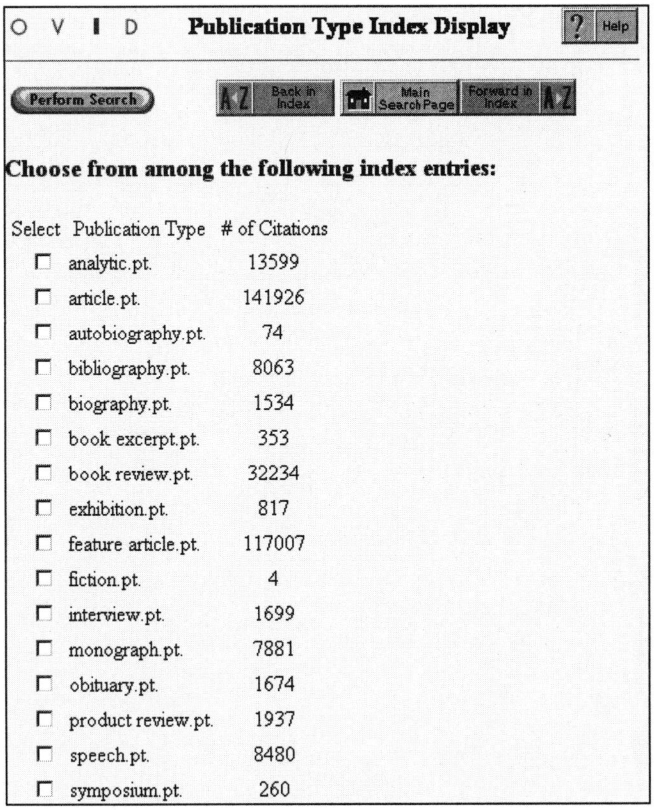

Fig. 5.7b. SilverPlatter's version of LibLit.

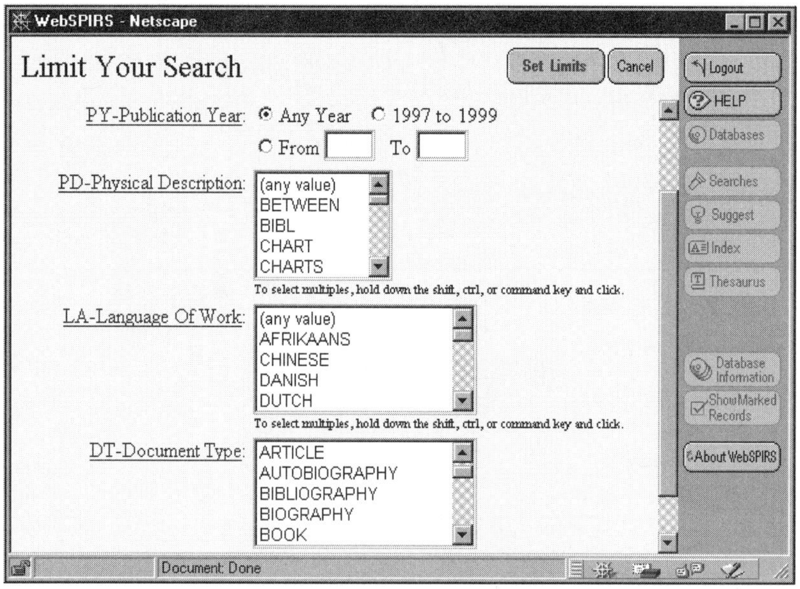

Fig. 5.7c. Ovid's version of LibLit.

In addition, the file producer may not have used the document type categories consistently. This is the case in ISA, where conference papers have been identified as "monographic" and "monographic chapter." This is not only grammatically awkward but also makes the document type index an unreliable search qualifier, as both terms are used for individual conference papers (as can be seen from the search results in figure 5.8). A record for the volume should be "monograph" as document type, and the paper "monographic chapter," but calling a spade a spade, or a conference paper a conference paper, would have helped to avoid this confusion. As mentioned earlier, in the latest twist of the document type saga of ISA, all records added in 1999 and 2000 are identified as "article" in the document type field, including conference papers. It is an extra burden that the user must search for these both in the JN (Journal Name) and SO (Source) index. The former is phrase indexed; the latter is word indexed. Hence, you cannot make the search in a single command.

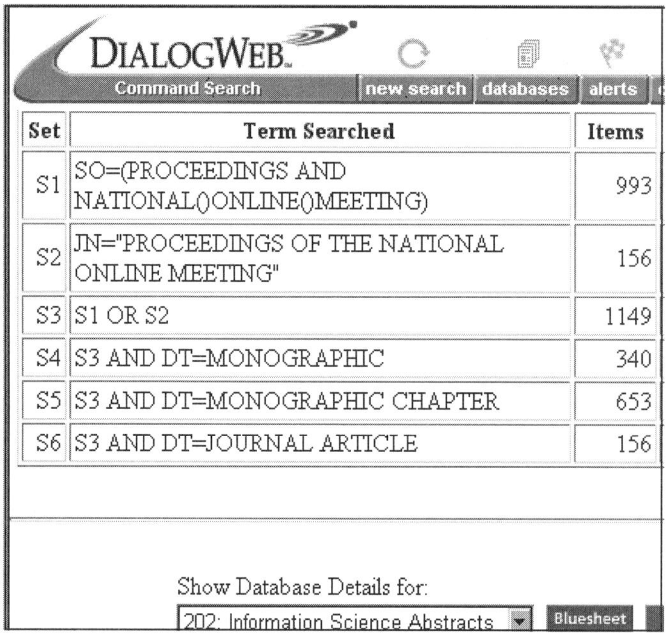

Set	Term Searched	Items
S1	SO=(PROCEEDINGS AND NATIONAL()ONLINE()MEETING)	993
S2	JN="PROCEEDINGS OF THE NATIONAL ONLINE MEETING"	156
S3	S1 OR S2	1149
S4	S3 AND DT=MONOGRAPHIC	340
S5	S3 AND DT=MONOGRAPHIC CHAPTER	653
S6	S3 AND DT=JOURNAL ARTICLE	156

Show Database Details for:

202: Information Science Abstracts

Fig. 5.8. Conference papers inconsistently identified in ISA.

Users may like or dislike the inclusion or exclusion of a certain document type. As long as the policy is made clear and is consistent, they know what they are getting. Although the introduction of patent records into the ISA database was not necessarily a good or bad decision by itself, its rate of yearly increase became suspicious, especially as the total number of records added annually to the database remained fairly constant (figure 5.9). The fact that the producer of the file, IFI/Plenum, imported these records from its own patent database did not make the case for it stronger. After Allcock (1997) and Jacsó (1997c) slugged it out in an exchange of letters in *Database* magazine, no more patent records were added to the database.

The H. W. Wilson databases have an unusually large proportion of records for various types of reviews. This could be a particularly useful source if review records would have abstracts, but they never do. The very specific subject headings and subheading combinations may help in some regard, but get in the way in other regards. This happens in the Biographies Plus Illustrated database. It is appealingly linked to the abstracting/indexing and full-text databases of H. W. Wilson. However, the user has to click on each and every review type just to get to the records (figure 5.10). Users are likely to be more interested in the review of the work itself than in the particular medium (laser disc, DVD, videocassette), and the records could be just collocated under the title of the work instead of being scattered.

Set	Term Searched	Items	
S1	DT=PATENT/1982	0	Display
S2	DT=PATENT/1983	45	Display
S3	DT=PATENT/1984	453	Display
S4	DT=PATENT/1986	463	Display
S5	DT=PATENT/1988	631	Display
S6	DT=PATENT/1990	588	Display
S7	DT=PATENT/1992	793	Display
S8	DT=PATENT/1994	1402	Display
S9	DT=PATENT/1996	2110	Display
S10	DT=PATENT/1998	0	Display

Show Database Details for:

202: Information Science Abstracts ▾ Blues

Fig. 5.9. Number of total records and patent records added to ISA.

Kubrick, Stanley

Click below for Records with Abstracts on the following topics

Autobiography
Biography
DVD review
Interview
Miscellaneous
Motion picture review
Reviews
Videodisc review
Videotape review
Works/Barry Lyndon
Works/Dr. Strangelove or: How I learned to stop worrying and love the bomb
Works/Fear and desire
Works/Full metal jacket
Works/Killing
Works/2001: a space odyssey

Fig. 5.10. Too many review types in Biographies Plus Illustrated.

JOURNAL BASE

Journals deserve special treatment when evaluating the source coverage of databases. Journals have been the most traditional and most essential type of source for indexing, abstracting, full-text, and page-image databases. Given the importance of journals, it is no wonder that their coverage receives primary attention in the evaluation of documentary databases. The journal base of a database is often the first criterion in comparing databases. The number of journals covered is a consistent component in even the most succinct database descriptions.

The sheer number in itself is not sufficient for evaluation. The extent of coverage may be wide but shallow, the coverage of articles may be too selective, and the absence of some essential journals (essential in the eye of the potential user community or its most vocal representatives) may exclude a candidate database from consideration. On the other hand, a database with a seemingly tiny journal base may be just the ticket for many researchers. The full-text Mental Health Collection of Ovid is a case in point. It has merely 10 periodical publications. Eight of them are journals monitored by the Institute for Scientific Information. Six of the 8 journals are ranked by impact factor as 1, 2, 4, 6, 7, and 8 among the 80 psychiatry journals in the Social Science Journal Citations Report database. Seven of the journals are among the top 20 journals of the combined psychology and psychiatry category, which includes 489 journals. The same 7 titles are ranked among the top 36 journals in the entire social science category, which includes 1,672 journals (figure 5.11). That is an outstanding journal base, a prime example of small is beautiful.

Titles in Mental Health Collection	All SocSCI rank	All Psyc. rank	All Psychiatry rank
American Journal of Psychiatry	5	4	2
Annual Review of Psychology	13	7	n/a
Archives of General Psychiatry	1	1	1
British Journal of Psychiatry	28	14	6
Current Opinion in Psychiatry	841	315	62
Journal of Clinical Psychopharmacology			
Journal of the American Academy of Child and Adolescent Psychiatry	16	9	4
Psychological Medicine	36	20	8
Psychosomatic Medicine	32	17	7
Year Book of Psychiatry and Applied Mental Health			
Total number of journals in this category	1672	489	80

Fig. 5.11. The rank of journals by impact factor in Ovid's Mental Health Collection.

Decision makers and potential users may prefer one database over another just by virtue of having one or two of their favorite journals covered. In such cases, it is a good idea to approach the file producer to add a few titles preferred by the library, as such requests can be easily accommodated. A survey by Hernon and Metoyer-Duran (1992) of 43 academic librarians in five academic and research libraries found that H. W. Wilson's LibLit fell short of covering journals relevant for those libraries. Knowing the attention given by H. W. Wilson to its customers and its systematic evaluation of journal coverage, this perceived shortcoming certainly would have been answered by the file producer had the needed titles been identified.

Although there are no formal lists of core journals for various disciplines that would please the librarians and faculty of every public, school, special, and academic library, let alone their entire user population, there are many useful sources that indirectly can be used to judge the adequacy of the journal base of a database. This is much easier in the case of a special library that is considering a discipline-specific database than in a large university library that needs both discipline-specific and multidisciplinary databases to serve a very diverse user community.

Nevertheless, the journal collection of the library can serve as a good starting point. This is based on the assumption that the library has had a well-defined policy for collection development with selection and de-selection criteria that are applied for journal subscriptions. Financial constraints certainly prevent a library from subscribing to all the desirable periodicals, but the ideal set of databases is expected to cover the majority of the journals subscribed to by a library. Additional titles may be welcome, especially if the full-text, or preferably the page-image, version of articles from those journals is available in the database. This availability may incur extra charges, as discussed in Chapter 12 on cost considerations.

Traditional collection development guides, such as *Katz's Guide to Magazines* and the Brandon-Hill list of journals for medical libraries, are also excellent resources for the evaluation of the journal base of databases. The latter is available free of charge at *http://www.nnlm.nlm.nih.gov/psr/outreach/branhill.html*. What makes the *ProQuest Medical Library* on CD-ROM an outstanding source for many medical schools and hospitals in developing countries and small medical centers in developed countries is that it covers most of the titles on the Brandon-Hill list.

The set and subsets of journals processed by the Institute for Scientific Information for the *Science Citation Index*, *Social Science Citation Index*, *Arts & Humanities Citation Index*, and the Journal Citation Reports (JCR) are, for many users, a de facto standard for journals that should be covered by a database meant for academic research. Even if the set for a given discipline should not be used without reservation, it is a very good starting point for evaluating the journal base of a database. For example, the choice for library and information science in JCR is rather limited (hovering around 65 titles), but about 90 percent of the journals are likely to be widely accepted as core titles for library and information science. The list can be further enhanced by titles not included in JCR but widely used and respected by professionals in their fields of specialization, such as *Cataloging & Classification Quarterly*, *Computers in Libraries,* and *Searcher* in the Library and Information Science (LIS) category.

If a database misses a few titles from the set of journals covered by ISI, it is not necessarily a bad sign. ISI has a few journals that made it to the privileged set more for political correctness than for scholarly merit. The Russian *Nauchno Tekhnicheskaiya Informatsiya* may have seemed to have some impact by ISI's measures, but its articles were cited by Russian and Eastern European researchers not so much for scientific relevance as for meeting expectations and being good soldiers. The *Zeitschrift für Bibliothekswesen und Bibliographie* (ZBB) may have been relevant for scholars in some German-speaking countries but certainly is not essential for inclusion for most of the users of library and information science databases. Not coincidentally, 15 of its 17 citations received in 1997 came from ZBB itself. Their appearance on the ISI list is more likely due to inertia rather than merit. To ISI's credit, since 1996 neither of the two journals of the Russian series appears among the LIS journals. I would assume ZBB will also be removed.

It is a serious deficiency of MHA that none of the 20 highest impact factor journals (figure 5.12) in the psychology and psychiatry section of the Journal Citation Reports are included in the database. The impact factor measures the ratio between the number of citations a journal received in the previous two years and the total number of citable publications in the journal for the same time period. The total lack of the top 20 psychiatry and psychology journals that received the most citations in absolute numbers (figure 5.13) is a crippling deficiency of MHA. It is no surprise that none of the 20 most productive psychiatry and psychology journals (figure 5.14) made it to the group of 227 journals that were processed in 1997 by the MHA database (figure 5.15). (For technical reasons, only the top 16 journals can be shown in one screen shot in all of the following figures. From MHA, the screenshot [figure 5.15] shows the 13 journals with the highest postings in 1997.)

Journal Citation Reports - 1997 Social Sciences Edition

File   Edit   View   Calculations   Options   Help

Journal Rankings

Mark	Rank	Journal Abbreviation	ISSN	1997 Total Cites	Impact Factor	Immediacy Index	1997 Articles	Cited Half-life
	1	ARCH GEN PSYCHIAT	0003-990X	23238	10.751	1.798	104	9.4
	2	BEHAV BRAIN SCI	0140-525X	2642	8.118	0.667	6	8.7
	3	PSYCHOL REV	0033-295X	9005	7.060	0.969	32	> 10.0
	4	AM J PSYCHIAT	0002-953X	22478	6.501	0.943	283	7.3
	5	PSYCHOL BULL	0033-2909	11572	6.038	1.206	34	> 10.0
	6	J COGNITIVE NEUROSCI	0898-929X	1500	4.844	0.927	55	5.0
	7	ANNU REV PSYCHOL	0066-4308	2087	4.841	1.409	22	7.7
	8	J CLIN PSYCHIAT	0160-6689	6784	4.003	0.351	171	6.0
	9	J AM ACAD CHILD PSY	0890-8567	6525	3.793	0.556	207	5.8
	10	LEARN MEMORY	1072-0502	317	3.673	0.119	42	2.6
	11	COGNITIVE PSYCHOL	0010-0285	2357	3.516	0.400	20	> 10.0
	12	SCHIZOPHRENIA BULL	0586-7614	3755	3.509	1.380	50	7.1
	13	J MEM LANG	0749-596X	1844	3.358	0.456	57	6.4
	14	BRIT J PSYCHIAT	0007-1250	13851	3.265	0.744	195	8.3
	15	CONTEMP PSYCHOL	0010-7549	107	3.200			4.0
	16	DEV PSYCHOPATHOL	0954-5794	1153	3.192	0.419	43	4.3

Sort: Impact Factor   Filter: Multiple Categories   422 Journals   14 marked

Fig. 5.12. Highest impact factor psychiatry and psychology journals in 1997.

Journal Citation Reports - 1997 Social Sciences Edition

File   Edit   View   Calculations   Options   Help

Journal Rankings

Mark	Rank	Journal Abbreviation	ISSN	1997 Total Cites	Impact Factor	Immediacy Index	1997 Articles	Cited Half-life
	1	ARCH GEN PSYCHIAT	0003-990X	23238	10.751	1.798	104	9.4
	2	AM J PSYCHIAT	0002-953X	22478	6.501	0.943	283	7.3
	3	J PERS SOC PSYCHOL	0022-3514	17864	2.986	0.500	216	> 10.0
	4	BRIT J PSYCHIAT	0007-1250	13851	3.265	0.744	195	8.3
	5	PSYCHOL BULL	0033-2909	11572	6.038	1.206	34	> 10.0
	6	CHILD DEV	0009-3920	9372	2.067	0.365	85	> 10.0
	7	PSYCHOL REV	0033-295X	9005	7.060	0.969	32	> 10.0
	8	PHYSIOL BEHAV	0031-9384	8062	1.250	0.167	360	8.6
	9	AM PSYCHOL	0003-066X	7688	3.076	2.118	76	8.4
	10	J CLIN PSYCHIAT	0160-6689	6784	4.003	0.351	171	6.0
	11	J AM ACAD CHILD PSY	0890-8567	6525	3.793	0.556	207	5.8
	12	ACTA PSYCHIAT SCAND	0001-690X	6245	1.588	0.136	169	8.5
	13	J ABNORM PSYCHOL	0021-843X	5882	2.678	0.290	69	> 10.0
	14	PSYCHOL MED	0033-2917	5740	3.017	0.550	131	8.5
	15	DEV PSYCHOL	0012-1649	5532	2.263	0.283	99	9.3
	16	J APPL PSYCHOL	0021-9010	5371	1.815	0.203	79	> 10.0

Sort: Total Cites   Filter: Multiple Categories   422 Journals   14 marked

Fig. 5.13. Most cited psychiatry and psychology journals in 1997.

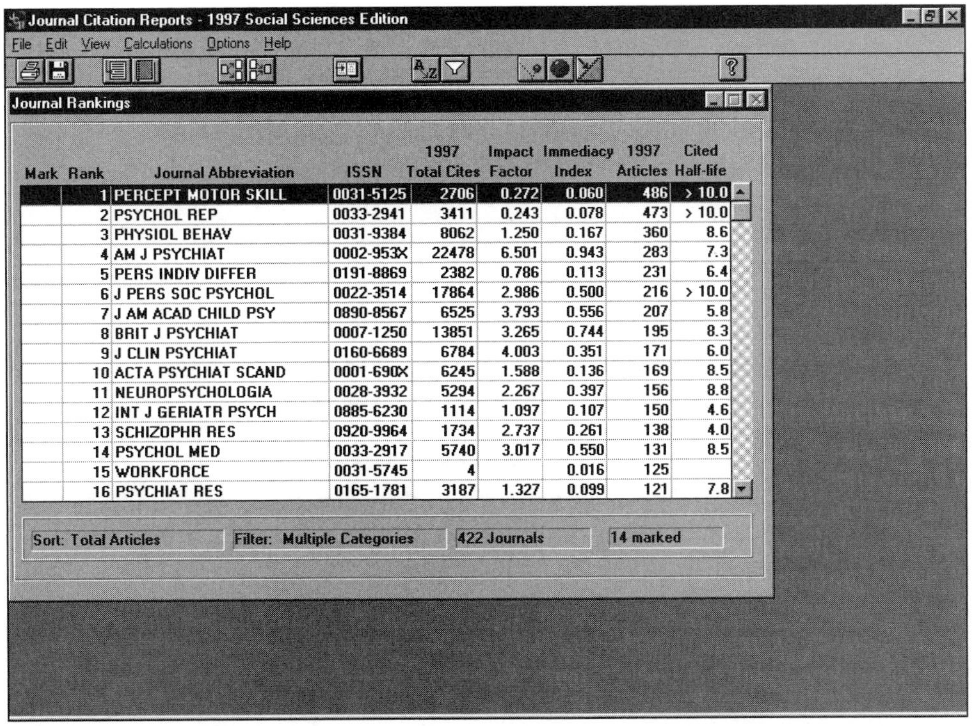

Fig. 5.14. Most productive psychiatry and psychology journals in 1997.

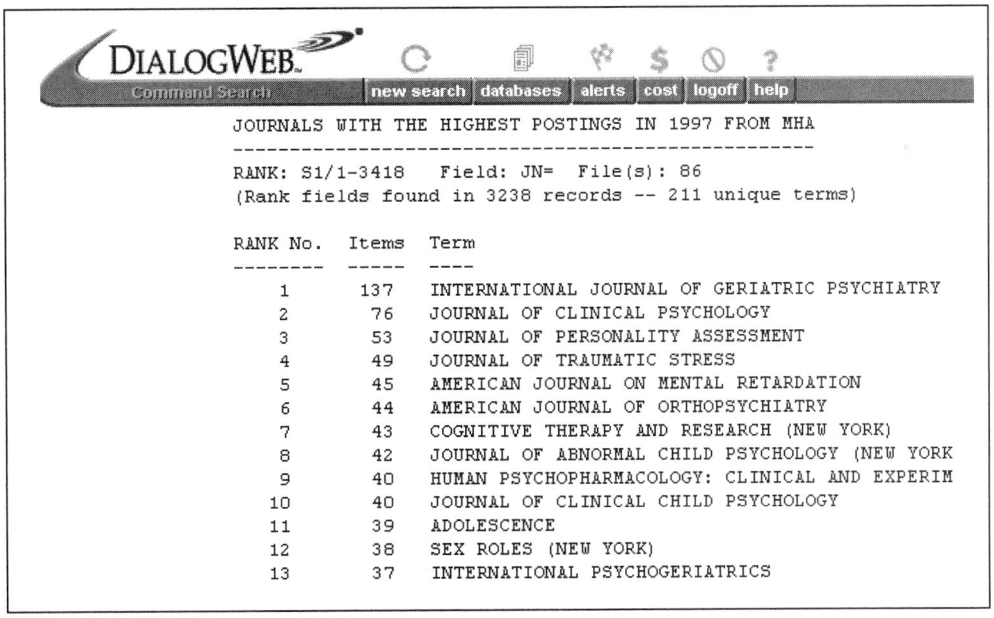

Fig. 5.15. List of journals processed by MHA in 1997 (excerpt).

Unofficial but informative prestige lists of journals of a discipline can also serve as a benchmark for evaluating the journal base of databases. In library and information science, there are quite a few prestige lists. Esteibar and Lancaster (1992) produced an informative ranked list of library and information science journals by analyzing 131 reading lists, 41 doctoral dissertations, and 114 publications of 13 faculty members of the Graduate School of Library and Information Science, University of Illinois at Urbana-Champaign.

The classic study of library and information science journals by Kohl and Davis (1985) is somewhat outdated by now and does not include increasingly important information technology journals. It still provides a good list of primarily library science titles ranked as the top ones by deans of ALA-accredited library schools and directors of 43 libraries of the Association of Research Libraries (ARL). The survey by Tjoumas and Blake (1992) also resulted in a prestige list based on the perception of professional journals by library school faculty specializing in school and public library topics. Jacsó (1998a) formed categories of subsets of these lists to compare them against the journal base of six databases with library and information science and technology coverage (figure 5.16).

TABLE 1
Sample Journals with Postings for Databases in the Peer Group

Abbreviated Journal Titles	INSPEC	SSCI	LISA	Pascal	LibLit	ISA
ANNU REV INFORM SCI		284	44	196		252
ASLIB PROC	654	1,282	938	1,005	493	698
B MED LIBR ASSOC	355	2,126	973	887	922	1,171
CAN J INFORM LIB SCI	16	94	70		82	32
CAN LIBR J	111	2,446	602	503	1,004	475
COLL RES LIBR	24	2,753	871	696	961	985
DATABASE	724	1,993	968	556	1,158	840
EDUC INFORM	51	622	280	77	411	92
ELECTRON LIBR	462	909	467	376	608	429
GOV INFORM Q	155	833	316		444	262
GOV PUBL REV	52	1,594	442	571	222	
IFLA J-INT FED LIBR		928	532	377	724	189
INFORM PROCESS MANAG	863	1,748	924	802	1,042	987
INFORM TECHNOL LIBR	400	1,022	527	431	809	467
INT FORUM INFORM DOC	192	550	413	424	284	184
INT J INFORM MANAGE	264	626	280	204		162
INTERLEND DOC SUPPLY	95	364	267	260	298	73
J ACAD LIBR		2,324	972	3	1,286	516
J AM SOC INFORM SCI	1,208	2,092	1,217	1,107	904	1,544
J DOC	260	1,737	485	366	793	903
J EDUC LIBR INF SCI	60	539	294	265	517	220
J INFORM SCI	503	1,007	685	677	536	617
LAW LIBR J	25	1,580	479		511	63
LIBR ACQUIS PRACT TH	112	1,235	773	553	914	459
LIBR INFORM SCI RES	51	530	301	216	337	302
LIBR J		27,108	1,407	1,383	7,346	1,015
LIBR QUART	26	2,487	412	265	934	397
LIBR RESOUR TECH SER	243	1,327	471	385	830	793
LIBR TRENDS	175	1,066	835	872	540	907
LIBRI	28	504	460	496	289	352
NACHR DOK	566	1,636	521	927	341	500
NAUCH-TEKHN INFORM 1	902	2,315	245		1,109	1,032
ONLINE	1,240	2,207	1,152	777	1,232	998
P ASIS ANNU MEET	36	2,342	106	120		1,527
PROGRAM-AUTOM LIBR	559	1,004	529	500	599	176
RQ	48	4,005	685		1,284	604
SCHOLARLY PUBL		743	210		330	159
SCIENTOMETRICS	45	1,124	689	689		644
SERIALS LIBR	374	1,159	827	376	730	691
SPEC LIBR		1,657	801	842	576	1,788
WILSON LIBR BULL		7,717	1,136		3,973	409
Z BIBL BIBL		1,270	210	626		23
Total for 42 sample titles	10,879	90,889	24,636	18,665	35,722	24,159
Total without LJ and WLB	10,879	56,064	22,093	17,282	24,403	22,735
Category A titles (bold)	7,332	30,892	13,479	10,095	13,984	14,421
Category B titles (italics)	1,197	49,773	8,656	5,713	18,777	6,064
Category C titles	2,350	10,224	2,501	2,857	2,961	3,674

Fig. 5.16. Coverage of prestigious library and information science journals in six databases.

A similar survey among faculty members specializing in information technology and among practicing information specialists could add the needed balance for these lists, which represent the traditional side of library and information science.

Ojala (1992) provided a good example for evaluating business and economics databases by determining the extent of coverage (not merely the presence) of journals that appeared on the prestige lists of faculty members in various university departments. Jaguszewski and Kempf (1995) compared the journal base of four current awareness services. They selected 44 chemistry journals and 50 mathematical journals for testing. Although in chemistry the coverage was good and comparable among the four databases, in mathematics two databases had very poor coverage, one had good coverage, and CARL Uncover had very good coverage (figure 5.17).

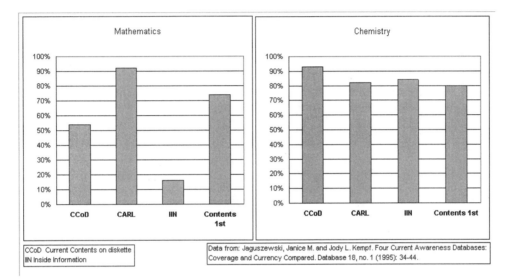

Fig. 5.17. Coverage of 94 chemistry and mathematics journals in four current awareness services.

Beaubien (1992) compared the journal coverage of IAC's Expanded Academic Index with a group of H. W. Wilson's databases. While the journal level overlap was very high in humanities, social sciences, and general sciences, it was only fair in general interest topics (represented by the Readers' Guide Abstracts database). The overlap in applied science and technology, biology, and agriculture was extremely low (4 percent and 9 percent, respectively), as summarized in figure 5.18.

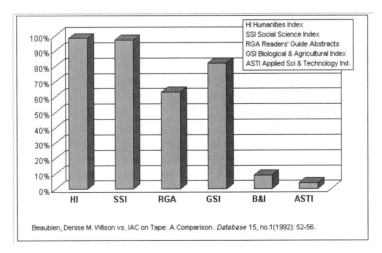

Fig. 5.18. Overlap of journals between IAC Expanded Academic Index and H. W. Wilson databases.

Matching the journal title coverage of databases with the collection of a library can be a decisive factor in selecting a database for subscription. Fry and Parsons (1994) compared the journal base of various databases of UMI, IAC, and H. W. Wilson for undergraduate research by major curricular categories and found that journals in the Wilson database family were the closest match to titles in the collection of the Iowa State Libraries.

One might expect that databases in a rather specific field would have much overlap in the journals covered. This may not be the case, as demonstrated by Giral and Taylor (1993). They found merely a 30 percent overlap (270 journals) between Avery Index (846 journals) and the Architectural Periodicals Index (609 journals) for the period between 1979 and 1986 (figure 5.19). For practical reasons, it is justified to use even a narrower window of time for comparison.

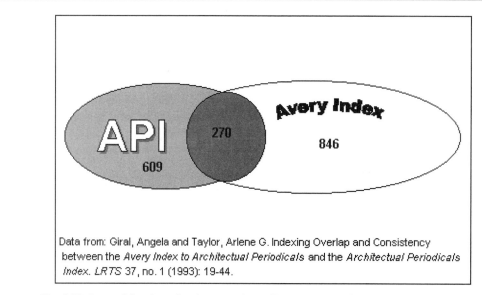

Data from: Giral, Angela and Taylor, Arlene G. Indexing Overlap and Consistency between the *Avery Index to Architectual Periodicals* and the *Architectual Periodicals Index. LRTS* 37, no. 1 (1993): 19-44.

Fig. 5.19. Journal-level overlap between Avery Index and Architectural Periodicals Index.

Even in databases that have exceptionally broad journal coverage, there is no guarantee that most of the journals relevant for the patrons of a library are available, let alone adequately covered. In a study by Holt and Schmidt (1995), sample searches that used the same search strategies found merely a 30 percent overlap of journal titles between Faxon Finder and Uncover2, both of which cover over 10,000 journals.

Making journal comparisons among databases can be a tiresome process of wading through and comparing hundreds or even thousands of journal names from a list typically made available by the file producer. For the largest databases, the journal list makes a hefty print volume, as is the case with BIOSIS, EMBASE, and INSPEC. PubMed made the MEDLINE journal list freely browsable and searchable on the Web at *http://www.ncbi.nlm.nih.gov:80/entrez/jrbrowser.cgi*. Although they offer in HTML format far more information than the simple journal lists of many other producers, it would be in the interest of many users to persuade the file producers to make available on the Web a searchable database version of their journal list.

An increasing number of file producers have published their journal lists on the Web. The best ones offer searching the journal lists by a combination of several criteria and producing a spreadsheet format output with columns defined by the user. Bell & Howell serves the best example for this at *http://www.umi.com/hp/Support/Titles/*, as illustrated later in this chapter.

Because of different abbreviations and description rules, the process of locating titles is more difficult in the printed version of a database than it may seem. Not even the online versions are a panacea, given the awkwardness of scrolling through long HTML pages. How many entry points in the alphabetically sorted journal list would you need to check to make sure that you don't miss the many variant format possibilities for the relatively simple title *Journal of the American Oil Chemists' Society*? As discussed in

Chapter 8 about consistency, the PASCAL database alone has well over a dozen variants for this journal name, many of them not even congregating close to each other, such as the version that consists of the acronym alone: JAOCS.

A number of file producers started to make available their journal lists on the Web free of charge. PAIS deserves credit as one of the pioneers. Its journal list is not a database, but beyond being browsable, it is also searchable—although to a limited extent—using the Find feature of the browser. The American Psychological Association also provides its list of journals on the Web (figure 5.20). It includes not only the journal name and the ISSN (where available) but also the first year of coverage of the title (figure 5.21).

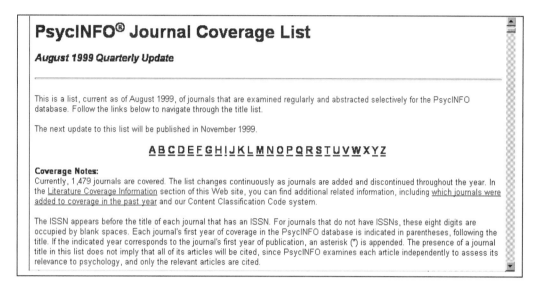

Fig. 5.20. Excerpt from the introduction to the journal list of PsycINFO.

```
0237-7896 Psychiatria Hungarica (1990)
0033-2674 Psychiatria Polska (1972)
0048-5713 Psychiatric Annals (1971)
0193-953X Psychiatric Clinics of North America (1982)
0955-8829 Psychiatric Genetics (1990)
0033-2720 Psychiatric Quarterly (1977)
1095-158X Psychiatric Rehabilitation Journal (1977*)
1075-2730 Psychiatric Services (1960)
0079-726X Psychiatrie de l'Enfant (1970)
1105-2333 Psychiatriki (1990*)
0165-1781 Psychiatry Research (1979*)
0925-4927 Psychiatry Research: Neuroimaging (1990*)
1321-8719 Psychiatry, Psychology & Law (1994*)
0033-2747 Psychiatry: Interpersonal & Biological Processes (1938*)
1023-0548 Psycho-analytic Psychotherapy in South Africa (1992*)
0377-3132 Psycho-Lingua (1975)
1057-9249 Psycho-Oncology (1992*)
0161-5289 Psychoanalysis & Contemporary Thought (1978*)
1460-8235 Psychoanalysis & History (1998*)
0736-508X Psychoanalysis & Psychotherapy (1983*)
1048-1885 Psychoanalytic Dialogues (1991*)
0735-1690 Psychoanalytic Inquiry (1983)
0736-9735 Psychoanalytic Psychology (1984*)
0266-8734 Psychoanalytic Psychotherapy (1985*)
0033-2828 Psychoanalytic Quarterly (1932*)
0033-2836 Psychoanalytic Review (1926)
0079-7308 Psychoanalytic Study of the Child (1945*)
```

Fig. 5.21. The PsycINFO journal list.

Some online service providers come to the rescue by offering searchable journal lists, sometimes even for nonsubscribers, or are willing to check the coverage against a list for the potentially lucrative business of contracting with a large university. You don't need to be a subscriber of Bell & Howell Learning and Information to find out which journals are covered by the various databases the company offers. You may choose the data elements (title, ISSN, UMI code, format availability, dates of coverage in different formats) to be included in the list that are generated on-the-fly in plain-text, HTML, or comma-delimited format (figure 5.22).

ProQuest databases: ABI/INFORM Research

This list is current as of August 23, 1999.

Title [1254]	Cit First [1254]	Cit Latest	Abs First [1250]	Abs Latest	FT First [688]	FT Latest	Img First [658]	Img Latest	T+G First [602]	T+G Latest
ABA Bank Compliance	7/1/84	current	7/1/84	current	10/1/94	current	5/1/96	current	11/1/96	current
ACM Computing Surveys	12/1/90	current	12/1/90	current	3/1/96	current	12/1/90	current	3/1/96	current
ARMA Records Management Quarterly	1/1/79	current	1/1/79	current	1/1/91	current	1/1/88	current	4/1/96	current
AS/400 Systems Management	10/1/79	current	10/1/79	current	10/1/97	current	10/1/97	current	10/1/97	current
ASCI Journal of Management	9/1/80	3/1/87	9/1/80	3/1/87						
ASEAN Business Quarterly	7/1/80	4/1/81	7/1/80	4/1/81						
AT & T Technology	1/1/87	1/1/96	1/1/87	1/1/96	1/1/92	1/1/96	1/1/88	1/1/96	1/1/96	1/1/96
AZB, Arizona Business [Selective Business Coverage]	10/1/71	current	10/1/71	current	1/1/91	current	12/1/87	current	6/1/96	current
Abacus [Full Text/Image Available via Fax]	12/1/74	current	12/1/74	current						
Absatzwirtschaft	3/1/81	10/1/86	3/1/81	10/1/86						
Academy of Management Executive, The	2/1/87	current	2/1/87	current	2/1/91	current	2/1/87	current	11/1/95	current
Academy of Management Journal	9/1/71	current	9/1/71	current	3/1/92	current	3/1/87	current	10/1/95	current
Academy of Management. The Academy of Management Review	1/1/76	current	1/1/76	current	1/1/92	current	1/1/87	current	1/1/96	current
Academy of Marketing Science. Journal	4/1/79	current	4/1/79	current	6/1/96	current	1/1/96	current	6/1/96	current
Accountancy	11/1/72	current	11/1/72	current	1/1/92	current	1/1/92	current	5/1/96	current
Accountants Digest, The	6/1/73	6/1/73	6/1/73	6/1/73						
Accounting Horizons	12/1/87	current	12/1/87	current	12/1/91	current	12/1/87	current	3/1/96	current
Accounting Review, The	10/1/71	current	10/1/71	current			1/1/88	current		
Accounting Technology	11/1/84	current	11/1/84	current	8/1/92	current	6/1/96	current	9/1/96	current
Accounting and Business Research	1/1/82	current	1/1/82	current	1/1/97	current	1/1/87	current	1/1/97	current
Accounting and Finance [Full Text/Image Available via Fax]	11/1/84	current	11/1/84	current						
Accounting, Organizations and Society	1/1/80	current	1/1/80	current						
Across the Board	8/1/71	current	8/1/71	current	2/21/85	current	1/1/87	current	11/1/95	current
Ad Forum	12/1/82	5/1/85	12/1/82	5/1/85						
Adherent	8/1/75	10/1/83	8/1/75	10/1/83						
Adhesives Age	8/1/91	current	8/1/91	current	8/1/92	current	6/1/96	current	9/1/96	current

Fig. 5.22. One of the UMI journal list formats.

Of course, once you subscribe to a service or have a trial period, you have more options. H. W. Wilson offers a journal list as part of the information about each database (figure 5.23). I often use it to verify serials information.

Library Literature & Information Science Journal List

Updated: September 28, 1999

Journal	ISSN	Peer Review	Index Start/End		Journal Note
AB Bookman's Weekly	0001-0340		10/1984		
African Journal of Library, Archives & Information Science	0795-4778	R	01/1993		
Against the Grain	1043-2094	R	01/1995		
ALA Washington News	1523-6005		01/1996		Formerly ALA Washington Newsletter; name changed with January 26, 1996
ALA Washington Newsletter	0001-1746		12/1984	12/1995	Name changed to ALA Washington News with January 26, 1996
Alabama Librarian	0002-4295		00/1998	03/1999	Ceased publication with Volume 49, No. 3, 1998
ALCTS Newsletter	1047-949X		01/1990	12/1998	Formerly RTSD Newsletter; name changed with Vol. 1, No. 1, 1990. Ceased publication in print form with Vol. 9, No. 6, 1998. Available in electronic format with 1999
ALCTS Newsletter (Online)	1047-949X		00/1999		Continues ALCTS Newsletter in electronic format with 1999
Alexandria	0955-7490		01/1993		
Alki	8756-4173		03/1993		
The American Archivist	0360-9081	R	10/1984		
American Libraries	0002-9769		11/1984		

Fig. 5.23. H. W. Wilson's journal list for a database.

In addition, most databases are also searchable by journal name. However, the journal name field is almost always phrase indexed, making it as difficult to spot a journal as from the printed list. Some of the special searchable journal list databases discussed next are word indexed, offering far more flexible searching.

On every CD-ROM database produced by H. W. Wilson (but not those published by SilverPlatter for H. W. Wilson's databases) there is a little-known gold mine: the journal name database. This database makes it possible to search for any word or combination of words (in full or abbreviated format) in the journal title field. The journal database includes all journals abstracted and indexed by H. W. Wilson, not only those that are covered for the CD-ROM database at hand.

WebSPIRS 4.0 offers a useful database selection tool. Its purpose is to allow a searcher to enter a combination of subject words to find the most promising databases for the subject, but it can just as well be used to run a search on journal names. This is very convenient when two or more of the competing prospective databases are available through SilverPlatter, like LISA and ISA. Unfortunately, you must know the exact format of the name of the journals as they appear in the database. It is hard enough to predict how a title such as the *Journal of the American Society for Information Science* will appear in a database (and in how many variations). It does not ease the task that SilverPlatter uses its own odd, hyphenated version of the journal name. Few users would guess correctly that *Online & CD-ROM Review* appears as ONLINE-AND-CD-ROM-REVIEW in the SilverPlatter implementation of databases (figure 5.24).

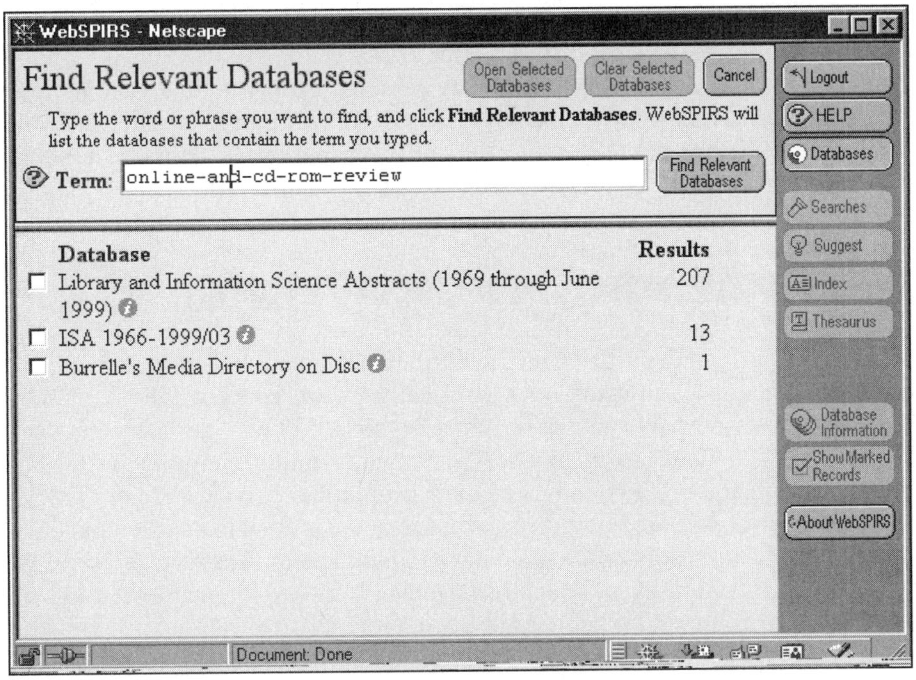

Fig. 5.24. Searching for journals in WebSPIRS databases.

DIALOG's Journal Name Finder (JNF) has been available for the longest time, and it is by far the most powerful tool for exploring journal coverage of databases. Its power has to do with two facts. One is that it covers all of the documentary databases of DIALOG, and the other is that it has word and phrase indexes, both with and without the JN= prefix. These variant indexes offer great flexibility in searching for even the most oddly abbreviated journal titles.

There is, however, a problem due to the illogical practices of some file producers. The Journal Name Finder database is created from the JN or JO tags of the records (figure 5.25), so in those cases where journal names appear only in the SO (source) field, the JNF results are unreliable because the SO field is not indexed in the JNF database. This is also a problem for searching in the database directly. For example, in the MHA and ISA databases, there are tens of thousands of records entered before the 1980s where the journal name appears in the source field alone but not in the journal name field. For a complete search by journal, both fields must be searched. It adds to the confusion that you need to have two different strategies, as the JN field is phrase-indexed while the SO field is word-indexed within the databases.

This serious deficiency in MHA and ISA should have been corrected a long time ago by IFI/Plenum, the producer of MHA (and ISA until 1998), using a smart conversion utility. Double searching databases both by the JN= prefix and the SO= prefix requires extra effort and likely remains unknown for many users who would assume that whatever results were found in searching the JN index represent the coverage of the given journal. This practice also debilitates the otherwise superb Journal Name Finder database.

Search History

Database Details

Set	Term Searched	Items	
S1	JN=JOURNAL OF SOCIAL PSYCHOLOGY	395	Display
S2	SO=(JOURNAL (1W) SOCIAL (W) PSYCHOLOGY)	2767	Display

Fig. 5.25. Searching in the JN and SO indexes of Mental Health Abstracts.

For a short time in 1998 the JNF database was free of charge for DIALOG password holders but now levies a reasonable charge. It was always updated very regularly every month, by the first weekend of the month. Lately, it has experienced significant delays. This is a unique database, and DIALOG should keep it as current as possible. It is a great asset in selecting the most appropriate database not only for an occasional search but also for licensing, as it allows the exploration of the journal coverage of databases considered for licensing.

GEOGRAPHIC COVERAGE

Database coverage is often described with the attribute "international." *International* is a politically correct term, but as is the case with many other politically correct concepts, the implementation needs scrutiny. Of the 426 databases that have a description in the DIALOG bluesheets database, 422 have a Geographic Coverage (GC) field. As many as 349 databases claim international coverage, 61 admit U.S.-only focus, and 12 claim other countries as their geographic coverage (figure 5.26). These statements should not be taken at face value. Covering one Canadian journal in addition to U.S. journals does not make a database really international. On the other hand, Education Abstracts of H. W. Wilson, for example, has the GC=other attribute even though its coverage is indeed international and would definitely justify the international attribute in the geographic coverage field.

International coverage presumes the inclusion of documents that 1) originate from several countries, or 2) focus on several countries in documentary databases. In directory databases, the word *international* implies the coverage of organizations, products, and objects from around the world. Many of the "international" databases, however, do not measure up to these requirements.

Just because a company directory includes data about U.S. and Canadian corporations, it may not really qualify as international, although semantically it is correct. The same applies to databases that include half a dozen British periodicals in addition to the several hundred U.S. journals. The essential criterion would be to provide some statistics in the documentation or as a help file about the geographic origin of the journals (as was done in the implementation of the PASCAL database by the file producer), as shown in figure 5.27. Without that information, the database evaluator has to do exploratory searches.

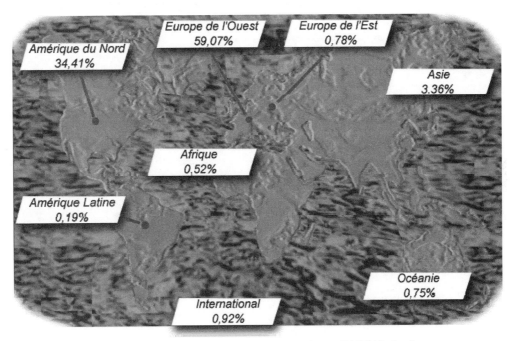

Search History
Database Details

Set	Term Searched	Items	
S1	UD=?	426	Display
S2	GC=?	422	Display
S3	GC=INTERNATIONAL	349	Display
S4	GC=US ONLY	61	Display
S5	GC=OTHER	12	Display

Show Database Details for:
415: DIALOG Bluesheets(TM) ▼   Bluesheet   Rates

Fig. 5.26. International coverage claims in DIALOG databases.

Europe de l'Ouest
59,07%

Europe de l'Est
0,78%

Amérique du Nord
34,41%

Asie
3.36%

Afrique
0,52%

Amérique Latine
0,19%

Océanie
0,75%

International
0,92%

Fig. 5.27. Geographic distribution of journals in the PASCAL database.

File producers should not be blamed for the bias of covering journals mostly from the United States, Great Britain, Canada, and Australia. These are the countries of the most interest for most of the users for advanced research, business dealings, contemporary arts, and entertainment and current events. One must realize, too, that the largest numbers of users of professional information services and databases are in those countries. Even in other countries, English has become the lingua franca of scientific, technical, and business communication (and also of entertainment). File producers are not bound by the principle of proportional geographic representation as is, for example, the United Nations and many international organizations and committees that often make their work inefficient due to the noble principle.

It is telling that the previously mentioned four countries publish more than 50 percent of the journals that appear in the Ulrich's database (figure 5.28), whose subtitle—rightly—is International Periodicals Directory.

Search History
Database Details

Set	Term Searched	Items	
S1	CN="UNITED STATES"	85891	Display
S2	CN="UNITED KINGDOM"	24184	Display
S3	CN="CANADA"	10197	Display
S4	CN="AUSTRALIA"	6566	Display
S5	S1:S4	126838	Display
S6	UD=?	230843	Display

Fig. 5.28. Dominance of U.S., British, Canadian, and Australian journals in Ulrich's.

The Serials Directory of EBSCO (figure 5.29) shows similar proportions (although there are significant differences between the two directories in the coverage of individual countries). EBSCO—in spite of its smaller size—has more comprehensive coverage of U.S., Canadian, Chinese, and South Korean serials, whereas Ulrich's has the lead for all other countries and regions.

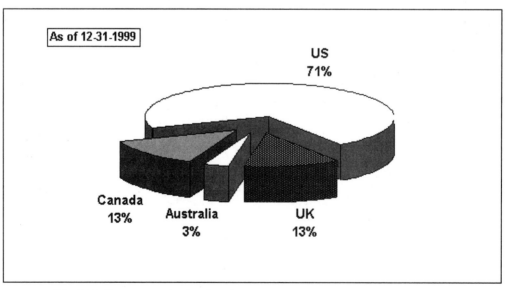

Fig. 5.29. Geographic distribution of serials in The Serials Directory of EBSCO.

In comparing these numbers, it is to be borne in mind that in Ulrich's, the record for the successor title absorbs the information of the former title, while EBSCO retains the record of the ceased titles. This is the typical policy of national serials catalogs, including the CONSER database of the Library of Congress. The OCLC Union Catalog follows the same policy. These resources are particularly interesting because they represent the geographic distribution of serials collections in actual libraries rather than merely the publishing of serials around the world.

Statistics from the far larger (900,000) and far more international directory compiled by the International Serials Data System (ISDS) reconfirm the distribution pattern seen in the other serials directories (figure 5.30). Data for ISDS are reported by nearly a hundred national libraries (which act like the national and sometimes regional ISDS centers).

Poland	4,869	5,799	6,811	8,008	9,084	10,028	10,574	12,614
Portugal	1,675	1,938	2,207	2,396	2,621	3,069	3,242	3,447
Romania	937	1,239	2,043	2,363	2,363	2,365	3,996	5,410
Saudi Arabia	82	83	85	268	376	491	634	628
Senegal	90	89	91	91	91	94	93	91
Singapore	2,014	2,217	2,366	2,424	2,515	2,680	2,713	2,712
Slovakia	na	na	552	551	551	552	552	844
Slovenia	na	na	701	956	1,383	1,604	1,707	1,932
Spain	7,901	9,247	10,129	11,060	11,895	13,114	14,365	14,969
Sri Lanka	136	140	142	152	255	320	402	477
Switzerland	2,779	2,989	3,023	3,199	4,051	5,237	6,411	7,319
Sweden	12,033	13,140	13,854	14,531	15,256	16,061	16,646	17,133
Tanzania	340	395	406	436	436	479	499	515
Thailand	1,205	1,450	1,452	1,485	1,490	1,769	1,810	2,859
Tunisia	262	264	269	279	295	305	318	320
Turkey	498	498	498	883	1,260	1,383	1,395	1,534
United Kingdom	33,157	36,143	39,688	43,098	46,324	50,113	53,983	57,145
United States of America	113,101	118,989	124,728	130,775	136,053	140,372	143,977	150,924
Uruguay	697	782	825	900	965	991	1,127	1,264
Venezuela	420	484	662	931	1,062	1,428	1,529	1,698
Yugoslavia[1]	4,484	4,726	2,391	2,391	2,391	2,389	2,722	2,722

Fig. 5.30. Geographic distribution of serials in the ISDS database.

It is one thing to recognize the pattern of serials publishing, and it is another to learn of their circulation (subscriptions), which would indicate their popularity. Such data are not readily available from any of the serials directories, even though Ulrich's and EBSCO claim to provide such data. Chapter 7 on accuracy and Chapter 9 on completeness illustrate how inaccurate and incomplete (and hence unreliable) these data may be.

The geographical distribution of journals monitored by the Institute for Scientific Information may indirectly, but well represent, how the professional science information consumer market perceives the importance of serials by country of publication (figure 5.31).

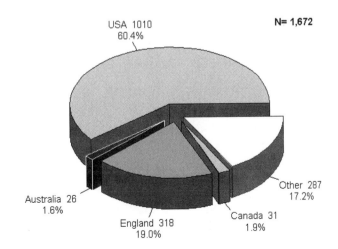

ISI SocSci

USA 1010
60.4%

N= 1,672

Australia 26
1.6%

England 318
19.0%

Canada 31
1.9%

Other 287
17.2%

Fig. 5.31. Geographic distribution of serials in the ISI social science edition of the Journal Citation Reports database.

These introductory data certainly help to put the geographic coverage of databases in the right perspective. Ultimately, it is the targeted user group whose interest must be reflected by the geographic coverage of a database. Beyond the national bibliographies and union catalogs, there are many databases that have a single country as the geographic origin of publications, or products or location of businesses. This is quite reasonable as long as it serves a viable market.

Single-source newspaper databases such as the *Guardian*, the *Irish Times,* or the *China Morning Star* obviously have a single country as the primary geographic source (even if they cover international events). The Canadian Newspapers database must have a large enough local market alone to justify the Canadian approach in terms of geographic coverage. SilverPlatter's Canadian database is possibly the largest digital information source dedicated to Canada. Dun & Bradstreet's Canadian Market Identifier database may be the ideal resource for those who need information about companies of the country that is the largest or second largest commercial partner for many other countries. The New Zealand Newspapers database, covering 13 newspapers, is perhaps a bolder project on DIALOG, but certainly helps Kiwis and Aussies get locally relevant information. The Australian databases are not available on the largest international online services, but the local and CD-ROM versions of Australian databases certainly help to remedy the problem of losing a nation's literature (described very convincingly in a classic piece by Byrne [1983], an Australian himself).

There is another aspect of geographic coverage that is independent of the country of publications and refers to the topical coverage of a country, region, or the entire world. AGRIBUSINESS is a case in point. It has only U.S. sources; still, these sources cover practically every country in the world—at least from an agricultural aspect. On the other hand, World Databases—among its many fatal deficiencies—does not really cover the world. It has a definite focus on U.S. and European databases. Actually, it has far less international coverage than the Gale Directory of Databases.

The Directory of Library and Information Professionals CD-ROM database of ALA boasts about its worldwide coverage. Formally, there are indeed many countries represented, but many of them by only one person (who is probably the ALA liaison of an institutional member). Less than 10 percent of the records refer to professionals outside the United States. Even Great Britain, whose Library Association has more than 20,000 members, is represented by only 34 individuals.

Regional coverage is also common in many databases. The Info Latino America database (produced in Florida) and the Latin American News database (produced in Mexico) have an obvious focus. However, the former covers a large number of journals (about 1,500), while the latter was originally restricted to two newspapers: *El Norte* and *Reforma,* which made up almost 90 percent of the database content (figure 5.32).

```
                    Dialog Response


     Ref     Items    Index-term
     E1          0    *JN=
     E2        136    JN=ANDEAN GROUP REPORT
     E3        135    JN=BRAZIL REGIONAL REPORT
     E4        217    JN=CARIBBEAN & CENTRAL AMERICAN REPORT
     E5     274059    JN=EL NORTE
     E6        842    JN=LATIN AMERICAN ECONOMY & BUSINESS
     E7        141    JN=MARKET: LATIN AMERICA
     E8        234    JN=MEXICO AND NAFTA REPORT
     E9     276283    JN=REFORMA
     E10       181    JN=SOUTHERN CONE REPORT
     E11      7733    JN=WEEKLY REPORT
     E12      9619    LA=ENGLISH
     E13    550339    LA=SPANISH
```

Fig. 5.32. The geographical source composition of Latin American News database.

The South American Business Information database, on the other hand, implies in its title somewhat more than it covers—merely five countries of South America: Argentina, Brazil, Chile, Peru, and Uruguay. The Asia-Pacific Business Journals database covers another region of primary science, technology, and business importance, both for its spectacular achievements and for its current financial doldrums. The Arctic & Antarctic Regions database has similar regional characteristics with a purely science and technology focus. The Eastern European Company Directory is obviously the number-one resource for information about companies in the region.

Sometimes the name of the producer implies the geographic coverage of a database, as is the case with the KIT database of the Royal Tropical Institute, the AGRIS database of the United Nations Food and Alimentation Organization, and the LILACS database of the Pan-American Health Organization. The name of the organization, however, is not always indicative of the subject coverage. The CAB Abstracts database of the Commonwealth Agricultural Bureaux (now CAB International) has a much broader spectrum than the Commonwealth in terms of both geographic origin and subject of documents. Common assumptions don't always pan out with geographic coverage of databases. PASCAL, the flagship multidisciplinary database of France, covers in information science 84 U.S. journals and only 14 published in France. This is below the proportion of serials publication in the two countries.

Just because the name of a database includes the name of a country or the geographic and political groups of countries does not mean that it would be limited to those categories. The British Education Index has a few thousand records from other European countries, such as Belgium, France, Germany, and the Netherlands.

Broad geographic coverage can be an asset or a liability depending on user preferences overall, or for a particular search. The average American may not be extremely interested in a journal published in Hungary, but her interest would skyrocket if she were to go to Hungary for a three-month consultancy on library automation as a Fulbright Fellow. A physician treating patients who use opiate derivatives may not bug the library to get interlibrary loan of the conference about the lifestyle of people in Chiang Rai, Thailand, but certainly would be interested when making a trip to the Golden Triangle. Lack of coverage of one or more countries may be a disadvantage—especially in a patent database where worldwide coverage is definitely an asset. In comparing Fast-Alert and Patents Preview, Cheeseman (1995) points out that the former does not cover patents issued in France and Germany.

Inspection of the geographic coverage in databases can reveal interesting traits. Whitney (1990, 1992, 1993) has done the most research surveying the coverage by major databases of the physical sciences, social sciences, medicine, and technology publications in general and authors in Third World and European countries in particular. Her studies analyze trends at the database and individual country levels, examining changes in patterns across two decades.

Coverage of some of the literature of a given country does not necessarily mean appropriate coverage. Amba and Naresh (1994) point out that although some journals from India are covered in CAB Abstracts, and articles about the leather industry are included, none of the leather industry core journals of India are covered, in spite of the fact that India holds a prominent position in leather research. Journals of less developed countries are rarely covered in international databases, although AGRIS, CAB Abstracts, MEDLINE, and LISA provide considerable coverage in their fields.

Databases of international cooperation are most likely to include journals from the Third World countries, as Hitti (1995) and Thomas (1990) point out. In the overcrowded medical database category, the ExtraMED database could possibly carve out a niche by processing nearly 3,000 biomedical journals not covered by other databases, especially ones from developing countries.

Journals from European countries may be a strong selling point of some databases. EMBASE has seen a decline in the coverage of its specialty, European journals (Briggs and Crowlesmith 1995). A few years ago, nearly half of the records in its database were for articles published in European journals. However, the trend is clear that both the non–U.S. journal portion of EMBASE and its non–English language subset keep decreasing (figure 5.33).

Search History

Set	Term Searched	Items	
S1	PY<1990	4183721	Display
S2	S1/NONENG	1041428	Display
S3	PY>1989	3519765	Display
S4	S3/NONENG	411669	Display

Show Database Details for:

73: EMBASE® (1974-present)   Bluesheet   Rates

Fig. 5.33. Diminishing share of records for non-U.S. and Canadian journals in EMBASE.

Freedman's study (1995) shows that, in the BIOSIS database, more than 50 percent of sources are from Europe and the Middle East, 31 percent from North America, 3 percent from Central and South America, and 2 percent from Africa. There is a decline in the coverage of Eastern European journals, as many of those countries have lost their researchers to brain drain or now have higher priorities than doing research. This may change later, as happened with Eastern European sociology journals covered by Sociological Abstracts, that bounced back by the mid-1990s (Chall and Owen 1995).

Changing political and economic circumstances may have an impact on the coverage of journals from a certain country or region. Ubico, Baily, and Weaver (1995) point out that the TULSA database of oil research witnessed a sudden increase in coverage of Chinese materials in 1982 when China opened opportunities to outside petroleum exploration. The changing reality of business potential in the former Soviet Union is reflected by the roller-coaster coverage of Russian materials. In other fields, the decline of Russian research in the 1990s is reflected in the shrinking coverage of Russian journals.

While at first blush the information and library science subset of Social SciSearch kept indexing and abstracting two Russian journals, there were merely 722 records added between 1990 and 1994, compared with the 3,200 records created before 1990. Not surprisingly, citations to Russian journals of library and information science have plummeted since the de facto independence of satellite countries of the former Soviet Union. Citing Russian language journals, in this author's opinion, has been motivated more by political savvy than by scientific reasons—at least in library and information science.

The absence of a data element identifying the country of publication of the source publication is surprising in LISA, which proudly (and rightly) brags about its worldwide coverage of library and information science journals. ExtraMED does not indicate the country of publication of the journal, but the geographic focus of the articles is searchable through descriptors.

Sometimes the relatively large number of records from a specific country may be surprising. Czech publications seem to have extraordinary coverage in the Business & Industry database of Responsive Database Services compared with Hungarian or Polish publications (figure 5.34). Beyond the appeal of the velvet revolution and the charismatic Václav Havel, nothing seems to justify this very strong preference in a database for the Czech Republic. Library Literature shows a good mixture of journals with international geographic origin (figure 5.35). Even if country of publication is not searchable, the language index is quite revealing about the internationalism of these two databases.

```
E3           0   *LA=
E4         326   LA=CHINESE
E5       29853   LA=CZECH
E6         944   LA=DANISH
E7     1393170   LA=ENGLISH
E8           2   LA=ENGLSIH
E9       13445   LA=FRENCH
E10      18359   LA=GERMAN
E11        769   LA=ITALIAN
E12      36653   LA=JAPANESE
E13         11   LA=KOREAN
E14       1837   LA=NORWEGIAN
E15      24522   LA=PORTUGUESE
E16      18321   LA=RUSSIAN
E17      25910   LA=SPANISH
E18         15   LA=SWEDEN
E19       1863   LA=SWEDISH
E20      16098   MT=ACCOUNT ACTIVITY
```

Fig. 5.34. Disproportionally large number of records in Czech language.

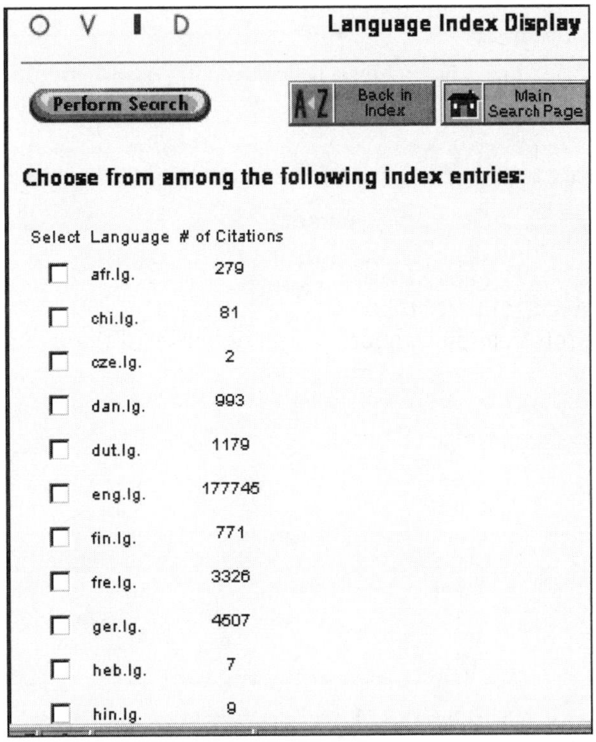

Fig. 5.35. Considerable mixture of international journals in LibLit.

Both of the largest, free movie directories provide a useful snapshot—without the need for searching—about the geographic origin of the movies. The All Movie Guide (AMG) provides an alphabetic list (figure 5.36), while the Internet Movie Database (IMDb) (figure 5.37) offers a subgroup of countries that are represented by more than 500 movies. It's obvious at first glance that IMDb offers more movies from Argentina, Austria, Brazil, China, East Germany, and Finland than AMG.

COUNTRIES:			
Albania	14	Algeria	53
Argentina	416	Armenia	26
Australia	928	Austria	331
Azerbaijan	12	Bangladesh	6
Belgium	310	Bolivia	10
Brazil	326	Bulgaria	146
Burkina Faso	20	Byelarus	74
Cameroon	18	Canada	1,567
Chile	70	China	260
Colombia	39	Croatia	11
Cuba	90	Cyprus	7
Czech Republic	19	Czechoslovakia	464
Denmark	494	East Germany	178
Egypt	86	Estonia	27
Finland	206	France	11,847
Georgia (Republic)	66	Germany	1,263
Ghana	11	Greece	296
Guinea	9	Hong Kong (China)	34
Hong Kong (U.K.)	689	Hungary	649
Iceland	33	India	656
Indonesia	32	Iran	110
Iraq	13	Ireland	123

Fig. 5.36. All Movie Guide's country snapshot.

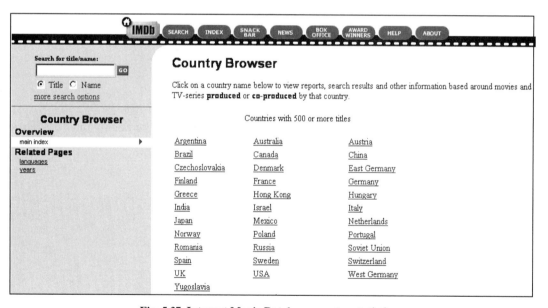

Fig. 5.37. Internet Movie Database country statistics.

LANGUAGE COVERAGE

Similar considerations apply to the language coverage of a database as to the geographic coverage. Diversity is attractive on the surface. It is useful for some of the potential users to find references to, say, Hungarian language articles, but for the vast majority of users, diversity may turn out to be a negative feature. Whereas multicontinental geographic distribution by origin of the source documents does not necessarily imply limited relevance for a target audience, diversity of language coverage is likely to do so.

In most cases U.S., Australian, and U.K. periodicals are potentially of the same relevance for a user who reads English. The same could apply to Canadian journals as long as they are from bilingual or English language publications. For an audience that is at ease reading French, a Canadian journal may be as relevant as a journal published in France, as long as it is in French or is bilingual. The same applies to the preferences of a user from Francophone, Africa.

In bibliographic databases, foreign language coverage also has additional implications, such as the difficulty of acquiring the journal or just the source document through interlibrary loan. In a survey of 43 academic librarians, Hernon and Metoyer-Duran (1992) found criticism of LISA for covering foreign language journals that are difficult to acquire.

The adequacy of the language coverage of a database is also in the eye of the beholder. The large number of Spanish language documents is an asset for users in Spain, Central and Latin America, and any user anywhere who has the required command of Spanish. For others, it is just a ballast that slows down searching and dilutes the results. This concern can be addressed by the system using intuitive language limiters prominently displayed near the search cell on the query template (as illustrated later in this section).

Language equality is a cardinal issue in many international organizations. The translation across languages and hiring of capable interpreters incur vast expenses. The European Economic Union (EEU) spends an enormous part of its budget to translate, for example, from Greek into the many other languages that are the official languages of the EEU.

Datafile producers face similar problems and have to balance the cost of indexing and abstracting foreign language journals and acquiring them in full-text format on the one hand and the real need for them on the other hand. Escalating costs may have forced Elsevier to cut back on the number of non–English language documents in EMBASE. We saw earlier (in figure 5.33) the drastic changes in the composition of EMBASE in terms of language before and after 1990. Figure 5.38 shows the decline in five-year increments from 1975, while the annual volume of records added to the database kept growing. The decline in the coverage of French, German, and especially Russian language documents was particularly strong. Interestingly, records of Polish language documents rose from 254 in 1990 to 402 in 1998.

Search History
Database Details

Set	Term Searched	Items
S1	UD=?	7815869
S2	S1/NONENG	1463013
S3	S2/1975	74019
S4	S2/1980	64591
S5	S2/1985	57752
S6	S2/1990	62825
S7	S2/1995	41111
S8	S2/1998	38324

Fig. 5.38. Declining foreign language coverage in EMBASE in five-year increments.

The Social SciSearch database clearly shows a decline in the proportion of non–English language documents. Prior to 1990, the non–English language documents represented 13 percent of the total collection. From 1990 onward, this rate is merely 3 percent (figure 5.39). Sociological Abstracts had a strong foreign language coverage in the 1960s; then it declined, but it was on the rise again in the late 1990s. The decline in Sociological Abstracts from 20 percent to 15.4 percent was not nearly as dramatic but definitely noticeable (figure 5.40).

The databases with library and information science coverage also showed a decline in adding records for non-English articles, although to a different extent. LISA, which is the most international among all the LIS databases, has seen a decline in non–English language documents from 32 percent to 18.7 percent (figure 5.41). LibLit went from 32 percent to 23 percent. ISA never had significant non–English language coverage, so the decline from 6.5 percent to 2 percent is not as bad as if we were just to say that coverage of non-English documents decreased by nearly 70 percent in ISA.

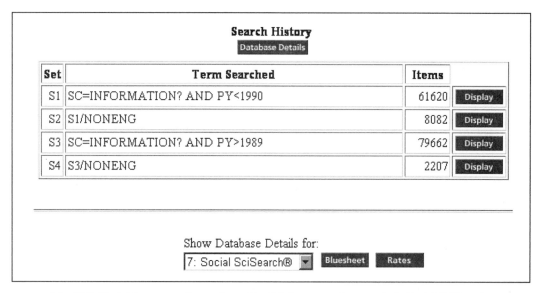

Fig. 5.39. Shrinking proportions of non–English language documents in Social SciSearch.

Search History
Database Details

Set	Term Searched	Items	
S1	PY<1990	309543	Display
S2	S1/NONENG	62985	Display
S3	PY>1989	242883	Display
S4	S3/NONENG	37570	Display

Show Database Details for:
37: Sociological Abstracts   Bluesheet   Rates

Fig. 5.40. Shrinking proportions of non–English language documents in Sociological Abstracts.

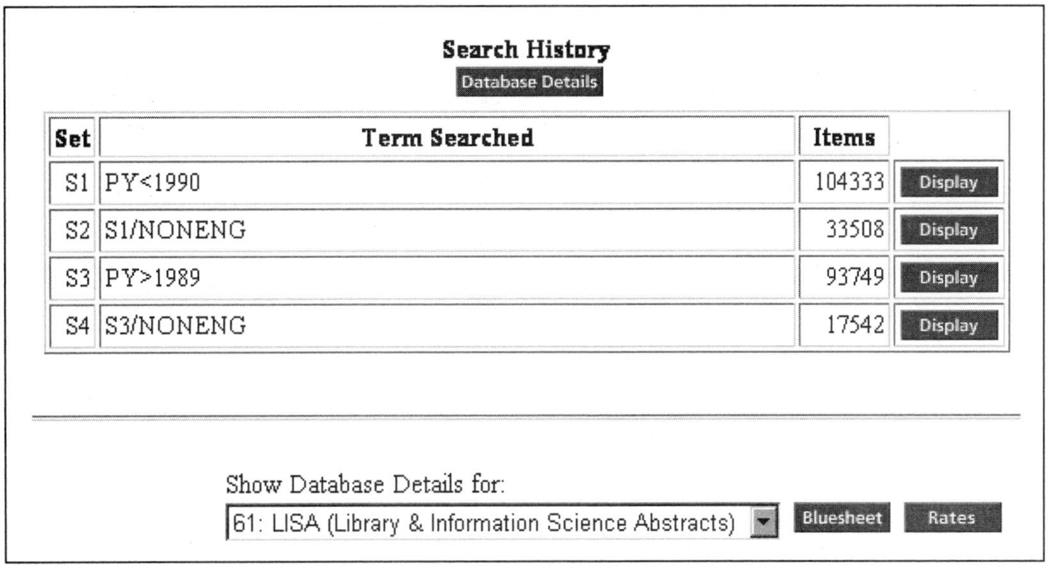

Fig. 5.41. Shrinking proportions of non–English language documents in LISA.

As long as limiting a search by language is easy and intuitive, foreign language materials are not a problem even for the English-only user. This is, of course, a function of search software and interface design. While most databases indeed allow restricting the search to one or more languages, it is not always intuitive. The command SELECT LIBRARIANSHIP AND LA=(ENGLISH OR GERMAN OR SPANISH) in DIALOG's command mode is easy for the experienced searcher but not for casual users. They may prefer pull-down menus of the language index or check boxes by language of documents.

In the case of pull-down menus, users may not realize that they may select more than one language by holding the Ctrl (Control) key while clicking on the language, so Ovid is applauded for clearly explaining this (figure 5.42). The check-box approach is certainly the most intuitive, but often the only option is English or non-English. In databases that have strong non–English language coverage, check-boxes for at least the top five languages would be useful. Even though ISA is not exactly a database with polyglot coverage, the WebSPIRS version shows the ideal check-box solution (figure 5.43).

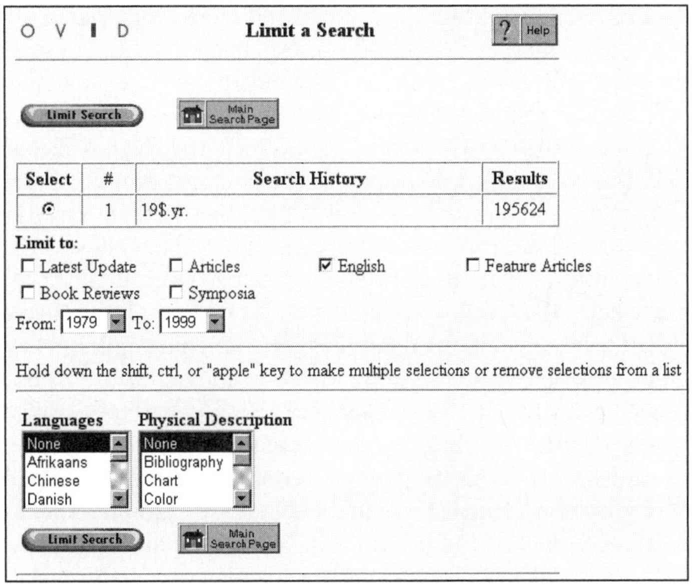

Fig. 5.42. Limiting by language in LibLit on WebOvid.

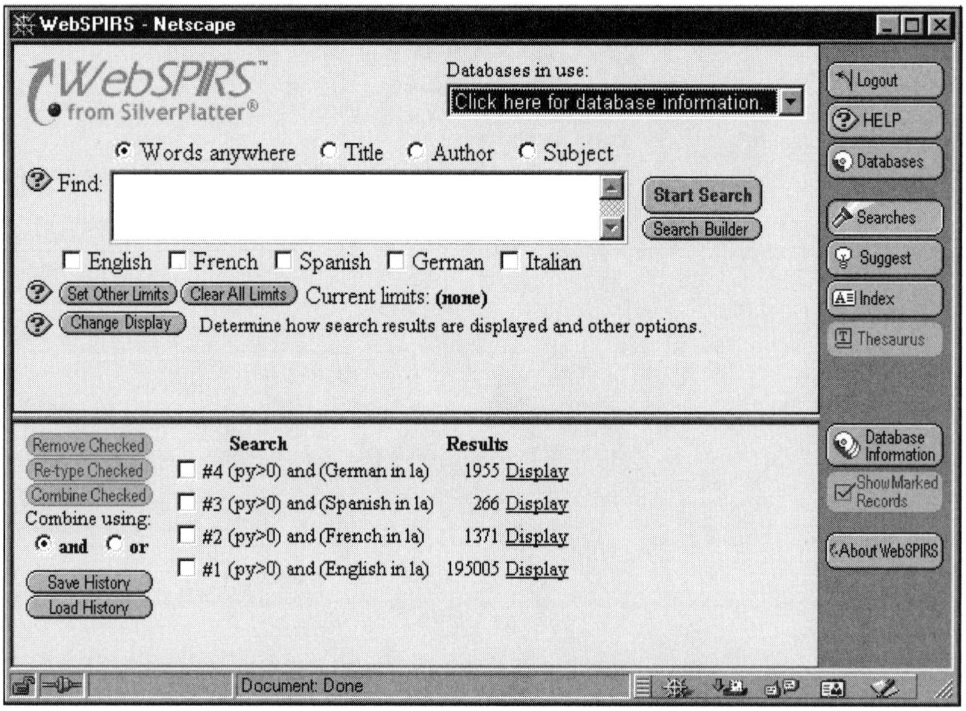

Fig. 5.43. Limiting by language in ISA on WebSPIRS.

It is surprising when, for an utterly polyglot database, there is no language index in any form (as is the case with Ulrich's database). It is a disservice, as searching by language of serials is obviously important (e.g., to find English language journals from Japan or French language newspapers in countries of western Africa). Economic Literature Index has some non–English language journals, but there is no search possibility to limit the search by language. Of the movie directory test databases, only IMDb can be searched by language.

Given the prominence of Japan in many research and development areas, learning of publications from Japan (especially those in English) is of high importance in many disciplines. It has such a viable marketplace that the Japan Information Center of Science and Technology compiled an English language database subset, JICST-E, for English language science and technology publications in Japan. Dueltgen (1991) provides an insightful comparison of four databases that cover Japanese journals, and Boykikeva (1994) compares the coverage of INSPEC, Compendex, and JICST-E. Compendex has the most comprehensive coverage for the test searches. Sodha (1993) found that 70 percent of the total English language Japanese papers could be found in JICST-E and in MEDLINE and EMBASE combined.

Among databases of library and information science coverage, only LISA has a noteworthy volume of records of Japanese language publications—slightly more than 3,000 in early 1999. LibLit has 135 and ISA 138, and ISA stopped adding such records a long time ago. Somewhat surprisingly, Social SciSearch has a relatively modest coverage of journals (9 titles) from Japan overall. None of them is in the Japanese language. The only area where MHA outperforms PsycINFO—though minimally—(before IFI/Plenum took it over) is the set of Japanese and Korean language documents (figure 5.44).

Merely scanning the language, language code index, or the help file of a database may give a false impression of its language coverage. Bowker's Complete Video Directory lists the languages where the language code is not identical to the first three characters of the language name (figure 5.45). Patrons who pine for getting some information about movies in Acholi, Aramaic, or Arapahoe languages may be somewhat disappointed to find that there is none in this database (and probably in the entire world). The help file merely lists languages and their codes for any language that linguists have ever unearthed, and for which the Library of Congress has assigned a code. This gem of help turns out to be the help file from *Books in Print*, as can be seen in figure 5.45.

The editor did not care to change the help file, and obviously no one checked how one of the sample examples would work in reality. You may sense the tumescence as the copywriter wrote the publicity material listing awesome capabilities (figure 5.46) and got a little carried away when suggesting to "Compile lists of videos that meet specific parameters, like 'all PG-rated comedies in English that were released in 1998'." The copywriter must have been unaware of the fact that English is assigned as a language only to multilingual movies. There are only 772 such movie records in this database. No wonder that the result is pathetic. There is only one record meeting the search criteria—not much of a list (figure 5.47).

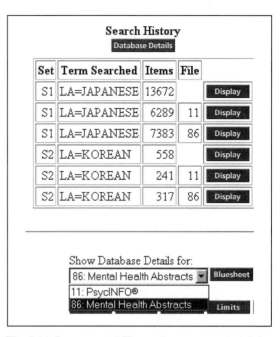

Fig. 5.44. Japanese and Korean language materials in MHA and PsycINFO.

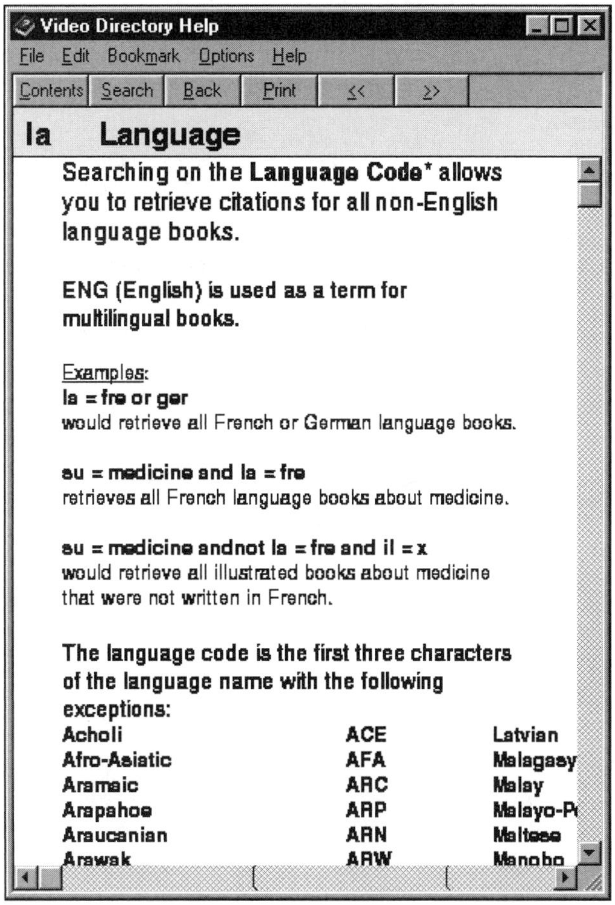

Fig. 5.45. "Help" information about language searching in Complete Video Directory.

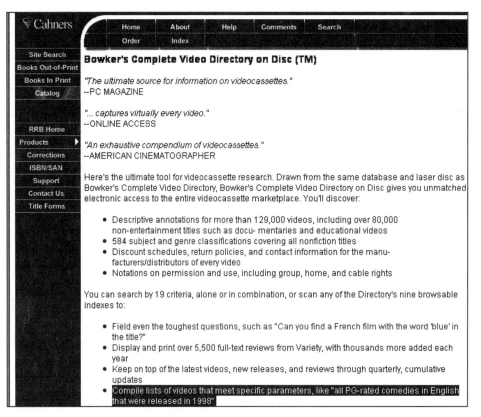

Fig. 5.46. Champagne promises about the possibilities of Bowker's Complete Video Directory.

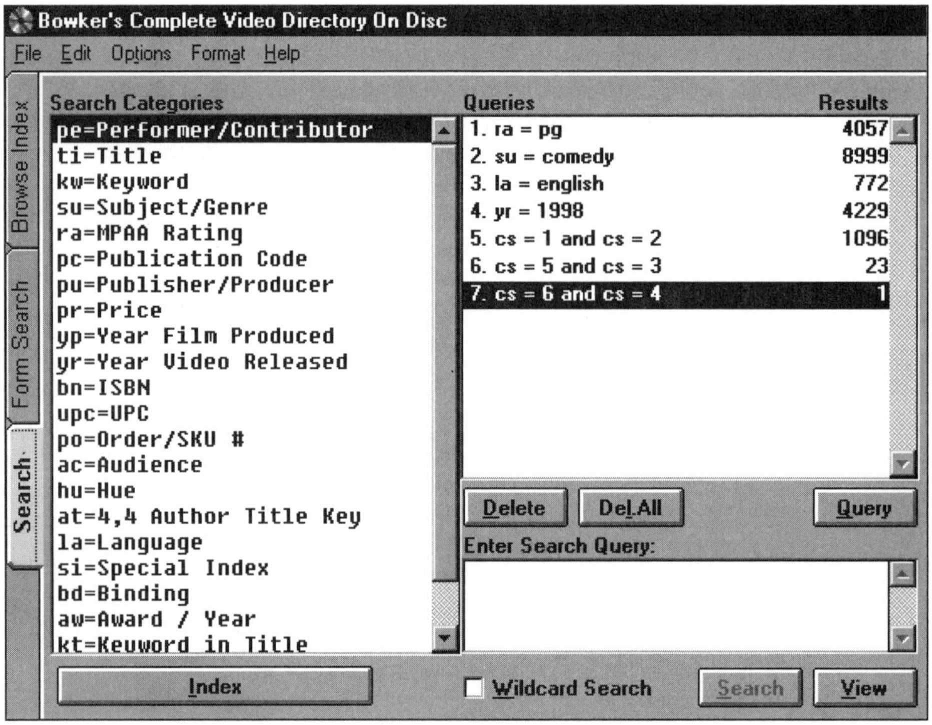

Fig. 5.47. Stale beer reality of the actual search.

Others also have difficulty providing appropriate help about foreign languages. EBSCO managed to pick a nonexistent language (Austrian) to illustrate language searching in the help file. The good news is that in the latest edition, the nonexistent Austrian is only one of the languages (figure 5.48), and if you search by Austrian as a language, no records will be retrieved. Austrian is as much a language as, say, Missourian, since in Austria people speak a dialect of German, not a language of their own.

Fig. 5.48. The help information about language searching in The Serials Directory.

CASE STUDY—THE (DIS)HARMONY OF DATABASE SCOPE AND SOURCE COVERAGE

The source coverage of a database can be correctly evaluated only in light of its subject scope. There must be a harmony among what the database claims it covers and the choice of its sources, as well as the consistency and appropriate breadth of coverage. We have looked at these elements on their own in the previous sections. In this section it is demonstrated—as a case study—how this plays out in one of the databases that is potentially among the most interesting ones for the readers of this book: Information Science Abstracts (ISA). The process is greatly facilitated by the unprecedented publicity that this database received from its editors in the past three years, which gives valuable insight into the efforts of maintaining, improving, and promoting a database. Editor-in-Chief, Donald T. Hawkins, and, to a lesser extent, editor Lynne A. Murray have been vigorously editorializing about the database through monthly editorials in the print version of ISA, on DIALOG's site, as well as on the ISA Web site (*http://www.infotoday.com/isa/editorials.htm*) after Information Today, Inc. acquired the database in mid-1998 (figure 5.49).

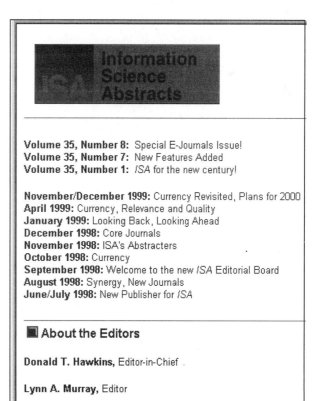

Fig. 5.49. List of editorials about the ISA database on its Web site.

Although the number of editorials decreased after the first few months, Hawkins has also extensively published articles describing the history of the database, the changes (to be) implemented, the poor quality of the database (before its takeover by the current owner), and ISA's standing among its peers. These contributions help immensely in learning about the difficulty of harmonizing the professed scope of a database with its source coverage, which is one of the cardinal issues in evaluating database quality.

I am particularly grateful to him for his ISA-related publications as they kept inspiring me to discover further the anatomy of a database that has such a prominent name in our profession, and also to confront my often differing opinion with his written (thus, quotable) statements for a reality check.

We know how much the study of anatomy is enhanced by post mortems alone, and especially when people offer their cadavers for research with accompanying daily activity diaries allowing researchers to analyze the post-mortem findings with this extra information in hand. The publications serve the function of the diary for my pre-mortem ponderings and maybe post-mortem conclusions later—in a final round, depending upon whether ISA will outlive me, or I will outlive ISA.

As for the peer acceptance and database quality, the editor-in-chief and the editor wrote that "we are conscious of the heritage of ISA and the position that it has enjoyed as a premier database among information scientists" (Hawkins and Murray 2000d). In the same article they also acknowledged that "the quality of the database was poor." This summary judgment also appears in another article (Hawkins 2001b) that was in response to the criticism that coverage of many essential journals ceased or nose-dived from the takeover in 1998. As the senior technical editor of ISA prior to 1998 and as the editor-in-chief of ISA from 1998, Hawkins was in the enviable position of being in the know, and he explained that the former coverage of those titles "is an outstanding illustration of the poor quality of ISA under its previous stewardship, when no selection policy existed." One cannot help but wonder what status ISA would have achieved among information scientists had its quality not been poor.

To the credit of the previous stewardship, vice president Harry Allcock, and editor Anne Meagher, at Plenum (the former producer of the datafile) ISA *did* have a selection policy. They identified 50 journals as core journals that were supposed to "receive complete coverage," while the other journals were to be "abstracted and indexed selectively" as it was stated in every issue of the print version. Hawkins himself (as part of the previous ISA team as senior technical editor from 1996) is to be credited with maintaining this targeting of core journals. Unfortunately, this distinctive mark was eliminated after the takeover by Information Today, Inc. By 1999 many of the former core journals of ISA were not covered by it at all. As discussed below, such dramatic changes can cause serious discrepancy between the professed and the real coverage of key topics in a discipline.

Obviously, Hawkins has been in a particularly good—although not necessarily impartial— position to assess the database quality, as he "became involved with ISA in 1996 as Sr. Technical Editor, and was astonished to learn that a working definition of information science had never been developed for this major A&I publication" (Hawkins 2001a). This astonishment is understandable considering that representatives of eight library and information science associations have been meeting regularly for years as members of an advisory board with members of the ISA stewardship.

The difficulty of defining the subject domain of a database, and choosing and processing the primary documents accordingly, is illustrated clearly by the past and current tests probing the coverage of ISA and its peer database by independent researchers.

As explained previously and shown in a quantitative format in figures 3.10 and 3.11, claims and reality of topical coverage by ISA have almost been poles apart. Unfortunately, this now prevails even more, and casts doubt on the chances of reconciling the two in the future.

A comparison of the topical coverage of ISA and LISA (Hawkins 2001a) clearly shows a lack of validation by the facts, and a grossly distorted reality. In this particular article, many of the topics claimed to be covered only by ISA but not by LISA (figure 5.50), are glaringly incorrect even without running a test search.

To help resolve this question, the subject classification of *Library and Information Science Abstracts* (LISA) was examined. Table 2 lists some of the differences. The left column lists the subjects that LISA covers that ISA does not. They are more related to librarianship. The right column lists the subject areas covered by ISA but not by LISA. These terms are more focused on "pure" information science. In general, ISA concentrates on the theoretical and practical aspects of the knowledge transfer process and its supporting technologies, while excluding coverage of basic librarianship issues such as library facilities, budgeting, personnel management, etc.[Note 4]

Table 2. Librarianship vs. information science.

Librarianship subjects	Information science subjects
Archives	Artificial intelligence, expert systems
Buildings	Basic information science research
Exhibitions	Behavioral sciences
Furniture	Fuzzy logic/fuzzy searching
Library organization	Information industry/marketplace
Library use and users	Information professionals
Loans	Information technologies technical aspects (i.e. computing, Internet, telecommunications)
Management, budgeting, finance	Law/legislation/regulation
Materials	Natural language processing
Microforms	Reading (literacy)
Museums	Subject area databases
Nonprint materials	Types of literature
Old and rare materials	
Promotions	
Removals	
Types of library staff	
Users (various types)	
Vehicles	
World librarianship	

Fig. 5.50. Claims about exclusive coverage of topics in LISA and ISA.

It would be one thing to purport that ISA covers some topics, such as artificial intelligence, expert systems, fuzzy searching telecommunications, and natural language searching more than LISA. Stating that LISA does not cover these topics is wishful thinking at best. Including in the sweeping statement such topics where LISA has and always has had better coverage than ISA, such as information industry and marketplace, information professionals, Internet, literacy (reading), law, legislation and regulation does not help the case of ISA.

One wonders how such a paper could pass the rigorous refereeing process of the respected *Journal of the American Society for Information Science* (JASIS). There is a reason that—as shown in figure 5.51— only 5.23 percent of the 746 articles published in JASIS between 1990–1999 were penned by authors from the commercial sector (Koehler et al., 2000, Table 11)—[*http://www.cindoc.csic.es/cybermetrics/ articles/v4i1p3.html*]. There is always the danger that commercial interest may inadvertently distort research methodology and interpretation of results to a smaller or larger extent.

This may be the case especially when authors discuss products in whose promotion they have a vested financial interest. Bias against the competition's products and services cannot be ruled out either. There are no statistics available about the number of such articles in JASIS, or if there was ever such an article accepted before. It is certainly a hot potato that demands extraordinary scrutiny by the referees for misrepresentation, whether subconscious or not. The temptation for touting one's own product is just too great. Such a paper can raise serious ethical questions, and can undermine the credibility of the journal in a situation when—despite of the presumed refereeing process—obviously wrong information is presented in the context of scientific research.

Presenting a summary of reproducible research data supporting a cardinal point in a research paper is a must. Unfortunately the JASIS article lacks this element. Relatively simple searches clearly indicate that the statements carving out a monopoly for the ISA database at the expense of its competitor, the LISA database in several information science topics, have no merit.

Table 11							
AD/JASIS Corporate First Authors – Parent Organization Distribution by Decade							
		Decades – Column Percent					All Years
Corporate Author	N	1950-59	1960-69	1970-79	1980-89	1990-99	1950-99
Commercial	386	27.38	40.68	16.06	16.67	5.23	17.79
Educational	1433	25.79	37.57	70.47	70.14	88.47	66.04
Government	147	23.81	7.63	4.92	6.02	2.01	6.77
Library	49	9.52	1.69	0.26	3.01	0.67	2.26
Hospital	1					0.13	0.05
Military	17	2.78	1.41	0.78		0.27	0.78
Organization	79	7.14	8.19	4.15	2.08	0.94	3.64
R&D	58	3.57	2.82	3.37	2.08	2.28	2.67
Total N	2170	252	354	386	432	746	

Fig. 5.51. Percentage of articles by type of author affiliation of JASIS articles.

Test searches were made in the summer of 2001 to compare the number of hits retrieved from both databases for queries that represent the topics in which the JASIS article claimed monopoly for the ISA database. Searches were done in the basic index (that consists of words extracted from the title, abstract, and descriptor fields).

It is important to note that, for comparison purposes, the title word searches are the most reliable as different wording and inconsistently applied vocabulary in the abstract, and especially in the descriptor field, may distort the results significantly. For example, one of the topics declared as covered only by ISA but not LISA is information professionals. ISA assigned this term to merely 11 records in different variations, whereas LISA assigned it to more than 1,000 records. A search involving the descriptor field would make LISA the absolute winner hands down. ISA prefers the descriptor "information specialists" and assigned it to 1,045 records, whereas LISA uses this descriptor for only 28 records, giving a knock-out win to ISA. There may be other descriptors used occasionally, such as information brokers, or searchers.

In light of the statement presented in the article that "ISA's controlled vocabulary has long outlived its usefulness," and knowing its very inconsistent use from experience, it would have been futile to rely in test searches on the use of the descriptor index. This deficiency in indexing would also implicitly distort the search results from the basic index. LISA has its own idiosyncrasies with the descriptor field. After Bowker-Saur acquired the database, a real thesaurus was developed replacing the old "controlled" vocabulary, but thesaurus terms were not retroactively applied to the old records, hence the descriptor index is not a reliable tool for the test in LISA either.

The title fields, on the other hand, are transcribed in a comparable way in these two databases as neither uses title enhancements. The searches were done in the basic index, the title index, and the descriptor index, but only the title search results are to be used for comparison being the most reliable indicators for leveling the playing field (figure 5.52).

In an effort to establish the "pure" information science coverage of ISA, the JASIS article turns a blind eye on tens of thousands of records in ISA for articles about such library science topics as archives, library organization, library use and users, museums, and non-print materials. (Figure 5.68 later in this section provides a reality check for those topics, too.)

Search terms	LISA	ISA	LISA	ISA	LISA	ISA	LISA	ISA	LISA	ISA	LISA	ISA
	basic	index	TI	TI	DE	DE	basic	index	TI	TI	DE	DE
artificial intelligence	2,059	9,606	227	702	1,445	6,870	869	629	55	9	717	346
expert systems	1,278	3,249	289	694	887	2,964	246	101	28	15	182	83
fuzzy (logic or searching)	95	208	23	78	26	6	50	39	12	13	13	0
fuzzy	330	1,007	161	641	157	774	138	175	75	118	73	139
information (industry or marketplace)	1,462	1,815	175	132	866	1,496	602	542	34	19	489	441
information professionals	2,368	1,130	361	175	1,007	35	980	524	144	80	423	3
information specialists	795	1,473	148	73	28	1,045	122	411	23	9	6	336
internet	13,184	7,075	4,033	1,769	7,575	5,082	8,398	4,662	2,669	988	4,919	3,194
telecommunications	5,405	11,258	562	925	3,878	4,121	776	649	133	27	473	211
natural language	1,131	1,898	236	550	404	1,051	219	168	52	29	83	76
reading (2N) literacy	224	85	12	2	164	70	34	10	0	0	15	8
information literacy	688	399	244	118	438	286	406	242	141	72	279	175
information science research	241	157	61	55	82	45	82	23	9	7	65	6
(behavioral or behavioural) sciences	72	116	19	29	14	31	9	7	2	2	2	0
behavi?	3,354	5,670	666	896	809	1,331	1,099	805	206	124	328	320
law or legislation or regulation	9,910	5,449	2,586	1,148	5,253	2,261	2,519	791	617	151	1,416	344
(scientific or technical or medical or business or government) databases	541	477	82	74	253	240	201	74	9	5	108	24

Fig. 5.52. Results from test searches in LISA and ISA.

The test results in the right part of the table also illustrate how ISA's coverage thinned after the contract with IFI/Plenum was terminated. In all the topics except for fuzzy logic/fuzzy searching where ISA's monopolistic coverage was claimed by the article, LISA yielded more and better results even when discounting non-English language articles that may be pertinent only for a tiny fraction of the users of library and information science databases. This happened not because the new management restricted the coverage only to the most relevant source documents but because of the termination of coverage and spotty coverage of many journals essential for the topics advertised by the bluesheet of ISA (shown in figure 4.31).

While there were some improvements in the database (such as the elimination of some of the duplicates, filling some of the gaps in journals considered by members of the former stewardship of ISA as core journals), the overall quality degraded further. The statement that "ITI quickly addressed and corrected the quality deficiencies identified by Jacsó" is about as accurate as the spelling of the name of this author in the article: two times wrong, one time right in a single paragraph (figure 5.53).

In 1995, Péter Jacsó of the University of Hawaii received the DAI grant. Jacsó studied the journal coverage of ISA, compared it to other A&I information science databases, and reported that the quality of ISA was significantly lacking in several areas. Jacsó's report (1997) ultimately led to the termination of DAI's contract with Plenum and the acquisition of ISA by Information Today, Inc. (ITI) on June 1, 1998.[2] With the sale of its only publication, DAI is in the process of disbanding and distributing its assets to the eight sponsoring societies.

ITI quickly addressed and corrected the quality deficiencies identified by Jacsó, and began to market ISA through its own marketing channels. Plans are currently underway to make ISA available on the Internet.

Fig. 5.53. The quick fix was about as effective as the spell checking of the paragraph itself that claims its success.

The fact is that many of the old deficiencies remained in the database as of summer 2001, such as the 12,000 patent records that were dumped in ISA at an alarming pace from the patent database (also created by the former producer of the file), thousands of the duplicate records, and all of the pre-1990 gaps in purportedly core journals. New gaps were also created. The list of core journals was eliminated, but not the gaps, making ISA totally inappropriate for tracking the literature of information science, which is what the title of the JASIS article promises.

We saw in Chapter 4 the massive gaps in some of the essential journals for topics touted by ISA, such as *Scientometrics* (figure 4.25) and *Program* (figure 4.24) that were not indexed for years. There are many other journals that have serious past and current gaps, such as the *NFAIS Newsletter* missing all the issues of 1999 (shown in figure 4.37), or the *Journal of Scholarly Publishing* that had year-long gaps after its name change from *Scholarly Publishing* in 1984.

After a short period of coverage it seems to have been abandoned after 1998 (figure 5.54), although it couldn't have become less important from the perspective of ISA's professed subject coverage. After all, if electronic publishing is among the 22 topics listed, and publishing by itself was added to the topics list of ISA in 2001, this journal must certainly be relevant. And indeed, it is, though users would not know from ISA about articles such as these, sampled here from the LISA database (figure 5.55).

```
------------------------------------------------------------
RANK: S7/1-202   Field: PY=   File(s): 202
(Rank fields found in 202 records -- 18 unique terms)


RANK No.   Items   Term
--------   -----   ----
   11        9     1970
   14        5     1971
   10       10     1972
    9       11     1973
    3       19     1974
    6       12     1975
    4       18     1976
    2       20     1977
    7       12     1978
   12        6     1979
    5       17     1980
    8       12     1981
   18        1     1984  <---
   15        5     1994
    1       29     1995
   13        6     1996
   16        5     1997
   17        5     1998
           ---end of results---
P =  next page       Pn = Jump to page n
```

Fig. 5.54. Old and new gaps in *Journal of Scholarly Publishing*.

There has always been some discrepancy between the purported subject coverage and the key journals of the appropriate subject areas. It is unfortunate if a database lists decision support systems as a prominent subject area in the database, but fails to cover such prestigious journals as *Decision Sciences, Decision Support Systems, Foundation of Computing and Decision Sciences, Information and Decision Technologies* to name a few journals that are the most cited in the category, and are very well covered by INSPEC, Compendex and ABI/INFORM. ISA does not have a single record for these journals, even though decision support is one of its claimed areas of coverage.

```
DIALOG(R)File  61:(c) 2001 Reed Reference Publishing. All rts. reserv.

 From Gutenberg to gateway: electronic publishing at university presses.


DIALOG(R)File  61:(c) 2001 Reed Reference Publishing. All rts. reserv.

 Fair use: a doubled edged sword.


DIALOG(R)File  61:(c) 2001 Reed Reference Publishing. All rts. reserv.

 Towards electronic journals: realities for scientists, librarians, and
 publishers.


DIALOG(R)File  61:(c) 2001 Reed Reference Publishing. All rts. reserv.

 The utility of publisher websites.


DIALOG(R)File  61:(c) 2001 Reed Reference Publishing. All rts. reserv.

 What do the readers think? A look at how scientific journal users see the
 electronic environment.


DIALOG(R)File  61:(c) 2001 Reed Reference Publishing. All rts. reserv.

 Competition and cooperation: libraries and publishers in the transition to
 electronic scholarly journals.
```

**Fig. 5.55. Some pertinent articles from the *Journal of Scholarly Publishing*
that ISA stopped covering after 1998.**

In the past, however, this was among the minor problems. The big problem was the inconsistency of covering high quality journals that matched the subject coverage of the database. This inconsistency has continued under the new stewardship, and coverage of many of the quality information science journals has been gradually shrinking in ISA. By the end of 1999 it had reached an alarming rate, and by 2000 it had further deteriorated, emaciating the database (Jacsó 2000b). Figure 5.56 shows the original illustration that demonstrated the sharp decline in the coverage of journals, most of which were declared core journals until this status was eliminated. (In 2001 a few records were added for some of the titles, but the trend clearly remained the same.)

	1996	1997	1998	1999	2000
Artificial Intelligence	32	52	48	4	0
IEEE Communications Magazine	66	15	5	6	0
IEEE Transactions on Information Theory	241	196	102	4	0
IEEE Transactions on Systems, Man,...	170	177	50	5	0
Information Sciences	121	92	31	0	0
Information Society	13	23	12	8	3
Information Systems	31	25	19	8	6
Information Systems Management	52	56	42	19	0
Journal of Supercomputing	15	14	0	0	0
M.D. Computing	28	42	23	1	0
MIS Quarterly	21	20	9	7	1
Neural Networks	113	98	7	1	0

**Fig. 5.56. Sharply declining trend of journal coverage in ISA
for ostensibly core topics of the database.**

The editor-in-chief did not share the concern about the sharp decline (Hawkins 2001a). He wondered if anyone could "make a rational argument that *Journal of Supercomputing* or *MD Computing* belong on the list of prestigious core information science journals?" Few may be inclined to answer this in the positive After all, who would argue with the senior technical editor, whose job included overseeing the selection of materials for inclusion in ISA? Well, I venture that *Journal of Supercomputing* is definitely a core journal if an information science database claims not only computer science but explicitly supercomputing among its 22 primary topics in the July 2000 edition of the bluesheet shown previously in figure 4.31. (Interestingly, both of them would be removed in early 2001 from the bluesheet's topic list after discussing this deficiency in the 2000 December installment of the Savvy Searching column [Jacsó 2000d] — figure 5.57).

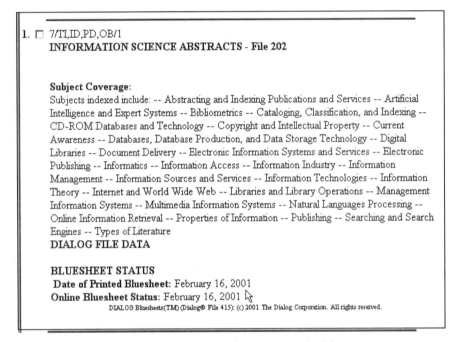

**Fig. 5.57. Major topics of ISA's purported subject
coverage in the February 2001 bluesheet.**

As for *M.D. Computing* of Springer Verlag, if medical informatics was releasing the February 2001 edition, one of the prominently mentioned topics on the database bluesheet (that was updated repeatedly under the new stewardship of the database, giving enough opportunity to modify it), then *M.D. Computing* cannot be ignored. And it definitely *was* ignored in the first couple of years of the senior technical editor's involvement in materials selection (as illustrated in figure 5.56), presumably based on a "rational argument." It remained, however, on the core journal list of ISA for a good reason. [*M.D. Computing* is among the three most cited sources by articles in social science journals discussing medical informatics as shown by the results of a citation search in the Social SciSearch database (figure 5.58). (Two entries, *MD Computing* and *M.D. Computing* were combined in the ranking to accommodate the variant spellings.)]

Later, of course, the core journal list itself was eliminated, probably having become an inconvenient and nagging piece of evidence illustrating how many sources designated as core journals of ISA by its stewardship were not covered at all.

Dialog Response

```
MD COMPUTING AS CW IN SOCSCI
----------------------------
RANK: S10/1-121    Field: CW=  File(s): 7
(Rank fields found in 112 records -- 1497 unique terms) Page 1 of 188
>>>The * indicates a user-precombined rank term;
>>>use DETAIL option to see which terms are precombined.

RANK No.  Items  Term
--------  -----  ----
    1       50   J AM MED INFORM ASSN
    2       44   METHOD INFORM MED
    3       39   JAMA J AM MED ASSOC
    4*      27   M D COMPUT
    5       26   B MED LIBR ASSOC
    6       23   ANN INTERN MED
    7       21   ACAD MED
    8       20   NEW ENGL J MED
P =  next page        Pn = Jump to page n
P- = previous page  M =  More Options      Exit = Leave RANK
```

Fig. 5.58. ***M.D. Computing*** **is among the most cited sources in social science journal articles discussing medical informatics.**

As for the other journals whose coverage hit bottom since 1998, Hawkins goes on to say that "*Artificial Intelligence* and *Neural Networks* occasionally publish articles relevant to information scientists, but they are hardly core journals in the field." Once again, instead of accepting an unsupported opinion to defend a practice, let's look at widely known scientific measures. In the artificial intelligence category of the Journal Citation Reports 2000, the journal *Artificial Intelligence* is ranked second by the number of citations received, and fifth in terms of impact factor. According to the JCR 2000, it received 4,320 citations in 2000 to articles published in the previous two years. As for *Neural Networks*, it is ranked 13th by impact factor and 6th by the number of citations received (2,481) within the artificial intelligence category (figure 5.59a). A simple search for cited works in articles about artificial intelligence would show loud and clear the clout of *Artificial Intelligence*, being far the most cited for the past 25 years whether looking at science journals (figure 5.59b) or social science journals (figure 5.59c), in the respective databases of the Institute for Scientific Information. It is irrational that its coverage by ISA has been plummeting and tanked (figure 5.59d).

Journal Citation Reports - 2000 Science Edition

File Edit View Calculations Options Help

Journal Rankings

Mark	Rank	Journal Abbreviation	ISSN	2000 Total Cites	Impact Factor	Immediacy Index	2000 Articles	Cited Half-life
	5	ARTIF INTELL	0004-3702	4320	2.029	0.364	77	9.2
	6	DATA MIN KNOWL DISC	1384-5810	131	1.931	0.417	12	3.1
	7	IEEE T FUZZY SYST	1063-6706	992	1.873	0.014	72	5.2
	8	INT J COMPUT VISION	0920-5691	1681	1.835	0.100	60	7.0
	9	ARTIF INTELL MED	0933-3657	355	1.793	0.083	36	3.5
	10	CHEMOMETR INTELL LAB	0169-7439	1326	1.462	0.232	69	5.2
	11	AI MAG	0738-4602	505	1.447	0.036	28	7.3
	11	MACH LEARN	0885-6125	1663	1.447	0.209	43	7.6
	13	NEURAL NETWORKS	0893-6080	2481	1.221	0.157	83	7.6
	14	IEEE T NEURAL NETWOR	1045-9227	3051	1.096	0.217	138	6.4
	15	COMPUT INTELL	0824-7935	326	1.091	0.346	26	6.6
	16	PATTERN RECOGN	0031-3203	3204	1.077	0.130	162	7.9
	17	J ARTIF INTELL RES	1076-9757	243	1.064	0.000	20	4.2
	18	KNOWL ENG REV	0269-8889	244	1.025	1.000	12	5.0
	19	APPL ARTIF INTELL	0883-9514	187	1.017	0.000	36	5.2
	20	IEEE INTELL SYST APP	1094-7167	120	1.000	0.161	56	2.0

Sort: Impact Factor | Filter: COMPUTER SCIENCE, | 71 Journals | 0 marked

Fig. 5.59a. Journals and their measures from the Journal Citations Report 2000 in the artificial intelligence category.

```
DIALOGWEB.                    C    ⊟    ꝑ    $    ⊘    ?
   Command Search          new search | databases | alerts | cost | logoff | help

                        Dialog Response
                 _____

Adding title to results...
MOST CITED SOURCES IN ARTIFICIAL INTELLIGENCE
-----------------------------------------------
RANK: S2/1-4750   Field: CW=  File(s): 34
(Rank fields found in 4247 records -- 42431 unique terms)

RANK No.   Items   Term
--------   -----   ----
     1     1380    ARTIF INTELL
     2      615    COMMUN ACM
     3      592    ARTIFICIAL INTELLIGE
     4      527    IEEE T SYST MAN CYB
     5      362    AI MAG
     6      311    SCIENCE
     7      294    COGNITIVE SCI
     8      287    PARALLEL DISTRIBUTED
     9      256    IEEE T PATTERN ANAL
    10      245    INT J MAN MACH STUD
```

Fig. 5.59b. *Artificial Intelligence* in variant spellings is the most cited journal in articles about artificial intelligence in the SciSearch database.

```
DIALOGWEB.                    C    ⊟    ꝑ    $    ⊘    ?
   Command Search          new search | databases | alerts | cost | logoff | help

                        Dialog Response
                 _____

Adding title to results...
MOST CITED SOURCES IN ARTIFICIAL INTELLIGENCE
-----------------------------------------------
RANK: S1/1-1412   Field: CW=  File(s): 7
(Rank fields found in 1305 records -- 16156 unique terms)

RANK No.   Items   Term
--------   -----   ----
     1      398    ARTIFICIAL INTELLIGE
     2      277    ARTIF INTELL
     3      162    COGNITIVE SCI
     4      151    COMMUN ACM
     5      144    SCIENCE
     6      129    MANAGE SCI
     7      118    IEEE T SYST MAN CYB
     8      110    PSYCHOL REV
     9      103    INT J MAN MACH STUD
    10       87    OPER RES
```

Fig. 5.59c. *Artificial Intelligence* in variant spellings is the most cited journal in articles about artificial intelligence also in the Social SciSearch database.

Set	Term Searched	Items	
S1	JN="ARTIFICIAL INTELLIGENCE"	581	Display
S2	S1/1997	52	Display
S3	S1/1998	48	Display
S4	S1/1999	4	Display
S5	S1/2000	0	Display
S6	S1/2001	0	Display

Show Database Details for:
202: Information Science Abstracts ▼ | Bluesheet | Rates

Fig. 5.59d. Coverage of *Artificial Intelligence* by ISA has tanked in spite of its absolute recognition by professionals.

As for the *IEEE Transactions on Information Theory*, Hawkins' article uses a table of contents page of an issue to illustrate that "only one of the articles is relevant to the subject of information science." It may not impress loyal ISA subscribers that their subscription price covered the cost of abstracting and indexing 2,035 documents from this serial alone in years before, including the period when the author was the senior technical editor of ISA, and kept the core journal designation of this publication. There were 241, 196, and 104 records created for papers published in this serial in 1996, 1997, and 1998, respectively.

After many years of complete coverage of this source that was ranked No. 4 in the information systems category by JCR (figure 5.60a), something must have convinced the editors of ISA that this IEEE publication is not relevant after all for information scientists. Merely four records were added to ISA in 1999 for it. If information theory is touted as a subject area covered by ISA, then one of the most cited sources (that also has the fourth highest impact factor) in information theory in the information systems category of JCR, it should not be suddenly almost wholly ignored.

◆IEEE

About IEEE | IEEE Memberships | Products & Services | Conferences | IEEE Organizations

| Search | Join | Newsroom | Shop | Site Map | Tour IEEE | Home |

IEEE Online Catalog & Store

What's New @ IEEE

Products & Services Index

More About Products

More About Services

Request your 2000 IEEE Publications Catalog

Overviews
Books
Conference Proceedings
Electronic Products
Merchandise
Self-Study Courses
Standards
Subscription Packages
Videos

Doing Business with Us

Year After Year, the Top-Cited Publications in the Field are from IEEE

According to ISI's annual Journal Citation Report, IEEE publications continually rank at the top of a variety of fields of technology. Following is a partial listing of some of the most cited publications based on the 1999 JCR.

Read more about IEEE's highly-cited journals.

Field	Highly Cited Periodicals
9 of the top 10 in electrical & electronics engineering	Proceedings of the IEEE (#2) IEEE Electron Device Letters (#3) IEEE Transactions on Medical Imaging (#4)
8 of the top 10 in telecommunications	IEEE Journal of Selected Areas of Communications Magazine (#1)
In Computer Science	
7 of the top 10 in hardware and architecture	IEEE Transactions on Networking (#1)
3 of the top 10 in software, graphics and programming	IEEE Transactions on Image Processing (#3)
2 of the top 10 in computer theory & methods	IEEE Transactions on Image Processing (#1)
4 of the top 10 in information systems	IEEE Transactions on Information Theory (#4)

Fig. 5.60a. The rank of *IEEE Transactions on Information Theory* by impact factor.

The article dismisses in one sweeping sentence four journals whose coverage has been dwindling since the editor-in-chief stewardship of ISA started at Information Today. He asserts that "despite their likely sounding titles, *Information Sciences, Information Society, Information Systems*, and *Information Systems Management* … are not journals of "information science" as most readers of IWR would define the term. They are on the fringe of information science."

I am one of the readers (and authors of multiple articles) of IWR and I definitely count these journals to belong to the realm of information science in general, and to the realm of information management in particular, which is another one of the 22 subjects listed prominently on the ISA bluesheet. Indeed, only a short time before, while acting as senior technical editor at ISA, Hawkins must have thought so too, as you can see from the trend of coverage of these journals in figure 5.56, not to mention other information scientists who rely in their research on these journals, and write for them as well, such as Blaise Cronin, one of the most influential authors in the information science field. Coverage of these journals started to dwindle, however, after the takeover, even though three of these four titles were designated as ISA core journals in 1997 (figure 5.60b), the last year before the core journal designation was eliminated.

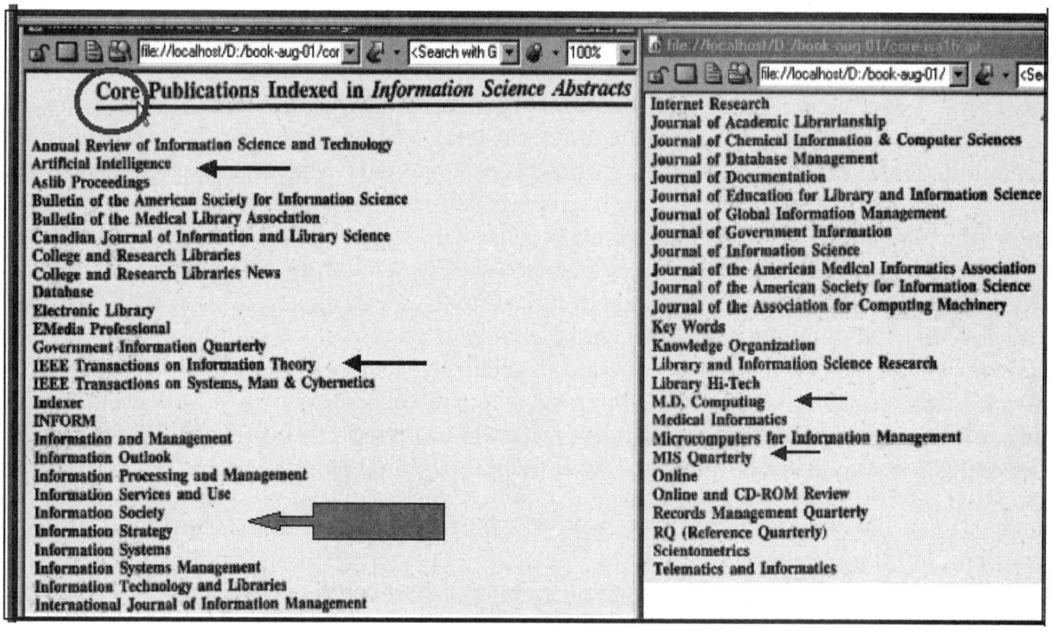

Fig. 5.60b. The last ISA core journals list.

There are no dismissive statements about *IEEE Transactions on Systems, Man, and Cybernetics* (also formerly an ISA core journal) whose coverage fizzled out by 2000 (at least until the November update of ISA) from 170 and 177 records per year in 1996 and 1997, respectively. Neither was *MIS Quarterly* criticized whose coverage plummeted to 1 in 2000 from 21 and 20 in 1996 and 1997 in ISA (a full coverage for this journal). It my not have been the best time to cut the coverage of *MIS Quarterly* as it landed the No. 1 position then the No. 2 position the next year by impact factor in the library and information science category of JCR, respectively. For an unbiased observer, this top ranking suggests that information scientists do read and cite these journals whose coverage plummeted after the takeover of ISA. There are more subtle problems that do not surface by looking at the number of records created for a core journal in ISA, but may cause discomfort for a librarian.

Maintaining an adequate level of coverage of these scientific journals still would have left room for the "new journals" announced by the editorial soon after the takeover. As you look at the list of those new titles two things may get your attention. One is the inclusion of several sources published by Information Today, Inc. such as *Multimedia Schools, Information Today*, and *Link-Up*. These are useful sources for the practitioners, and I am privileged to have contributed a few articles to the former, and several regular columns to the latter two for many years (and I hope to keep doing so even after this book is published).

Still, I would not call them information science journals. Neither would I for almost any of the "new journals" that appeared in the announcement, especially after taking the "No pasaran!" stand publicly with the firmness of the defenders of the short-lived Republic of Spain, pledging that "one thing that we will *not* do is to compromise quality by adding "filler" items or by falsely expanding the coverage of ISA into subject areas unrelated to information science (Hawkins and Murray 2000d) and in a slightly modified version also at *http://library.dialog.com/products/f202.html).*

The second is that 27 of the "new journals" have been covered by Microcomputer Abstracts (later Internet and Personal Computing Abstracts — IPCA). The synergy was meant to be created by reusing IPCA abstracts in ISA. They are good quality abstracts but are available at a fraction of the price from IPCA directly — whether in print or online format, therefore not much of a benefit for the users who can easily make multi-database searches, or for IPCA whose stewardship does an outstanding job in the same office building in New Jersey, keeps a low profile, and presumably resigned to the synergy plan without such fight that we see sometimes in the television show "The Sopranos."

From a purely return on investment perspective, of course, this synergy project may have looked attractive. Using existing bibliographic records with minimal adjustments (such as assigning ISA descriptors and section headings), relying more on in-house journals, and on existing subscriptions for consumer-oriented inexpensive journals (like *PC World, PC Magazine*), cutting back on abstracting expenses and subscription fees to the science journals (the most significant cost elements of maintaining an indexing and abstracting database), is a vigorous business plan while maintaining and even raising the subscription price of the printed and CD-ROM versions, and the usage fee for the online version.

It is quite telling about the soundness of journal selection policy at ISA from 1998 that not a single record was added to articles from issues of 2001 of any of those new journals; at least not until July 2001. Only for a very few of the new journals were some records added in 2000 (figure 5.61).

NEW journals announced for ISA	1998	1999	2000	2001
AI Magazine	5	0	0	0
Booklist	5	3	0	0
Bottom Line: Managing Library	16	0	0	0
Bulletin of the Japan Spec. Libr. Associ.	18	18	18	0
Byte	1	0	0	0
Computer Life	2	0	0	0
Computerworld	10	4	3	0
DBMS	1	0	0	0
Digital Publishing Strategies	0	0	0	0
Fee for Service	0	0	0	0
Forbes	1	1	1	0
Fortune	2	0	2	0
Home Office Computing	1	0	0	0
Imaging	4	2	0	0
Information Today	134	84	56	0
InfoWorld	2	2	3	0
Inside the Internet	0	0	0	0
International Journal of Information Sciences and Decision Making	3	2	0	0
Internet World (was WebWeek)	44	16	2	0
IntraNet Professional	8	11	6	0
LAN Times	2	0	0	0
Link-Up	18	26	19	0
Multimedia Schools	5	6	27	0
Network	3	1	0	0
New Media/NewMedia	2	0	0	0
PC Magazine	29	2	2	0
PC Week	9	6	1	0
PC World	2	2	0	0
Proc Geoscience Info Society	8	0	0	0
Proceedings of the Off-Campus Library	27	0	0	0
School Libraries Worldwide	6	0	0	0
Software Magazine	6	0	0	0
WebWeek (now Internet World)	0	0	0	0
Windows Magazine	2	0	0	0

Fig. 5.61. The coverage of the "new" journals as of July 2001.

It is also quite telling about the philosophy behind maintaining this database that after the publication of the "Endangered Database Species" article, wherein ISA made the list of endangered species, the ISA bluesheet was replaced, once again, in February 2001. There was no announcement and DIALOG did not send out the new printed bluesheet as usual with its *Chronolog Newsletter*. In response to my inquiry, customer service representatives of DIALOG advised me that the bluesheet was replaced at the request of the information provider, and no announcement was made because of the minor nature of the changes.

This is remarkable, because previously DIALOG published and distributed a new bluesheet when a single word was changed on the ISA bluesheet. For example, when the update frequency was identified as irregular (figure 5.62a) in the bluesheet of May 2000, DIALOG replaced it with a new bluesheet in July 2000, changing the update frequency to nine times a year (figure 5.62b). This would be understandable perhaps, had this correction been justified. As the UD index field clearly shows the history (figure 5.63a), the update frequency was reduced to eight times a year already in the previous year, so it was really no big news in mid-1999, although it is certainly bad news for users that it will remain like that.

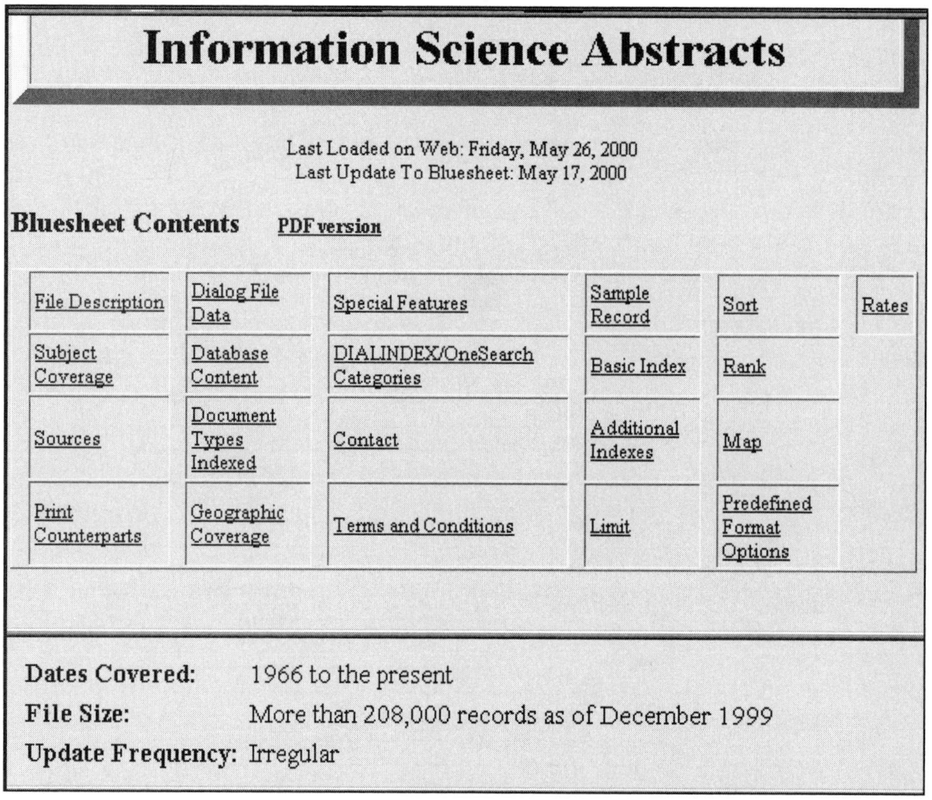

Fig. 5.62a. The bluesheet correctly identifies the updating pattern of ISA as irregular.

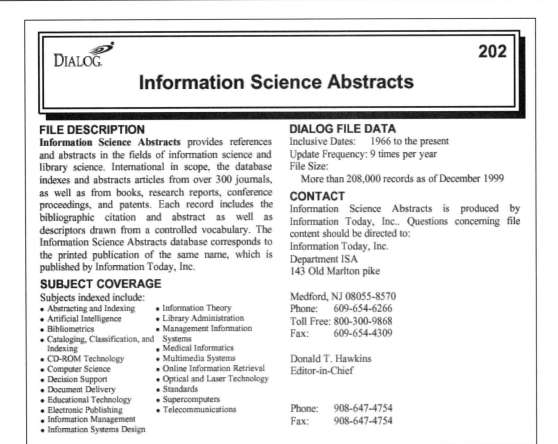

Information Science Abstracts

202

FILE DESCRIPTION

Information Science Abstracts provides references and abstracts in the fields of information science and library science. International in scope, the database indexes and abstracts articles from over 300 journals, as well as from books, research reports, conference proceedings, and patents. Each record includes the bibliographic citation and abstract as well as descriptors drawn from a controlled vocabulary. The Information Science Abstracts database corresponds to the printed publication of the same name, which is published by Information Today, Inc.

SUBJECT COVERAGE

Subjects indexed include:

- Abstracting and Indexing
- Artificial Intelligence
- Bibliometrics
- Cataloging, Classification, and Indexing
- CD-ROM Technology
- Computer Science
- Decision Support
- Document Delivery
- Educational Technology
- Electronic Publishing
- Information Management
- Information Systems Design
- Information Theory
- Library Administration
- Management Information Systems
- Medical Informatics
- Multimedia Systems
- Online Information Retrieval
- Optical and Laser Technology
- Standards
- Supercomputers
- Telecommunications

DIALOG FILE DATA

Inclusive Dates: 1966 to the present
Update Frequency: 9 times per year
File Size:
    More than 208,000 records as of December 1999

CONTACT

Information Science Abstracts is produced by Information Today, Inc.. Questions concerning file content should be directed to:
Information Today, Inc.
Department ISA
143 Old Marlton pike

Medford, NJ 08055-8570
Phone: 609-654-6266
Toll Free: 800-300-9868
Fax: 609-654-4309

Donald T. Hawkins
Editor-in-Chief

Phone: 908-647-4754
Fax: 908-647-4754

Fig. 5.62b. The subsequent release of the ISA bluesheet breaks the news that it is to be updated nine times a year.

DIALOGWEB.

Guided Search | new search | favorites | settings | cost | logoff | help

Dynamic Search: Information Science Abstracts :

Browse a List

Enter Update |1999| browse

select
all none   Update   Records   cancel   add to search »

	Update	Records
☐	199901	609
☐	199902	469
☐	199903	433
☐	199904	495
☐	199906	452
☐	199908	422
☐	199910	385
☐	199912	419

Fig. 5.63a. The real update pattern of the ISA database.

The regularity of updating has always been a big problem with ISA, and was never acknowledged, let alone fixed. Promises have been made, and promises have been broken. The latest public promise was made in an ISA editorial, along with the reduction of update frequency, and an approximately 6-week interval was contemplated for the print version, and a similar one for the online version (figure 5.63b). The reality was quite dissimilar. Just after the editorial was penned, updating of ISA (File 202) once again became erratic and was not updated in March, April, and May, while its peers, LISA (File 61) and Library Literature (File 438) were updated with fair regularity.

We have discussed the problem of currency in a previous Editorial, and in this final issue of 1999, we would like to revisit the issue and present our plans for ISA in 2000. As Editors, we have become increasingly concerned about the false impression of poor currency that ISA's updating dates give to our users. The reason that ISA appears to be delinquent in publication is purely because of the slow receipt of journals from the publishers, not because of any backlog in database production. Indeed, ISA has no backlog; journals are entered into the next issue of the database following their receipt. During the summer of 1999, the problem became especially critical; the receipt rate of journals fell to approximately half its normal rate. We are unaware of any special circumstances which would explain this.

We are addressing the problem described above by instituting the following measures:

- This is the final issue of 1999, and it is dated November/December.
- In 2000, ISA will be published nine times, at approximately six week intervals. The issue numbers will not correspond to a specific publication date or month. The next issue you receive will be designated "Volume 35, Number 1, 2000". The online database will follow a similar updating schedule. The CD-ROM database will continue to be published at quarterly intervals.
- We are planning a significant expansion in ISA's coverage by including other types of literature (ISA is currently comprised totally of journals and conference proceedings). We hope that the volume of literature will grow enough to support resumption of the previous monthly publication schedule in 2001.
- As the field of information science grows to encompass new areas, such as knowledge management, ISA's coverage will also grow as these new areas are included.

One thing we will not do is to compromise quality by adding "filler" items or by falsely expanding the coverage of ISA into subject areas unrelated to information science. We are acutely aware that database quality is of paramount importance to the users of databases, and currency, albeit significant, is only one consideration that searchers make when deciding which database to use to meet their information needs. We are conscious of the heritage of ISA and the position that it has enjoyed as a premier database among information scientists. We therefore especially invite readers of this Editorial who have comments or suggestions on any of the issues pertaining to ISA to contact us. Such comments and suggestions are most welcome. User feedback is by far the most valuable form of input to database Editors.

Donald T. Hawkins, Editor-in-Chief

Lynn A. Murray, Editor

Fig. 5.63b. The commitment to approximately 6-week update intervals.

When starting a multiple database search, the short file identifier labels allude to the problem of outdatedness of the ISA database (figure 5.63c). The optimist may hope that DIALOG merely forgot to update the label (that should be automatic, by the way). Unfortunately, the file label update date correctly alerted the user of the problem as can be seen in the ZD index that reflects the actual dates when an update was added to a database (figure 5.63d) in three LIS databases.

```
                  Dialog Response

ABI/INFORM(R) 1971-2000/May 25
(c) 2000 Bell & Howell
Social SciSearch(R) 1972-2000/May W3
(c) 2000 Inst for Sci Info
Gale Group Trade & Industry DB 1976-2000/May 25
(c)2000 The Gale Group
LISA(LIBRARY&INFOSCI) 1969-2000/Apr
(c) 2000 Reed Reference Publishing
Library Literature 1984-2000/Apr
(c) 2000 The HW Wilson Co
Internet & Personal Comp. Abs. 1981-2000/May
(c) 2000 Info. Today Inc.
Information Science Abs. 1966-2000/Jan
(c)  Information Today, Inc
```

Fig. 5.63c. Update labels indicate the currency problem.

```
               Dialog Response

     File    Items    Total   Index-term
      61               1708   ZD=19991207
     438               1681   ZD=19991218
    ------                 0  *ZD=2000
      61               1152   ZD=20000106
     438               1338   ZD=20000119
     202               1374   ZD=20000201
      61               1018   ZD=20000204
     438               2434   ZD=20000301
      61               1116   ZD=20000307
      61               1520   ZD=20000407
     438               2531   ZD=20000425
     438               3312   ZD=20000426
     438               2350   ZD=20000510
      61               1018   ZD=20000516
```

Fig. 5.63d. The reality of update intervals in the first half of 2000.

In the light of the traditional policy of DIALOG regarding the printing and distributing of bluesheets, it is particularly interesting that when the Subject Coverage section of the bluesheet was significantly changed after two articles demonstrated the disharmony between the professed subject coverage and the plummeting coverage of important journals of the subject fields, it was not enough reason for printing and distributing a new bluesheet with the *Chronolog Newsletter*.

What is a significant change? Seven of the 22 subjects formerly listed were unceremoniously removed while new ones were added (figure 5.64). That's a significant change. Which subjects were removed? Computer science, decision support, educational technology, information systems design, medical informatics, optical and laser technology, standards, supercomputers, and telecommunications were removed. Many of them were exactly the subjects that the two articles two months before (Jacsó 2000b and Jacsó 2000d) used as examples to demonstrate how dramatically the coverage of primary sources for the subjects touted by the bluesheet — computer science, supercomputers, decision support and medical informatics — declined or bottomed out since the takeover of the ISA database.

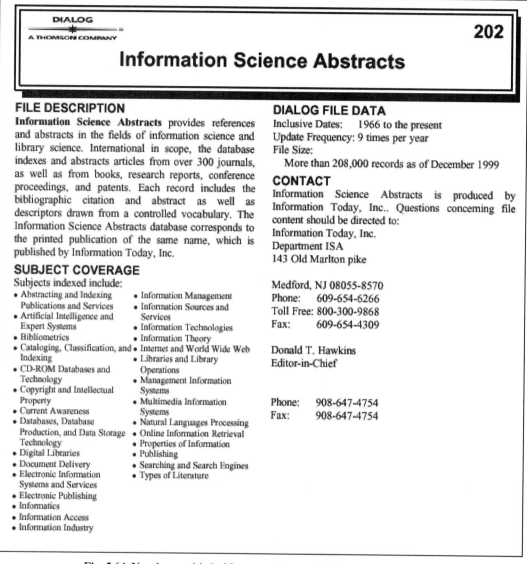

Fig. 5.64. Nearly one-third of former subjects of ISA were eliminated
from the February 2001 version of the ISA bluesheet.

Doing away with almost 30 percent of the subjects prominently listed in four consecutive issues of the bluesheet is not something that should be taken lightly. If appropriately advised, users — especially information scientists and researchers in general and those interested in the topics (and their sources) in particular, eliminated or drastically reduced — may decide to take their business to other databases, such as the impeccable INSPEC database that has far better (if not perfect) coverage of the most respected sources of information science and information systems, and that is much more current than ISA, has a very good thesaurus, and has a price tag almost identical to that of ISA.

It may motivate them more to do so when the editor-in-chief declares that many of the information science journals that used to have substantial (if not consistent) coverage in the previous decades are considered to be on the fringe of information science, or contain only occasionally relevant articles for information scientists, and therefore would be covered minimally. If such a decision is made it should not be announced in *Information World Review*, a UK-based journal that does not widely circulate in the U.S., especially since the predominant user base of ISA is in the U.S. DIALOG itself has been exceptionally accommodating for requests and announcements by ISA stewardship in other matters recently, so it would only be fitting for this kind of major change in topical coverage to be prominently featured in DIALOG publications and publicity announcements. Not even the house organ of ISA made any announcement about the elimination of topics from ISA.

There is a greater issue about the real and advertised subject scope of the ISA database which emerged first in a debate on the pages of *Online Information Review,* originally about the diminutive growth rate and the lack of currency of the ISA database in comparison with LISA and Library Literature. The editor-in-chief of ISA wrote that "ISA covers information science, which is the smallest discipline (in terms of the size of the literature) of those compared by Jacsó, so it is not surprising that its database, ISA, has added the fewest records. Simply comparing the total number of records added to several disparate [sic!] databases in an 'apples and oranges' fashion, as Jacsó did, does not take into account the variations in the size of the literature of each subject. Jacsó states that ISA is a 'library and information science' database, but it is important to recognize that ISA is an information science database" (Hawkins and Murray 2000d). To see these three databases characterized as disparate could easily be interpreted by seasoned practitioners and LIS database connoisseurs as a desperate move to deny the library science coverage of ISA, in order to explain the shrinking of the yearly volume of records added to ISA since the takeover (figure 5.65).

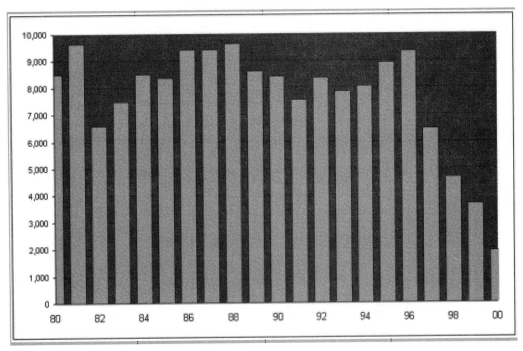

Fig. 5.65. Declining growth rate in ISA since the takeover.

Describing the comparison with LISA and LibLit as an "apples and oranges" comparison is a classic spin doctoring maneuver to dismiss the work of your opponent, but it may not sit well with many of the information scientists who have been comparing LISA and ISA for decades, and LibLit for more than a decade as databases with library and information science coverage. Users may find this denial of library science coverage odd — as not only do the two commercial hosts, DIALOG and SilverPlatter, but also all the college libraries that subscribe to ISA mention that it is a library and information science database — sometimes using different word order or phraseology (such as librarianship), but never omitting library science or its synonyms (figure 5.66).

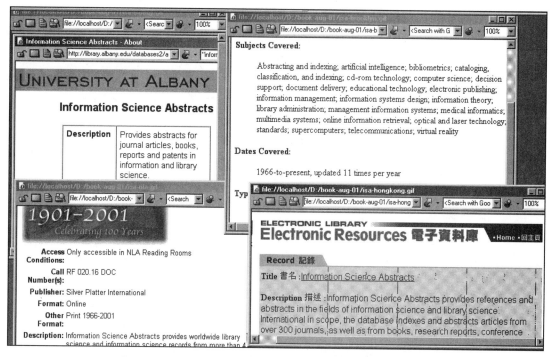

Fig. 5.66. Collage of ISA database descriptions at college sites.

The home page of ISA itself (figure 5.67) also acknowledges that "ISA has provided worldwide library science and information science records from more than 450 publications dating back to 1966." Although the JASIS article (Hawkins 2001a) in another effort to strengthen its information science focus, denies that it covers such library science topics as archives, library organization, library use and users, microforms, museums, and non-print materials, this is obviously not true as shown by sample search results (figure 5.68). I did not bother with such topics as old and rare materials, removals, furniture, types of library staff, or other vehicles that the article generously relegated to LISA's exclusive domain (omitting, however, dust protection, mildew prevention, and bug extermination).

Fig. 5.67. Reference to the coverage on ISA's home page.

Searched terms	All years						1997-2001					
	LISA basic index	ISA basic index	LISA TI	ISA TI	LISA DE	ISA DE	LISA All	ISA All	LISA TI	ISA TI	LISA DE	ISA DE
archives	7,526	3,263	2,278	683	5,198	1,690	1,794	527	473	75	1,230	278
library organi?ation	317	222	64	29	3	38	49	23	6	1	1	0
library (use or users)	3,212	1,447	515	244	41	130	648	227	74	27	10	0
library and loan?	4,590	1,924	2,468	1,035	2,152	1,487	522	220	271	85	252	177
museums	1,298	1,964	203	97	559	439	408	234	59	17	192	81
(nonprint or non()print) materials	151	207	33	31	32	57	24	4	3	1	11	0

Fig. 5.68. Coverage of library topics in ISA that are denied by the JASIS article.

ISA covers the library science topics listed by the article, much more than certain information science topics that it has been listing prominently on the bluesheet for many years, such as multimedia information systems. The search phrase brings up two records from the entire database (figure 5.69). The exclusion of library science from ISA coverage is not in harmony with the subjects listed on even the most recently updated bluesheet that saw the removal of seven subjects, but not document delivery, or library administration, and included among the newly added subjects the topic of libraries and library operations.

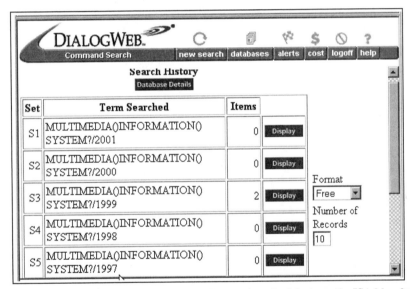

Fig. 5.69. Coverage of one of the prominently mentioned subjects on the ISA bluesheet.

This apparent change of heart about the scope of ISA being exclusively information science could harm its business as librarians may feel abandoned (if they accept the claim that ISA covers information science but not library science), and may cancel their subscription of ISA in favor of LISA or Library Literature & Information Science Full Text. It may also disappoint business partners, such as the ISA product manager at SilverPlatter who expressed strong belief in a letter to the editor that "SilverPlatter's offering is an excellent resource for library science research" (Hern 2001). If indeed, ISA were a strictly information science database, and not a library and information science database, then it may not be such an excellent resource for library science research, and after SilverPlatter's intensive cooperation with the editors of ISA as mentioned by Hern, it may not have been the most lucrative investment.

A few reality checks, however, may alleviate these concerns. If you look at the coverage of traditional library science journals by ISA in the past three to five years you will see that ISA did not abandon or drive into the ground such primarily library science oriented journals that are listed in figure 5.70. Actually, almost all of them are among the most consistently covered journals in ISA, much more so than many of the high quality information science journals.

ACQUISITIONS LIBRARIAN
AGAINST THE GRAIN
AMERICAN LIBRARIES
ART LIBRARIES JOURNAL
BEHAVIORAL AND SOCIAL SCIENCES LIBRARIAN
CATALOGING & CLASSIFICATION QUARTERLY
COLORADO LIBRARIES
IFLA JOURNAL
JOURNAL OF LIBRARY ADMINISTRATION
KONYVTARI FIGYELO (LIBRARY REVIEW)
LIBRARIAN'S WORLD
LIBRARIES & CULTURE
LIBRARY & ARCHIVAL SECURITY
LIBRARY ACQUISITIONS: PRACTICE AND THEORY
LIBRARY ADMINISTRATION & MANAGEMENT
LIBRARY COLLECTIONS, ACQUISITIONS, & TECHNICAL
LIBRARY JOURNAL
LIBRARY MANAGEMENT
LIBRARY PHILOSOPHY AND PRACTICE
LIBRARY RESOURCES & TECHNICAL SERVICES
LIBRARY REVIEW
LIBRARY TRENDS
LIBRI
NEW LIBRARY WORLD
PUBLIC LIBRARY QUARTERLY
RECORDS MANAGEMENT JOURNAL
SERIALS LIBRARIAN
SERIALS REVIEW
TECHNICAL SERVICES QUARTERLY
TUDOMANYOS ES MUSZAKI TAJEKOZTATAS
VJESNIK BIBLIOTEKARA HRVATSKE

**Fig. 5.70. Predominantly library science oriented journals
remain being abstracted and indexed.**

It must also be a sign of commitment to library science by ISA that certain journals in foreign languages that are not widely spoken by the primary target audience of ISA were picked up or picked up again after the takeover of ISA in 1998. The last two items on the list are especially to be noted from the geographic and language aspects of source coverage. These will not enable ISA to compete in the world librarianship topic that was designated in the JASIS article as the exclusive domain of LISA. Those ISA subscribers who are not fluent in Hungarian and Croatian may wonder if the relevance of these two journals is indeed higher than that of the aforementioned journals.

Although the journals are in Hungarian and Croatian, respectively, at least the Hungarian journal has informative English language summaries that can be used without much extra effort, and are available almost immediately after the publishing of the original issue, providing instant secondary service to the user community (assuming that a regular updating pattern will be achieved by ISA). No wonder that it seems to enjoy a de facto core journal coverage status in ISA from 1999 onward, after a 10-year gap under the previous stewardship of ISA. [I feel compelled to disclose that I am on the advisory board of that Hungarian journal but had nothing to do with its revitalization for ISA after its acquisition in 1998.]

Along with another Hungarian language journal, *Hungarian Library Review*, it can be safely assumed that most of the interest by the predominant user base of ISA for developments in librarianship and to some extent information science and technology in that country can be satisfied. Although coverage of Russian, Polish, and Czech language library science journals has not been revitalized, the recent embracing of the Croatian language library science journal may console the user community of ISA that certainly mourned the loss of coverage of *Informatologia Yugoslavica* (and its successor title). They may now cherish the coverage given to the Croatian Library News that after an inconsistent start in 1997 also got core journal treatment coverage in 2000.

The disharmony between the ostensible subject coverage and the source base in this database of potentially central interest to library and information science professionals definitely grew in the past few years. It started with the sharp decline in the coverage of many English language information science journals in the subject fields listed prominently by the ISA bluesheet. Many of the information science journals that were practically abandoned are top-ranked by information scientists by virtue of citing (and presumably) reading them.

The latest statements by the editor-in-chief of the database add a further discomfiting tone to the disharmony from two aspects. One is the lack of realization that the emperor is wearing fewer and fewer clothes, and that the continuation of this trend may leave it with merely a fig leaf because in many of the subject areas its major competitor, the LISA database, has forged ahead of ISA in the past five years. The other aspect is the odd disengagement by ISA from the library science field.

It was not yet denied thrice, but the two denials, especially the very strong second one in JASIS, may result in librarians abnegating the use of this database for the wrong reason. It does cover library science, and it does cover many of the subject areas relegated to LISA in the JASIS article (although not at equal depth). ISA has better choices of journals for library science, and more consistent and better coverage of those journals than for many of the information science topics. Oddly, the domain that showed harmony between official claims of subject scope and the source base of the respective fields can turn cacophonous by singing some false tunes in an almost self-destructive way.

After the acquisition of the ISA database, the first editorial contemplated the reload of the database by the end of the year. This was in June 1998. Three years later, the reload still did not happen, many of the deficiencies remained, and new ones were introduced. It is hoped that it will happen, and then an update will be posted at *http://www2.hawaii.edu/~jacso/isa-faqs* to appraise the long-heralded and long-awaited changes.

There are indications that, when the database will be reloaded, its size will decrease significantly. I thought that it would grow by adding records to fill the significant gaps in many of the core information science journals that would still offset the decrease caused — hopefully — by the elimination of thousands of duplicate records, and the vast majority of the irrelevant patent records. Hopefully, the records for information science journals that were designated as core journals until 1998 will not be trimmed down in the process to make the increasingly more shallow coverage of them less apparent.

It is also hoped that the newly introduced gaps in the indexing and abstracting of journals that undoubtedly deserve full coverage will also be filled. These are less obvious than the dramatic changes in other journals, but the gaps are definitely there. Take, as an example, the *Journal of the American Society for Information Science* that has been ranked No. 1 or No. 2 for decades in the library and information science category of JCR. A futile search, yielding zero results in ISA for articles about the Conference on Fair Use (known as CONFU) in 1999, led to the discovery that the entire issue was missed by ISA along with many other articles in various issues in the past few years.

Luckily, all the articles are indexed and abstracted by LISA (figure 5.71) that many information specialists use for its lower cost, more predictable (but not perfect) coverage, good thesaurus (in the Cambridge Scientific Abstracts implementation), and better currency.

Not even LISA can always help with deficiencies of the indexing and abstracting coverage in ISA, as is the case with the other top-ranking periodical, the *Annual Review of Information Science & Technology (ARIST)*, because, inexplicably, LISA does not cover it at all. The problem is that ISA does not cover it right, either. It is immediately alarming when the search for this outstanding publication brings up merely 94 records (figure 5.72). Anyone slightly familiar with *ARIST* would know that it has between 8 and 10 articles (actually they are chapters) in each volume. It is in its 34th volume, so the number of records should be close to 300. It is ironic that *ARIST* has been a very valuable asset of Information Today, Inc. for a number of years. Still, its substandard coverage in another Information Today, Inc. product goes unnoticed by the database editors. If any source should have complete coverage in this database, it is *ARIST*.

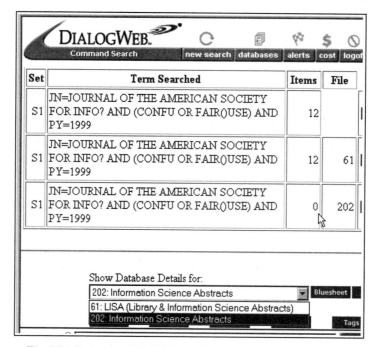

Fig. 5.71. Entire 1999 JASIS issue missing in ISA, found in LISA.

Fig. 5.72. Substandard coverage of the top-ranked
Annual Review of Information Science and Technology (ARIST) **in ISA.**

In light of the serious disharmony between the scope and source coverage of ISA, the accomplishments in the highly upbeat and satisfied January 1999 editorial seem to be a bit prematurely listed (figure 5.73).

The addition of the many new journals announced in 1998 was apparently a harried move, and none of them survived by 2001. The relevance of the records added for some of those journals is highly questionable from an information science perspective, especially if we put the emphasis on science. The reference to completion of efforts to fill gaps is not unlike Dewey claiming victory over Truman.

The institution of tighter serial control to ensure that coverage gaps will not occur in the future obviously does not work even for such a prominent journal as JASIS where selectivity cannot be an excuse. The hope to roll out a completely new controlled vocabulary and subject structure in 1999 remained a hope in 1999, then in 2000, and in the first part of 2001. It can be done, as we saw that Bowker-Saur could do that in 1992 within a year. Maybe it takes a village and then some to do it.

Although these predicted improvements did not happen, the total number of records added each year to the database since 1998 was reduced to half of the previous volume. The editor-in-chief addressed this concern in the April 1999 editorial about currency (figure 5.74) saying that "in the past, additions to ISA were governed more by a numerical "abstract quota" than subject relevance; the result was that many irrelevant records found their way into ISA. Such irrelevant items are no longer being included in ISA, so its quality has improved. However, this improvement has had undesired side effects. Because fewer records are being added, the monthly issues of ISA are not only smaller than they were previously, but it is also taking longer to accumulate enough material for each issue." He then goes on to acknowledge delay in publishing issues.

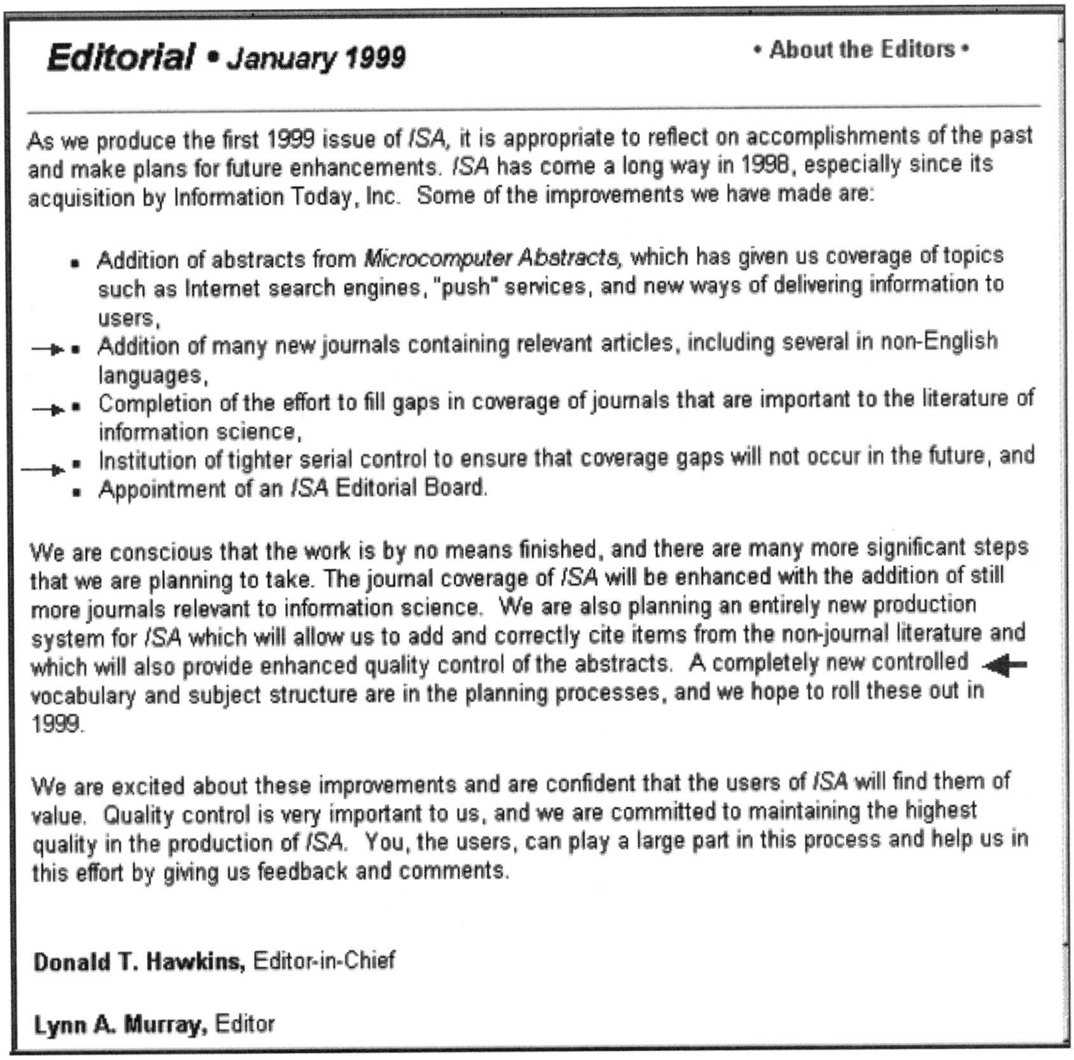

Editorial • January 1999   • About the Editors •

As we produce the first 1999 issue of *ISA*, it is appropriate to reflect on accomplishments of the past and make plans for future enhancements. *ISA* has come a long way in 1998, especially since its acquisition by Information Today, Inc. Some of the improvements we have made are:

- Addition of abstracts from *Microcomputer Abstracts*, which has given us coverage of topics such as Internet search engines, "push" services, and new ways of delivering information to users,
- Addition of many new journals containing relevant articles, including several in non-English languages,
- Completion of the effort to fill gaps in coverage of journals that are important to the literature of information science,
- Institution of tighter serial control to ensure that coverage gaps will not occur in the future, and
- Appointment of an *ISA* Editorial Board.

We are conscious that the work is by no means finished, and there are many more significant steps that we are planning to take. The journal coverage of *ISA* will be enhanced with the addition of still more journals relevant to information science. We are also planning an entirely new production system for *ISA* which will allow us to add and correctly cite items from the non-journal literature and which will also provide enhanced quality control of the abstracts. A completely new controlled vocabulary and subject structure are in the planning processes, and we hope to roll these out in 1999.

We are excited about these improvements and are confident that the users of *ISA* will find them of value. Quality control is very important to us, and we are committed to maintaining the highest quality in the production of *ISA*. You, the users, can play a large part in this process and help us in this effort by giving us feedback and comments.

Donald T. Hawkins, Editor-in-Chief

Lynn A. Murray, Editor

Fig. 5.73. The highly optimistic January 1999 editorial of ISA.

This point is further elaborated (Hawkins and Murray 2000d) in response to a criticism: "Jacsó's suggestion that ISA has a quota is not correct. It is true that the former owners were under a contractual obligation to add at least 800 records per month to the database. These owners found it difficult to sustain that rate of abstract production (as we would) because of the limited scope of the field of information science, and their practice was to add "filler" records to each update to make up the shortfall. It is important to note that most of those "filler" records were not relevant to the subject of information science, so the quality of the database was poor."

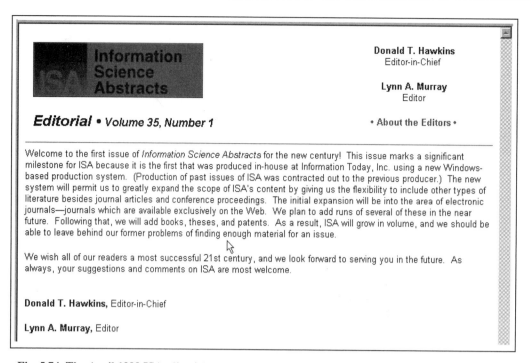

Fig. 5.74. The April 1999 ISA editorial about the reason for the decline in the number of abstracts.

There are two very confusing points in this single paragraph. One is the reference to the owners. Documentation Abstracts, Inc. (DAI) was the owner of the database, assisted by representatives of seven library and information science associations. These people were not under any obligation to sustain the rate of abstract production simply because they were not supposed to produce any abstracts. The file producer, Plenum, did that, and DAI paid for it, and the buck stopped at the senior technical editor, who among others, had to oversee publication. Therefore, the reference to "their practice" is odd finger pointing. The reference to the poor quality of the database is correct.

Not finding enough relevant source documents about the topics identified as the subjects of the ISA database is difficult to understand. There has been a surge in the past few years in publishing about those issues. Just the relevant articles that were not covered by ISA from the journals it scanned could easily add several hundred items. In addition, there are other journals and conference proceedings not covered by ISA (such as the Digital Libraries conferences of ACM, and IEEE, respectively, that would more than alleviate the editor-in-chief's concern about the lack of relevant materials for the database). If the editors would focus their attention on the important issues for the survival of this database, and fill the past and current gaps in cleaning up the database, it would reduce the disharmony between database scope and source coverage.

On the other hand, spending energy on too much spinning of the database will spin it out from the playing field where INSPEC has already the best coverage for information science; LISA for library science; Library Literature for full-text library and information science; and Internet & Personal Computing Abstracts for information technology. The writing is on the wall, and the major cause of death will be the disharmony between the claimed scope and actual source coverage of the ISA database, and its long-time denial.

Record Content

Databases differ significantly in the amount of information they provide about source documents, persons, or objects described. They also differ very much with regard to the structuring of the information presented. All these will have an impact on the way the content can be indexed, searched, and presented on the screen or in print. Most important, it will make much of a difference in the end result: what the user will get.

BIBLIOGRAPHIC DATA ELEMENTS

The scope of data elements that should be included in a record is very much database-specific. Beyond the essential bibliographic items (author, title, journal name, chronological and numerical designation, and pagination), it is the set of additional data elements that distinguishes databases the most. These data elements are referred to as value added information and include elements that enhance the previously mentioned citation information, such as the following:

- Title enhancements that clarify the title

- Total number of pages, lines, or words

- Indication of graphics, photos, and illustrations

Comparing these citation elements for the same article in three databases illustrates the differences. The page count in ProQuest (figure 6.1a) and the line and word count in Magazine Database are good for orientation. In ProQuest, however, the various identifiers are distractive and should not be shown in a citation record. Readers' Guide Abstracts (RGA) (figure 6.1b) has the cleanest source citation, but in other regards this format does not show RGA's biggest asset—the very informative abstracts (to be discussed later). Gale Group's Magazine Database has the best title information, with a long subtitle and informative title enhancement (figure 6.1c).

New Search
by word
for publication
BELL&HOWELL ProQuest
RESULTS LIST | MARKED LIST | PREFERENCES

Article 51 of 100
NEXT ARTICLE
TO KEYWORD
EMAIL ARTICLE
PRINT ARTICLE
Mark article
Cite/Abstract
Full Text
Text+Graphics
Page Image
Publisher Info.

BUILD PAGE | MAKE LINK | PREVIEW LINK | MODIFY LINK
HELP ?

Burial at sea
Maclean's; Toronto; Aug 2, 1999; Andrew Phillips; Susan Oh;

Volume:	112
Issue:	31
UMI Publication No.:	04403445
Start Page:	26-29
Page Count:	4
Text Word Count:	2258
Document Type:	Feature
Source Type:	PERIODICAL
ISSN:	00249262
Subject Terms:	Death & dying
	Celebrities
	Aircraft accidents & safety
	Memorial services
Personal Names:	Kennedy, John F Jr
	Bessette, Carolyn
	Bessette, Lauren
Companies:	Navy-US
UMI Article Re. No.:	GMAC-2178-12
UMI Journal Code:	GMAC

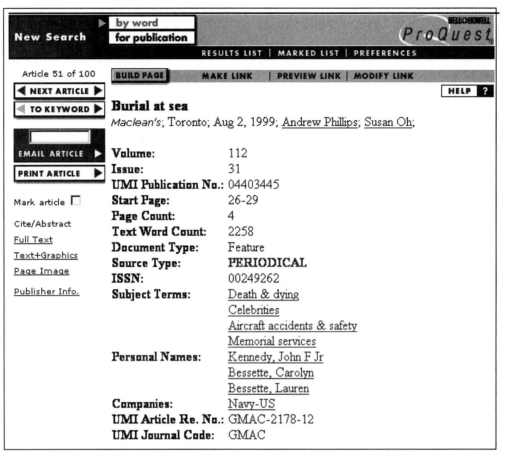

Fig. 6.1a. Comparison of bibliographic citations for the same article (ProQuest).

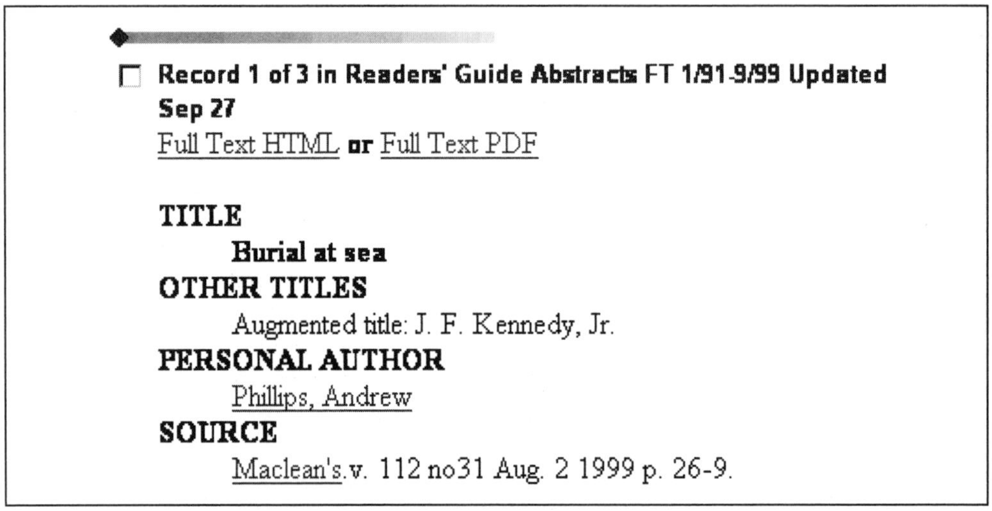

Record 1 of 3 in Readers' Guide Abstracts FT 1/91-9/99 Updated Sep 27
Full Text HTML **or** Full Text PDF

TITLE
Burial at sea
OTHER TITLES
Augmented title: J. F. Kennedy, Jr.
PERSONAL AUTHOR
Phillips, Andrew
SOURCE
Maclean's v. 112 no31 Aug. 2 1999 p. 26-9.

Fig. 6.1b. Comparison of bibliographic citations for the same article (RGA).

```
05406400    Supplier Number: 55272717 (USE FORMAT 7 OR 9 FOR FULL TEXT )
Burial At Sea: A massive search locates the bodies of John F. Kennedy Jr., his wife and his
sister-in-law.(ceremony from USS Briscoe at recovery site)

PHILLIPS, ANDREW; OH, SUSAN
Maclean's , 26
August 2 , 1999
Document Type: Biography
ISSN: 0024-9262
Language: English    Record Type: Fulltext
Word Count: 2289   Line Count: 00175
Geographic Codes: 1U1MA Massachusetts
Biographee: Kennedy, John F., Jr.--Rites and ceremonies; Kennedy, Carolyn Bessette-- Rites and ceremonies;
Bessette, Lauren G.--Rites and ceremonies
File Segment: MI File 47
              Gale Group Magazine DB(TM) (Dialog® File 47): (c) 1999 The Gale group. All rights reserved.
```

Fig. 6.1c. Comparison of bibliographic citations for the same article (Gale Group Magazine Database).

In company directories, the essential elements include the name, address, telephone and fax numbers, and e-mail address (these days also the URL) of the companies. In a serials directory, the minimum bibliographic requirements include the title, former title, successor title, ISSN, country of publication, publisher, and start year (also end year if applicable) of the journal (and again the URL of the publisher or the journal itself). Although it is a software issue, it is worth mentioning that DIALOG is doing a disservice by not offering a hotlink from the displayed records to ones with the same author, subject heading, or journal name, which is common practice in most online information services. The lack of this feature also means that URLs included in records are cold (i.e., passive) in DIALOG. In the Ovid version of Ulrich's, the same serials record has a hot URL, and clicking on it will take you to the Web site of the publisher or the journal (figure 6.2).

```
Title
       E Media Professional
Alternate Title
       Variant title: EMedia Professional. Former
       titles (until 1997): C D - R O M Professional. ISSN
       1049-0833. Incorporates (in 1994): C D - R O M News Extra. ISSN 1075-1106.
       (until May 1990): Laserdisk Professional. ISSN 0896-4149
Publisher
       Online, Inc.
Status Code
       Active
Country Code
       United States (US)
ISSN
       1090-946X
Dewey Decimal Number
       025.04
Circulation
       17,000 (paid)
Editor
       Stephen Nathans
LC Call Number
       TA1635
E-mail Address
       E-mail: emedia@onlineinc.com; URL:
       http://www.emediapro.net
```

Fig. 6.2. Ovid's version of Ulrich's provides hotlink to publisher and journal Web sites.

In a biographical directory, the bare essentials include name, gender, birth and death date, avocation or profession, and claim to fame. Figure 6.3 shows the variety of categories available in the Gale Group Biography Resource Center. What Gale calls a thumbnail biography is often far more than that—close to a biographical essay. H. W. Wilson's Biographies Plus Illustrated database shows an excerpt from the well-structured biography of JFK Jr. (figure 6.4). These two biographical sources are in sharp contrast—even just looking at the basic biographical information—with the painfully unstructured biographical entries in the Merriam-Webster Biographical Dictionary (figure 6.5). They reflect the crowded structure of the print edition and do not offer any distinct access point beyond the last name of the subject. It is the textbook example for how not to make a digital version out of a print reference source.

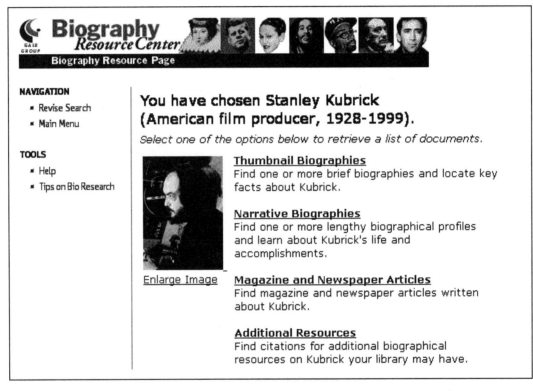

Fig. 6.3. Excerpt of an entry from the Biography Resource Center of the Gale Group.

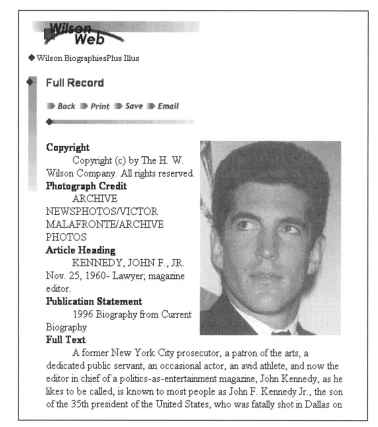

Fig. 6.4. Excerpt of an entry from the Biographies Plus Illustrated database of H. W. Wilson.

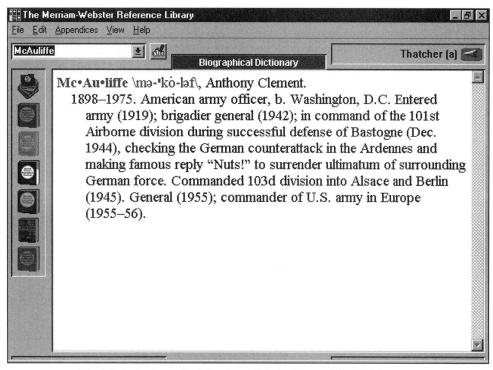

Fig. 6.5. Entry from the Merriam-Webster Biographical Dictionary.

VALUE ADDED DATA ELEMENTS

Seemingly minor elements can make searching much more efficient and can make the selection of the most relevant articles from the results set easier. Some of them are really easy to provide (such as language and document type), and others may require more work (such as author affiliation, especially in a consistent format). It is surprising why simple elements are not used to enhance records. For example, it is difficult to understand why Ulrich's International Periodicals Directory does not have a language field; why LISA does not have a document type field (except for current research reports) to distinguish conference papers from journal articles and from reviews; why LISA does not have a country of publication field; and why the Merriam-Webster Biographical Dictionary does not include gender, an often-required search criterion. The inclusion in the record and indexing of such data elements is an utterly simple way to add value to records and to make searching far more powerful.

The need for additional data elements depends on the particular database. One would not expect a language field for the ABI/INFORM database (but it still has them), as 99.99 percent of the records are for English-language documents.

Classifying articles by length in UMI's Magazine Express database (short, medium, and long) is an excellent tool to limit the search to only substantial articles to avoid a deluge of short articles about a hot event, such as the impeachment trial of the president. Magazine Express also gets credit for indicating in some of its databases the type of journal (academic, general interest, etc.) to limit a search and orient the user in scanning the output.

EBSCO offers a somewhat similar option, allowing the search to be limited to peer-reviewed journals using this additional data element. (The reliability of that information about the peer-reviewed status of journals is another question.) As discussed in Chapter 7 on accuracy, this information is often inaccurate in the Serials Directory of EBSCO (and also in the Ulrich's database). Obviously, this undermines the use of that data element as a filter. H. W. Wilson, in its own WilsonWeb implementation of its databases, also provides such value added information as the refereed status of journals and—as usual—it is accurate in the library and information science field where I could judge it. This kind of value added data element is unique, as it is not assigned to each and every record, but to the journal.

Value added information may be helpful in the browsing, searching, and the output phase(s). Although it is unlikely that anyone would want to browse the ISSN index of journals in an abstracting and indexing database fishing for a promising ISSN, displaying the ISSN of a journal is particularly useful when the user may need an interlibrary loan request. Bell & Howell's use of journal codes that stay with the journal even if its title changes can simplify the search.

Instead of specifying all the former and current titles of a journal in a search, such as FIND JN=(Laserdisk Professional OR CD-ROM Professional OR E Media Professional) in DIALOG, a single search in ProQuest using the journal code JC (LDP) will retrieve records from any of the three versions of this journal (figure 6.6). It is another question that the new title of a journal should never replace the former title in the records retroactively as it happens in ProQuest with some journals such as *Database,* which changed its title to *EContent* in 1999. It is improper to display records from, say, the 1996 issues of that journal with the *EContent* name.

In the case of book reviews, the additional bibliographic elements may include the ISBN of the reviewed book and also a review grade assigned by the indexer after analyzing the reviewer's comments. The latter is also applicable to reviews about movies, theatrical performances, and exhibits (figure 6.7).

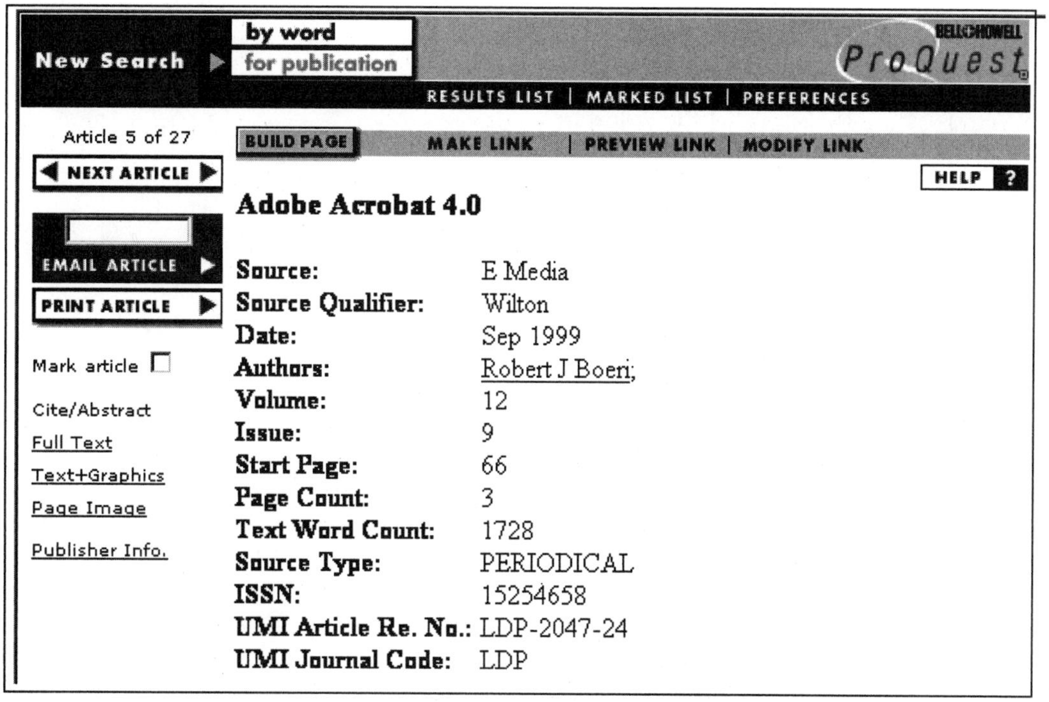

```
                by word
New Search  ▶  for publication                      ProQuest
                        RESULTS LIST | MARKED LIST | PREFERENCES
```

Article 5 of 27   BUILD PAGE   MAKE LINK | PREVIEW LINK | MODIFY LINK

◀ NEXT ARTICLE ▶   HELP ?

Adobe Acrobat 4.0

EMAIL ARTICLE ▶
PRINT ARTICLE ▶

Mark article ☐

Cite/Abstract

Full Text

Text+Graphics

Page Image

Publisher Info.

Source:	E Media
Source Qualifier:	Wilton
Date:	Sep 1999
Authors:	Robert J Boeri;
Volume:	12
Issue:	9
Start Page:	66
Page Count:	3
Text Word Count:	1728
Source Type:	PERIODICAL
ISSN:	15254658
UMI Article Re. No.:	LDP-2047-24
UMI Journal Code:	LDP

Fig. 6.6. Using the permanent journal code to find the former and current titles.

```
Adding title to results...
REVIEW SUMMARIES FOR BRIDGET'S DIARY
--------------------------------------
RANK: S4/1-30   Field: DT=  File(s): 484
(Rank fields found in 30 records -- 4 unique terms)


RANK No.  Items  Term
--------  -----  ----
       1     29  PERIODICALS
       2     19  BOOK REVIEW-FAVORABLE
       3      9  BOOK REVIEW-COMPARATIVE
       4      2  BOOK REVIEW-MIXED
              ---end of results---
```

Fig. 6.7. Review grades in the Periodical Abstracts database.

The identification of document types is quite customary and is a good tool for filtering out document types not relevant for the user, such as reports or book reviews. It is much less common when articles are qualified to distinguish between theoretical and practical papers, as is done in the INSPEC database using a treatment field (figure 6.8). ERIC uses similar value added information to distinguish the target audience for the documents processed. It is both searchable and browsable in the Ovid version of the database (figure 6.9). In neither of these two databases is this value added information available for all records.

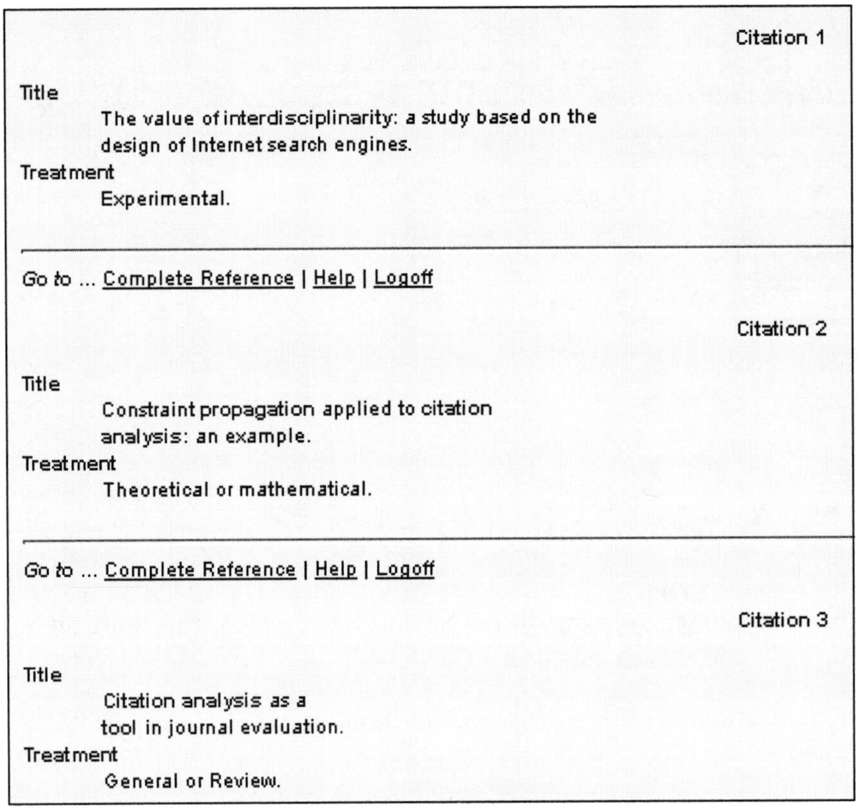

Citation 1

Title
    The value of interdisciplinarity: a study based on the
    design of Internet search engines.
Treatment
    Experimental.

Go to ... Complete Reference | Help | Logoff

Citation 2

Title
    Constraint propagation applied to citation
    analysis: an example.
Treatment
    Theoretical or mathematical.

Go to ... Complete Reference | Help | Logoff

Citation 3

Title
    Citation analysis as a
    tool in journal evaluation.
Treatment
    General or Review.

Fig. 6.8. INSPEC's article treatment code.

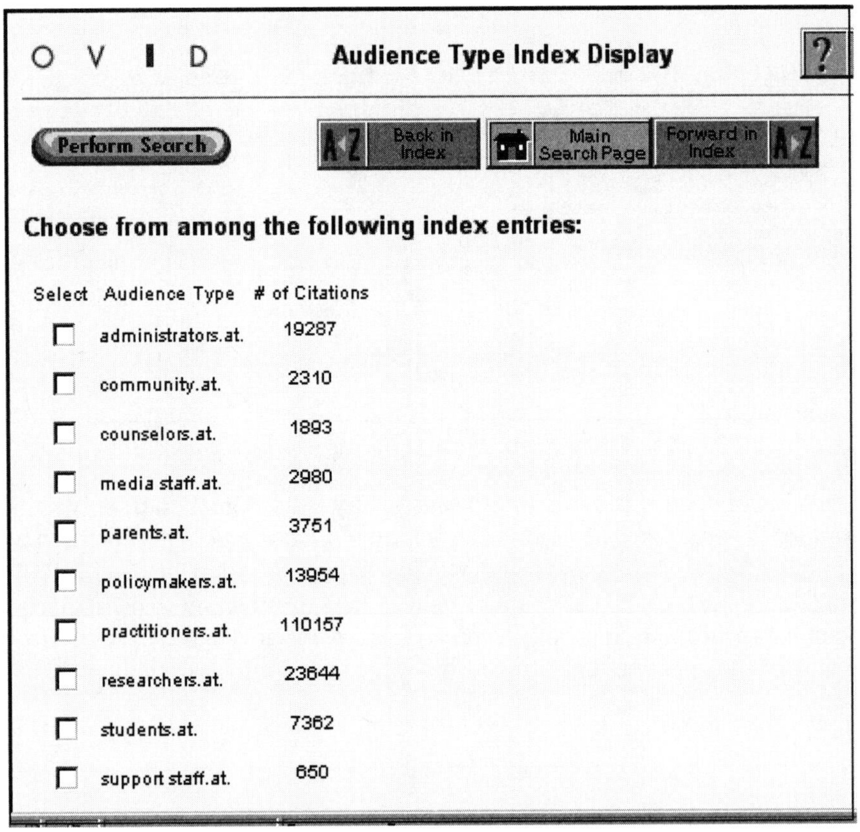

O V I D   **Audience Type Index Display**   ?

(Perform Search)   A-Z Back in Index   Main Search Page   Forward in Index A-Z

Choose from among the following index entries:

Select	Audience Type	# of Citations
☐	administrators.at.	19287
☐	community.at.	2310
☐	counselors.at.	1893
☐	media staff.at.	2980
☐	parents.at.	3751
☐	policymakers.at.	13954
☐	practitioners.at.	110157
☐	researchers.at.	23644
☐	students.at.	7362
☐	support staff.at.	650

Fig. 6.9. ERIC's target audience index in Ovid.

The next level in value added information is represented by the classification and subject terms assigned to source documents. There is great variation also in this regard among databases, as discussed in detail in Chapter 10 on the quality of subject indexing.

Abstracts or summaries of original documents remain of added value, even when the full text of the document is also available. The structuring, readability, and informativeness of abstracts can be an important distinguishing function in most databases of general interest periodicals. In that genre, the primary sources covered by such databases do not have author abstracts. This is different from the majority of scholarly and academic journals covered by scientific, technical, and medical databases. The producers of these files usually include the original abstracts and occasionally modify them rather than create their own.

Evaluation of abstracts is discussed in detail in Chapter 11 on the quality of abstracts. Suffice it to say here that abstracts are the information elements that require the most intellectual work, unless they are lifted from the journal. Note, too, that the length of the abstract is not necessarily an indicator of a more informative record, but obviously longer abstracts are likely to have more information. Additionally, the presence of fields of value added information is not sufficient in itself. The added value must be applied consistently and accurately to fill its role. This is discussed in Chapter 7 on accuracy, Chaper 8 on consistency, and Chapter 9 on completeness.

The availability of the full text of primary documents in the records is obviously a great asset. There are different ways, however, how the full text is made available. Plain ASCII format just includes the text without preserving the original typography. Even at that level, however, there are differences in the legibility of the text and in the quality of the OCR (optical character recognition) process. Figures 6.10 and 6.11 show the same excerpt from the same full-text document.

```
The variety of databases, modestly listed under the subcategory "Forbes
Lists" which doesn't reflect the fact that most are searchable files with
dynamic output capabilities, cover a really impressive spectrum-200 Best Small
Companies, Forbes  Platinum 400, Forbes  Annual Report on American Industry,
Top 800 CEOs (by compensation), the International 800, the 400 Richest People
in America, The World Richest People, the Forbes  Celebrity 100, the Top 40
Entertainers, and Athletes, among others. Not all have the three-year
retrospective coverage and the dynamic search and output generation
capabilities of the 500 lists, but most do, with appropriate criteria. The
International 800 database, for example, offers sorting by country, and two
years of retrospective data.
(Illustration Omitted)
Captioned as: The usercustomizable Forbes  500 list on the Forbes  Digital
Toolbox site
```

Fig. 6.10. Excerpt from an ABI/INFORM record in DIALOG.

Full text may be enhanced by including captions of the figures, charts, tables, and photographs that are not reproduced in the full-text version of the article. ABI/INFORM provides a caption and indicates that a figure was omitted where it fits in the text. The Wilson Business Abstracts and Full Text database does not specifically mention the omission and provides the caption only at the very end of the article. ProQuest Direct offers three full-text formats for many of the articles. The simplest is the plain-text format, which includes captions and indicates the location of an illustration (figure 6.12). The text-plus-graphics format includes a thumbnail version of the illustration (figure 6.13). It can be enlarged two or four times the size of the thumbnail and is quite legible (figure 6.14). Reproducing the typography of the original article's text portion is a definite asset.

> The variety of databases, modestly listed under the subcategory "**Forbes** Lists" which doesn't reflect the fact that most are searchable files with dynamic output capabilities, cover a really impressive spectrum-200 Best Small Companies, **Forbes** Platinum 400, **Forbes** Annual Report on American Industry, Top 800 CEOs (by compensation), the International 800, the 400 Richest People in America, The World Richest People, the **Forbes** Celebrity 100, the Top 40 Entertainers, and Athletes, among others. Not all have the three-year retrospective coverage and the dynamic search and output generation capabilities of the 500 lists, but most do, with appropriate criteria. The International 800 database, for example, offers sorting by country, and two years of retrospective data.
>
> (Illustration Omitted)
>
> Captioned as: The usercustomizable **Forbes** 500 list on the **Forbes** Digital Toolbox site

Fig. 6.11. Excerpt from an ABI/INFORM record in Ovid.

Many newspapers and journals have characteristic fonts and layout, and the reproduction of the original boldfacing and italicizing in the original text may significantly improve understanding. ProQuest's third format reproduces the entire image of the original page. The text usually is as good as if it were done on a copy machine (figure 6.15). The quality of the figures seems to depend much more on the original than on the quality of the text portion. Although there are more scaling options in this format than in the text-plus-image format, the quality is not as good and the entire page is enlarged, which makes navigation somewhat awkward but still worthwhile (figure 6.16).

The variety of databases, modestly listed under the subcategory "Forbes Lists" which doesn't reflect the fact that most are searchable files with dynamic output capabilities, cover a really impressive spectrum-200 Best Small Companies, Forbes Platinum 400, Forbes Annual Report on American Industry, Top 800 CEOs (by compensation), the International 800, the 400 Richest People in America, The World Richest People, the Forbes Celebrity 100, the Top 40 Entertainers, and Athletes, among others. Not all have the three-year retrospective coverage and the dynamic search and output generation capabilities of the 500 lists, but most do, with appropriate criteria. The International 800 database, for example, offers sorting by country, and two years of retrospective data.

[Illustration]
Caption: The usercustomizable Forbes 500 list on the Forbes Digital Toolbox site

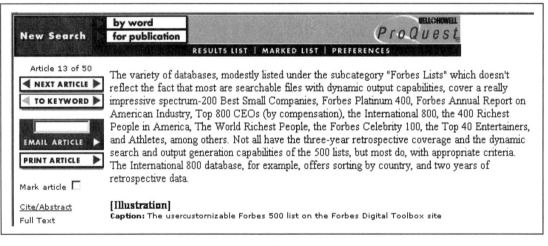

Fig. 6.12. Excerpt from an ABI/INFORM record in ProQuest.

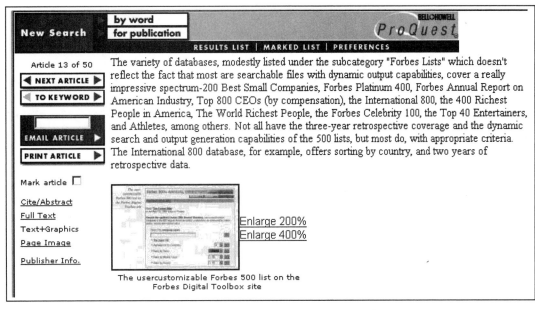

Fig. 6.13. The text-plus-graphics format in ProQuest.

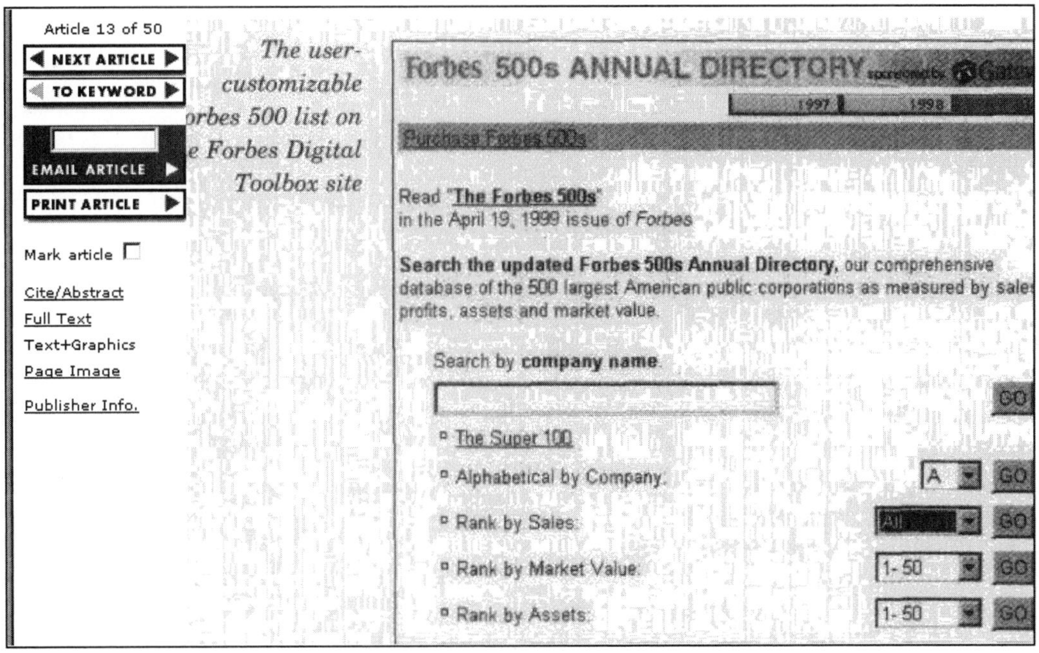

Fig. 6.14. The image component enlarged in ProQuest.

Fig. 6.15. Excerpt from the page-image version of an ABI/INFORM record in ProQuest.

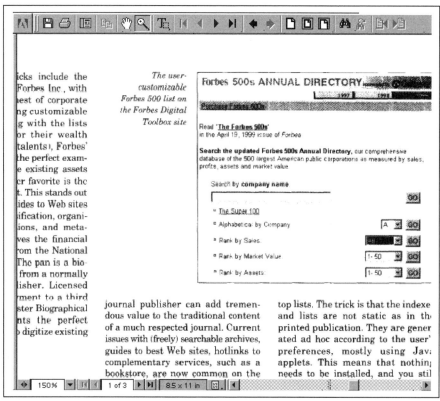

Fig. 6.16. The page enlarged in ProQuest.

Some online service providers offer special features that make use of the aggregation of different abstracting and indexing and full-text databases. Ovid has pioneered the technology and made the most impressive progress in this area. Assuming that users have access to the appropriate files, they can click on the REFERENCES section at the end of the article in a full-text database and display its full bibliographic record, including the abstract from an indexing and abstracting database.

Figure 6.17 shows an excerpt from a full-text record in the Mental Health Collection database of Ovid. Clicking on the REFERENCES line will display the list of cited references. Some of them will have links to PsycINFO, MEDLINE, or BIOSIS (or a combination of these) (figure 6.18). Clicking on one of the links will display the full bibliographic record with abstract from the chosen database. The reverse is also possible—that is, jumping from an indexing and abstracting database to a record in a full-text database that the user is authorized to access. The link is so well designed that it can fetch the record even if it misspells the author's name, as is the case with the BIOSIS citation that spells *Kanin* as *Kianin* (not shown here).

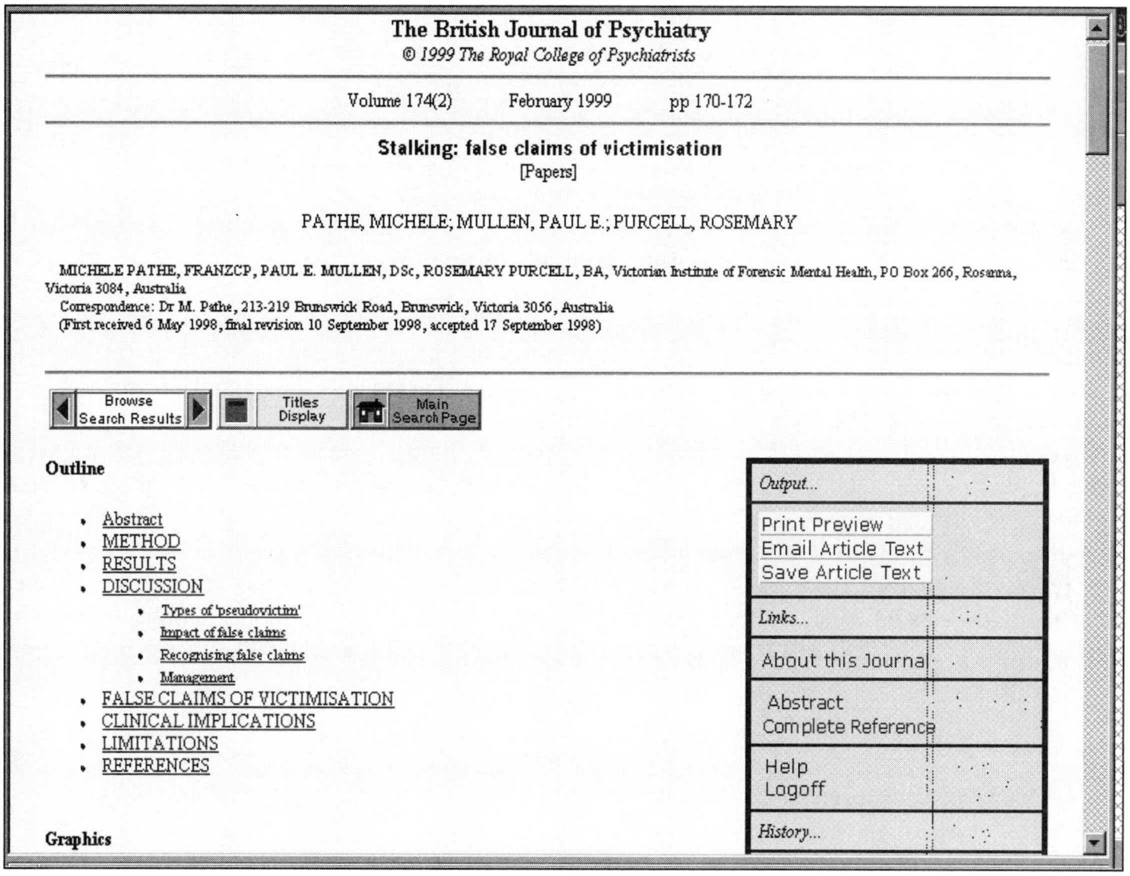

Fig. 6.17. Excerpt from a full-text record in Mental Health Collection of Ovid.

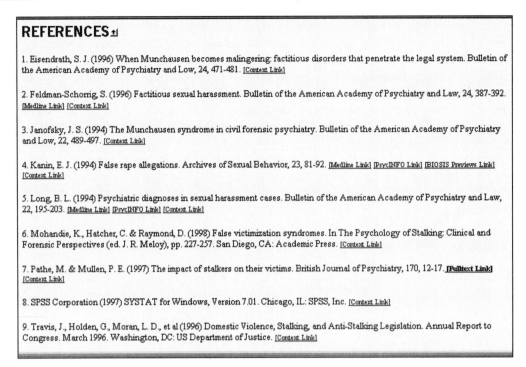

Fig. 6.18. The references with links to bibliographic records with abstracts.

In the directory category, both the Biography Resource Center of the Gale Group (BRC) and the Biographies Plus Illustrated of H. W. Wilson qualify as full-text resources because of their substantial and excellently structured and edited biographies. They offer much value added information, such as gender, nationality, and birth and death locales and dates, making their searching very efficient.

In other biographical sources, this information is mostly lumped together with the body of the rather short text, making it difficult to search for the previous information without retrieving many false records. The biography databases of the Gale Group (figure 6.19) and H. W. Wilson (figure 6.20) also add the photo of the subject for many biographees, as shown in figures 6.3 and 6.4.

The two biographical databases from Gale Group and H. W. Wilson also offer special added values by linking to review articles and news items that are available in the dozens of full-text databases in their stable. (The Gale Group acquisition of IAC in 1999 enriched its collection of reference databases significantly.)

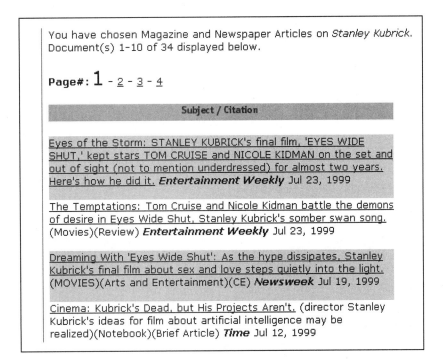

Fig. 6.19. Link to full-text review articles from BRC.

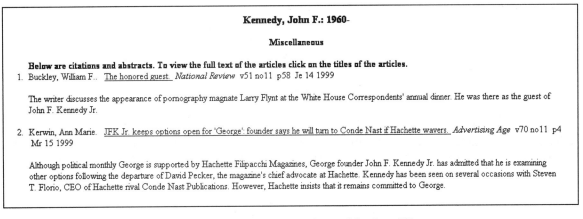

Fig. 6.20. Link to full-text review articles from BP.

Searchability makes it necessary to spell out information, which, for readers of a printed abstracting and indexing service, is probably obvious when scanning the pages of the printed volume, such as the language or the type of the original document (conference paper, article, or book review). Such attributes must be made explicit for the efficient filtering of the results. Even the structuring of the bibliographic citation may become important for indexing and searching purposes. The producer of the National Criminal Justice Reference Service (NCJRS) database does not separate the chronological and numerical designation of the issues from the name of the journal (figure 6.21).

This backfires when the user wants to browse the journal name index and must scroll through several screens to get from one journal to the other across dozens (if not hundreds) of entries for different volumes and issues of the same journal. Wading through all the entries for Adolescence would make even parents with teenagers impatient. Similarly, in PaperChem, scrolling through the *Abbey Newsletter* entries (figure 6.22) would test the patience of a saint. Not only is this an unprofessional solution defying the collocation purpose, but is also costly for the user.

```
E5        1   JN=ADOLESCENCE, V 12, N 48 (WINTER 1977), P 523-5
E6        1   JN=ADOLESCENCE, V 12, N 48 (WINTER 1977), P 559-5
E7        1   JN=ADOLESCENCE, V 13, N 49 (SPRING 1978), P 21-28
E8        1   JN=ADOLESCENCE, V 13, N 49 (SPRING 1978), P 29-43
E9        1   JN=ADOLESCENCE, V 13, N 50 (SUMMER 1978), P 209-2
E10       1   JN=ADOLESCENCE, V 13, N 50 (SUMMER 1978), P 339-3
E11       1   JN=ADOLESCENCE, V 13, N 50 (SUMMER 1978), P 365-3
E12       1   JN=ADOLESCENCE, V 13, N 51 (FALL 1978), P 375-392
E13       1   JN=ADOLESCENCE, V 13, N 51 (FALL 1978), P 401-410
E14       1   JN=ADOLESCENCE, V 13, N 51 (FALL 1978), P 461-482
E15       1   JN=ADOLESCENCE, V 13, N 51 (FALL 1978), P 483-493
E16       1   JN=ADOLESCENCE, V 13, N 52 (WINTER 1978), P 531-5
E17       1   JN=ADOLESCENCE, V 13, N 52 (WINTER 1978), P 643-6
E18       1   JN=ADOLESCENCE, V 13, N 52 (WINTER 1978), P 675-6
E19       1   JN=ADOLESCENCE, V 13, V 52 (WINTER 1978), P 543-5
```

Fig. 6.21. Entries with chronological-numerical designation in the journal index in NCJRS.

Browsing the subject code index in ISA is utterly confusing because of the ill-structured text equivalent of the codes (figure 6.23). Is code 04.08, for example, both for Information Generation and Promulgation and for Information Recognition and Description, as the first two entries in the figure would suggest? Are codes 04.09 and 04.10 also for these two concepts? Why are there so many different codes for Information Processing and Control and for Information System and Applications without any distinction in the text equivalents?

The answer is that these are the main headings, and the distinguishing subheadings cannot be seen in the index—and cannot even be searched. You see them in the records (figure 6.24). When they are displayed in a database about information science, applying a little information technology and common sense could go a long way. Splitting the section heading text field into two subfields (main section and subsection) would solve the problem simply.

```
        E9      1   JN=ABBEY NEWSL. 17, NO. 6
        E10     1   JN=ABBEY NEWSL. 17, NO. 7-8
        E11     1   JN=ABBEY NEWSL. 18, NO. 3
        E12     1   JN=ABBEY NEWSL. 18, NO. 8
        E13     3   JN=ABBEY NEWSL. 19, NO. 3
        E14     1   JN=ABBEY NEWSL. 19, NO. 5
        E15     2   JN=ABBEY NEWSL. 19, NO. 6/7
        E16     1   JN=ABBEY NEWSL. 20, NO. 2
        E17     1   JN=ABBEY NEWSL. 20, NO. 3
        E18     4   JN=ABBEY NEWSL. 20, NO. 4/5
        E19     1   JN=ABBEY NEWSL. 20, NO. 8
        E20     2   JN=ABBEY NEWSL. 21, NO. 1
        E21     1   JN=ABBEY NEWSL. 21, NO. 3
        E22     1   JN=ABBEY NEWSL. 7, NO. 3
        E23     1   JN=ABBEY NEWSLETTER 11, NO. 3
        E24     1   JN=ABBEY NEWSLETTER 11, NO. 4
        E25     1   JN=ABBEY NEWSLETTER 11, NO. 6
```

Fig. 6.22. Entries with chronological-numerical designation in the journal index in PaperChem.

```
    Ref    Items   Index-term
    E1         6   SC=04.08 INFORMATION GENERATION AND PROMULGATION
    E2      3075   SC=04.08 INFORMATION RECOGNITION AND DESCRIPTION
    E3        10   SC=04.09 INFORMATION GENERATION AND PROMULGATION
    E4      4897   SC=04.09 INFORMATION RECOGNITION AND DESCRIPTION
    E5         3   SC=04.10 INFORMATION GENERATION AND PROMULGATION
    E6       834   SC=04.10 INFORMATION RECOGNITION AND DESCRIPTION
    E7      3838   SC=05.00 INFORMATION PROCESSING AND CONTROL
    E8      1554   SC=05.01 INFORMATION PROCESSING AND CONTROL
    E9      6938   SC=05.02 INFORMATION PROCESSING AND CONTROL
    E10      102   SC=05.03 INFORMATION PROCESSING AND CONTROL
    E11     2949   SC=05.04 INFORMATION PROCESSING AND CONTROL
    E12     4619   SC=05.05 INFORMATION PROCESSING AND CONTROL
    E13    10111   SC=05.06 INFORMATION PROCESSING AND CONTROL
    E14     2651   SC=05.07 INFORMATION PROCESSING AND CONTROL
    E15     3655   SC=05.08 INFORMATION PROCESSING AND CONTROL
    E16     1397   SC=05.09 INFORMATION PROCESSING AND CONTROL
    E17     1650   SC=05.10 INFORMATION PROCESSING AND CONTROL
    E18     5401   SC=05.11 INFORMATION PROCESSING AND CONTROL
    E19      612   SC=06.00 INFORMATION SYSTEMS AND APPLICATIONS
    E20     6211   SC=06.01 INFORMATION SYSTEMS AND APPLICATIONS
    E21        1   SC=06.02 BIBLIOGRAPHIC SEARCH SERVICES, DATABASE
    E22     6023   SC=06.02 INFORMATION SYSTEMS AND APPLICATIONS
    E23     1911   SC=06.03 INFORMATION SYSTEMS AND APPLICATIONS
    E24      795   SC=06.04 INFORMATION SYSTEMS AND APPLICATIONS
    E25     5602   SC=06.05 INFORMATION SYSTEMS AND APPLICATIONS
    E26     6314   SC=06.06 INFORMATION SYSTEMS AND APPLICATIONS
    E27     1573   SC=06.07 INFORMATION SYSTEMS AND APPLICATIONS
    E28     3371   SC=06.08 INFORMATION SYSTEMS AND APPLICATIONS
    E29     3513   SC=06.09 INFORMATION SYSTEMS AND APPLICATIONS
```

Fig. 6.23. Different subject codes for the seemingly same subject concepts in the ISA index.

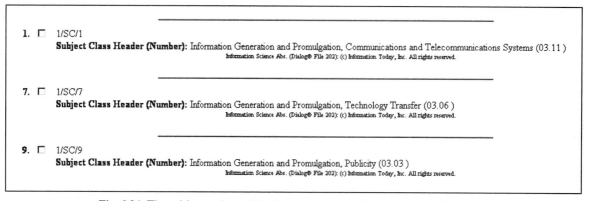

1. ☐   1/SC/1
Subject Class Header (Number): Information Generation and Promulgation, Communications and Telecommunications Systems (03.11)

7. ☐   1/SC/7
Subject Class Header (Number): Information Generation and Promulgation, Technology Transfer (03.06)

9. ☐   1/SC/9
Subject Class Header (Number): Information Generation and Promulgation, Publicity (03.03)

Fig. 6.24. The subject codes and their text equivalents in the records displayed.

Accuracy

Accuracy of information retrieved from a database is often taken for granted. For many users, the fact that the information is delivered by and presented not merely on paper but on a computer lends extra credibility to CD-ROM and online databases. For the past 30 years, an increasing volume of printed output has been the by-product of computer processing of data. The databases can hardly be more accurate than the print version derived from them. Many other databases are created from data existing in print-only format. Computer processing of printed data can and does introduce further mistakes. Some of these are caused by technical difficulties—for example, when the scanner/conversion software does not recognize a letter or number correctly.

When data are manually entered from printed text, catalog cards, work forms, and questionnaires, additional errors are bound to occur. Though it is true that opportunity also arises to use sophisticated data entry verification programs, few file producers are willing to invest in it. When they do it retrospectively, the volume of errors detected and corrected is staggering.

This is clearly seen in cataloging records that were created manually by typing in data from catalog cards or the primary source itself. The dimension of the problem is well illustrated by OCLC, which reported that 30,000 errors were corrected daily during the cleanup of its Online Union Catalog. Although this number included all types of errors, such as coding and typographical ones, the number is still striking.

Printed primary sources are responsible for a large number of errors. The public rarely knows about them unless the error can cause harm and necessitates the recall of a book. *American Libraries* (1996) reported a number of cases. For example, this happened with Carol Walter's *Great Cakes,* which Ballantine, the publisher, recalled "because a recipe listed lilies of the valley, a poisonous flower, as an ingredient." Not a healthy recipe, indeed. "Only" intellectual harm would have been caused by a series of history textbooks under consideration for adoption in Texas to the tune of over $20 million when an advocacy group uncovered more than 5,200 errors before the book purchase was approved.

One of Dr. Ruth's books had to be recalled when her designation of two time periods as unsafe for avoiding pregnancy was changed to "safe" in the final copy. Pedersen (1992) in *Publishers Weekly* reported the recall of a textbook that claimed that President Truman "easily settled" the Korean War by dropping the atomic bomb.

It is quite telling that of the total of 3,244 records added in January 1999 to the *New York Times* in Newspaper Abstracts Daily, 121 were identified as corrections to information reported in a previous issue. Not all of them were earthshaking errors, but they were serious enough for the *New York Times* to run a correction. According to a quick search, the ratio of errors to new records in the *Washington Post* (15 of 2,114), *Wall Street Journal* (16 of 4,117), and *Los Angeles Times* (10 of 1,153) was much lower, but it may have to do with different correction policies of the newspapers.

It is surprising how obvious errors can sneak through or originate even from librarians who appreciate accuracy highly. According to *American Libraries* (1996), the first edition of a historical calendar in 1996 compiled by the Chicago Public Library had such errors as Michael *Jordon* for Michael *Jordan*, Lord *Tenneyson* for Lord *Tennyson*, and pegged both the birth and death years of Jean Baptiste Point du Sable as 1818. Few, if any, could have achievements as an infant that would deserve a spot in the calendar.

The calendar also listed under two separate years the election of Richard Daley as his first-time election. In politics anything is possible, but letting Richard Daley be elected twice for the first time is unlikely, even considering the checkered election history of Chicago. Errors abound in fiction and nonfiction, including children's biographies. As more printed materials are mounted as online databases, their digital versions spread the errors.

Spelling and typographical errors are the most common types of inaccuracy in databases. Online catalogs have been analyzed the most often to explore the variety of inaccuracies. O'Neill and Vizine-Goetz (1988) gave a comprehensive analysis of this literature in 1988. The magnitude of the problem of misspelling is striking. Klemmer and Lockhead (1962) found error rates ranging from two to six errors per 10,000 keystrokes. Errors per word as calculated by Pollock and Zamora (1975) in the Chemical Abstracts Service database may be more relevant, as a single error in a word may render a record irretrievable.

They found 2 misspelled words for each 1,000 words in this expensive database. They also found that 90 to 96 percent of the errors fall in one of the four most common error types: omission of character(s), 30 to 40 percent; insertion of character(s), 25 to 35 percent; substitution, 15 to 20 percent; and transposition, 10 to 15 percent.

These are scientific and scholarly sources, most of which go through refereeing and editing, which presumably contribute to the high cost and professed esteem of these journals. The situation in general interest sources such as newspapers is certainly worse.

The more dissective analysis of errors by Yannakoudakis and Fawthrop (1983) revealed that many errors occur with vowels and with words that include the letters *w, y,* and *h*. Dittography and haplography (duplication of letters that should be singular and omission of letters when they should be duplicated, e.g., such errors as *leter dupplication*) are very common. The detailed analysis of error types and patterns can be very useful for developing defensive search strategies.

In the late 1990s, the problem was alleviated by the implementation of automatic error checking and correction procedures in many online catalogs, but abstracting and indexing services have not embraced this idea adequately. The merging of the legendarily clean Western Library Network (WLN; formerly Washington Library Network) bibliographic utility and OCLC in 1999 will likely improve the remarkable cleanup efforts of OCLC. It is also encouraging that more databases are built through direct file transfer from the file producers. This direct feed reduces the chance of introducing additional errors in retyping bibliographic citations, abstracts, and full text. This is especially true in light of the results of the earlier cited studies that assert that most typing errors are associated with the use of the QWERTY keyboard. It is somewhat ironic that the far superior Dvorak keyboard, which, according to tests, drastically reduces typing errors (and carpal tunnel syndrome), has never taken off.

Spelling errors in abstracting and indexing databases have been analyzed using the host software of the database as early as 1977 by Charles Bourne, who analyzed 3,600 index terms (subject headings, words from abstracts and titles) drawn from 11 different databases. The percentage of index terms misspelled ranged from 0.4 percent for BIOSIS to 22.8 percent in ABI/INFORM, with ISMEC (Information Service in Mechanical Engineering) 0.6 percent; ERIC (4.2 percent); Social Science Citation Index (6.1 percent); and NTIS (6.5 percent) in the low range and the PATS database of Predicast (12.4 percent) and Compendex (12.3 percent) in the high range. I find it ironic that ISMEC is misspelled as *ISMES* in the label of a figure of Bourne's article (1977) in a vigorously refereed and edited journal, *Information Processing & Management*. ABI/INFORM later went through a massive cleanup that eliminated the majority of misspellings.

Jeffrey Beall's dirty database testing idea may be less scholarly, but is very pragmatic for getting a feel for spelling accuracy in databases by using often-misspelled words such as *Wensday, goverment, grammer,* and a dozen other error-prone terms. *Database Searcher* credited Harold Way (1988) for calculating the accuracy score of 14 databases using Beall's test words. Dwyer (1991) refined the deficiency of Bourne's and Beall's methods by calculating the ratio between the misspelled and correctly spelled versions of the same word, which Bourne himself recommended. Jacsó (1995) checked the correct and misspelled versions of a few words in five library and information science databases. He found LibLit squeaky clean and ISA the most error-prone, followed by ERIC. ISA misspelled the root term *accommodat* in more than 200 records; nearly 20 percent of the correct spelling.

Cahn (1994) enhanced this methodology—among others—by examining whether the record also contained the correct spelling of the misspelled word, thus reducing or eliminating the impact on searching. Once again, it is interesting to note that the *Harvard Business Review* of John Wiley (a journal with utmost clout, and from the publisher of very expensive scholarly journals) was head and shoulders above the other 13 databases—in producing the most errors in the majority of Cahn's tests.

Ballard and Lifshin (1992) eyeballed all 117,000 terms in the keyword index of the online public access catalog of a university and analyzed the errors by data field, part of speech, and error type. There were 1,082 erroneous index terms. Given the prominence of title field searching in book catalogs, it is unnerving that terms generated from the title field accounted for 60 percent of the errors. Luckily, more than half of them were in the subtitle, which is less critical in browsing and searching. On the positive side, there were no errors in the subject heading field, and only 2 percent of the author fields had misspellings. (It is, however, not clear from the article how the accuracy of author names was checked.) As for the distribution of errors by error types, it was close to the one reported previously.

The position of the error within the title field was also analyzed. The bad news is that more than 14 percent of the errors occurred in the first word of the title and nearly 41 percent in the first three words of the title. Entries with misspelled lead terms dramatically reduce the probability of finding a book by title browsing. Misspelled second and third terms also decrease the chance of finding a known item, but to a lesser extent, which depends on how many short entries are displayed on the screen and how far the misspelled entry is from the correct entry. More short entries increase the chance that the user spots the misspelled entry, and the distance from the correct spelling variant may be close if the typo is at the end of the word. The misspelled *Jacsu* is closer to *Jacsó* than the also misspelled *Jascó*. Ironically, when referring to the most commonly misspelled words in the catalog, including *commerical, reseach,* and *adminstration,* the authors also list *government*; i.e., with the right spelling. Then again, it may have been the printer's devil.

Such full-blown tests for the entire population require an enormous amount of time. The method of using problem terms in one or more of the commonly misspelled format(s) and in the correct format is sufficient for getting an impression of the magnitude of misspellings. For a start, you may want to check out a Web site (*http://www.sentex.net/~mmcadams/spelling.html*) for commonly misspelled words, along with the correct spelling and see how often the wrong one occurs in a database that you use often (figure 7.1).

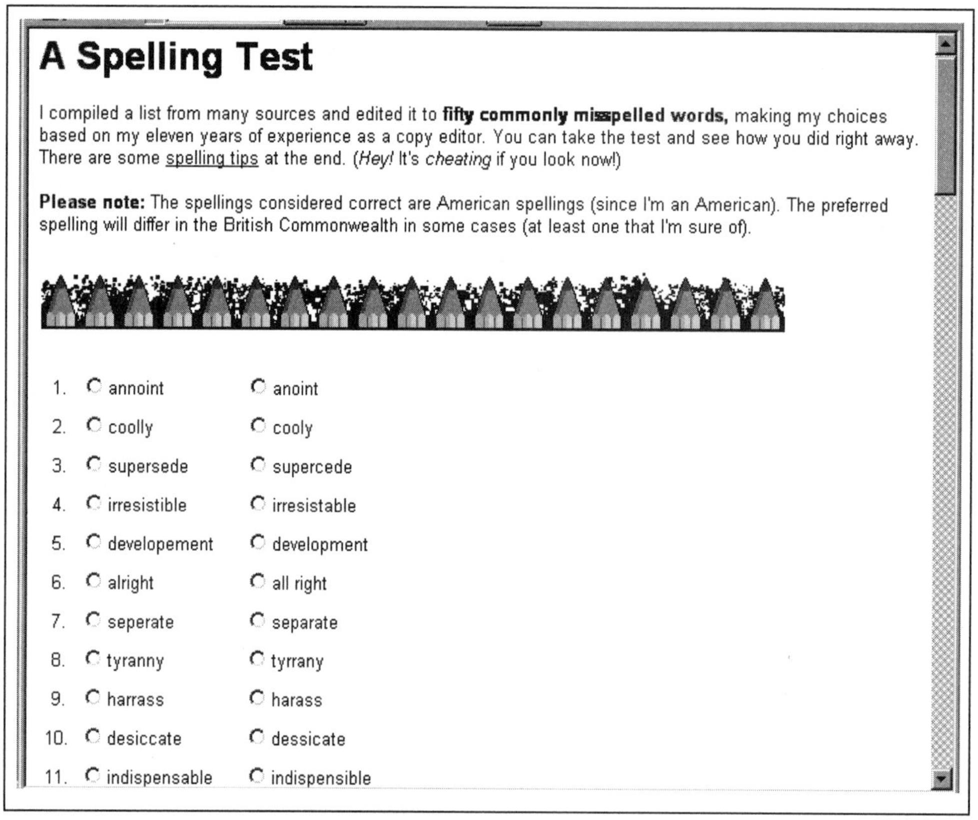

A Spelling Test

I compiled a list from many sources and edited it to **fifty commonly misspelled words,** making my choices based on my eleven years of experience as a copy editor. You can take the test and see how you did right away. There are some spelling tips at the end. (*Hey!* It's *cheating* if you look now!)

Please note: The spellings considered correct are American spellings (since I'm an American). The preferred spelling will differ in the British Commonwealth in some cases (at least one that I'm sure of).

1.	○ annoint	○ anoint
2.	○ coolly	○ cooly
3.	○ supersede	○ supercede
4.	○ irresistible	○ irresistable
5.	○ developement	○ development
6.	○ alright	○ all right
7.	○ seperate	○ separate
8.	○ tyranny	○ tyrrany
9.	○ harrass	○ harass
10.	○ desiccate	○ dessicate
11.	○ indispensable	○ indispensible

Fig. 7.1. Most commonly misspelled words.

A distinction should be made between fields that are the exclusive sources for a search criterion (such as the country of publication) and fields whose words may appear in other fields as well. A misspelling in the abstract is not that critical, as the correct spelling may occur in the title or in the subject heading field (or both). This distinction is very similar to the distinction between fields using controlled vocabulary versus fields with free text. The misspelling of *Rorschach* in the abstract is not a problem in PsycINFO (figure 7.2) because it also appears correctly in the first sentence of the abstract, so the record will be retrieved. The misspelled version in the title field in MHA is unappealing (figure 7.3), but because it appears correctly in the original Spanish language title field, it is only an eyesore, as long as the original title field (i.e., the Spanish title) is also used for the creation of the keyword or basic index.

Even when the misspelled version is the only occurrence in the abstract (as in the second record), it is not a serious problem when the term appears correctly in the subject heading field. When the misspelled version, *Rorshach,* is the only format in which the name appears, the record will be irretrievable by the correct name, *Rorschach* (figure 7.4). In case of databases such as Inside Conferences that don't have abstracts and that use very broad subject categories, misspellings in the title can be fatal. Two of the five records that misspell the word *toxoplasma* as *taxoplasma* in the title are shown in figure 7.5. In light of the enormous number of typos, it is to be applauded that some search programs get smarter and either automatically correct the user's term or offer both the alphabetically closest terms and the ones that sound like the word entered by the user. The former is used with the file producer's version of the National Criminal Justice Reference Service database; the latter was used on the subscription-based version of *Encyclopaedia Britannica* until 1999.

3/TI,AB/6 (Item 6 from file: 11)
La problematica existencial del enfermo alcoholico cronico.

Translated Title: The existential problem of the chronic alcoholic.

Abstract: (30 male chronic alcoholics (median age 44.9 yrs) and a matched group of nonalcoholics were administered the **Rorschach** and the TAT. The **Rorshach** test assessed Ss' affective stability and their social contact; the TAT

Fig. 7.2. One correct and one incorrect spelling of *Rorschach* in the abstract.

3/8/19 (Item 9 from file: 86)
0046269
IPA1970-01382
Psychodiagnosis of Rorshach, and delinquency.
Psicodiagnostico de Rorschach y delincuencia.
Descriptors: Behavioral Sciences; Crime and Delinquency
Identifiers: Journal Article; maturation

Fig. 7.3. Correct spelling in the original (Spanish) title and misspelling in the English title.

1/TI,AB,DE,ID/8 (Item 3 from file: 86)
Graphology -- an art, science, or fraud?

Cases are made for and against the validity of graphology. Graphologists find considerable acceptance in industrial personnel departments. In courts of law, handwriting analysis generally is considered to be reliable with respect to the validation of a signature, but not with respect to personality analysis. A random survey of 10 police departments found that only one of them had ever used the services of a graphologist in compiling a personality profile, and that this analysis did not result in the apprehension of the writer. It is suggested that the law enforcement profession should regard graphology with skepticism, although graphologists insist on handwriting analysis as a valuable projective technique on a par with the Rorshach dream interpretation, and free association to reveal a person's character traits.
Descriptors: Crime; Personality; Psychometrics
Identifiers: Journal; Evaluation; Human; Overview

Fig. 7.4. Only occurrence of the name *Rorschach* misspelled in the abstract.

Fields that have a limited number of possible values, such as the language, the country of publication, or the document type, are rather simple to check and calculate the accuracy score—the ratio between the number of records with correct and incorrect spelling. It is also easy to correct by a competent file producer who has some respect for the customer. The language index of a database covering documents in a handful of languages requires only a single once-over, as the number of languages is usually only a dozen or two.

A large number of erroneous entries makes the language index scatter across several screens and may make users miss relevant records if they don't spot the misspelled variations. It is quite obvious from the language index of ISA, for example, that it needs someone to check how to spell *Czech*. At least in this case the misspellings are adjacent, but the correct version of *Serbo-Croatian* is several screens away from the nonexistent language *Croato-Serbian* (figure 7.6).

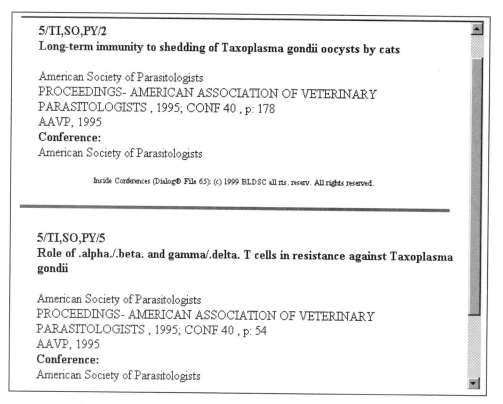

Fig. 7.5. Only occurrence of the word *toxoplasma* misspelled in the title.

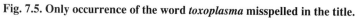

Fig. 7.6. Misspellings in the language field in ISA.

While the misspelled version of *Portuguese* is next to the correct one in figure 7.7, the fact that the in-accurate version occurs half as often as the correct one does not increase the appeal of the ISA database. All these become appalling in the DOS CD-ROM version of this database, because this version does not allow browsing of the language index or, for that matter, the country of publication and the document type index. It hides these deficiencies from users, depriving them of half of the references to Portuguese language documents if they spell the language correctly in the query.

Some databases are even worse, where the misspelled versions of just this language outnumber the correct spelling. Figure 7.7 shows the proportion of misspelled and correct versions of *Portuguese* in some databases as of February 1999. In FLUIDEX (file 96) and Pollution Abstracts (file 41), there are nearly three times as many misspelled versions than correct ones. In file 16 (PROMT) there are merely 9 correct spellings of *Portuguese* and 232 wrong versions. Sometimes a spelling variant is considered acceptable by dictionaries, but the variant *Portugese* is just plain wrong.

HOME	DATABASES	COMMAND SEARCH	GUIDED SEARCH		COST
S1	LA=PORTUGESE		638		Display
S1	LA=PORTUGESE		147	202	Display
S1	LA=PORTUGESE		25	96	Display
S1	LA=PORTUGESE		95	41	Display
S1	LA=PORTUGESE		139	28	Display
S1	LA=PORTUGESE		232	16	Display
S2	LA=PORTUGUESE		500		Display
S2	LA=PORTUGUESE		290	202	Display
S2	LA=PORTUGUESE		71	96	Display
S2	LA=PORTUGUESE		37	41	Display
S2	LA=PORTUGUESE		93	28	Display
S2	LA=PORTUGUESE		9	16	Display

Fig. 7.7. Ratio of misspelled and correct versions of *Portuguese* in the language index.

Why would the typical user search for the misspelled version of a language if some records are indeed found with the correct version? From this perspective, the Compact Cambridge version of PsycLIT was better because it misspelled the word *Portuguese* in all the 1,375 records (i.e., the absence of any records may have alerted the user that there may have been a problem with the language field). The same applies to two of the IAC databases, AeroSpace/Defense Markets & Technology and Marketing & Advertising Reference Services, which do not have a single record with the correct spelling of this language.

The same is true about Mental Health Abstracts. Not a single record spells the word *English* correctly in the language field. Interestingly, the database documentation instructs the indexer that "if the language of the document is English it is not to be entered." One wonders if this decision was made after nearly 100 efforts failed to spell this not-too-difficult word correctly. The person who wrote the DIALOG bluesheet for MHA using S LA=ENGLISH as an example must have been out of the loop regarding this decision and did not test the recommended example for the use of this field. Users who browse the language index at least can see the struggle if they care to scroll screen after screen to find out how many ways there are to misspell the word *English* (figure 7.8). By 1992 ISA learned how to spell Portuguese correctly; so, by now it has twice as many correct spellings as misspellings.

Competency and respect for the users may achieve squeaky-clean language names as shown in Library Literature and in all the H. W. Wilson databases (figure 7.9). It is another question as to why so many records include the variable "undetermined" for the language. It turns out that all these entries are in book review records and refer to the original language of the book, not that of the reviews. The indexer could probably figure out the language of the book from the review and use the appropriate language name in the record.

```
      new search  databases  alerts  cost  logoff
   File      Items    Total   Index-term
     86                   1   LA=EMGLISH
     86                   1   LA=ENBLISH
     86                   5  *LA=ENG
     86                   1   LA=ENGIISH
     86                  24   LA=ENGISH
     86                   1   LA=ENGLAIH
     86                  25   LA=ENGLAND
     86                   1   LA=ENGLIAH
     86                   2   LA=ENGLIDH
     86                   2   LA=ENGLIGH
     86                   1   LA=ENGLIISH
     86                   1   LA=ENGLILSH
     86                   3   LA=ENGLIS
     86                   5   LA=ENGLISH ENGLISH
     86                   1   LA=ENGLISH 12
     86                   8   LA=ENGLISH.
     86                   2   LA=ENGLISH/JAP.
     86                   1   LA=ENGLISH,
     86                   1   LA=ENGLISH'
     86                   3   LA=ENGLISN
     86                   1   LA=ENGLLISH
     86                   1   LA=ENGLSH
     86                  20   LA=ENGLSIH
     86                   1   LA=ENGLUSH
     86                  10   LA=ENLGISH
```

Fig. 7.8. Numerous misspellings of *English*
in Mental Health Abstracts language field.

```
                        Dialog Response

   Ref   File   Items    Total   Index-term
   E1    438                 0   *LA=
   E2    438               246   LA=AFRIKAANS
   E3    438                60   LA=CHINESE
   E4    438               980   LA=DANISH
   E5    438              1013   LA=DUTCH
   E6    438            143494   LA=ENGLISH
   E7    438               768   LA=FINNISH
   E8    438              2930   LA=FRENCH
   E9    438              4054   LA=GERMAN
   E10   438               191   LA=HUNGARIAN
   E11   438                 2   LA=IRISH
   E12   438               532   LA=ITALIAN
   E13   438               135   LA=JAPANESE
   E14   438                 6   LA=MULTILINGUAL
   E15   438              1675   LA=NORWEGIAN
   E16   438              1001   LA=POLISH
   E17   438               508   LA=PORTUGUESE
   E18   438              5285   LA=RUSSIAN
   E19   438               132   LA=SPANISH
   E20   438               281   LA=SWEDISH
   E21   438             25880   LA=UNDETERMINED
   E22   438                 3   LA=URDU
```

Fig. 7.9. Squeaky-clean language names in the LibLit database.

It is more difficult to ensure the correct spelling of the tens of thousands of author names that many databases have. Correct author names are essential for many searches, and in most databases, accurate author names cannot be taken for granted (and consistency of name format is even more unlikely). The H. W. Wilson databases, the WLN bibliographic utility, and the Internet Movie Database stand out for their impeccable authority control, including name authority. Although the Library of Congress (LC) was among the first to develop and apply name authority files, the files have deficiencies. These deficiencies are critical because those errors trickle down to all the catalogs that use LC MARC records. It is disappointing to see that F. W. Lancaster's first name appears incorrectly (as *Wilfred*) in the LC authority file next to the correct one, *Wilfrid*.

Testing the accuracy of author or other personal names in a database cannot be comprehensive, as even in a small database there are too many names. It is also more difficult to do sampling than checking the accuracy of terms in the free-text fields and most controlled vocabulary fields unless you have an absolutely reliable source for the names of the person. Jacsó (1989) used business cards in his Rolodex and the catalog of the School of Library Services of Columbia University to check the accuracy of the names of his acquaintances and fellow faculty members in the Directory of Library and Information Professionals.

A total of 469 persons were searched by name, but records could be found by this approach for less than half of the library and information professionals. A follow-up search by other criteria improved the hit rate somewhat and also revealed that misspelled names are common in the database. Such additional search criteria are not consistently available and/or are not current (such as affiliation) in this database; therefore, they can't be relied upon as a fallback if name searches don't yield results. The many misspellings in this directory are more painful than usual because it was made with the cooperation of the American Library Association.

For two faculty members (out of ten) at Columbia University, the typos were lethal, as they occurred in the first letter (*Fres, Beth* instead of *Eres, Beth* and *Tetherbridge, Guy* instead of *Petherbridge, Guy*). Other inaccuracies were at the end of the name, so could be alleviated by using truncation. In this database, personal names are the only data elements present in every record; thus, any error may render the record inaccessible.

In this example, the responsibility for accuracy lies with the file producer, but this is not always the case. The file producers can't be blamed if the original source document misspells the name. *Serials Review* managed to misspell *Jacsó* as *Jascó* twice (figure 7.10) in spite of vocal protest of the author after the first time. As publishers of refereed journals don't pay the authors, the only reward for them is the potential for being acknowledged and cited, but it is nearly useless when the author's name is misspelled.

Serials Review is a refereed journal, but the copy editor's work may not go through as rigorous a process as the authors' manuscripts. It is exceptional that H. W. Wilson, in its bibliographic record, correctly overrode in both cases the misspelled name of the author, and LISA overrode it in one case. Looking up a small sample of fairly unique and distinguishable names in the author index would give a good indication of the accuracy of author names.

The results of a cross-database search illustrate the extent of the most common misspelling for this author's name (figure 7.11). Surprisingly, even databases that care about quality, such as Microcomputer Abstracts, have a relatively high number of misspellings in this example.

Fig. 7.10. Inaccurate entry in the source documents in *Serials Review*.

Your select statement is **'S AU=JASCO, P?'**.

	File	Database Name	Hits
☐	202:	Information Science Abstracts	18
☐	233:	Microcomputer Abstracts(TM)	13
☐	148:	IAC(SM) Trade & Industry Database(TM)	11
☐	484:	Periodical Abstracts PlusText(TM)	5
☐	15:	ABI/INFORM®	5
☐	61:	LISA (Library & Information Science Abstracts)	4
☐	47:	IAC(SM) Magazine Database(TM)	4
☐	2:	INSPEC (1969- present)	2
☐	239:	MathSci®	1
☐	211:	IAC(SM) Newsearch(TM)	1
☐	13:	Business & Management Practices®	1
☐	1:	ERIC	1

There are **12** databases matching your statement **'S AU=JASCO, P?'**.

Fig. 7.11. Frequency of the most common misspelling variant of this author.

The Institute for Scientific Information cannot be blamed for the misspelling of cited author names (and otherwise inaccurate citations) when the original documents misspell the citation elements. Tenure-track faculty can hardly afford to have 15 records with their names misspelled (figure 7.12) in this coveted database—especially as cited author, which is more important than contributing author. This represents nearly 20 percent of the number of items that cite this author. One can only guess what the proportion of misspellings is for really long Thai names or Polish names with many consonants.

The consequences of not finding records by author names can be more serious than just missing an entry. Pao (1989) found a 4.5 percent rate of misspellings (and inconsistencies) of author names in MEDLINE. The result clearly proved that the proportion of misspellings distorted the author productivity distribution to such an extent that it no longer conformed to Lotka's law of distribution. After extensive correction of misspelled names, the distribution became conformant.

Obviously, misspellings of author names may have a significant impact on promotion, tenure and grant applications, and faculty productivity rankings if data retrieved from databases are taken at face value. Persons with compound names, prefixes, or just slightly unusual names are particularly handicapped in this regard. Differences in punctuation, capitalization, and inversion of prefixes scatter their names in the index, in addition to the problems caused by transposition, common even with simple names.

While misspellings in journal names are rampant, inconsistent spellings and abbreviations are more rampant; therefore, this issue will be discussed in the next chapter.

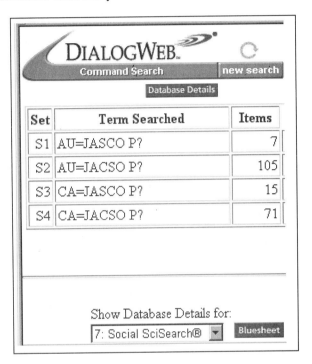

Fig. 7.12. Misspelled and correctly spelled author and cited author names in the Social SciSearch database.

One area that deserves special mention is the inaccuracy in references in the original documents. This has an obviously serious implication for all citation indexes, and to a lesser extent for the full-text databases that include bibliographies and endnotes. Smith (1981), in her seminal paper about citation errors, warned nearly 20 years ago that inaccurate citations may distort the conclusions drawn from bibliometric studies.

Pandit (1993) checked the accuracy of citations in top-ranking scholarly journals of library and information science, such as *College & Research Libraries*, *Library Resources & Technical Services*, *Library Quarterly*, *Library Trends,* and the *Journal of Academic Librarianship*. A total of 1,094 citations in 131 articles were examined. In 193 citations, 223 errors were identified. *Library Resources & Technical Services* and *College & Research Libraries* had the largest percentage of errors (31.6 percent and 27.2 percent, respectively), while *Library Trends* had a 3.8 percent error rate. Ironically, *Library Trends* is the only non-refereed journal (although it is an invitation-only serial and is among the most respected ones). *Library Trends* receives manuscripts with the usual error rate, but the exceptionally careful editing eliminates most of the errors before the final print—in this experiment, 92 percent of them.

The hypothesis of this author that refereed journals pay more attention to forcing the authors to comply with their particular citation style than to ensuring the accuracy of the content of citations seems to be reinforced by Pandit's research. Of course, the types of citation errors have different weight. This is the consolation for we librarians and information specialists who seem to make the same amount of mistakes in citations as the authors in medicine. Our mistakes, however, are somewhat less serious, according to a study by Benning and Speer (1993). They examined 555 citations in articles in *Library Trends*, *Library*

Resources & Technical Services, and the *Bulletin of the Medical Library Association*. The results of the analysis of 525 of the 555 citations were compared with citation errors in medical journals, and the error rates were almost identical between the two groups (28 percent and 29 percent). The significant difference was that only 2 percent of the citation errors were major ones in library and information science journals, but 7 percent were so in the medical journals.

Moed and Vriens (1989) examined 25,000 citations from 4,500 articles in five medical journals and found that nearly 10 percent of the citations contained at least one discrepancy. An analysis of such magnitude is beyond the capacity of mere mortals, but the moral is worthy of attention. Interestingly, both Sweetland (1989) (who made a richly illustrated review of the literature about citation errors) and Moed and Vriens conclude that inaccurate citations can often be traced back to the fact that authors of citing documents have not seen the cited documents.

Noncompliance with national and international standards in catalogs is also a form of inaccuracy. Boissonnas (1979) analyzed 151 LC MARC records and 150 OCLC records input by members that needed modification by catalogers at Cornell Law Library. Only 29 percent of LC records and a mere 1.3 percent of OCLC member records were found to comply with AACR2, ISBD, and published LC rule interpretations.

In directory databases, error detection is more difficult without intimate familiarity with the subject, unless the errors are obvious at a glance or the data are self-contradictory. This is the case with the World Databases of G. K. Saur, where even the sample record in the documentation contains nonsense data, and so did all the other records examined by this author (Jacsó 1998e) for the databases mentioned in this book. The magnitude of factual errors in this database is astonishing. It is even more astonishing that a respected file producer and online service keeps charging unsuspecting users a hefty price for such erroneous data. The only consolation is that—in spite of the yearly update promise—no new records (and no new mistakes) were added to this database since the day it was first loaded at the end of 1997.

Looking up records about journals that you are familiar with can reveal serious inaccuracies in serials directories. Ulrich's, for example, declared dead (ceased) *Computers in Libraries* and *Multimedia Schools* (two journals of Information Today, Inc.) in the fall 1998 edition of the database (figure 7.13). By the winter 1999 edition, Ulrich's brought both of them back to life, realizing that the rumors this misinformation spread about the death of these two journals were not only premature but also baseless. Those who had a subscription to the journals were not affected, but potential subscribers may have been. One also wonders from where the information about the cessation of these journals originated. Certainly not from the publisher, which is supposed to provide the information to Bowker. The extent of such serious errors in the entire database is not known but is certainly worth sampling by the searchers in their specific fields.

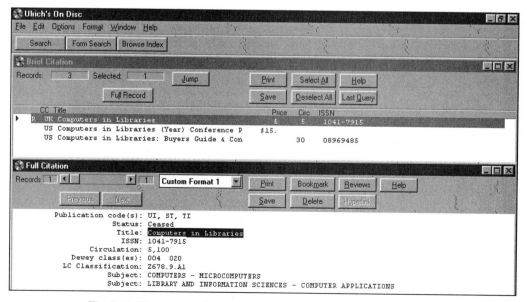

Fig. 7.13. Wrong status information in the fall 1998 edition of Ulrich's.

Systematic error detection is possible in directories, at least for some data elements. Searching by U.S. state codes should not retrieve any record with a code starting with the letters *B, E, J, Q, Z, X,* or *Y,* obviously. Similarly, a company directory should not yield any result when searching for the U.S. Standard Industry Classification code 18, as this code was left unassigned. Searching for records with a publication year earlier than 1400 should not produce any results except in databases that use two digits for the publication year or that have invalid data in that field. Neither should the query PY>2001 yield records except for *Books in Print* and a few other databases that include records for forthcoming books in print and upcoming events. Eyeballing long lists of index entries for structural discrepancies can shed light on problems in fields such as ISSN, ISBN, area codes, and U.S. telephone and fax numbers that have a fixed length or a pattern (or both).

Making a search for extremes in directories is always a good way to spot inaccuracies. Searching for library journals with the largest circulation brings up titles whose circulation data is obviously false. It's hard to believe, for example, that a ceased Argentine archive journal would have had a circulation of more than 700,000 copies (figure 7.14), but that's what Ulrich's claims. If it had, surely it would not have ceased publication.

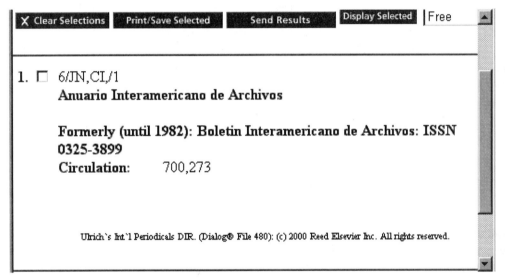

Fig. 7.14. An Argentine archive journal with an unlikely high circulation figure.

Another way of large-scale and systematic checking of facts is to compare two directories to find out if they yield results that agree. Jacsó (1991a) compared the coverage of 19 abstracting and indexing services as reported in Ulrich's and The Serials Directory of EBSCO and found tenfold differences between the two sources. Two years later, Eldredge (1993) did a similar comparison on a larger scale, also including the SERLINE directory of the National Library of Medicine, to compare the accuracy of indexing coverage information. Eldredge's conclusion that "librarians need to view the reporting on indexing service coverage in these three serials sources with skepticism" is an understatement. Even if data are available from only a single source, the erroneous information can be obvious.

EBSCO does not have any information about ISA in either its acronymic or fully spelled out version. Ulrich's has information about the ISA abstracting and indexing publication and claims that it covers 91 journals (figure 7.15). The journal base of ISA has shrunk, but not that badly. The documentation of ISA claims to abstract and index more than 300 journals. Neither is correct. There are more than 3,500 serial names in the Journal Name Finder Database for ISA (including many inconsistent versions and misspellings), which indexed and abstracted them sometime in its 35-year history. For the past few years, the number of journals covered to some extent was around 230.

Neither of the two serials directories has information about Mental Health Abstracts, and only Ulrich's includes information of Microcomputer Abstracts as an abstracting and indexing journal, although under its old title, Microcomputer Index, which changed in 1994. The title changed from Microcomputer Abstracts to Internet & Personal Computing Abstracts in early 2000, but this is not reflected in the A&I index of Ulrich's and has not prompted EBSCO to include it in its abstracting and indexing sources. One cannot help wondering about the quality control processes in updating the serials directories.

```
DIALOGWEB.              C      ▣     ⚑    $    ⊘    ?
   Command Search          new search  databases  alerts  cost  logoff  help

                            Dialog Response
                            ─────────────────

   File    Items    Total   Index-term
   480               55     AI=INDUSTRIAL HYGIENE DIGEST
   480               44     AI=INFORMATION MEDIA AND TECHNOLOGY
   480               91    *AI=INFORMATION SCIENCE ABSTRACTS
   480              870     AI=INFORMATION    SERVICE    IN    MECHANICAL
                            ENGINEERING
   480             2160     AI=INPHARMA
   480             5315     AI=INSPEC: COMPUTERS & CONTROL ABSTRACTS
   480              522     AI=INSTITUTE OF MINING & METALLURGY ABSTRACTS
   480              668     AI=INSTITUTE    OF    PAPER    CHEMISTRY    ABSTRACT
                            BULLETIN
   480                4     AI=INSTITUTE ON THE CHURCH IN URBAN INDUSTRIAL
                            SO
   480                3     AI=INT.G.CLASS.STUD.
   480              357     AI=INT.IND.MUS.PER.
   480               21     AI=INTERACTIONS BIBLIOGRAPHY
   480              351     AI=INTERNATION LABOR DOCUMENTATION
   480              126     AI=INTERNATIONAL    ABSTRACTS    IN    OPERATIONS
                            RESEARCH
```

Fig. 7.15. Number of journals indexed by ISA according to Ulrich's.

Similarly revealing is the fact that two of the commercially available serials directories cannot agree on such important issues as what are the refereed journals in a discipline. The first sign of trouble is that the directories have striking differences in the number of refereed serials in some of the disciplines. Minor differences may occur because of different classification (e.g., a refereed journal may be classified under sociology in one directory and psychology in the other). However, the differences are major even in disciplines where the classification would seem to be straightforward and unambiguous, and both directories use identical or almost identical subject terms (figure 7.16).

At first sight, the difference in the total number of journals reported as refereed (11,407 for The Serials Directory and 13,124 for Ulrich's) seems to be congruent with the difference in the total number of journals. But the numbers in the identical categories reveal odd differences. Ulrich's reports twice as many refereed journals in Oceanography and nearly three times as many in the Water Resources category as EBSCO, which in turn has 30 percent more refereed journals in Anthropology than Ulrich's.

These figures were retrieved from the fall 1997 editions of the two CD-ROM directories, and the numbers keep changing. Two years later, EBSCO had 106 refereed journals (from 127) in library and information science, while Ulrich's reported 194 titles as such (up from 131). The total number of refereed journals in Ulrich's went up from 13,124 in 1997 to more than 20,000 by the end of 2000—an unlikely growth. There are similar discrepancies in the number of refereed journals when limiting those titles by country (figure 7.17) or by publisher (figure 7.18). The numbers are the oddest for Austria, Sweden, Denmark, Norway, and Australia in the country comparison, and for John Wiley, Allerton Press, and Elsevier in the publisher comparison.

	TSD	TSD-r	ULR	ULR-r	TSD/ULR	TSD-r/ULR-r
All records	187,161	11,407	218,002	13,124	0.86	0.87
LIS	2,514	127	2,633	131	0.95	0.97
Anthropology	737	197	1,118	151	0.66	1.30
Arch(a)eology	1,090	84	1,636	135	0.67	0.62
Oceanography	409	41	603	87	0.68	0.47
Geograph$	1,037	90	1,236	112	0.84	0.80
Linguistic$	2,388	200	2,799	276	0.85	0.72
Music$	2,545	78	3,316	106	0.77	0.74
Pharmac$	1,505	180	1,762	291	0.85	0.62
Publishing	1,348	21	1,583	29	0.85	0.72
Veterinary$	734	105	619	105	1.19	1.00
Water Res$	644	24	783	65	0.82	0.37

Fig. 7.16. Significant differences in refereed journals by subject areas.

	TSD	TSD-r	ULR	ULR-r	TSD/ULR	TSD-r/ULR-r
Hungary	611	25	753	29	0.81	0.86
Portugal	284	3	602	8	0.47	0.38
Austria	789	39	1,826	17	0.43	2.29
Sweden	921	46	2,233	62	0.41	0.88
Denmark	793	74	2,700	108	0.29	0.69
Finland	786	20	870	24	0.90	0.83
Norway	425	35	1,047	26	0.41	1.35
Australia	4,350	337	6,228	257	0.70	1.31
Canada	17,912	504	9,852	379	1.82	1.33
UK	15,263	1,647	21,995	2,045	0.69	0.81
USA	88,956	5,456	81,562	6,045	1.09	0.90

Fig. 7.17. Significant differences in refereed journals by countries.

	TSD	TSD-r	ULR	ULR-r	TSD/ULR	TSD-r/ULR-r
Wiley	803	158	573	295	1.40	0.54
McGraw	671	5	558	4	1.20	1.25
Haworth	212	135	171	152	1.24	0.89
Ablex	64	8	94	13	0.68	0.62
Academic	553	157	465	222	1.19	0.71
Allerton	136	2	102	11	1.33	0.18
AMA	53	10	49	10	1.08	1.00
Blackwell	505	177	471	258	1.07	0.69
Bowker	190	3	207	1	0.92	3.00
Elsevier	1,734	927	1,748	1,364	0.99	0.68

Fig. 7.18. Significant differences in refereed journals by publishers.

Even when the two directories report an almost identical number of refereed journals in a discipline, the overlap between the two may be distressingly low, considering the importance attached to the refereed status of journals by many in academia. In the library and information science category, for example, Urlich's still does not list among the refereed ones such titles as *College & Research Libraries* (figure 7.19), *The American Archivist*, or *Library Resources & Technical Services*. Both companies claim that they get their data from the publishers. It is unlikely, however, that the publishers would report the refereed status of their journals differently on the two questionnaires.

One has to know the field well to recognize the absurdity of some titles present and others missing from the list of refereed journals. By definition, such serials as *Montana Library Directory*, and *OCLC Selected Titles* cannot be refereed journals as The Serials Directory claims (figure 7.20). Similarly, the titles that are not reported by EBSCO as refereed is stunning for a librarian, such as the omission of *Information Processing & Management*, *Information Services & Use*, *Journal of Government Information*, *Knowledge Organization*, *Research Strategies*, and *Serials Review*.

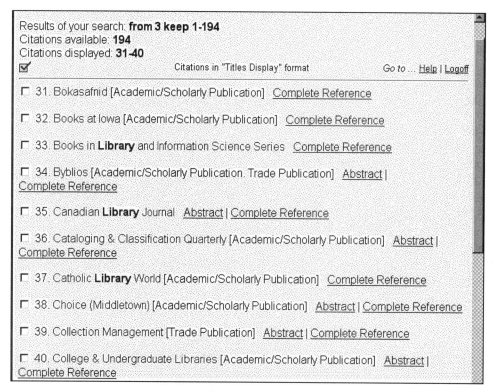

Fig. 7.19. List of refereed LIS journals in Ulrich's (excerpt).

Sometimes such lists can be compared against the most authentic list; the one compiled by the publisher. The Association for Computing Machinery (ACM) identifies 16 journals as refereed on its home page (figure 7.21). Ulrich's reports only four of them as refereed (figure 7.22). It is certainly an improvement of the situation two years ago when it listed only a single ACM journal as refereed. The Serials Directory correctly identifies only eight ACM titles as refereed, but incorrectly reports as refereed two titles: the *Communications of ACM* and *Data Base* (figure 7.23).

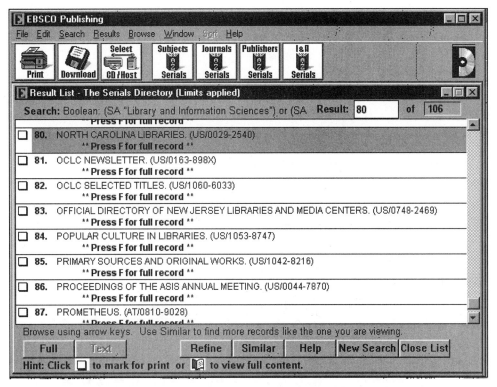

Fig. 7.20. List of refereed LIS journals in The Serials Directory (excerpt).

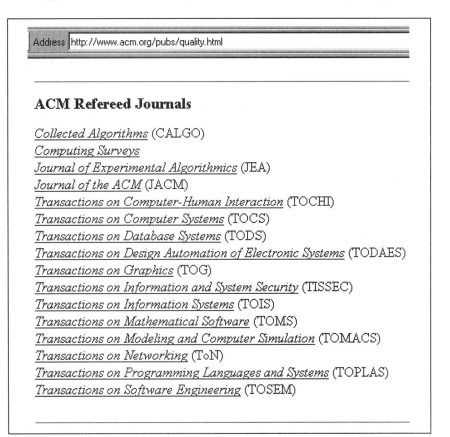

Fig. 7.21. Refereed journals of ACM as reported by ACM.

```
REFEREED JOURNALS OF ACM ULRICH'S DECEMBER, 1999
--------------------------------------------------
RANK: S3/1-4   Field: JN=  File(s): 480
(Rank fields found in 4 records -- 5 unique terms)

RANK No.   Items   Term
--------   -----   ----
     1       1     A C M  TRANSACTIONS  ON  GRAPHICS
     2       1     A C M  TRANSACTIONS  ON  MATHEMATICAL  SOFTWARE
     3       1     SHORT TITLE: T O C S
     4       1     TRANSACTIONS  ON  COMPUTER  SYSTEMS
     5       1     TRANSACTIONS  ON  DESIGN  AUTOMATION  OF  ELECTRONI
```

Fig. 7.22. Refereed journals of ACM as reported by Ulrich's.

Print	Full Text	Select Result For More Detail
□	.	ACM COMPUTING SURVEYS. (US/03600300)
□	.	ACM JOURNAL OF EXPERIMENTAL ALGORITHMICS [COMPUTER FILE].ACM JOURNAL OF EXPERIMENTAL ALGORITHMICS (US/10846654)
□	.	ACM TRANSACTIONS ON COMPUTER SYSTEMS. (US/07342071)
□	.	ACM TRANSACTIONS ON DATABASE SYSTEMS. (US/03625915)
□	.	ACM TRANSACTIONS ON GRAPHICS. (US/07300301)
□	.	ACM TRANSACTIONS ON MATHEMATICAL SOFTWARE. (US/00983500)
□	.	ACM TRANSACTIONS ON PROGRAMMING LANGUAGES AND SYSTEMS. (US/01640925)
□	.	COMMUNICATIONS OF THE ACM. (US/00010782)
□	.	DATA BASE. (US/00950033)
□	.	JOURNAL OF THE ASSOCIATION FOR COMPUTING MACHINERY. (US/00045411)

Fig. 7.23. Refereed journals of ACM as reported by The Serials Directory.

Doing a comparative search between the two directories would likely yield similar discrepancies in other disciplines as well. Such a comparison sheds some light also on two other attributes of journals that are reported as value added information by the two directories: the number of copies that a journal is circulating and the subscription price. This information is presumably collected and reported because it is used in reference, collection development, and some business decisions, such as the consideration of advertisement charges.

Obviously, they don't serve these purposes well when there are serious discrepancies between the two directories. The differences speak for themselves. Some of them can be checked easily against the information printed in the serials or made available by the publishers in their catalogs. Often neither directory is accurate. Such comparisons can be extended to other data elements as well, but these are perhaps the most important ones.

Occasionally, it is the database publisher that introduces inaccuracies in a database. This is the reason for one of the oddest, large-scale mistakes in the DIALOG implementation of Ulrich's. Searching for the journal titles that start with *Excerpta Medica*, one of the largest abstracting and indexing services, retrieves 49 journals such as *Excerpta Medica*, Section 16: Cancer. However, searching for journals that are indexed and abstracted by *Excerpta Medica* yields zero results (figure 7.24). On processing input, the database designer must have specified the misspelled words *Exerta Medica* to replace the original code (say, EXM). That's why there are 5,654 records under the misspelled entry (figure 7.25). The Ovid version of Ulrich's lists the name of the abstracting and indexing service correctly for 5,630 records (figure 7.26).

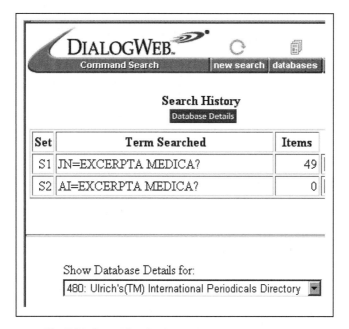

**Fig. 7.24. Searching for journals that are abstracted
and indexed by *Excerpta Medica* on DIALOG.**

```
E5      5654   AI=EXERTA MEDICA
E6         1   AI=EXERTA MEDICA (UNTIL 1983)
E7        20   AI=EXERTA MEDICA (UNTIL 1992)
E8         1   AI=EXERTA MEDICA (UNTIL 1992; 1994- )
E9         2   AI=EXERTA MEDICA (UNTIL 1992; 1995- )
E10       50   AI=EXERTA MEDICA (UNTIL 1993)
E11        2   AI=EXERTA MEDICA (UNTIL 1993; 1996- )
E12        2   AI=EXERTA MEDICA (UNTIL 1994)
E13      205   AI=EXERTA MEDICA (1993- )
E14      124   AI=EXERTA MEDICA (1994- )
E15      120   AI=EXERTA MEDICA (1995- )
E16      106   AI=EXERTA MEDICA (1996- )
E17      150   AI=EXPLORATION AND PRODUCTION HEALTH, SAFETY AND
E18      127   AI=EXTRAMED
E19      120   AI=FABABEAN ABSTRACTS
E20        1   AI=FAM.IND..
E21      780   AI=FAMILY INDEX
E22       45   AI=FAMILY MEDICINE LITERATURE INDEX
E23        1   AI=FAMILY MEDICINE LITERATURE INDEX (1980-1992)
```

**Fig. 7.25. Erroneously coded abstracting and indexing
service name in DIALOG's version of Ulrich's.**

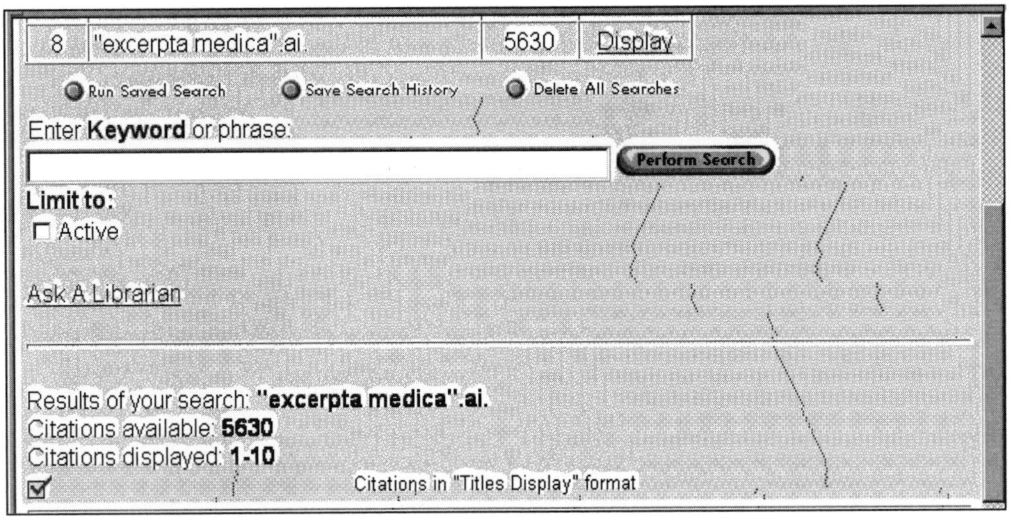

Fig. 7.26. Correctly coded *Excerpta Medica* in Ovid's version of Ulrich's.

In database directories, some inaccuracies are immediately obvious for a practitioner, as in the case with the record about the Social SciSearch database in the World Databases directory. If it were indeed updated by 780,00 records every week, it would double its size in about 15 weeks. This type of error is prevalent in the exceptionally inferior World Databases directory.

For the uninitiated, inaccuracies are simply pinpointed when comparing essential information such as database size, update frequency, update volume, hourly rate, cost per printing, or license price of the database between two databases (figure 7.27).

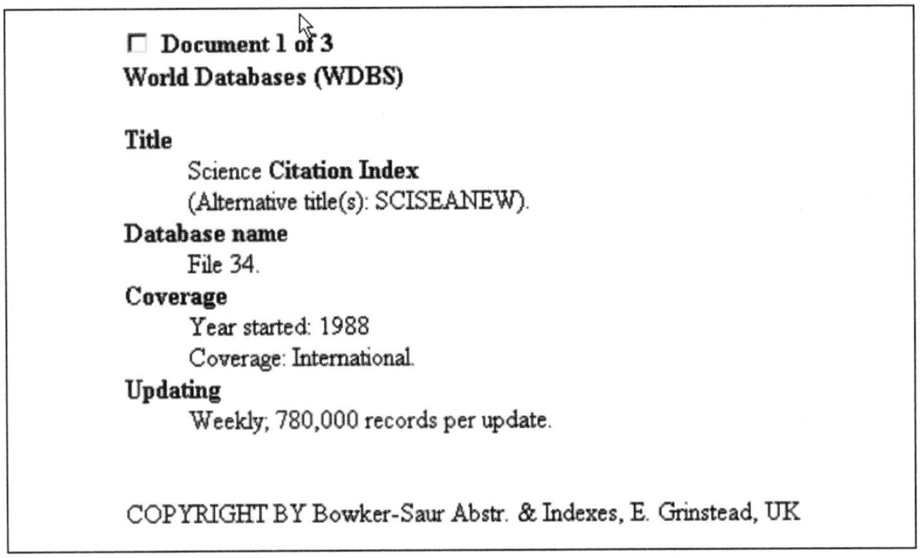
Document 1 of 3
World Databases (WDBS)

Title
Science **Citation Index**
(Alternative title(s): SCISEANEW).
Database name
File 34.
Coverage
Year started: 1988
Coverage: International.
Updating
Weekly; 780,000 records per update.

COPYRIGHT BY Bowker-Saur Abstr. & Indexes, E. Grinstead, UK

Fig. 7.27. Obvious inaccuracy in World Databases of G. K. Saur.

Sometimes, inaccuracies cannot be blamed on the publishers of the directory, as they appear incorrectly in the primary source. It caused some problems for librarians when Sage Publications identified the February 1999 issue of *Journal of Contemporary Ethnography* as the first number of the volume, when the journal itself claimed to be published in April, July, October, and January (figure 7.28). It just added further to the confusion that Sage plans to publish six issues a year, but because its commitment to this frequency is not firm, libraries were not advised (figure 7.29).

From: Jeanette Skwor   **To:** SERIALST@LIST.UVM.EDU
Subject: Journal of Contemporary Ethnography

Subject: Journal of Contemporary Ethnography

I am not having a good day.

The February issue of this title was on my Problem Pile with a note from my
student, that the month does not match the pattern. So I looked inside,
and found: "Published four times annually -- in April, July, October and
January."

What are others doing with it, and if I stop banging my head against the
wall now will the pain go away?

Jeanette Skwor
Cofrin Library
UW-Green Bay
SKWORJ@GBMS01.UWGB.EDU

Fig. 7.28. E-mail regarding confusing chronological designation.

From: Sarah Peaden, Serials   **To:** SERIALST@LIST.UVM.EDU
Subject: Re: Journal of Contemporary Ethnography

I called Sage Publications and was told that "Journal of Contemporary
Ethnography" had been upgraded to a bimonthly publication as 1999. So,
February is the first issue for this year. However, when I asked if
Sage would be sending out a letter informing its subscribers of this
change, the operator did not know. While she was helping me, I heard
her murmur that Sage's computers had not been completely updated to show
the new months. I hope this helps. Please stop banging your head
against the wall. Instead, make a bulls eye for the different
publishers that do this and throw darts at it. ;)

Fig. 7.29. E-mail regarding erroneous information by Sage about frequency in one of its publications.

Libraries and information professionals feel the burden to be held responsible for information that they dispense to their patrons. Using either Ulrich's International Periodicals Directory or The Serials Directory to verify the refereed status of journals in a dispute over tenure application is irresponsible. Making cancellation decisions based on the information provided by these two databases, regarding which abstracting and indexing journals cover certain serials, is equally irresponsible. Not finding in a database some of the works of a potential candidate for a position because her name is more often misspelled than correctly spelled may have an impact on the hiring decision. Providing obviously bad data for thousands of databases in World Databases to customers is akin to medical malpractice. Charging premium prices for such data is immoral.

Many librarians are very vocal in criticizing free Web databases for their deficiencies. They are right to do so, but they should know that respected traditional information providers from ritzy corporate headquarters often deliver far more deficient databases for nifty fees. Compiling databases of accurate information costs a lot of money that few content providers are willing to pay.

H. W. Wilson is one of the few companies in the information industry that has been especially keen on verifying their information and correcting wrong information retrospectively if errors or changes are detected. It is certainly more expensive than hiring PR mavericks and spin doctors who sell snake oil and can find excuses and explanations for many of the shortcomings of their databases.

These practices don't help the librarians who are sometimes the end-users themselves or face the end-users directly. Large-scale and serious inaccuracies in expensive databases are among their worst enemies. They should be detected first, then the providers should be confronted.

Format and Content Consistency

In a perfect world, almost every data element would be entered into a database using a controlled vocabulary or some standard list. Even then, there would be differences among the databases in terms of the format and content of personal and corporate names, journal names, or descriptors, but at least *within* a database the spelling of words, abbreviations of journal titles, and company names could be predictable. In turn, this would facilitate users finding every article taken from a journal, all references to a company, and all mention of famous and infamous persons who make the news in a variety of transliterated forms. Just think of the variations for the leader of Libya, the prime minister of Thailand, or the capital of North Korea.

Some of these variations are due to changes in transliteration rules. They could be controlled using cross-references in a browsable list. Indeed, such solutions work fine with the CD-ROM versions of the H. W. Wilson database family or with PAIS, and to a lesser extent with the databases of EBSCO. In the online world, however, there are usually no cross-references from one format of a name to another—with the exception of descriptors in those few databases whose thesaurus has been implemented online. (The quality of indexing, including indexing consistency, is discussed in Chapter 10. Consistency in covering journals and other types of documents is discussed in Chapter 5 about source coverage.)

Establishing consistency is especially needed in databases that use many different source documents that often have their own in-house standard. One may assume that the *Washington Post* has such a standard; therefore, within that single online file, the names of countries, persons, movements, and companies appear consistently. However, the producer of an aggregate indexing, abstracting, or full-text database (such as the Gale Group, Bell & Howell, and EBSCO) needs to standardize these names and assign them consistently to the records created from thousands of newspapers, journals, and magazines. Many datafile producers may have an authority list on paper, but data entry is apparently not checked against the items on those authority lists.

H. W. Wilson is one of the very few content providers that achieve an almost impeccable level of consistency. Interestingly, a free Web-born database, the Internet Movie Database, is another "squeaky-clean" and consistent resource that also provides cross-references from title variations and pseudonyms. It is done in a way that should be taught in fine schools.

Just like misspellings and other inaccurate data elements, inconsistency is likely to result in missing highly relevant items when searching in a database. Users who apply defensive search strategies may minimize the impact of inconsistency, but it takes time to browse and search around for variants, and it costs money to do so time and again, especially in systems that still base part of their charges on connect time. Many of the information retrieval systems don't provide adequate browsing options that could alleviate some of the problems of inconsistency.

Browsing around and searching the field-specific indexes (author index, publisher index, journal name index) will shed light on inconsistencies. Systems that offer only a lump index to browse, such as the DOS version of SilverPlatter, hide the inconsistencies. It doesn't help to have index entries generated from a number of fields without distinctive prefixes that would identify the data element from which the entry was taken. It harms users when they cannot browse the language, document type, and country of publication indexes.

For example, in Sociological Abstracts the name of the language is *Romanian* (figure 8.1a), while the country of publication is *Rumania* (figure 8.1b), and the descriptor for the country is *Romania* (from 1985 onward) and *Rumania* (until 1984). Neither is incorrect, but the entries are certainly inconsistent, and in the DOS version of SilverPlatter, you would never know about them. Luckily, in the DIALOG version of the databases (and in most others, too), the language and country indexes can be looked up. Some of the online thesauri can be consulted to find the preferred subject terms and the broader, narrower, and related terms (figure 8.1c).

```
┌──────────────────────────────────────────────────────────────────────┐
│   │new search│databases│ alerts │cost│logoff│help│                    │
│                           Dialog Response                              │
│                         ───────────────────                           │
│                                                                        │
│  Ref   File   Items   Total   Index-term                               │
│  E1     37            2606    LA=PORTUGUESE                            │
│  E2     37            2952    LA=ROMAN                                 │
│  E3     37             608   *LA=ROMANIAN                             │
│  E4     37            7216    LA=RUSSIAN                               │
│  E5     37            1105    LA=SERBIAN                               │
│  E6     37            4057    LA=SERBO                                 │
│  E7     37            1105    LA=SERBO-CROATIAN WITH CYRILLIC ALPHABET/SERB-│
│                                IAN                                     │
│  E8     37            2952    LA=SERBO-CROATIAN WITH ROMAN ALPHABET/CROATIAN│
└──────────────────────────────────────────────────────────────────────┘
```

Fig. 8.1a. Language index terms in Sociological Abstracts.

```
                        Dialog Response

        Ref   File   Items   Total   Index-term
        E1     37             238    CP=RICA
        E2     37             248    CP=RICO
        E3     37             530   *CP=RUMANIA
        E4     37            1946    CP=RUSSIA
        E5     37              55    CP=SALVADOR
```

Fig. 8.1b. Country of publication index terms in Sociological Abstracts.

```
        Dialog Response


  Total  Type  RT   Index-term
   535          5  *ROMANIA
     0    S          (FORMERLY   (1964-1985)   DC  397650,
                     RUMANIA/R...)
   333    F    1    RUMANIA
   116    B    8    BALKAN STATES
  1166    B    12   EASTERN EUROPE
    12    N    2    BUCHAREST, ROMANIA
```

Fig. 8.1c. Descriptor terms in Sociological Abstracts' thesaurus.

Although DIALOG offers many field-specific browsable indexes, there is no separate descriptor index to browse, such as DE=, which would help users choose the right terms (especially when the thesaurus is not implemented online to provide guidance) and learn about inaccuracies and inconsistencies. On the other hand, Ovid makes every feasible indexed data element browsable and, uniquely, allows the user to create on-the-fly combined indexes. For example, in the Ovid version of Sociological Abstracts, the user can create a combined index of the language, country of publication, and the descriptor field indexes. In the results list, the variant terms for the language, country of publication, and descriptor will be interfiled.

Browsing the author index in every database will give a feel for the level of inconsistency. Often, misspellings and inconsistent spellings are filed near each other. In its Ulrich's database, Bowker uses a number of inconsistent formats for its own name (figure 8.2). Some of the variants are legitimate, but many just show the lack of a corporate name authority file—and some care. Note that there were many more variants (such as R. R. Bowker, RR Bowker, and R R Bowker) several years ago, which by now have mostly been eliminated.

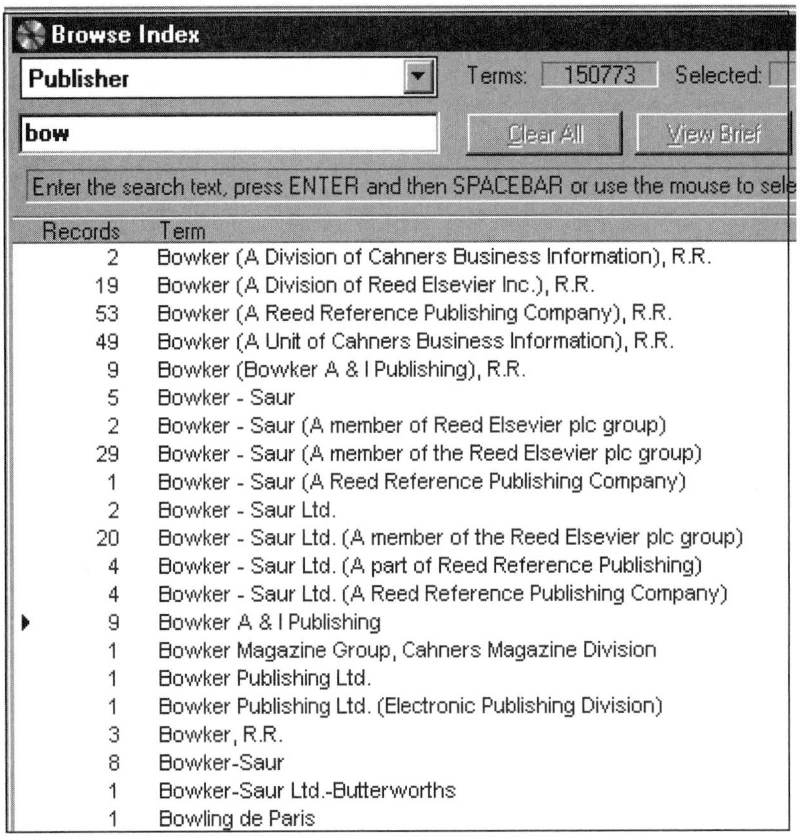

Fig. 8.2. Congregating variants for Bowker in a Bowker database.

When inconsistent entries are not adjacent, the user may miss the majority of the records that include the name searched for. Once the user spots the entry John Wiley & Sons, Inc., in the publisher index of Ulrich's (figure 8.3), chances are she will not also try the section starting with Wiley, thus losing hundreds of records that appear under one of these variants of the British, Australian, and American arms of the conglomerate (figure 8.4).

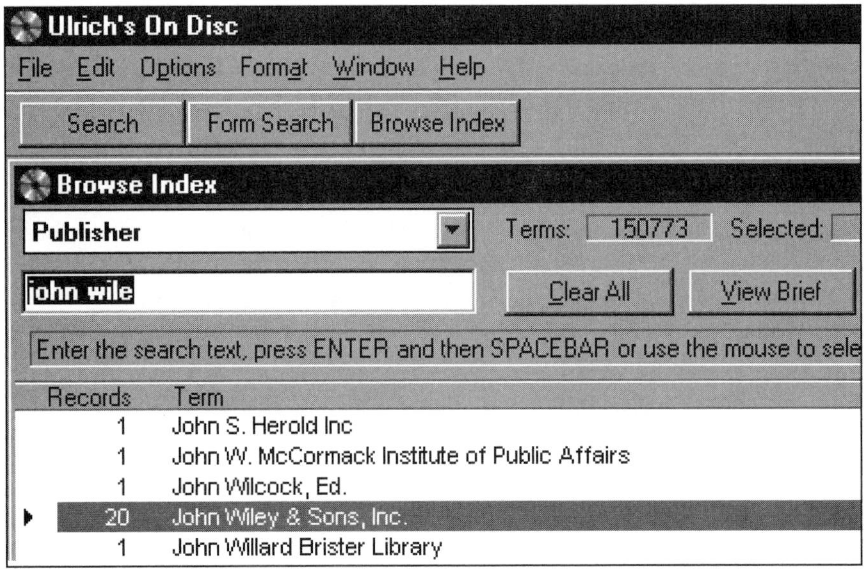

Fig. 8.3. Items under John Wiley & Sons, Inc., in Ulrich's.

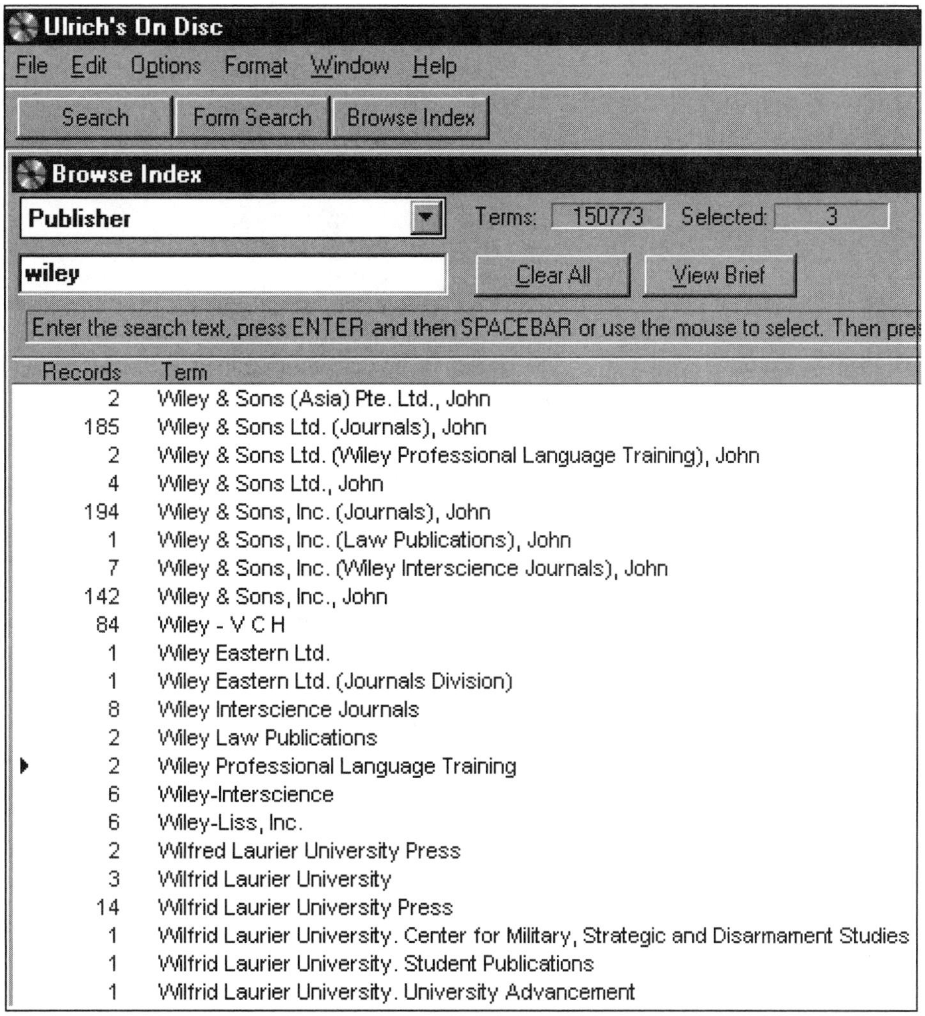

Fig. 8.4. Hundreds more items under Wiley & Sons, Inc. in Ulrich's.

Searching for scattered entries in the journal name field is much facilitated in DIALOG by the Journal Name Finder database, which creates both word- and phrase-indexed entries from the journal name fields of the databases. Savvy searchers can use a search such as SELECT news AND world AND report to find variants of the popular magazine in different databases. It is not encouraging that the ERIC database alone uses three formats for the 37 articles it included from this newsweekly. Other databases also have their share of variants, such as the Transportation Research Information Services database (File 63 in DIALOG) (figure 8.5).

Inconsistencies can originate from the different primary sources that have different policies—for example, for the second and third middle initials of authors. The authors themselves may have used them inconsistently in different publications. The beauty of the H. W. Wilson Name Authority File is that it collocates under one entry the works of the authors even if they or the primary sources are not spelling their name consistently or correctly.

A relatively systematic way to gauge the problem is to browse the author name index and to look for prefixed Dutch and German last names such as Van Brakel or Von Seggern, and then try to find variations under the names that make the prefix a suffix. A quick check tells you a lot about how consistently a file producer may handle personal names.

```
FILE      RECORD   JOURNAL
NUMBER    COUNT    NAME
------    ------   --------------------------

18        3975     US NEWS & WORLD REPORT
18        275      U.S. NEWS & WORLD REPORT
63        23       US NEWS AND WORLD REPORT
63        1        US NEWS & WORLD REPORT
63        1        U.S. NEWS AND WORLD REPORT,
63        1        U.S. NEWS & WORLD REPORT.
149       2082     U.S. NEWS & WORLD REPORT
485       432      US NEWS & WORLD REPORT
485       379      U.S. NEWS & WORLD REPORT
570       101      US NEWS & WORLD REPORT
570       727      U.S. NEWS & WORLD REPORT
1         16       U.S. NEWS AND WORLD REPORT
1         17       U.S. NEWS & WORLD REPORT
1         2        U. S. NEWS & WORLD REPORT
```

Fig. 8.5. Variant formats for *U.S. News & World Report*.

It is quite disappointing that in LISA there are so many spelling variants for personal names. Take, as an example, Pieter van Brakel who is listed under the letter *V* 41 times in four different spelling variants, and under the letter *B* 30 times in three variants (figure 8.6). ISA has the name listed 31 times under *V* in two formats and only once under the letter *B*. LibLit—not surprisingly— has all of its 58 postings for Pieter van Brakel under the letter *B* in a single format. The same pattern shows up in many other test searches.

The Getty Name Authority File shows how idiosyncrasies in different sources can be handled through controlled vocabulary by providing cross-references from the variant name formats to the standard one preferred by the Getty databases (figure 8.7).

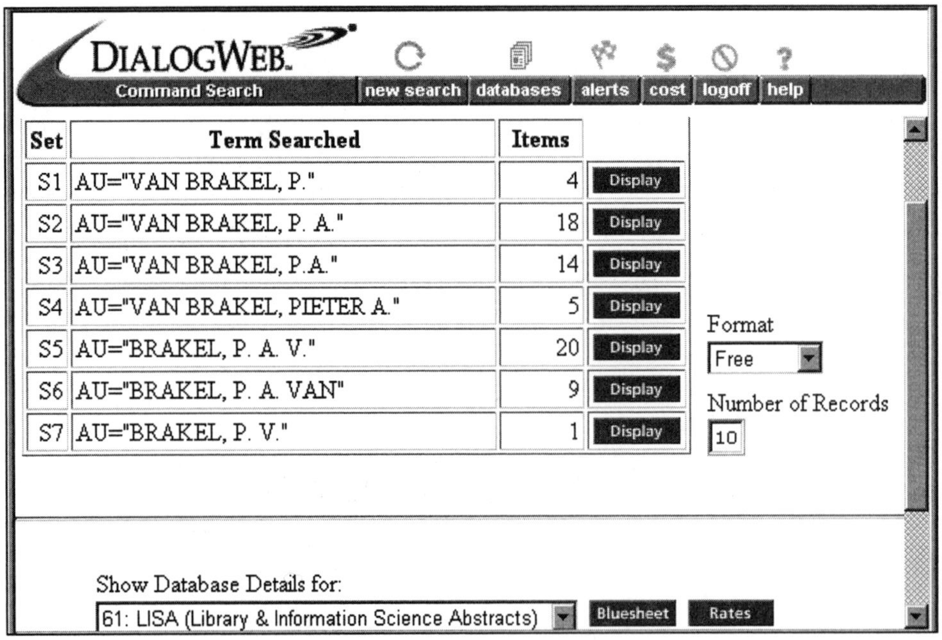

Fig. 8.6. Severe inconsistency in the author index in LISA.

```
┌──────────┐
│   New    │
│  Search  │   GETTY VOCABULARY PROGRAM          calendar c
└──────────┘                                         retu
                                                Getty Research Ins


                                                ULAN Name Record


Bosch, Hieronymus (Hieronymus van Aken)    [BA,GC,PR]
   (Netherlandish painter, ca.1450-1516)                    [PR]
   (Netherlands artist, op.1474-m.1516)                     [WC]
   (North Netherlandish painter, ca.1450-d.1516)            [GC]
   (early Netherlandish painter, ca.1450-1516)              [BA]
      Aeken, Hieronymus van                                 [BA]
      Aken, Hieronymus van                                  [BA]
      Ambrosius Bosch                                       [PR]
      Bosch                                                 [PR]
      Bosch, Hieronymous                                    [PR]
      Bosch, Hieronymous (Hieronymus van Aken)              [PR]
      Bosch, Hieronymus                                     [GC,PR]
      Bosch, Hieronymus (Hieronymus or Jerome van Aken)     [WC]
      Bosch, Jerome                                         [PR]
      Hieronymous Bosch                                     [PR]
      Hieronymus Bosch                                      [PR]
      Hieronymus van Aken                                   [PR]
      J. Bos                                                [PR]
      Jer. Bos                                              [PR]
      Jeronimus Bosch                                       [PR]

Bibliography:
 *Encyc. world art; *Friedländer, Early Neth. ptg.;
    *Kindlers Malerei Lex.; *RILA/BHA; *Thieme-Becker
```

Fig. 8.7. Excerpt from the exemplary Getty Name Authority File.

Journal names are even more inconsistently entered than author names because of the possibilities of the use of acronyms versus fully spelled out versions of issuing bodies, abbreviations for many of the title words, the haphazard inclusion and omission of subtitles, the inconsistent dropping of *and* and *of*, or their replacement by the ampersand (&) and the hyphen (-) characters, not to mention tinkering with the publication place qualifiers to distinguish two otherwise identical journal titles. The seemingly utterly simple title *Database* shows up in a great variety within the same database, PASCAL (figure 8.8).

No database can compete with the inconsistencies and inaccuracies in the journal name field of the PASCAL database published by the French Center for Scientific Research. In this author's estimate, there is an average of 4.3 title variants and typos (excluding the legitimate abbreviations) for every title. This ratio can be achieved by having a dozen variants for longer titles, as illustrated by the *Bulletin of the American Society for Information Science* (figure 8.9) and the *Journal of the American Oil Chemists' Society* (figures 8.10a and 8.10b). In the former example, most of the entries are fairly close, but for the second title the entries are widely scattered. They are listed continuously only for the sake of limiting the list to one page in this book. (It's fortunate that the word *oil* cannot be abbreviated to spawn another dozen or so title variants.)

Search History
Database Details

Set	Term Searched	Items	
S1	JN="DATABASE"	38	Display
S2	JN="DATABASE (U.S.)"	1	Display
S3	JN="DATABASE (USA)"	3	Display
S4	JN="DATABASE (WESTON)"	2	Display
S5	JN="DATABASE (WESTON, CONN.)"	3	Display
S6	JN="DATABASE : (WEST.)"	1	Display
S7	JN="DATABASE : (WESTON)"	1	Display

Fig. 8.8. Variations for the journal title *Database* from a single database, PASCAL.

```
            DIALOG(R)File 414 :Dialog Journal Name Finder(TM)
                 (c) 1999 The Dialog Corp. All rts. reserv.

  FILE     RECORD   JOURNAL
  NUMBER   COUNT    NAME
  ------   ------   ---------------------------------------------

  144      250      BULLETIN OF THE AMERICAN SOCIETY FOR INFORMATI
  144      1        BULL. AMER. SOC. INFORM. SOC.
  144      130      BULL. AMER. SOC. INFORM. SCI.
  144      244      BULL. AM. SOC. INF. SCI.
```

Fig. 8.9. Variations for a longer journal title within PASCAL (adjacent entries).

```
          DIALOG(R)File 414 :Dialog Journal Name Finder(TM)
               (c) 1999 The Dialog Corp. All rts. reserv.

  FILE     RECORD   JOURNAL
  NUMBER   COUNT    NAME
  ------   ------   --------------------------------------------

  144      1        JOURNAL OF THE AMERICAN OIL CHEMITS'SOCIETY.
  144      2        JOURNAL OF THE AMERICAN OIL CHEMITS' SOCIETY.
  144      1        JOURNAL OF THE AMERICAN OIL CHEMISTS'SOCIETY.
  144      49       JOURNAL OF THE AMERICAN OIL CHEMISTS' SOCIETY.
  144      3450     JOURNAL OF THE AMERICAN OIL CHEMISTS' SOCIETY
  144      1        JOURNAL OF THE AMERICAN OIL CHEMISTS' SOC.
  144      379      JAOCS, J. AM. OIL CHEM. SOC.
  144      547      JAOCS - J. AM. OIL CHEM. SOC.
  144      2        J. AMER. OIL. CHEMISTS'SOC.
  144      17       J. AMER. OIL. CHEMISTS' SOC.
  144      1        J. AMER. OIL. CHEMISTS' SOC
  144      75       J. AMER. OIL CHEMISTS'SOC.
  144      2        J. AMER. OIL CHEMISTS'SOC
```

Fig. 8.10a. Variations for a longer journal title within PASCAL (scattered entries).

```
144      2       J. AMER. OIL CHEMISTS'SOC
144      2       J. AMER. OIL CHEMISTS'S SOC.
144      1       J. AMER. OIL CHEMISTS'. SOC.
144      1       J. AMER. OIL CHEMISTS' SOC.,
144      1235    J. AMER. OIL CHEMISTS' SOC.
144      9       J. AMER. OIL CHEMISTS' SOC
144      1       J. AMER. OIL CHEMISTS/ SOC.
144      1       J. AMER. OIL CHEMISTS. SOC.
144      9       J. AMER. OIL CHEMISTS SOC.
144      2       J. AMER. OIL CHEMISTRS' SOC.
144      59      J. AMER. OIL CHEMIST'S SOC.
144      5       J. AMER. OIL CHEMIST' SOC.
144      5       J. AMER OIL CHEMISTS' SOC.
144      1       J. AMER OIL CHEMISTS SOC.
144      4       J. AM. OIL. CHEM. SOC.
144      1       J. AM. OIL CHEMISTS SOC.
144      3807    J. AM. OIL CHEM. SOC.
144      1       J. AM. OIL CHEM SOC.
144      1       J. AM OIL CHEM. SOC.
144      22      AM. OIL CHEM. SOC.
```

Fig. 8.10b. Variations for a longer journal title within PASCAL [continued].

Even in a smaller database with far fewer journals than in PASCAL, the scatter can easily make users miss a variantly spelled journal name and miss a large percentage of the records from the journal under that entry version. For example, in ISA there is the journal name *MIS Quarterly* and *Management Information Systems Quarterly* (figure 8.11). The more commonly used name has far fewer records than the name that is less likely to be searched for and that is used in most of the other databases sporadically.

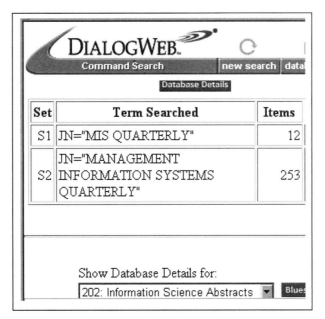

**Fig. 8.11. Scatter of posting between two
nonadjacent forms of journal names.**

Inconsistencies can also show up in such seemingly simple fields as document types. Periodical Abstracts PlusText is not the only database that assigned a different document type to installments of the same column ("Péter's Picks and Pans") , as shown in figure 8.12.

```
                          Dialog Response
              ──────────────────────────────────────


Adding title to results...
DOCUMENT TYPES FOR PETER'S PICKS AND PANS COLUMN FILE 484
------------------------------------------------------------
RANK: S2/1-11   Field: DT=  File(s): 484
(Rank fields found in 11 records -- 4 unique terms)

RANK No.  Items  Term
--------  -----  ----
      3      3   COMMENTARY
      2      6   FEATURE
      1     11   PERIODICALS
      4      2   PRODUCT REVIEW-COMPARATIVE
              ---end of results---
```

Fig. 8.12. Inconsistently assigned document types to the same column.

Completeness

Inconsistencies in databases can represent problems for searchers. Inaccuracies can have serious consequences. Incompleteness can be lethal for a search. Inconsistencies and inaccuracies are visible. Incompleteness—that is, when one or more taken-for-granted data elements often used to filter a search are missing from a large number of records— by definition is not visible. Sometimes the help file warns the user about incompleteness; sometimes the savvy user can explore incompleteness in a database, but often no one knows about it. Errors of commission may be visible to the naked eye; errors of omission obviously are not. Yet, they can drastically distort results without the user even being aware of it.

Despite their serious implications, errors of omission have not been discussed to the same extent as errors of commission. Basch (1990a) states that omissions or blank (empty) fields often cause searchers to miss relevant records. Quint (1989) says they result in misleading and costly output when results are sorted by data elements that are not present in all the records. This may be even less apparent for users who do not realize that sorting the output by publication year will simply throw out those records that have no value in the publication year field. Tenopir (1992, 1995) warns repeatedly about the dangers of missing data elements. Jacsó (1993b) shows the extent of incompleteness in several databases of good reputation, as well as the methods of exploring the volume of omissions.

The problem is aggravated by the widely touted advantage of electronic databases over their printed counterparts; namely that they can be searched by a variety of data elements not available in the print version. It is true, but it is also true that search you may, but find you may not, as in the case of massive omissions. For example, serials can be searched in the Ulrich's Plus database by Library of Congress classification code. It is proudly listed as an access point in the Bowker's product catalog, and it is displayed prominently on the search template. What the naïve user would not know is that only 43,118 of the 226,276 records (19 percent) are assigned this code (figure 9.1). It should not be offered as an access point, as using it automatically restricts the search to a fifth of the database.

When this very significant omission was brought up by this author in a conference presentation, a then-representative of Bowker argued that few users would search by LC classification code or use it as a filter. This is unlikely. All university libraries and many special libraries use the LC classification code instead of the Dewey code (which, by the way, is available in every record). It would be much better to be forthcoming and indicate clearly on the search screen or at least in the help file that only 19 percent of the records have this code. At least in the CD-ROM version of the database published by Bowker, the extent of omission can be discovered by a search, as illustrated in figure 9.1.

However, in implementations that put the two classification codes in the same field, or don't allow full truncation searching of prefixed indexes, this deficiency remains hidden. The results of searches by LC classification code grossly mislead the users. In the DIALOG version, the LC and Dewey classification codes were merged into one index; therefore, not even the savvy searcher would be able to find out how unacceptably incomplete the records are.

The extent of missing price and circulation data in Ulrich's is also a warning sign for not searching by these data elements even when you are enticed to do so by the publicity blurb of Bowker. Price is not searchable in the DIALOG version. Although the publisher field is absent in "only" less than 10,000 records in Ulrich's, it is odd because the data are supposedly provided by publishers of the journals, so this data element should be readily available.

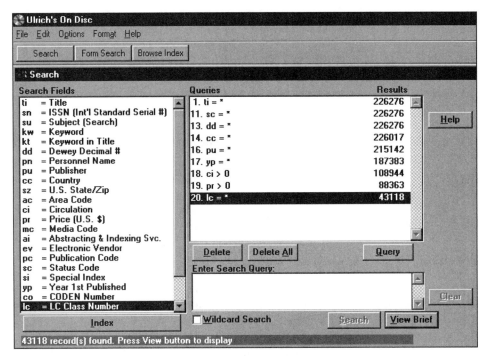

Fig. 9.1. Massive omission of LC classification data in Ulrich's Plus.

Most of the databases omit taken-for-granted data elements, although few of them to the extent just illustrated. Still, it is discomforting to see that the file producer and the database publisher do not warn you that ERIC does not have the document type field for 28 percent of its records; Compendex for 32 percent; NTIS for 72 percent (figure 9.2); Packaging Science and Technology for 78 percent; and GeoArchive for 90 percent (figure 9.3). Even seemingly small-scale omissions of data elements may be very significant in the case of mega databases. In AGRICOLA, 5 percent of the records do not have a language field, which does not sound that bad until you realize that this is a 4-million record database, so the omissions exclude almost 200,000 records if someone limits the search by language.

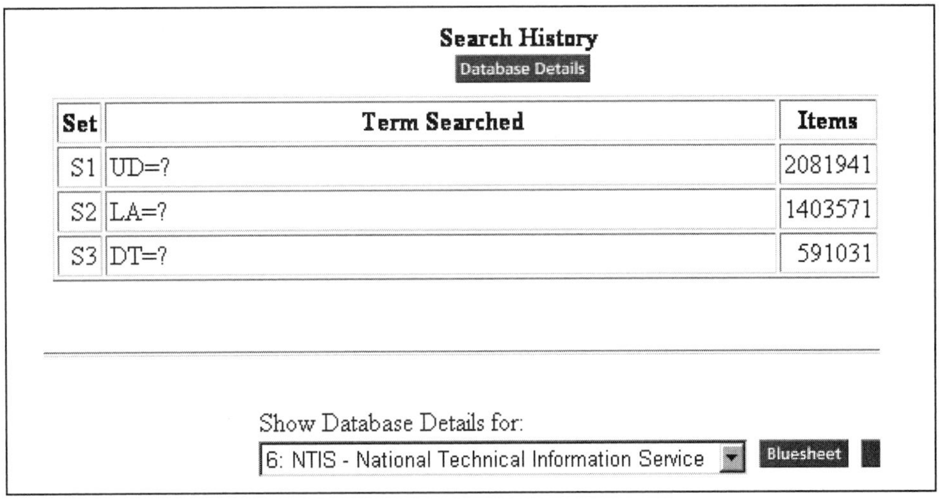

Search History
Database Details

Set	Term Searched	Items
S1	UD=?	2081941
S2	LA=?	1403571
S3	DT=?	591031

Show Database Details for:
6: NTIS - National Technical Information Service   Bluesheet

Fig. 9.2. Omission of document type field without any explanation in NTIS.

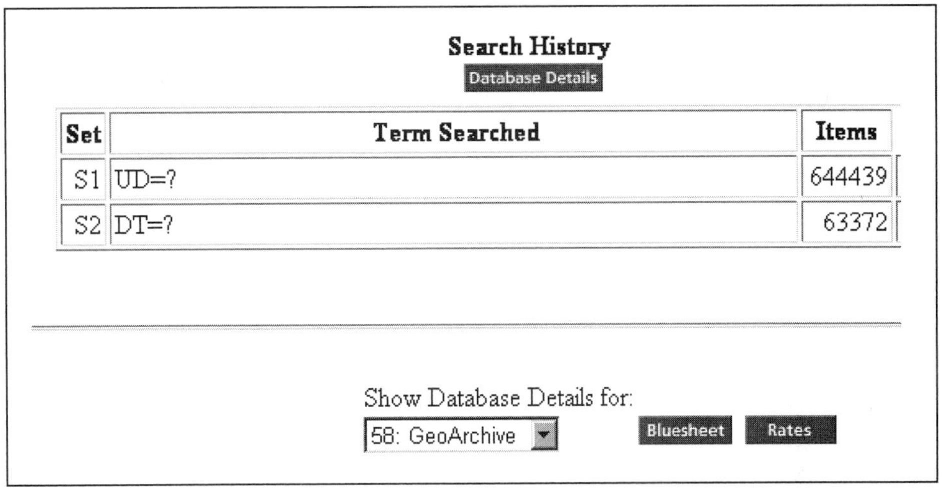

Search History
Database Details

Set	Term Searched	Items
S1	UD=?	644439
S2	DT=?	63372

Show Database Details for:
58: GeoArchive   Bluesheet   Rates

Fig. 9.3. Omission of document type field without any explanation in GeoArchive.

The three library and information science databases (figure 9.4) fare pretty well in providing such often-used search criteria as publication year, language, and document type. (LISA does not promise document type, so its zero posting is acceptable, although it is a very lamentable design concept.) As shown in figure 9.5, PsycINFO also does well, but Mental Health Abstracts has document type for only 82,133 of its 513,017 records (16 percent). The language field in this database is also absent for almost 90 percent of the records, but this is understandable once you know that the in-house policy is not to assign English as a language. It is another question that the DIALOG bluesheet of MHA uses LA=ENGLISH as a search example (figure 9.6), which—not surprisingly—yields zero results (figure 9.7). While one can sympathize with the producer of this file to have struggled so fiercely with spelling this word correctly (figure 9.8), users should be warned about the policy of giving up assigning English as a language.

Set	Term Searched	Items	File
S1	UD=?	609082	
S1	UD=?	195544	438
S1	UD=?	207262	202
S1	UD=?	206276	61
S2	PY=?	600522	
S2	PY=?	195544	438
S2	PY=?	205814	202
S2	PY=?	199164	61
S3	LA=?	597128	
S3	LA=?	189176	438
S3	LA=?	207261	202
S3	LA=?	200691	61
S4	DT=?	394923	
S4	DT=?	187661	438
S4	DT=?	207262	202
S4	DT=?	0	61

Fig. 9.4. Checking the presence of fields in LIS databases.

Search History
Database Details

Set	Term Searched	Items	File
S1	UD=?	2093197	
S1	UD=?	513017	86
S1	UD=?	1580180	11
S2	PY=?	2092586	
S2	PY=?	512457	86
S2	PY=?	1580129	11
S3	LA=?	1636034	
S3	LA=?	55854	86
S3	LA=?	1580180	11
S4	DT=?	1662313	
S4	DT=?	82133	86
S4	DT=?	1580180	11

Fig. 9.5. Checking the presence of fields in PsycINFO and MHA.

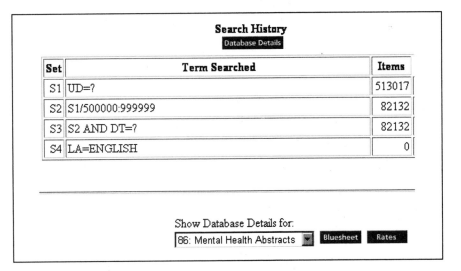

ADDITIONAL INDEXES [return to top]

SEARCH PREFIX	DISPLAY CODE	FIELD NAME	INDEXING	SELECT EXAMPLES
None	AN	DIALOG Accession Number		
AN=	AN	NIMH Accession Number [2]	Phrase	S AN=APA1968-06726
AU=	AU	Author	Phrase	S AU=SCOTT, K.S.
BN=	BN	International Standard Book Number (ISBN) [5]	Phrase	S BN=0-02-904330-1
CC=	None	Contractor Code [3]	Phrase	S CC=HIS
None	CP	Country of Publication		
CS=	CS	Corporate Source	Word	S CS=(HOFFMAN(W)LA(W)ROCHE)
DT=	DT	Document Type [4,5]	Phrase	S DT=JOURNAL
JN=	JN	Journal Name [5,6]	Phrase	S JN=HUMAN RELATIONS?
LA=	LA	Language	Phrase	S LA=ENGLISH
PY=	None	Publication Year	Phrase	S PY=1997
None	RF	Number of References		
SN=	SN	International Standard Serial Number (ISSN) [5]	Phrase	S SN=0018-7267
SO=	SO	Source Information [7]	Word	S SO=(HUMAN(W)RELATIONS)
UD=	None	Update	Phrase	S UD=9999

[3] Only NIMH records (1969-1982).

[4] Also searchable as /ID.

[5] Only IFI records (1983+).

Fig. 9.6. Excerpt from the bluesheet of MHA.

Search History
Database Details

Set	Term Searched	Items
S1	UD=?	513017
S2	S1/500000:999999	82132
S3	S2 AND DT=?	82132
S4	LA=ENGLISH	0

Show Database Details for:
86: Mental Health Abstracts | Bluesheet | Rates

Fig. 9.7. No record with English in the language field in MHA.

The PsycINFO database is among the highest quality databases, and it is no surprise that a test in its Ovid version (figure 9.9) shows that all 1,594,013 records had a document type field. The population field also used to be a field that had either the term *human* or the term *animal*, but a current test reveals that 20 percent of the records do not have this data element.

databases	alerts	cost	logoff	help		
E5	86			1	LA=E NGLISH	
E6	86			1	LA=EEN	
E7	86			2	LA=EGLISH	
E8	86			3	LA=EGNLISH	
E9	86			2	LA=EIGLISH	
E10	86			4	LA=EINGLISH	
E11	86			1	LA=EMGLISH	
E12	86			1	LA=ENBLISH	
E13	86			5	LA=ENG	
E14	86			1	LA=ENGIISH	
E15	86			24	LA=ENGISH	
E16	86			1	LA=ENGLAIH	
E17	86			25	LA=ENGLAND	
E18	86			1	LA=ENGLIAH	
E19	86			2	LA=ENGLIDH	
E20	86			2	LA=ENGLIGH	
E21	86			1	LA=ENGLIISH	
E22	86			1	LA=ENGLILSH	
E23	86			3	LA=ENGLIS	
E24	86			5	LA=ENGLISH ENGLISH	
E25	86			1	LA=ENGLISH 12	
E26	86			8	LA=ENGLISH.	
E27	86			2	LA=ENGLISH/JAP.	
E28	86			1	LA=ENGLISH,	
E29	86			1	LA=ENGLISH'	
E30	86			3	LA=ENGLISN	
E31	86			1	LA=ENGLLISH	
E32	86			1	LA=ENGLSH	
E33	86			20	LA=ENGLSIH	
E34	86			1	LA=ENGLUSH	
E35	86			10	LA=ENLGISH	

Fig. 9.8. Excerpt from the language index in MHA.

O V I D   **PsycINFO**   [?] Help
                   1887 to July 1999

Author Title Journal Search Fields Tools Combine Limit Basic Change Database Logoff

#	Search History	Results	Display
1	19$.up.	1594013	Display
2	("authored book" or "book" or "chapter" or "dissertation abstract" or "edited book" or "journal article" or "report" or "secondary publication").pt.	1594013	Display
3	("animal" or "human").po.	1286235	Display

Fig. 9.9. Determining the total number of records and presence of two fields in Ovid.

Omission could be categorized as a special kind of inconsistency. However, the inconsistency of providing essential data elements, such as language, country, year of publication, or document type, has such important implications that it deserves special treatment. It should be noted that not all data elements are expected to be present in all the records. Obviously, author name cannot be provided for anonymous publications. Not all serial publications have ISSN, and not all of them identify the editor as a data element—for example, as in Ulrich's.

But for every publication, there should be a language name or a document type. It often happens that such data elements were not used in the early years of the database; they were introduced later. In such cases, the user should be warned of this. ABC-Clio does so with its American History & Life and Historical Abstracts databases, explaining that the language field was assigned since 1980 only (and the databases go back to 1963 and 1973, respectively).

So does Oceanic Abstracts (figure 9.10), noting that document type was used only between 1971 and 1973, which explains why only 8 percent of the records have a document type field. The Searchable Physics Information Notices (SPIN) database explains that document type is assigned only for non-journal articles. Sometimes the reason can be deduced by experienced users. The Occupational Health and Safety database has a language field for only 8 percent of the records. However, a look at the language index indirectly serves an explanation: there is no entry for English, so obviously that is the default value.

In *Books in Print*, only the absurdly small result set of English language documents would give a hint to the experienced searcher that English is specified only in cases of bilingual or multilingual documents (such as dictionaries).

In some cases, warning is given for the large-scale omission of one data element but not the other. In ERIC there is no warning for omitting the document type field for 28 percent of the records, but there is a note that language was added only from 1979 onward. The same applies to NTIS (figure 9.11). BIOSIS warns that language was added to records only from 1978, but there is no warning or explanation for why 65 percent of the records have no document type field. In the case of a 12-million record database, this proportion of omission is gigantic.

ADDITIONAL INDEXES [return to top]

SEARCH PREFIX	DISPLAY CODE	FIELD NAME	INDEXING	SELECT EXAMPLES
None	AN	DIALOG Accession Number		
AN=	AN	OA Accession Number [4]	Phrase	S AN=71-1A-00061
AU=	AU	Author	Phrase	S AU=KING, K.
BN=	BN	International Standard Book Number (ISBN) [5]	Phrase	S BN=0-930118-03-0
CL=	CL	Conference Location	Word	S CL=FLORIDA
CO=	CO	CODEN [1]	Phrase	S CO=MPNBAZ
CS=	CS	Corporate Source	Word	S CS=(USFWS(S)PATUXENT)
CT=	CT	Conference Title [1]	Word	S CT=(NORTH(W)SEA)
CY=	CY	Conference Year [1]	Phrase	S CY=1985
DT=	DT	Document Type [1]	Phrase	S DT=JOURNAL PAPER
JA=	JA	Journal Announcement [5]	Phrase	S JA=V25N1
JN=	JN	Journal Name	Phrase	S JN=COLONIAL WATERBIRDS?
LA=	LA	Language	Phrase	S LA=JAPANESE
PU=	PU	Publisher [1]	Word	S PU=(PERGAMON(W)PRESS)
PY=	PY	Publication Year	Phrase	S PY=1987
SN=	SN	International Standard Serial Number (ISSN) [5]	Phrase	S SN=0093-3651
None	SO	Source Information [6]		
TC=	TC	Treatment Code [7]	Phrase	S TC=I
UD=	None	Update	Phrase	S UD=9999

[4] Present in records entered in the database from 1971 through 1973.

[5] Present in records from January 1980 to the present.

[6] Includes Journal Name, Corporate Source, Publication Year, and Pagination.

Fig. 9.10. Bluesheet information for Oceanic Abstracts.

CP=	CP	Country of Publication [6]	Word & Phrase	S CP=(UNITED(W)STATES) S CP=UNITED STATES
CS=	CS	Corporate Source	Word & Phrase	S CS=(DEPARTMENT(2W)NAVY) S CS=DEPARTMENT OF THE NAVY, WASHINGTON? S CS=110050
DT=	DT	Document Type	Phrase	S DT=PATENT
JA=	JA	Journal Announcement	Phrase	S JA=GRAI9801
LA=	LA	Language [7]	Phrase	S LA=ENGLISH
NT=	NT	Note	Word	S NT=(FOREIGN(W)LICENSING)
None	PC	NTIS Price Code		
PY=	PY	Publication Year	Phrase	S PY=1997
RN=	RN	CAS(R) Registry Number [9]	Phrase	S RN=8001-35-2
RN=	RN	Report Number	Word & Phrase	S RN=(AD(W)D018(W) 520) S RN=PATAPPL8854511 S RN=PAT-APPL-8-854 511
SC=	SC	Section Heading Code [9]	Phrase	S SC=90F
SH=	SH	Section Heading	Phrase	S SH=ELECTROTECHNOLOGY--GENERAL S SH=49GE
None	SO	Source Information [9]		
SP=	SP	Sponsoring Organization [10]	Word & Phrase	S SP=(DEPARTMENT(1W)ENERGY) S SP=DEPARTMENT OF ENERGY, WASHINGTON?
UD=	None	Update	Phrase	S UD=9712B1

[3] Searchable in the Basic Index and in the Additional Indexes.

[4] Also searchable as RN=

[5] For best results, search without punctuation.

[6] For records from 1980 forward.

[7] For records from 1979 forward.

Fig. 9.11. Missing note about massive omission of document type field in NTIS.

Not warning users about such omissions is akin to a restaurant manager who does not set off the fire alarm when the kitchen catches on fire, to make sure that all patrons pay their checks and do not flee the restaurant. Searchers may burn their fingers if they don't pay attention to the serious deficiency of record incompleteness. The powerful tool of filtering search results by language, document type, and classification code can easily become a harmful tool.

A very few databases at least make omissions of data elements clear right in the search process. The Multimedia and CD-ROM Directory, for example, clearly shows how many records do not have price information (figure 9.12).

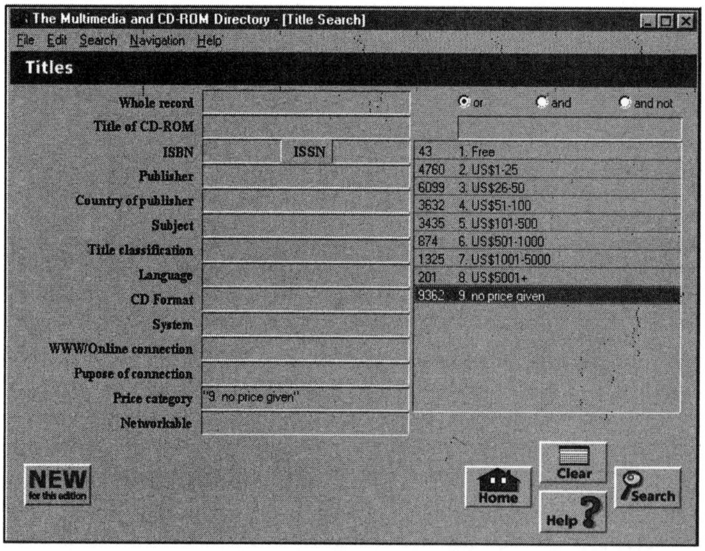

Fig. 9.12. Clear identification of missing data elements.

The Directory of Library and Information Professionals, which uses the same software, does not use the same technique to alert the user that only a fraction of the data elements offered for searching is indeed available in the records. The only exception is the gender of the information professional, as the print documentation warns the user that less than half of the records have gender information. (It is another question as to how many users would have access to and/or would be willing to read the print documentation.)

The easiest way to learn about the extent of omission of data elements is when the database volunteers this information, as shown in figure 9.12. Another way to explore incompleteness is to look for index entries such as N/A, Not Available, or Undetermined in abstracting and indexing databases. It seems not only excessive but also odd why there are 25,880 records in Library Literature with undetermined language until you do some exploration and realize that H. W. Wilson's practice is to not assign language fields for records of book reviews (figure 9.13). This is not logical, and from the review, the language of the critiqued work certainly can be determined.

Search History
Database Details

Set	Term Searched	Items
S1	LA="UNDETERMINED"	25880
S2	S1 AND DT=REVIEWS	25880

Show Database Details for:
438: Library Literature   Bluesheet   Rates

Fig. 9.13. Records with undetermined language in LibLit.

These kinds of confessional entries still cannot always be taken at face value. Even when counting entries with the words *Undetermined* or *Unavailable*, in the particular index, the sum does not add up to the total number of records in the database. This is quite obvious in the Marquis Who's Who database, which has four entries for the gender field (figure 9.14), but their postings still don't equal the total number of records. Also, even just glancing through the records with undetermined gender makes one wonder why it is so difficult to determine the gender of persons with first names such as Tatiana or Charles, and from the other clues of the biography.

Search History
Database Details

Set	Term Searched	Items
S1	UD=?	965187
S2	SX="FEMALE"	281456
S3	SX="MALE"	681677
S4	SX="N"	2
S5	SX="UNAVAILABLE"	2026
S6	S1 NOT S2:S5	26

Show Database Details for:
234: Marquis Who's Who®   Bluesheet   Rates

Fig. 9.14. Unavailable gender information and then some in Marquis's Who's Who.

In directory databases, the common code to indicate unavailability of a numeric data element is 9999. For example, if the Standard Industry Classification (SIC) code could not be determined for a company, this number is used. The text equivalent of this code varies. In some databases, it is nonclassified or unclassified establishment, and in some it is nonclassifiable establishment. One may wonder by whom it is nonclassifiable. This convention gives file producers quite a leeway and seems to be abused.

In the American Business Information directory (ABI), there are over 100,000 records with 9999 SIC codes (figure 9.15). It's hard to fathom why companies such as Office Machines & Furniture and Office Depot are nonclassifiable (figure 9.16). One would think that the SIC 502112 (OFFICE FURNITURE & EQUIP-DEALERS [WHOL]) or one of its variants would be appropriate, as indeed it has been assigned to 15,000 companies in this database.

The Moody's Corporate News database assigns 9999 to the Walt Disney Company (figure 9.17). It seems to be child's play to figure that out. Dun & Bradstreet may not impress the customers when it slaps the 9999 code to companies such as America Online, American Eagle Airlines, and Burger King Corporation (figure 9.18). By the price this company charges, you would expect that it could afford to hire people who can figure out what SIC codes would fit these companies the best.

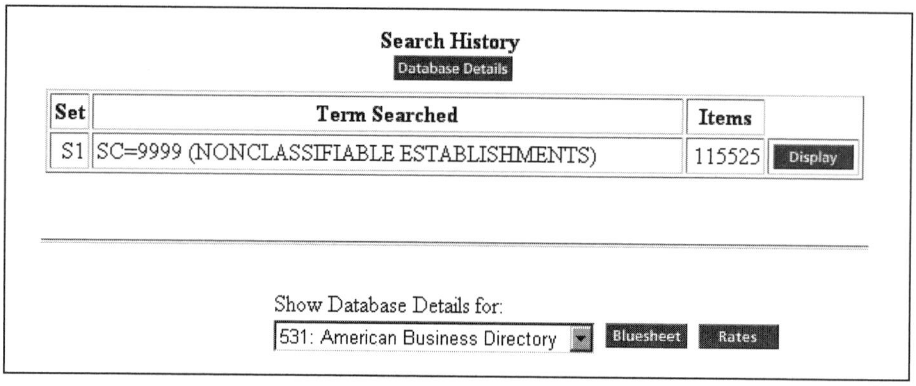

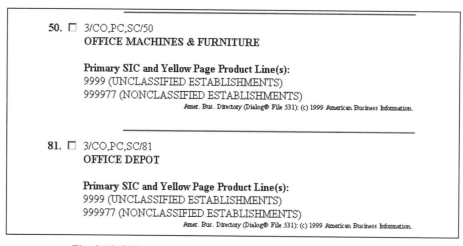

Fig. 9.15. Excessive number of records in the ABI directory with 9999 SIC code.

Fig. 9.16. Office Depot as a nonclassifiable establishment in ABI.

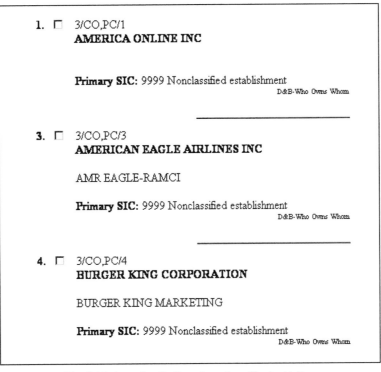

3/CO,PC/15 (Item 1 from file: 556)
DISNEY (WALT) CO. (THE)

COMPANY INFORMATION:

Primary SIC: 9999

Moody`s(R)CorpNews

Fig. 9.17. The Walt Disney Company gets a 9999 code from Moody's.

1. ☐   3/CO,PC/1
AMERICA ONLINE INC

Primary SIC: 9999 Nonclassified establishment
D&B-Who Owns Whom

_____

3. ☐   3/CO,PC/3
AMERICAN EAGLE AIRLINES INC

AMR EAGLE-RAMCI

Primary SIC: 9999 Nonclassified establishment
D&B-Who Owns Whom

_____

4. ☐   3/CO,PC/4
BURGER KING CORPORATION

BURGER KING MARKETING

Primary SIC: 9999 Nonclassified establishment
D&B-Who Owns Whom

**Fig. 9.18. America Online, American Eagle Airlines,
and Burger King get a 9999 code from Dun & Bradstreet.**

Bowker uses this 9999 value when the year of publication is not known. This would be an acceptable solution, but it has problems in many databases. Very often such codes or warnings are not consistently entered and thus misinform users. Once you know the total number of records in a database, try a fully truncated search, such as PY=? which means "Find all the records that have any value in the Publication Year field." If the resulting set is smaller than the total number of records, then you know how many records have no value in the given field—not even a warning code or text. In this case, 66 records do have the special code 9999 in the PY field, but even with those records included, nearly 80,000 others do not have any value in the PY field (figure 9.19). This defies the purpose of using the 9999 value in *Books in Print*.

Search History

Database Details

Set	Term Searched	Items
S1	UD=?	2359042
S2	PY=?	2271291
S3	PY=9999	66

Fig. 9.19. Misleading use of the 9999 code in *Books in Print*.

How would you know the total size of the database? You can take the word of the content provider or the database publisher (although with a grain of salt). It is better to do a search on the UD (update) index—using either a full truncation search or an arithmetic operation—because typically this field is automatically generated when the database is updated.

Figure 9.20 shows such a search in DIALOG's version of ERIC, which reveals a significant volume of omissions. Note that sometimes the UD field stands for the reload date of the database. This is because many directories are not updated but reloaded (i.e., records are deleted and modified as the objects of the directory change). This happens, for example, when the headquarters of a company is moved or its CEO is replaced by a new one. If a UD field is not available, some other data elements that are most likely to be available in every record (and have a few possible values only) may be searched. These may be corroborated by the additional search results.

Figure 9.21 shows a completeness verification search in Bowker's Complete Video Directory. Although there is no UD field, it is safe to say that there are 192,166 records in the database. The full truncation search in the keyword index (kw=$) is the best proof of the size of the database because it counts every record that has any information in any of the fields, regardless of the content of the field. It is quite revealing to learn that nearly one-third of the records have no data in the PC (publication code) field, 43 percent have no year of production, more than 75 percent of the records have no release year, and about 8,000 records have no subject information.

A similar test can be done in the Ulrich's Plus database published on CD-ROM by Bowker. A combination of fully truncated and numeric searches of several indexes clearly shows that there were 226,276 records in this database. The numbers also show how badly incomplete many of the records are (figure 9.22).

Search History

Database Details

Set	Term Searched	Items
S1	UD=?	990090
S2	PY=?	966799
S3	LA=?	656004
S4	PY>1978	617028
S5	DT=?	712423

Show Database Details for:

1: ERIC ▾   Bluesheet   Rates

Fig. 9.20. Searching for the total number of records in DIALOG's ERIC.

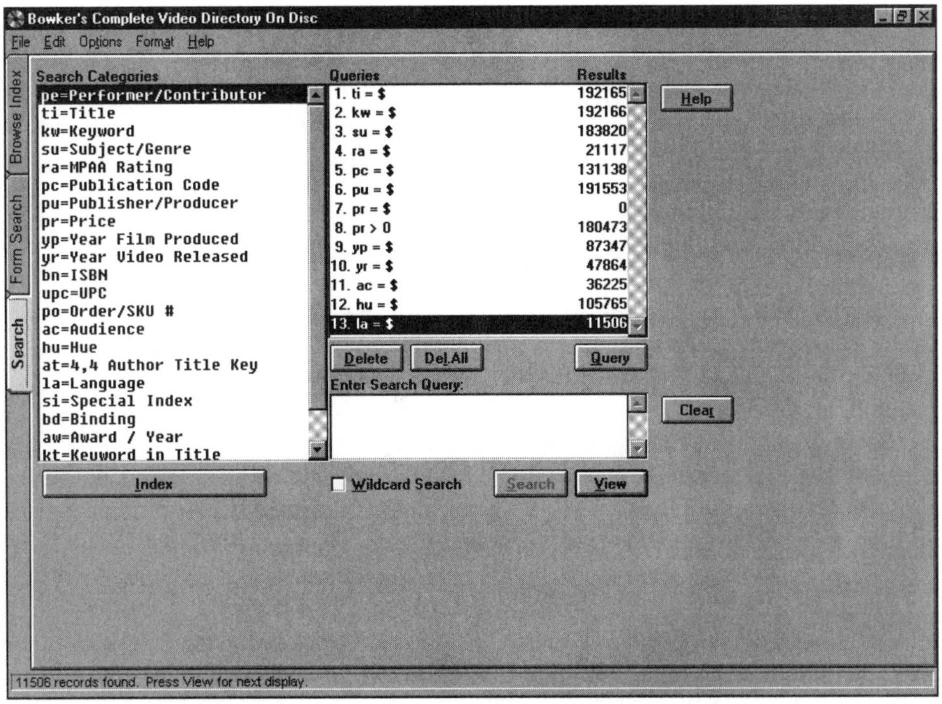

Fig. 9.21. Completeness searching in Bowker's Complete Video Directory.

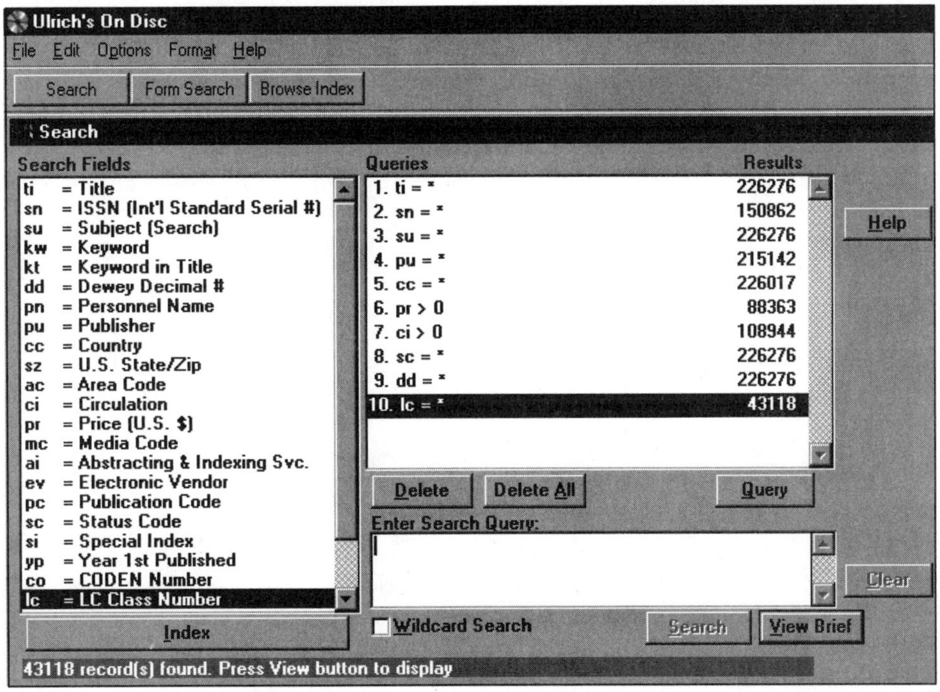

Fig. 9.22. Completeness searching in Bowker's own CD-ROM version of Ulrich's.

Completeness test searches are always database-specific and assume knowledge about the conventions applied in the database. In some databases, the language field is entered only for non–English language documents, considering English as the default value. The same applies in some databases if the country of publication is the United States. Similarly, the total number of records in ERIC can be easily determined, using any software, by making two searches and comparing the results of other searches to these results.

In ERIC every record is either an RIE (Resources in Education) or a CIJE (Current Index to Journals in Education) record. Sometimes the eyeballing of the field-specific indexes would immediately indicate if there are serious problems of incompleteness in some data elements. The many field-specific indexes in the Ovid version of databases illustrate this well. For example, eyeballing the values in the status code index in Ulrich's instantly informs us that its total posting is in the neighborhood of 236,000 records promised in the file (figure 9.23).

Some fields' presence can be determined easily by clicking on filter boxes or by applying predefined limits after a search that yields the total number of records. In Ovid the total number of records can be determined by using the 19$.ud. command, which will retrieve all the records that were added between 1900 and 1999. Then, in Ovid's version of PAIS, searching by all publication types and all languages will retrieve the same number of records, proving that all records have both publication type and language fields (figure 9.24).

In WebSPIRS, a search for any record with an update date greater than zero will yield the total number of records. This set can then be limited to the English and then to the non–English language documents to see if there is any difference. In DIALOG this process is done using the limit suffix in the SELECT statement to find, for example, that only every second record has circulation information (figure 9.25).

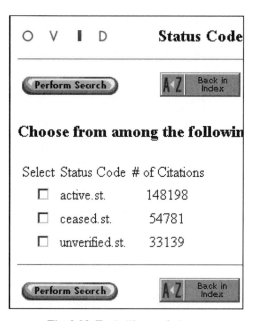

Fig. 9.23. Eyeballing an index
with few values in Ovid.

#	Search History	Results	Display
1	("book or monograph" or "journal article").pt.	467620	Display
2	("english" or "french" or "german" or "italian" or "portuguese" or "spanish").lg.	467620	Display

Run Saved Search   Save Search History   Delete All Searches

Fig. 9.24. Comparing the completeness of the publication type and
language field in Ovid's version of PAIS.

Set	Term Searched	Items
S1	UD=?	236155
S2	S1/NOCIRC	116992

Show Database Details for:

480: Ulrich's(TM) International Periodicals Directory ▾ Blue

Fig. 9.25. Determining completeness of the circulation field in Ulrich's on DIALOG.

Knowing the incompleteness of fields in databases is essential for efficient searching. These data should be made readily available not only in the publicity materials but also prominently on the screen when the database is invoked. Such data would alert the searcher, for example, that finding the top circulating journals in the Ulrich's database is hopeless, as half of the records don't have such data and thus are excluded from such a search. At least for this database, the user may learn how many records don't have certain data elements.

In the case of The Serials Directory, the user doesn't have the slightest clue. Large-scale absence of data elements that are often used to limit a search can distort the results dramatically. The culminating effect of absent fields can totally cripple the search—as, for example, when publication year, document type, and language are used to limit a search.

It adds insult to injury when the author of the publicity material is not aware of these limitations and recommends a search that yields a zero result. The spring 2000 edition of Bowker's Complete Video Directory (BCVD) illustrates this case and sums up the consequences of the absence of multiple fields used to refine a search.

The incompleteness of records in terms of many of the search criteria has a crippling effect on most of the searches. The test search (figure 9.26) for verifying the completeness of the records shows unnerving results even in the most current edition. Although subject descriptors are assigned to 95 percent of the records, year of publication is present in only 45 percent of the records, year of video release in 28 percent, audience code in 21 percent, hue in 63 percent, and language in 6 percent.

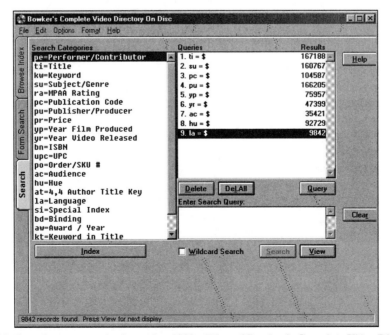

Fig. 9.26. Completeness test in the spring 2000 edition of Bowker's Complete Video Directory.

This massive omission does not deter the copywriter to sell this database on its searchability (figure 9.27). You certainly can search by 19 criteria, but you certainly will not find what you hope, as the absence of many of the 19 search criteria in tens of thousands of records will limit the search to a subset implicitly, without the user having the faintest idea about it.

The copywriter, in the bubbling style of midnight infomercials, challenges you to compile lists of videos that meet specific parameters, such as all PG-rated comedies in English that were released in 1988. For a starter, release year is available in only 28 percent of the records, so the search domain is automatically restricted to 47,399 records. Only 3,249 movies meet this criterion. Rating is available in 11 percent of the records (you don't expect a very high percentage for this data element because many of the films are not rated).

> You can search by 19 criteria, alone or in combination, or scan any of the Directory's nine browsable indexes to:
>
> - Field even the toughest questions, such as "Can you find a French film with the word 'blue' in the title?"
> - Display and print over 5,500 full-text reviews from Variety, with thousands more added each year
> - Keep on top of the latest videos, new releases, and reviews through quarterly, cumulative updates
> - Compile lists of videos that meet specific parameters, like "all PG-rated comedies in English that were released in 1998"
> - Offer library or retail store patrons a self-service video information center, and turn untrained staff into instant video experts
> - Streamline ordering by locating titles and printing order slips in one easy session
>
> Updated quarterly.
> Available in Windows and MS-DOS.
>
> 1-year Subscription: $520.00

Fig. 9.27. The challenge and implied promise of the catalog—and the reality.

As can be seen in the query progress (figure 9.28), the combination reduced the choices to 145 records. Adding the comedy criteria narrows the search to 44 flicks (figure 9.29). The last step makes the search a comedy when you limit it to English language movies, yielding a zero result (figure 9.30). The message refers to the *Books in Print* database (as does much of the help file), even though the video directory was being searched, as can be seen on the top of the screen.

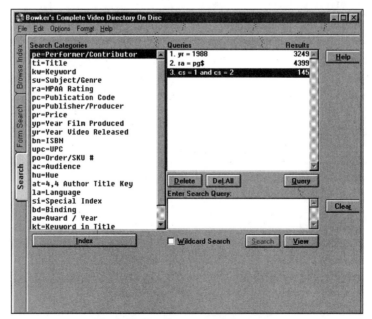

Fig. 9.28. The first steps of the query.

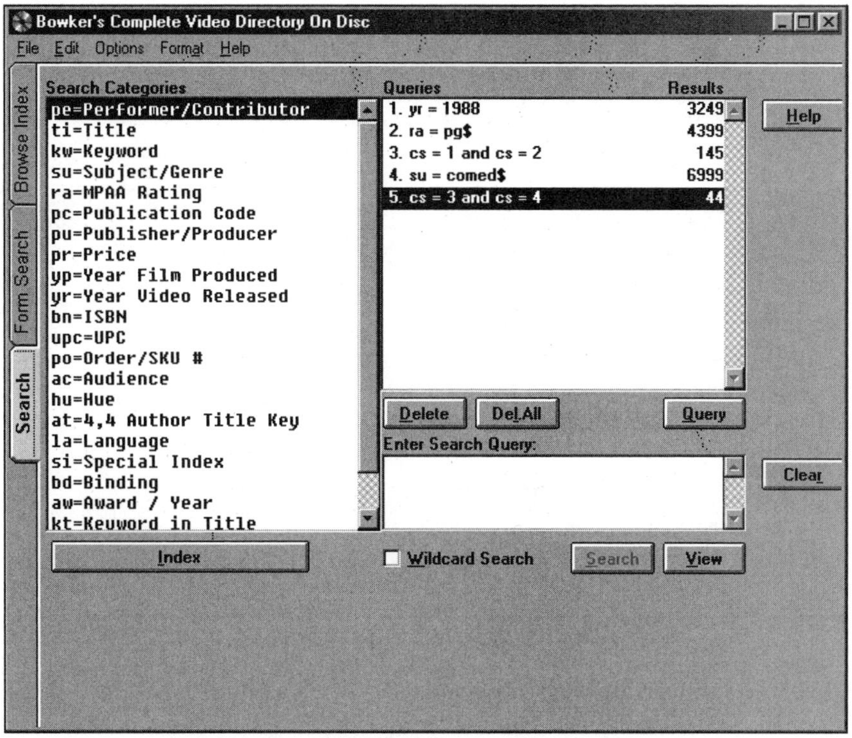

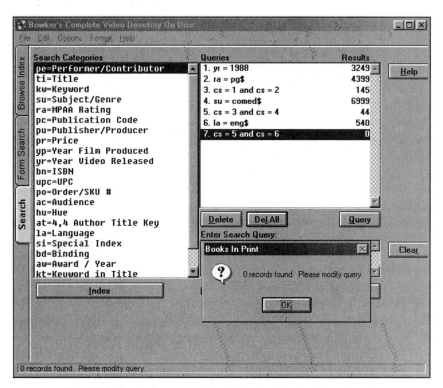

Fig. 9.29. Limiting the search to comedy genre.

Fig. 9.30. Producing no results, but makes the search a comedy.

The happy copywriter did not check the sorry help file (and I am afraid users would not either), which tells you that "ENG (English) is used as a term for multilingual books" (figure 9.31). If you replace *books* with *movies*, then it would mean multilingual movies. There are only 540 such records, and none of them are for comedies released in 1988. That's why you get a zero result.

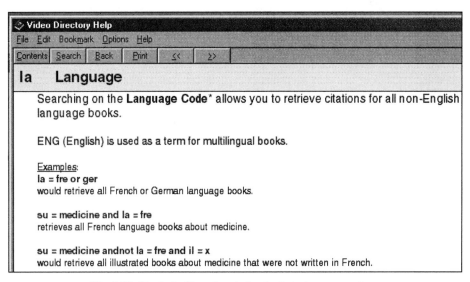

Fig. 9.31. The help file refers to books but gives some clue.

Keeping the database in such an inferior shape is one thing. Keeping the nonsense publicity blurb is another, as it could be removed immediately from the Web. Obviously, Bowker is not much interested in doing so because there are enough libraries that happily pay $520 for BCVD.

With the many information-rich, current, accurate, and free databases, BCVD has no future. Librarians will realize that the well-known name of Bowker adorns a sorry database.

Quality of Subject Indexing

Appropriate subject indexing of documents is a prerequisite of efficient retrieval. This has been obvious in the printed world because in abstracting and indexing journals, the most often used access points are the subject index entries of the individual and cumulative volumes. The importance of subject indexing seems to have been somewhat downplayed in electronic databases because of the accessibility of records by many data elements that carry subject content, such as title, abstract, and subject identifier fields. Measurement of the quality of subject indexing has been given the most substantial treatment within the area of evaluating database quality; therefore this chapter provides more references for background reading than other chapters.

CONCEPTS AND LITERATURE

Milstead (1994a) proves that the amount of research in indexing, as reflected by entries about indexing issues in ARIST, has been declining. While in the first decade of ARIST there were 25 to 30 entries per volume under Indexing and related terms, the average in the past 20 years has decreased to 10 to 12 entries in each volume. She convincingly argues for a set of measures that would allow the testing of indexing systems and could compensate for the deficiencies of recall/precision methodology, predominantly used for evaluation of indexing quality. There are four major aspects in evaluating the quality of subject index term assignment:

1. exhaustivity
2. specificity
3. accuracy
4. consistency

Soergel (1994) gives a refined definition for these evaluation criteria, distinguishing entity and descriptor views for indexing accuracy and consistency, and viewpoint and importance exhaustivity for the extent of coverage by descriptors of the concepts discussed in a document. (He argues against the use of the term "depth of indexing" for its possible ambiguity, but because several other authors prefer this term in referring to the number of descriptors assigned to documents, this chapter uses the term to denote this concept later.) Soergel (1994) discusses the impact of all of these indexing characteristics on retrieval performance, as well as the underlying reasons for studying and evaluating these measures of indexing.

One of the few large-scale studies to evaluate indexing quality in operational systems by quantitative terms was developed for the National Library of Medicine to compare the indexing quality of MEDLINE, PsycINFO, BIOSIS, and *Excerpta Medica* by Griffith et al. (1986). Their study—using clusters of closely related documents—analyzed how appropriately index terms link related documents, discriminate broadly among the linked documents within the entire database, and discriminate finely among individual documents. Their methodology to calculate the term discriminating index for databases of varying size was refined by Ajiferuke and Chu (1988). They used this revised measure to evaluate the quality of indexing in Library Literature, LISA, and ISA (1989), but the methodology is equally applicable to other databases.

Beaubien (1992), in discussing indexing quality of IAC and H. W. Wilson databases, argues that IAC's single controlled vocabulary appears much more "controlled" than Wilson's efforts, but admits that Wilson tends to use more precise terms at the expense of consistency, and asserts that the library has to decide whether patrons would be better served by the more consistent indexing of IAC or by the more precise indexing of Wilson.

No studies are needed to realize the implications of inaccurate and inconsistent subject indexing on retrieval performance. The results of checking these two criteria in the purportedly controlled vocabulary index entries in databases speak for themselves, as illustrated by Jacsó (1998c). Martin and Bergerhoff (1991) analyzed the terms beginning with the letter *A* in the controlled term index of Chemical Abstracts Service database and compared it with the printed subject heading list of valid terms. In the latter they found only a single misspelling.

However, there were 1,713 terms that appeared in the online but not in the printed controlled vocabulary for the sample entries, and the reasons were more disappointing. Misspellings accounted for 9.4 percent, 6.8 percent had differed from the preferred singular or plural form, and 61 percent could not be found in the printed vocabulary. These data suggest that many of the terms were used as descriptors without any control.

Good quality of subject indexing in MEDLINE was indirectly proven in the Drexel project reported by McCain, White, and Griffith (1987). They found that failure to retrieve records from MEDLINE is attributable mostly to lack of indexing of the journal, the issue, or the article, rather than inappropriate or inaccurate indexing.

Inaccurate indexing sometimes is not the fault of the indexer but of the creators of the controlled vocabulary. Miller (1996) illustrates how basic rules of thesaurus construction were violated by the 1994 edition of the Sports Thesaurus, including erroneous interpretation of relations between descriptors, elimination of homonyms and synonyms, and ignoring substantial historical changes in geographical names, which led to incorrect indexing, low precision, and low recall. Problems were further aggravated by the inconsistencies between the printed and CD-ROM versions of the Sports Thesaurus.

It's difficult to quantify or judge objectively the adequacy of terms in a controlled vocabulary or their assignment to records (or both). Nevertheless, the side results of an experiment meant to test the validity of the strategy of unlimited aliasing by Brooks (1993) yielded noteworthy observations about indexing quality.

In that experiment, records were selected from the ERIC, LISA, and ISA databases for the same 21 documents. The descriptors were aggregated, and the lists of descriptors in various combinations (such as ERIC only, ISA/LISA mix, and ERIC/ISA/LISA mix) for each record were shown along with the title and abstract of each record.

The time it took 40 searchers to find the right matching descriptor was measured. The results that refuted the advantage of unlimited aliasing claimed by previous experiments have also indicated that the matching of records by single ISA index terms required a significantly higher mean time for the right selection, more choices, and caused far more failures than the other single-type indexes. These findings suggested that "the ISA index is a poor performer," and searchers "were thwarted by the ISA index that offered few . . . simple words or phrases."

Sievert and Sievert (1991), in comparing overlapping coverage between FRANCIS and Philosopher's Index, found that 49 of 104 records that could not be retrieved, but were present in the latter, were irretrievable because the relevant concept or name was not indexed. While appropriateness of topical subject heading assignment is subjective, the missing names as index terms were clearly indexing errors in light of the clear guidelines of the Philosopher's Index Thesaurus. It mandates "indexing by the name of the person if two pages or half the article concern the said person."

In a study that was rather unique in terms of the subjects surveyed, Braam and Bruil (1992) examined to what extent authors were satisfied with the indexing terms assigned to their papers by Chemical Abstracts Services (CAS). Of 211 authors who responded to the questionnaire, only 52 percent agreed that the index headings assigned to their articles by indexers of CAS adequately represented the subject matter. Forty-eight percent would have liked to change the list of index headings (adding, deleting, or replacing terms). As for the adequacy of the CA section codes, 19 percent of the authors thought their articles were not placed in the proper main CA section.

Giral and Taylor (1993) compared—among other characteristics—the most common access points (named persons, geographic names, topical descriptors, etc.) between records describing the same articles in Avery Index and Architectural Periodicals Index. They found that only 55 percent of the personal or corporate names, 50 percent of the geographic names, and about 40 percent of the architectural site names used in common in both sources matched exactly, or—in the case of geographic names—at least partially. (Use of the same elements, regardless of the order [i.e., Portland (Maine) and Maine–Portland] was considered to be matching.)

Assignment of the right Chemical Abstracts Services Registry Numbers (CASRN) was tested by Buntrock (1994) in six databases, then again by Buntrock (1995) in three databases. He found that those databases that use an algorithm to select chemical names from the full text or abstracts and match it with a CASRN have a margin of inaccuracy much higher than in those databases whose producers use a "live" CAS registry system.

Even worse is the chance for efficient indexing and searching if controlled vocabulary is not available. Controlled vocabulary is a prerequisite for quality indexing (along with a classified scheme for broader classification). Jacsó (1997b) asserts that the lack of controlled vocabulary for Information Science Abstracts in its early years proved detrimental to the quality of subject indexing in ISA.

Hood and Wilson (1994) attribute the far from exemplary indexing policy and practice of LISA to some extent to the fact that the "thesaurus (or controlled vocabulary) LISA uses [is] not compiled according to standard thesaurus construction principles." They state that the "first edition of the LISA Online User Manual which calls the 'thesaurus' a 'Preferred Terms List' " is a "more honest assessment of the source of DE terms in the LISA database." Note that the new owner of the LISA database, G. K. Saur, discontinued the use of the LISA vocabulary in 1992 and devised a new controlled vocabulary, but although it is not published in print, it is available in the far-the-best implementation by CSA.

Even professionally compiled thesauri may prove to be a hindrance for novices who may not be able to comprehend, let alone apply in searching, the sophisticatedly structured subject heading lists, such as MeSH. Killion (1995) explains that one of the reasons for developing the RNdex Top 100 database was to allow indexers and searchers to use a thesaurus that is more simple than MeSH or the CINAHL Thesaurus. There were additional reasons, too, such as better currency of terms, better scope notes, extensive cross-references, and more natural subject headings using direct instead of inverted forms.

As for depth (exhaustivity) of indexing, there are no universally valid magic numbers. The first comprehensive experiment of the Sparck Jones (1973) studies has shown that indexing depth does matter; it increases recall (in Boolean search systems), but beyond a certain point drastically reduces precision.

Although the degree of indexing exhaustivity is generally proportional to the number of descriptors assigned to documents, a higher number of descriptors does not guarantee appropriately exhaustive indexing. Depth of indexing, however, may be an important indicator for exhaustivity, especially in comparing the number of index terms assigned to the same documents by two or more indexing services.

In comparing the indexing practices of CINAHL and MEDLINE for the same nursing articles, Brenner and McKinin (1989) found that while both databases have the same number (3) of major descriptors, MEDLINE used three times as many minor descriptors as CINAHL. More important, however, is the finding that the average number of common major descriptors is fewer than 0.5, indicating little agreement in the choice of major descriptors, even though 70 percent of CINAHL's descriptors are derived from MeSH.

This lack of commonality has serious implications for cross-database searching. The study did not examine the reasons for incongruence between the choice of major descriptors, but it clearly illustrated that users of CINAHL who use more than two descriptors in a Boolean AND relation in their query greatly reduce the possibilities for retrieval.

Ahmad (1991) examined the indexing practices of an international assortment of newspaper indexes. He states that comprehensiveness (exhaustivity) and consistency in newspaper indexing depend on the effectiveness of subject analysis of news items, and the number of index terms assigned—which ranged from one to two dozen—is not a determinant factor for the quality of indexing. Jacsó (1992a) claims that limiting the number of subject headings to one in Magazine Article Summaries (MAS) (the limit was eliminated in 1993) could not ensure adequate depth of indexing. He also notes that the high number of descriptor terms in LISA (as was the case with the majority of records until 1994) is not a guarantee for quality indexing either. In fact, he contends that extreme redundancy has been a major flaw of indexing in the LISA database.

In comparing records for the same articles in Avery Index and Architectural Periodicals Index (API), Giral and Taylor (1993) analyzed how many descriptors and name access points were assigned in the two sources. For the 444 matched records from the Avery Index sample, Avery indexers made 687 name access points, and the API indexers made 688 name access points. For the 671 matched records from the API sample, Avery indexers made 1,192 name access points, and API indexers made 1,203 name access points.

The numbers may seem to be very impressive, but they are misleading by themselves. Nearly one-third of the names were not used in common by the two sources. As for the form of the names, the match was only 55 percent (though the matching criteria were strict, only capitalization differences were considered nonsubstantial). As for topical descriptors, the average number of descriptors per record was also very close, and 40 percent of the first element of descriptors in one source were present in the descriptor string of the other source, in spite of the fact that the sources use different thesauri.

Turner (1995) compared user-assigned terms with indexer-assigned terms for storage and retrieval of moving images. Shot-level indexing of the stock shot collection of the National Film Board of Canada was used to find the degree of agreement between the terms users think of when searching film and video shots and those assigned by professional indexers. Participants, numbering 181, screened 44 stock footages and supplied words or phrases that they felt were obvious keys for retrieval at a later date by themselves or others. Results showed a high rate of indexer-requester consistency and a higher rate of consistency at the pre-iconographical (ofness) level than at the iconographical (aboutness) level. This confirmed the hypothesis of Layne (1994) that there is more agreement on the principal and more objective aspects of an image, and less on the secondary and subjective aspects.

Changes in both the classification scheme and the controlled vocabulary over time are necessary to introduce more specific terminology and neologisms. As Mintz (1990) observes, searchers cringe when learning about such changes because they are not implemented retrospectively in records created prior to the formal acceptance of a new classification scheme or terms as descriptors. The practice of yearly updating the thesaurus and mapping new subject headings to old ones retrospectively in MEDLINE and CINAHL is exemplary but rare. In lack of such conversions, however, Mintz (1995) warns that it is the user's responsibility to adapt the search strategy for the differences in terminology throughout the time span of a database. When introducing new descriptors, H. W. Wilson adds those terms retrospectively to existing records. This implies substantial cost but facilitates the searcher's job.

Depth or exhaustivity and specificity of indexing have been studied primarily in relation to their effect on retrieval. The optimal depth and specificity of indexing always depends on the individual documents and on the target audience; therefore, it is hard to agree on the optimal number of descriptor terms and on their specificity. However, Svenonius and McGarry (1993) proved that objectivity in assessment of subject heading assignments is indeed feasible.

Their hypothesis was that, at least 80 percent of the time, there is a clear-cut right and wrong to Library of Congress Subject Headings (LCSH) subject heading assignment. This was confirmed by authors' assigning of subject headings to 100 books on scientific subjects, with the understanding that subject headings can be assigned if 20 percent of the book is about the topic indicated by the heading. Out of 202 subject headings, there were only six where the authors disagreed on the choice and form of subject headings.

Omitting expected descriptors can significantly decrease the results if users limit their search to the descriptor field to ensure the appropriate level of precision. Jacsó (1992a) analyzed a subset of LISA that contained any of the variants of the term *CD-ROM* (i.e., with or without a hyphen, space, or slash) in the title, but not in the descriptor field. He found the omission of the appropriate descriptor particularly perplexing in light of the large number of inappropriately broad and redundant descriptors in LISA records. Although some indexing rules advise indexers to avoid redundancy by omitting descriptors that match words in the title, it is arguable and is not applicable to LISA, because the printed version must provide access points through subject headings, and these may coincide with terms in the title.

Although over-indexing is not as harmful as under-indexing, it can reduce the relevance of search results. Extreme redundancy of descriptors offsets the advantages of indexing. Jacsó (1995) contends that in the case of LISA, quantity not only does not make quality, but even weakens what may be good in indexing. He assumes that the double, triple, and quadruple occurrences of identical descriptors in tens of thousands of records in LISA are due to the automatic generation of descriptors from the classification code used by LISA, as humans are unlikely to be so extremely redundant.

With regard to specificity of indexing, the survey of Hernon and Metoyer-Duran (1992) had an interesting finding. In the focus interviews conducted with 43 librarians at five academic and research libraries, there was recurring criticism against H. W. Wilson's Library Literature that the subject headings are too general and that there are too few subject headings. This is the opposite of this author's opinion that subject heading–subheading combinations of Library Literature are too specific. By mere eyeballing of the controlled vocabulary, it is quite clear that the majority of index entries are singletons (i.e., are assigned to one record only). This is the typical symptom of overly specific indexing.

Hood and Wilson (1994) went much further than sampling records in examining exhaustivity and specificity. They analyzed—among other features—exhaustivity and specificity of indexing based on the entire population of records in LISA rather than on a sample. They looked at all the records in LISA and—after eliminating duplicate descriptors—analyzed all 669,403 occurrences of 28,191 unique descriptors. The authors found that since 1979, LISA has been consistently assigning an average of about six to seven descriptor terms per record, but 64 percent of the descriptors occurred only once in the entire database. This yields an unusually high concentration level. They conclude in a measured tone that the indexing policy and practice of LISA are far from exemplary.

Judging the appropriateness of the choice of subject index terms, as opposed to descriptive cataloging and bibliographic descriptions, is also highly subjective. It is even more difficult to evaluate the consistency of subject indexing within one database (though not the inter-indexer consistency among different databases). No wonder that relatively few articles have been published about the consistency of indexing within one indexing and abstracting service.

The study by Leininger (2000) of testing indexer consistency in 60 duplicates inadvertently entered twice into the PsycINFO database is an exception to the dearth of current publications about the subject. Cooper's often-cited criticism in 1969 (consistent indexing can't be but consistently bad) may have discouraged researchers from engaging in studies of consistency. Fugmann (1992) claims that Cooper's statement has never been refuted (and seems to agree with him).

Nevertheless, he also states that it is intuitively felt that (subject) indexing should, in some hitherto unexplored way, be related to indexing quality and search effectiveness. He then argues that "predictability instead of consistency ... should be the goal in indexing both in the selection of the essence of the documents, and also in the description of this essence."

Measuring the consistency of indexing the same documents by the same person or same database at different time intervals (intra-indexer consistency), or by two or more persons or indexing services (inter-indexer consistency) using identical or similar controlled vocabularies and indexing policies, has been a very popular topic of research. One reason is that such research can also shed light on the extent of consistency of a single source. The many inter-indexer consistency studies—reviewed by Leonard (1977) for the period between 1954 and 1975 and by Markey (1984) to 1984—clearly suggest that there is a direct correlation between retrieval effectiveness and inter-indexer consistency.

Chan (1989) compared 100 pairs of OCLC member-supplied records with LC records for the same edition or issue of English language works that did not have Cataloging in Publication (CIP) information, for the purpose of identifying variations among the LC subject headings assigned. The small sample was acceptable, as the primary purpose of the study was to test the methodology of consistency evaluation.

The study found that 15 percent of the record pairs were perfect matches (identical headings or, in the case of six pairs, no headings at all). Partial matches totaled 80 percent (some headings matched completely or partially; e.g., differences in subdivisions). Five percent were totally unmatched (two of them for the reason that the non-LC records had no subject heading).

While the ideal would be total consistency, it is almost impossible to achieve. Analysis of the 80 partial matches showed that the majority of the records on the same subject shared common subject words that can ensure partial success in recall using systems that allow keyword searching in the subject heading fields. The majority of no matches was due to incorrect synthesis of subject headings and subheadings. It is suggested that LCSH consider the move from a predominantly pre-coordinate system to a post-coordinate one. The very small number of records that showed total inconsistency in main headings did not allow any generalization.

Reich and Biever (1991) discuss inter-indexer consistency as measured by the number of identical terms independently assigned to the same articles by AGRICOLA and CAB using the CAB Thesaurus (slightly modified by the National Agricultural Library when adopting it for AGRICOLA to cater to American spelling and additional terms for subject areas not covered well by the CAB Thesaurus). A total of 236 articles from two journals were selected, and their descriptors were compared.

Although the average number of descriptors assigned by the two indexing services show no significant difference (8.2 versus 8.9), the number of assigned descriptors on a per-article basis shows few instances of identical indexing depth, which in turn may explain the low match rate of 27 percent. Another reason is the availability of synonyms as valid descriptors for the same concept (e.g., cold stress and winter hardiness or developmental stages and growth stages), which is not conducive to consistent assignment of index terms.

Tonta (1991) compares indexing consistency between the Library of Congress (LC) and the British Library (BL) in 82 items in library and information science that were cataloged by both LC and BL (the latter assigning LC subject headings beyond the PRECIS term strings). The average number of terms assigned to items differed significantly (3.44 by LC and 1.55 by BL) because BL does not rely exclusively on the Library of Congress Subject Headings. Despite these differences, nearly 21 percent of the items had the same number of subject headings, but for 74 percent, LC catalogers assigned more LCSH terms than BL did. Nearly 40 percent of the BL-assigned subject headings exactly matched the LC-assigned subject headings, and an additional 35 percent had partial matches (when the main headings matched but not the subdivisions). The indexing consistency measure for the combined exact and partial matches was found to be 36 percent—a rather low value that nevertheless confirmed the findings of previous studies. The findings can have important implications for copy catalogers using the records of the other agency on both sides of the Atlantic Ocean.

Sievert and Andrews (1991) conducted an intra-database consistency study using Information Science Abstracts. They selected 71 genuine duplicate record pairs from four journals to examine the consistency of descriptors and identifiers. Main headings showed 52 percent consistency, and subheadings had a consistency of 45.5 percent, yielding a combined consistency of 48 percent. Identifier consistency was found to be 33 percent. These figures must be interpreted in light of the fact that in the case of ISA, there is a small vocabulary from which indexers can choose terms, and only one main heading can be assigned. Both of these factors increase the probability of agreement.

The fewer terms there are, the more likely it is that two indexers would choose the same descriptor, and as indexing depth increases, indexing consistency decreases. Though the sample was relatively small, the findings that confirmed the results of a similar test in MEDLINE by Funk, Reid, and McGoogan (1983) revealed a low level inter-indexer consistency for documents with perfect semantic similarity. It was used as a factor in interpreting the results of this novel research about semantic relationships between cited and citing articles by Harter, Nisonger, and Weng (1993).

THE PROCESS OF EVALUATING INDEXING QUALITY

The best way to put theory into practice is to perform some test searches. But the first step in evaluating the quality of indexing precedes the search. As indexing depends on the quality of the thesaurus, or at least on the controlled subject vocabulary used to find and assign index terms to the documents by indexers, it is very useful to study the controlled subject vocabulary of a database. Unfortunately, many file producers do not publish their vocabulary in print (like H. W. Wilson in our sample group), but at least it can be studied online or on CD-ROM if the information provider has implemented it. Although this is a software issue, note that there are tremendous differences between the implementations of the same thesaurus by different information providers.

Ovid has by far the most intuitive and most informative representation of thesauri among the online and CD-ROM publishers followed by the excellent implementation in CSA. DIALOG has the thesaurus function for a disappointingly low percentage of its database collection, and it is often substandard, as in the handling of the scope notes of the ERIC Thesaurus, which are often chopped off. SilverPlatter has good implementations of various thesauri in the Windows CD-ROM and the Web version.

The best choice for the preliminary step is to use the printed version of the controlled subject vocabulary, reading the preface, then spot-checking entries and cross-references to get a feel for the implementation.

The size of the controlled vocabulary is not a decisive factor in itself, although the extremely slim ones for a specific discipline, such as the list of terms of ISA and MHA, immediately raise a red flag. In multidisciplinary databases, it is more difficult to get a grasp of the extent of terminological coverage of a discipline. Finding library and information science and technology terms in INSPEC (essentially an electric and electronic engineering database), or ERIC (primarily an educational database), or ABI/INFORM (a business database with very good coverage of information technology) is a time-consuming process.

One would expect that databases focusing on the information and library science field would have exemplary controlled vocabulary for the discipline. LISA and ISA certainly do not confirm this hypothesis. Both have substandard vocabularies, but at least LISA changed to a new vocabulary in 1993. ISA should have switched a long time ago to the ASIS *Thesaurus of Information Science*.

LISA was taken over from the British Library Association by G. K. Saur at the end of 1992, and after a year of suspension, it was re-launched with a completely revised and far better controlled vocabulary. You still have to be familiar with the old controlled vocabulary, however, because more than 20 years of materials have been indexed with it. Users doing retrospective searches, including the pre-1993 time period, will have to live with the "mummy's curse," as Reva Basch (1990b) colorfully called such legacies in the database industry. The last printed version of the vocabulary, which, inexplicably, is titled *LISA Thesaurus*, has about 6,000 entries. It is no thesaurus: the LISA online manual itself states that "it does not pretend to be an exhaustive list of all the terms used in LISA since 1969, but it does provide a substantial core list of the most important and most widely used terms."

It pretends, nevertheless, to be far more than it is. It is certainly not a thesaurus with consistent and extensive cross-references; narrower, broader, and related terms; and scope and usage notes. Occasionally, LISA provides some scope notes and cross-references to preferred terms, but many of those entries are absurd. A single page (figure 10.1) illustrates how erroneous and confusing the notes and references can be. The note about LIBRARY SCHOOL STUDENTS* does not make much sense and is redundant. The ones about LIBRARY RELOCATION and LIBRARY REMOVALS suggest ROMOVALS TO NEW BUILDINGS. Typos are not nice in articles, but in a thesaurus they are considered a sin.

---

*References to descriptions are in uppercase for clarity. They appear in the sample records sometimes in lowercase and sometimes in uppercase.

Lisa Online User Manual: Thesaurus

AREA MATERIALS (post-1978)
and also under specific countries.

SEE LIBRARY MATERIALS

LIBRARY OF CONGRESS:CLASSIFICATION
USE LIBRARY OF CONGRESS
(Since references are indexed under both this term and:
LIBRARY OF CONGRESS CLASSIFICATION
For best results a search on both terms is advised)

LIBRARY OF CONGRESS:SUBJECT HEADINGS
USE LIBRARY OF CONGRESS (combined with)
SUBJECT HEADING SCHEMES

LIBRARY ORGANISATIONS
SEE LIBRARY ASSOCIATIONS

LIBRARY ORIENTATION
SEE USE INSTRUCTIONS

LIBRARY PERIODICALS
UF LIBRARY PERIODICALS
LIBRARIANSHIP:LIBRARY PERIODICALS
RT ARCHIVES PERIODICALS
PUBLISHED MATERIALS
(Occasionally and incorrectly as:
LIBRARY PERIODIALS)

LIBRARY PROGRAMMES
(Since references are indexed under both this term and:
EXTENSION WORK
For best results a search on both terms is advised)

LIBRARY PROJECTS

LIBRARY PUBLICITY
SEE PUBLICITY (post-1977)
PUBLICITY (LIBRARY PUBLICITY) (pre-1978)

LIBRARY RELOCATION
SEE ROMOVALS TO NEW BUILDINGS

LIBRARY REMOVALS
SEE ROMOVALS TO NEW BUILDINGS

LIBRARY RESEARCH
SEE RESEARCH (post-1977)
RESEARCH (LIBRARY RESEARCH) (pre-1978)

LIBRARY RESOURCE CENTRES
SEE RESOURCE CENTRES (post-1977)
SCHOOL LIBRARIES (pre-1978)

LIBRARY RESOURCES

LIBRARY SCHOOL LECTURERS
SEE LECTURERS

LIBRARY SCHOOL STUDENTS
(Occasionally and incorrectly used instead of:
LIBRARY STUDENTS)

LIBRARY SCHOOLS
UF SCHOOLS OF LIBRARIANSHIP
GRADUATE LIBRARY SCHOOLS
RT EDUCATION (PROFESSIONAL)
LIBRARIANSHIP (pre-1978)
PROFESSIONAL EDUCATION (post-1977)

LIBRARY SCHOOLS:STUDENTS
SEE LIBRARY STUDENTS

LIBRARY SCIENCE
SEE LIBRARIANSHIP

LIBRARY SKILLS

LIBRARY STAFF
SEE STAFF (post-1977)
STAFF (LIBRARY STAFF) (pre-1978)

LIBRARY STANDARDS
SEE STANDARDS (post-1977)
STANDARDS (LIBRARY STANDARDS) (pre-1978)

LIBRARY STATISTICS
SEE STATISTICS (post-1977)
STATISTICS (LIBRARY STATISTICS) (pre-1978)

LIBRARY STOCK
SEE LIBRARY MATERIALS
STOCK (post-1977)
STOCK (LIBRARY STOCK) (pre-1978)

LIBRARY STUDENTS
UF LIBRARY SCHOOLS:STUDENTS
(Occasionally and incorrectly as:
LIBRARY SCHOOL STUDENTS)
(Since references are indexed under this term and:
STUDENTS (post-1977)
STUDENTS (ACADEMIC STUDENTS) (pre-1978)
STUDENTS (LIBRARY STUDENTS) (pre-1978)
For best results a search on all terms is advised)

LIBRARY SUPPLIERS
(Since references are indexed under both this term and:

184

**Fig. 10.1. Confusing and erroneous cross-references under
LIBRARY SCHOOL STUDENTS and LIBRARY RELOCATION.**

There is a UF (used for) cross-reference from SEAS to OCEANOGRAPHY, but the term OCEANS just floats around by itself. OLDER WOMEN is a term that occurs only once in the entire database and has a cross-reference to WOMEN in the controlled list but not to the term OLD PEOPLE. It is also odd that there is no term for OLDER MEN.

One can't refrain from wondering what makes such terms as "oceans" or "oil shales" "the most important and most widely used" in a library and information science database. The former is assigned to 14 records, but the latter does not appear at all in the entire database. It is hard to believe that the British Library Association could get away for so long with such a poorly organized controlled vocabulary.

In the case of ISA, it is surprising that IFI/Plenum has continued using a poorly compiled list of terms without any scope notes or cross-references, when the well-built ASIS *Thesaurus of Information Science* would have been a natural choice to adopt for this database when its first edition became available in 1994.

Another problem that may become evident by scanning a printed thesaurus is the lack of an appropriate term. The ERIC Thesaurus has many very specific and well-chosen LIS terms, but offers neither the most commonly used term, "CD-ROMs," nor its spelled-out form. The nearest term is OPTICAL DATA DISKS. It is not appropriate to assign this term when the species rather than the genus is discussed in an article—it is just too broad a term. (At least ERIC indexers can use the identifier field for terms that have not yet become thesaurus terms. Note, however, that in the ERIC database, not all the records were assigned the identifier "CD-ROM" that should have been.)

A similar problem is when the term chosen for the thesaurus is not the one used in the literature (i.e., does not have literary warrant). For example, Compendex had for "CD-ROM" the rather artificial term DATA STORAGE DIGITAL - ROM until the mid-1990s. Many databases use a modified version of the Library of Congress Subject Headings (LCSH), which is rather outdated when it comes to new terminology, and was meant for pre-coordinated catalogs rather than online systems that accommodate and encourage post-coordination. The H. W. Wilson and the IAC families of databases are examples for the pre-coordinated index terms. To their credit, both introduce more contemporaneous terms than LCSH would offer.

A special problem of controlled vocabulary can be seen in the French PASCAL database, which offers a multilingual controlled vocabulary but bites off more than it can chew. Obviously, the compilers of the English, Spanish, and German vocabularies are not purists and zealots when it comes to respecting languages other than French. The Spanish terms seem to have been translated by a computer rather than by a bilingual specialist. Many lack literary warrant, even if the prepositions had not been removed. Without the prepositions (e.g., DETECCION ERROR instead of DETECCION DE ERROR or rather in plural form, DETECCION DE ERRORES), these terms sound like tourists on a Tijuana shopping spree and mean DETECTION ERROR instead of ERROR DETECTION.

Actually, many of the tortured descriptors of PASCAL get a different meaning. Take, as an example, the record in figure 10.2. MOTOR INVESTIGACION means ENGINE INVESTIGATION—what the Federal Board of Aviation would do after an airplane crash. What they meant was "search engine." "Search engine" is BUSCADOR in the Spanish computer technology magazines. For software, the Spanish term is PROGRAMA, not LOGICIAL which is a "Spanishized" word for the French "*logiciel.*"

German descriptors make Spanish ones look good in PASCAL. (It is also worth mentioning that the Spanish descriptors are always fewer than the French ones, and German ones never exceed three terms.) German terms are so general that they are useless for searching. BESCHREIBUNG ("description") is the one most often used, and I would rather spare the description of my opinion about such a choice as the only descriptor.

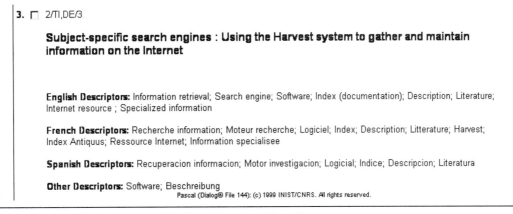

Fig. 10.2. Spanish terms without literary warrant.

Not even the best thesaurus can help if the terms entered by the indexer do not go through quality control and are not matched against the list of valid terms. MHA shows the most extreme examples for the total disregard of at least spell checking the subject descriptors, the most sacred cows (figure 10.3).

```
                    DIALOGWEB.        C        🗐    🕊    $    ⊘    ?
                    Command Search          new search  databases  alerts  cost  logoff  help
                                    Dialog Response

        Ref    Items   Index-term
        E1       57   BEHAVIORAL SCIENCE
        E2        1   BEHAVIORAL SCIENCE>
        E3    35542  *BEHAVIORAL SCIENCES
        E4        1   BEHAVIORAL SCIENCES CHILDREN AND YOUTH
        E5        1   BEHAVIORAL SCIENCES INTELLIGENCE STUDIES
        E6        1   BEHAVIORAL SCIENCES MENTAL OR EMOTIONAL DISOR
        E7        1   BEHAVIORAL SCIENCES PSYCHOLOGY
        E8        1   BEHAVIORAL SCIENCES PSYCHOSOMATIC MEDICINE
        E9        1   BEHAVIORAL SCIENCES SUBCOMMITTEE RECOMMENDATI
        E10       3   BEHAVIORAL SCIENCES.
        E11       1   BEHAVIORAL SCIENCES. DRUG DEPENDENCE AND ABUS
        E12       2   BEHAVIORAL SCIENCIES
        E13       1   BEHAVIORAL SCIENCWES
        E14       2   BEHAVIORAL SCIENES
        E15       1   BEHAVIORAL SCIENSES
        E16       2   BEHAVIORAL SCINCES
        E17       1   BEHAVIORAL SEICNCES
```

Fig. 10.3. Blatant and pervasive misspellings in the descriptor field in MHA.

Selecting the wrong term from the thesaurus is also a common problem. This is, of course, often arguable, but not in cases where the descriptor selected is clearly the wrong term. English terms fare better, but there is the problem of using linguistically correct but semantically inappropriate terms. It is surprising when it happens even in the case of articles where the original title clearly suggests the right term, which happens to be a valid descriptor. For example, PASCAL uses the term LEGIBILITY when READABILITY is called for. The example in figure 10.4 clearly illustrates that the article discusses how easily documents can be understood (readability) rather than how difficult they are to read (legibility) because of poor-quality printing or handwriting that would make a pharmacist blush. Most of the records about readability have the wrong descriptor assigned in PASCAL.

2. ☐ 6/TI,DE/2

Three ways to improve the clarity of journal abstracts

English Descriptors: Abstract; Writing; Text; Legibility; Verbal comprehension; Language; Human

French Descriptors: Resume; Redaction; Texte; Lisibilite; Comprehension verbale; Langage; Homme; Clarte

Spanish Descriptors: Resumen; Redaccion; Texto; Legibilidad; Comprension verbal; Lenguaje; Hombre
Pascal (Dialog® File 144): (c) 1999 INIST/CNRS. All rights reserved.

Fig. 10.4. Ill-chosen English descriptor in PASCAL.

CASE STUDY FOR EVALUATING THE QUALITY OF SUBJECT INDEXING

Some aspects of the four major measures to evaluate the quality of subject indexing will be illustrated through a set of records that were created for the same articles in different databases. The articles were selected to be related to online or CD-ROM technology. Some were selected because they provide a good testing ground for illustrating consistency of subject indexing for one of the following reasons: They are either records for two-part articles that cover the same subjects (although from different angles, occasionally) or records for an article that was published in English, then translated for a Hungarian journal.

You need to make many more tests to reach a conclusion about the quality of indexing. Space limits here the number of examples to use. Testing the quality of subject indexing requires familiarity with the subject and with primary documents, so evaluators should choose records for documents well known by them. This gives an excuse for the inclusion of records for articles by this very author. Some of these articles will also be used in Chapter 11 about evaluating the quality of abstracts.

Specificity is the basic indexing principle of assigning the most specific term available in the controlled vocabulary for the concept. This is difficult to do when the thesaurus terms are very generic and there are no guidelines on how to assign subheadings or subdivisions, if they are allowed at all. This is an obvious problem for the PIRA database, which avoids compound terms at all costs and does not use subdivisions. A case in point is the indexing of both parts of the "Searching for Skeletons" article (figure 10.5). One uses the terms DATABASE, SOFTWARE, and TECHNIQUE. The other has DATABASE, METHOD, and TECHNIQUE. The terms cry out for pluralization and qualification, such as "search techniques" and "evaluation methods," if subdivisions are not used.

```
8/TI,DE,SC/1
Title: SEARCHING FOR SKELETONS IN THE DATABASE CUPBOARD PART II: ERRORS OF COMMISSION

Descriptors: DATABASE; METHOD; TECHNIQUE
Section Headings: Databases (8680)
                    PIRA (Dialog® File 248): (c) 1999 Pira International. All rights reserved.
```

```
8/TI,DE,SC/2
Title: SEARCHING FOR SKELETONS IN THE DATABASE CUPBOARD. PART 1: ERRORS OF OMISSION

Descriptors: DATABASE; SOFTWARE; TECHNIQUE
Section Headings: Databases (8680)
                    PIRA (Dialog® File 248): (c) 1999 Pira International. All rights reserved.
```

Fig. 10.5. PIRA records for the "Searching for Skeletons" article.

One might think that ABI/INFORM could be blamed for the same deficiency for the very same record pair (figure 10.6), but it is a different situation. ABI/INFORM also uses generic terms, such as TECHNIQUES (correctly in the plural format), but it is used along with an important term, SEARCHES. Note, however, that the term DATA BASES ignores the concept of literary warrant. The form DATABASES is used far more often in the literature, as a search in ABI/INFORM clearly reveals. There are 101,918 full-text records where this is the term used, and only 30,895 records when the format preferred by ABI/INFORM for descriptor (i.e., data bases) appears in the full text.

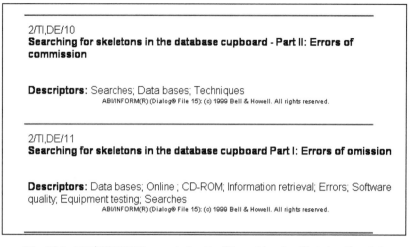

Fig. 10.6. ABI/INFORM records for the "Searching for Skeletons" articles.

In the record for part 2 of the "Data Transfer," article, the terms PROBLEMS and FUNCTIONS are very generic, but they are listed along with several specific terms, so the context would make the implications clearer (figure 10.7). The odd descriptors MANYPRODUCTS and MANYCOMPANIES are not typos. They are used for articles that discuss many products and many companies, and can be useful for someone looking for a wide range of, say, printers or companies dealing, for example, with the Y2K problem.

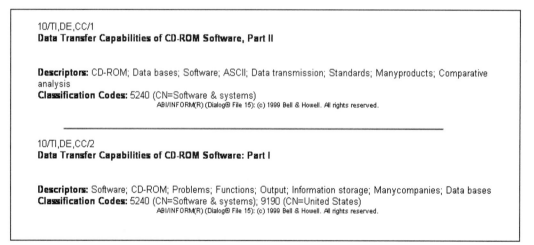

Fig. 10.7. ABI/INFORM records for the "Data Transfer" articles.

Even if compound terms are assigned, required specificity may be lacking. For example, one of the highest quality databases, INSPEC, performs poorly in this test. It assigns generic and redundant terms to both "Searching for Skeletons" records (figure 10.8), missing the most important one related to the concept of quality checking, even though there is a perfect descriptor for it in the INSPEC Thesaurus: quality control.

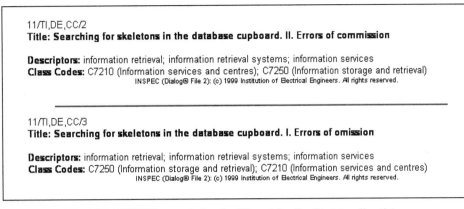

11/TI,DE,CC/2
Title: Searching for skeletons in the database cupboard. II. Errors of commission

Descriptors: information retrieval; information retrieval systems; information services
Class Codes: C7210 (Information services and centres); C7250 (Information storage and retrieval)

11/TI,DE,CC/3
Title: Searching for skeletons in the database cupboard. I. Errors of omission

Descriptors: information retrieval; information retrieval systems; information services
Class Codes: C7250 (Information storage and retrieval); C7210 (Information services and centres)

Fig. 10.8. INSPEC records for the "Searching for Skeletons" articles.

The two single terms assigned by LISA from the revised controlled vocabulary are much better for the same records (ERRORS and DATABASES and QUALITY and DATABASES) (figure 10.9).

12/TI,BL,DE/2
Searching for skeletons in the database cupboard part II: errors of commission.

BLDSC Shelf Mark: 3535.802200

Descriptors: Databases; Quality

12/TI,BL,DE/3
Searching for skeletons in the database cupboard Part 1: errors of omission.

BLDSC Shelf Mark: 3535.802200

Descriptors: Databases; Errors

Fig. 10.9. LISA records for the "Searching for Skeletons" articles.

In PASCAL the French, English, and—in our examples—even most of the Spanish descriptors are adequate. Some of them are very good, such as SEARCH STRATEGY or DATABASE QUERY. The German descriptors are so generic in almost every record that they are useless. The very haphazard assignment of too few of even those generic terms doesn't provide any clue about the content of the articles. In the record shown in figure 10.10 for part 2 of the "Searching for Skeletons" articles, the German descriptor ABWEICHUNG, which means DEVIATION, DISCREPANCY, or ABNORMALITY, does not make any sense alone. A quick test for the adequacy of the choice of terms is to consider the probability of using the term(s) in a search. ABWEICHUNG alone does not stand a chance.

Exhaustivity of indexing means to assign as many relevant index terms as is warranted by the article. Too few index terms can significantly limit the recall of the search. Too many can lead to false hits, though good post-coordination of index terms in a query can reduce false hits. For this reason, it is safer for the indexer to err on the side of assigning more index terms than less, though not to the extent LISA stretches it.

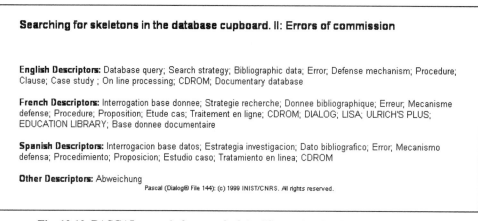

Searching for skeletons in the database cupboard. II: Errors of commission

English Descriptors: Database query; Search strategy; Bibliographic data; Error; Defense mechanism; Procedure; Clause; Case study ; On line processing; CDROM; Documentary database

French Descriptors: Interrogation base donnee; Strategie recherche; Donnee bibliographique; Erreur; Mecanisme defense; Procedure; Proposition; Etude cas; Traitement en ligne; CDROM; DIALOG; LISA; ULRICH'S PLUS; EDUCATION LIBRARY; Base donnee documentaire

Spanish Descriptors: Interrogacion base datos; Estrategia investigacion; Dato bibliografico; Error; Mecanismo defensa; Procedimiento; Proposicion; Estudio caso; Tratamiento en linea; CDROM

Other Descriptors: Abweichung

Fig. 10.10. PASCAL records for part 2 of the "Searching for Skeletons" articles.

The terms assigned by LISA for the "Data Transfer" articles shown in figure 10.11 (INFORMATION STORAGE AND RETRIEVAL, COMPUTERIZED INFORMATION STORAGE AND RETRIEVAL, INFORMATION RETRIEVAL) are obviously redundant and generic, as are the terms for the other concept of STORAGE MEDIA, OPTICAL DISCS, DISCS, and COMPACT DISCS when "CD-ROM" would suffice. The terms COMPUTERIZED SUBJECT INDEXING, SUBJECT INDEXING, and once again SUBJECT INDEXING are not only absurdly redundant but also irrelevant, as the article nowhere mentions subject indexing. The three best, more specific terms are UPLOADING, DOWNLOADING, and EXCHANGE FORMATS, and they would have sufficed along with the term "CD-ROM."

13/TI,BL,DE/2
Data transfer capabilities of CD-ROM software Part 2.

BLDSC Shelf Mark: 3096.303980

Descriptors: Information storage and retrieval; Information work; Subject indexing; Computerized information storage and retrieval; Computerized subject indexing; Discs; Optical discs; Storage; CD-ROMs; Compact discs; Software; Uploading; Exchange formats; Formats

13/TI,BL,DE/3
Data transfer capabilities of CD-ROM software. Part 1.

BLDSC Shelf Mark: 3096.303980

Descriptors: Information storage and retrieval; Information work; Subject indexing; Computerized information storage and retrieval; Computerized subject indexing; Discs; Optical discs; Storage; CD-ROMs; Compact discs; Databases; Information services; Software; Downloading; Output

Fig. 10.11. LISA records for the "Data Transfer" articles.

The repeated use of the same descriptors is so unprofessional that the only explanation is that the thousands of records showing this symptom must have been assigned descriptors by a program to which no one paid attention. The records in figure 10.12 speak for themselves. The records chosen for illustration are not accidentally for articles about — what else, redundancy. A human would not have been able to assign so many redundant terms for articles about redundancy.

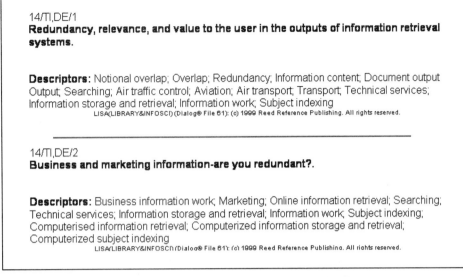

Fig. 10.12. LISA records for articles about redundancy.

Specificity is often achieved by subdividing a more generic term to indicate some aspect of the main heading. The Trade & Industry Database (T&I) shows a good example of this in the record for the "Negotiating" article (figure 10.13) by assigning the terms LIBRARIES–AUTOMATION and CD-ROM–INSTALLATION.

17/TI,SC,DE/3
Negotiating your way through the pitfalls of CD-ROM installation.

Descriptors: Online searching--Usage; CD-ROM--Installation; Libraries--Automation
Product/Industry Names: 3652 Prerecorded records and tapes; 3571 Electronic computers;
8231 Libraries

Fig. 10.13. T&I records for the "Negotiating" article.

The same happens in the record for the "Quality of Abstracts" article (not shown here), where both main headings get the perfect subdivision: QUALITY CONTROL to make the terms appropriately specific. Strangely, for part 1 of the "Searching for Skeletons" article, the indexer assigns the good subdivided term QUALITY CONTROL, but part 2 of the "Searching for Skeletons" article has the less appropriate subject heading–subheading combination: DATA BASES–USAGE (figure 10.14). The same applies to the use of the format DATA BASES instead of DATABASES, discussed previously for ABI/INFORM. The differences in the sequence of title proper and subtitle in the records, as well as the variance in the identification of the parts, should also be noted.

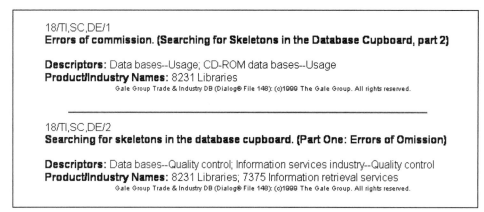

Fig. 10.14. T&I records for the "Searching for Skeletons" articles.

This kind of subdivision is characteristic of the H. W. Wilson databases, which have good specificity but fall somewhat short in exhaustivity. Such an issue should always be examined in light of the content of entire records. H. W. Wilson is known to provide very good title enhancement, which is as good for online searching as are additional descriptors. Among the sample records from the H. W. Wilson databases, the Business Abstracts database strikes the perfect balance between frugal and excessive indexing (figure 10.15). It also illustrates the strong adherence to the traditional pre-coordinated indexing.

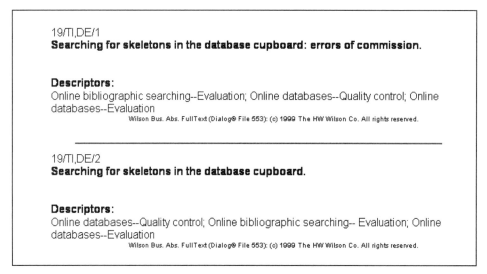

Fig. 10.15. Business Abstracts records for the "Searching for Skeletons" articles.

A larger number of index terms assigned to articles does not necessarily provide adequate exhaustivity, as was clearly the case with the unprecedentedly redundant indexing in LISA. PIRA shows another reason for not relying merely on the number of descriptors assigned to records in judging the quality of subject indexing. Showering the "Quality of Abstracts" article with 12 index terms (all but one single word) is to be taken with a grain of salt (figure 10.16).

PIRA seems to give utmost preference for single terms in its subject descriptors. The terms FORM, GRAPHIC, and PROFESSIONAL by themselves may seem more like KWOC (keyword out of context) index entries than descriptors, and the use of singular format for most nouns except for ABSTRACTS is not common practice. In the case of the descriptor OBJECTIVE, this becomes confusing.

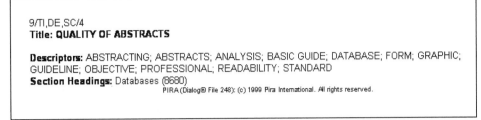

Fig. 10.16. PIRA record for the "Quality of Abstracts" article.

The ideal candidates for consistency checking are multipart articles, conference papers later developed into journal articles, and translated versions of original articles.

There is an obvious indexing inconsistency between LISA records for the original English language "Negotiating" article and its Hungarian translation (figure 10.17). The record for the original article has seven terms, mostly unnecessarily broad, for CD-ROM, but at least includes that most specific term as well. The record for the Hungarian translation omits the descriptor CD-ROMs and provides only the generic and unnecessary terms.

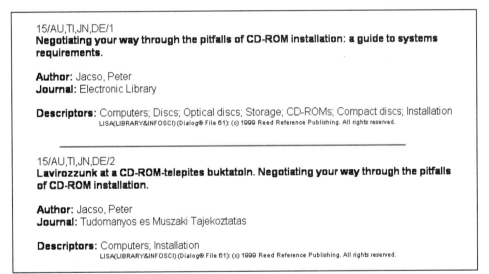

Fig. 10.17. LISA record for the original and the Hungarian translation of an article.

In the case of INSPEC, the two descriptors assigned for the English language article are perfect (CD-ROMs and INSTALLATION). The descriptors for the Hungarian translation of the "Negotiating" article are of questionable relevance (DP MANAGEMENT and INFORMATION SERVICES) because they are too generic. The wrong initial for the author is also to be noted, although it does not have an impact on subject indexing (figure 10.18).

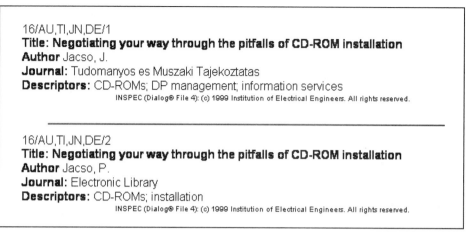

Fig. 10.18. INSPEC records for the "Negotiating" article.

ISA provides a fertile ground for checking consistency in subject indexing, as it has several thousand genuine duplicate pairs, discussed in detail by Jacsó (1998a). Most of them show an interesting cyclic pattern (figure 10.19). The duplicates were typically added three to five years after the first copy. This practice was the most prevalent in the early and mid-1990s when the number of records added to ISA in each update was enviably round (figure 10.20), although it did not always reach the volume of 800 to 900 monthly records promised by IFI/Plenum, the former producer.

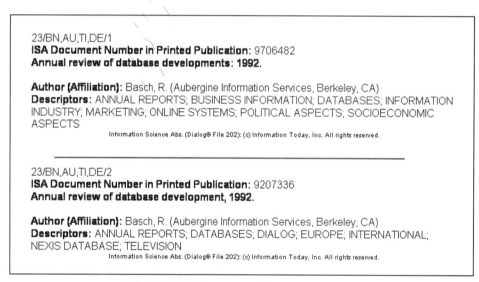

Fig. 10.19. Cyclic pattern of duplicates in ISA.

An analysis of the descriptors in the duplicate pairs shows a lower level of consistency than was found by Sievert and Andrews (1991). This applies also to the broad subject categories as illustrated by the sample records (figure 10.21). Considering that there are only 170 subject category and subcategory codes, and they did not change during the period of most excessive duplicate additions, this appears to be an unusually high level of inconsistency. This may explain, on the other hand, why the longtime editor of ISA may not have been cognizant of the extent and persistence of duplicate entries, and was compelled to announce that, from 1986, duplicate entries have not been added to the database (Allcock 1997).

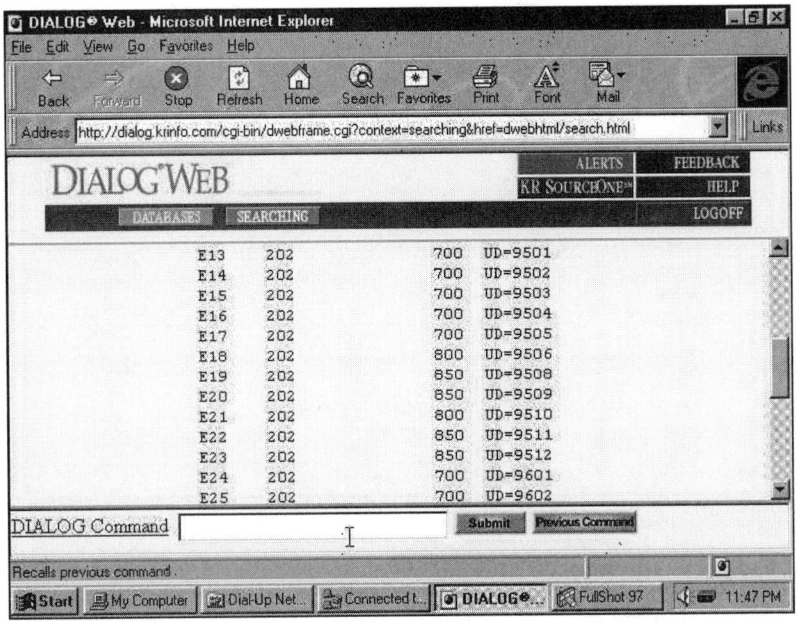

Fig. 10.20. Perfectly round number of update records in ISA.

Indeed, duplicates appeared in different sections (i.e., not congregating under the same category) to facilitate for readers and the editor the spotting of this problem in the printed version, which organizes the entries by broad subject categories. The other side of the issue is that neither did the subscribers complain about duplicates, as mostly they consult a specific section of the abstracting and indexing journal and don't read it through from *A* to *Z*.

The new management of the database promised to put ISA through a "vigorous clean-up process," including the elimination of duplicate records. This vigor is enhanced by the fact that the former senior technical advisor of IFI/Plenum, in ISA matters, joined the new owner's organization and undoubtedly provides the bridge between the old and the new ISA. Eliminating the thousands of duplicates may be more time-consuming than it was to add them to the database.

In spite of efforts, there are still duplicates and new ones continue to be introduced. Although this is not good for the customers, it is good for researchers who may explore different aspects of indexing consistency beyond subject indexing. However, researchers must take care when interpreting bibliometric data retrieved from ISA in analyzing publishing and topical trends until all the duplicates are eliminated.

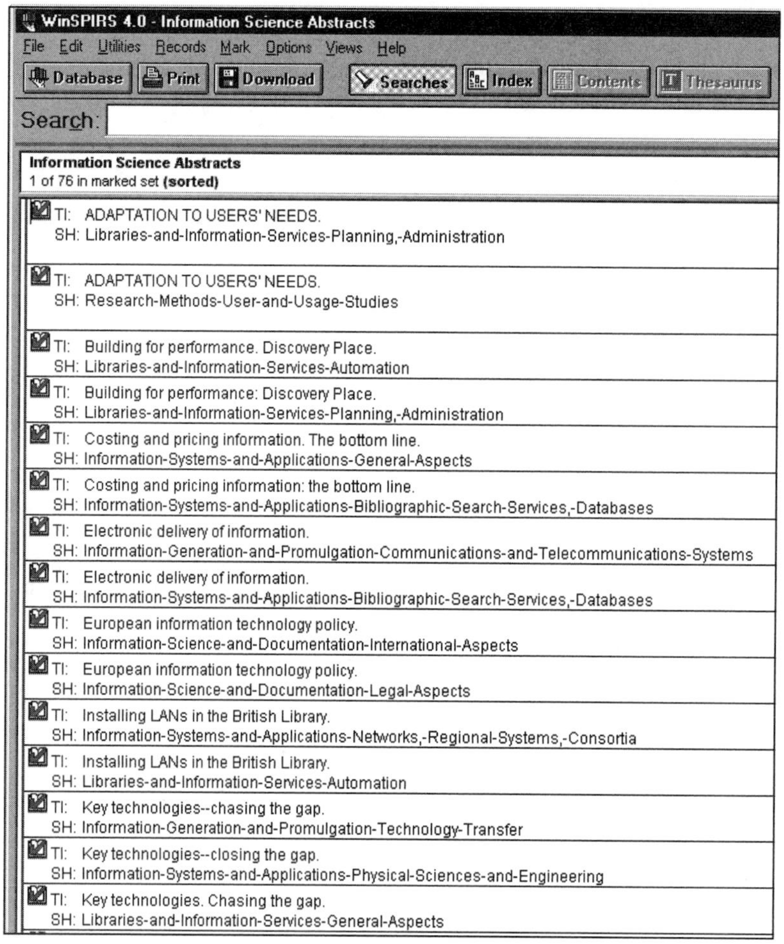

Fig. 10.21. Inconsistent broad subject category names in ISA duplicates.

Quality of Abstracts

An abstract is meant to provide a brief (150- to 250-word) summary of the original document. Although publishing abstracts of papers historically predates journal indexing services, the automation of information services started with using computers to produce indexing databases. It was quite a breakthrough when indexing services to journals and conferences started to include abstracts. By the late 1990s, the number of indexing-only databases (but not the number of printed indexes) plummeted.

The British Education Index, Anthropological Index, National Newspaper Index, and Library Literature are among the few exceptions in the database market, and as of the summer of 1999, Library Literature was enhanced with full-text articles (but not abstracts) from nearly 80 prominent LIS journals. This enhanced version is named Library Literature & Information Science Full Text Database. The Population Index database just ceased adding new records from 2000 despite its excellent quality and reputation. The lack of abstracts makes the indexing-only databases more and more an endangered species.

The other classic indexes of H. W. Wilson, such as Art Index, Humanities Index, and Applied Science &Technology Index, were enhanced earlier with abstracts (although only for the past few years and not in their entirety), and for hundreds of journals with the full text of original articles. Increasingly, full texts of the documents or their page image versions (or both) are expected to be available in databases.

In spite of these developments, abstracts will have a place under the sun. Good abstracts can help users in the selection of what documents should be read in their entirety. An abstract may allude to the content of source documents (journal articles, patents, congressional hearings, books, movies) or summarize the content. The former is an indicative abstract, the latter an informative abstract, which presents directly some of the specific information in the source. Both types are illustrated in this chapter. The third type of abstract, the critical abstract, adds to the summary evaluative and critical comments by the abstractor, who is a specialist in the field. Critical abstracts are mostly produced for in-house use, and lately for classified Web directories. Their evaluation is not discussed here.

Good abstracts are also excellent filters in the search process. Limiting the search to those records that have the terms "Microsoft," "Department of Justice," and "antitrust" in the abstract is likely to increase the relevance of records retrieved by eliminating those items that include these words only in the full-text part. They may passingly mention the ongoing trial or include the three terms, but in an unrelated context.

Online and CD-ROM versions of indexing and abstracting services make the analysis and comparison of abstracts much easier. Selecting abstracts from a database meeting specific criteria (such as topic, type, and language of source documents) and finding matching records in another database for comparative analysis are not time-consuming processes anymore. Grammatical and stylistic analysis of a large number of abstracts to determine their readability level is far less tedious than it was using manual analysis. Comparison of abstracts with the source documents, however, remains a domain in evaluating abstracts that requires human skills and competence, as well as time. Finding how well an abstract summarizes the content of the source documents remains a time-consuming process.

CONCEPTS AND LITERATURE

Several excellent books discuss at length what makes an abstract good and what types of abstracts are used for different purposes (Borko and Bernier 1975; Cleveland and Cleveland 2001; Tenopir and Lundeen 1988; Lancaster 1998). The second edition of Lancaster's book also provides a current review of the literature.

Abstracts have been the subject of a joint standard of the American National Standards Institute (ANSI) and the National Information Standards Organization (NISO). The original standard, developed in 1971, was revised twice. The latest edition of Guidelines for Abstracts ANSI/NISO Z39.14-1997 was made available in early November 2000 free of charge on the Web by NISO at *http://www.techstreet. com/cgi-bin/detail?product_id=52600.*

This unusually succinct standard summarizes the principles discussed in the monographs mentioned previously. It is enhanced by a useful appendix with different types of abstracts to illustrate the guidelines. The appendix is not part of the standard itself, and neither is the foreword, which gives background about the history of standardizing abstracts. Although the efforts are laudable, especially the special attention given to desired traits of abstracts from the perspective of computer-based searching, note that few abstracting and indexing services follow the guidelines in every regard.

There is a good collection of books and articles about the qualitative aspects of abstracts, although studies about operational systems are few and far between, despite the agreement of scholars that abstracts can significantly contribute to retrieval efficiency.

The consensus about the importance of abstracts is so high that there was only one study found in the current literature that alluded to the fact, in a side comment, that users may not appreciate the presence of abstracts as much as information professionals assume. Watson and Perrin (1994) compared the coverage of MEDLINE and CINAHL in the allied health areas and found in their survey that 6 out of the 10 faculty members involved in the evaluation did not feel that the lack of abstracts was limiting.

The importance of the abstract as a source to increase recall in retrieval is illustrated by the experience of Sievert and Sievert (1991), who found that 12 percent of the records that could be retrieved through subject searches from the FRANCIS database, but not from Philosopher's Index, did not have abstracts or did not have the term in the author-written abstract to match the term in the query. Weston and Lauderdale (1988) attribute the lack of abstracts in PsycINFO for dissertations to the low recall of these documents by keyword searching.

Although there is consensus about the potential added value of abstracts, there is disagreement in separating the indexing and abstracting process, and in the appreciation of author-written abstracts. Everett Brenner (1989) says that abstracting and indexing skills are significantly different, that a good indexer is not necessarily a good abstractor, and that changing one's mind-set between indexing and abstracting at each document may not be efficient. On the other side of the debate, Lancaster (1991) argues that abstracting is a small step from indexing, and requires the same conceptual analysis of the document after reading and skimming it, so it makes the process more efficient if the two activities are combined.

On the matter of author-written abstracts, Froehlich (1994) argues that, while in the hard sciences it is possible that an author-written abstract enhances its value and credibility, "in other subject domains, this may not be the case, because the author only articulates his or her understanding of the subject matter, which is an understanding that may or may not map to an orthodox approach to or understanding of the subject domain." (Ironically, the high-quality, informative abstract written for this very article by the author contradicts his opposition of author-written abstracts.)

Milas-Bracovic and Zajec (1989), on the other hand—in concert with the stipulations of the 1979 version of the ANSI standard for writing abstracts—argue that having authors write abstracts saves time and improves the quality of abstracts "since it may be expected that the authors, being the subject specialists, are the best possible abstractors provided that they are also made familiar with the rules for writing abstracts."

The most prominent issue about abstracting in the past few years has been the use of structured abstracts in clinical medical journals. While library and information science journals have hardly taken notice of this development (with the notable exception of a comprehensive, statistically sound, and information-rich study by Harbourt, Knecht, and Humphrey [1995], to be discussed later), editors and contributors of medical journals have discussed the merit or the lack of merit of structured abstracts intensely, as cited by Haynes et al. (1996), and Johnson and Bevan (1996). Their pro and con arguments can be highly relevant for information professionals in any discipline as, with some adapting, the structured abstracts may be applicable for other disciplines of science and—to a lesser extent—social science.

Structured abstracts show up in increasing numbers in medical and other life science databases as well. As quoted by Froom and Froom (1993), the American College of Physicians Ad Hoc Working Group for the Critical Appraisal of the Medical Literature developed (and later modified) comprehensive guidelines about the content and format of abstracts that should accompany original research and review articles of clinical investigations. The guidelines suggest that the maximum 250-word abstract should have labeled segments identifying the objective, design, setting, patients, treatment, outcome measures, results, and conclusions of original research studies. Somewhat different aspects of reviews are suggested.

Dixon (1988) was among the ones to praise structured abstracts, while Heller (1990) felt that they are "yet another blow against creative medical communication." Beyond the emotionally heated exchange of opinions, some quantitative and qualitative evaluations were published, and journals took sides. While the *Journal of Clinical Epidemiology* refused to use structured abstracts, the highest impact journals, such as *New England Journal of Medicine*, *Journal of the American Medical Association*, *Chest*, and *Gut*, adopted somewhat different versions of structured abstracts.

Narine et al. (1991) found marked deficiencies in the quality of 33 abstracts published in the *Canadian Medical Association Journal*, one of the early adopters of the guidelines. Taddio et al. (1994) extended the study of Narine et al. (1991) to 150 nonstructured and 150 structured abstracts using his scoring model and found that the overall mean quality scores for the two strata were 0.57 and 0.74, respectively.

Froom and Froom (1993) studied abstracts and full texts of 130 articles published in the *Annals of Internal Medicine,* which was the first to adopt the concept of structured abstracts. They examined to what extent the structured abstracts conformed to the guidelines and helped clinicians decide whether the information was relevant for their own patient population. They found structured abstracts significantly deficient in presenting information related to patient selection factors and authors' conclusions.

In a dissenting but well-balanced paper, Haynes (1993) points out the limited scope of the survey and notes that more detailed studies would be needed. Although he admits that it is "distressing that so much information was missing" from the structured abstracts, he warns that the key question is not how well the abstracts meet the guidelines but rather how well structured abstracts meet their objectives. These objectives are better communication with readers, improved peer review, and improved retrieval from bibliographic databases.

Salager-Meyer (1991) evaluated 77 abstracts published in 33 biomedical journals between 1987 and 1989, and found that 48 percent of them had one or more structural flaws, such as the omission of an important segment, or the illogical ordering of segments, such as the conclusion preceding the results.

Harbourt, Knecht, and Humphreys (1995) have made perhaps the most important step so far in the direction of evaluating the characteristics and impact of structured abstracts from the online and CD-ROM retrieval perspective. The authors profiled the characteristics of nearly 1 million records added to MEDLINE from early 1989 to the end of 1991, including 3,873 records with structured abstracts. They found that records with structural abstracts had 3.5 more MeSH terms than the overall MEDLINE sample, though this increase was less when the comparison was made with records of clinical articles (2.1) and reviews (1.9). Also, the structured abstracts (without the labels) were nearly 70 percent longer than the abstracts in the overall MEDLINE sample. Statistics clearly indicate that both the number of clinical journals and the number of articles featuring structured abstracts keep growing, though 79 percent of the sample records with structured abstracts were clustered in 17 percent of the journals.

Kulkarni, Gupta, and Viswanathan (1996) looked at the growth rate of MEDLINE records with structured abstracts from the perspective of the total number of English language clinical journal articles from 1990 and found that only 28.5 percent of them had structured abstracts. Although it may take a long time for the structured abstracts to become mainstream in clinical medicine articles, the significantly increased number of access points is likely to assist searchers in both the retrieval and the display processes.

This assumption was tested by Hartley, Sydes, and Blurton (1996) on a small sample of 30 pairs of structured and unstructured abstracts for the same articles from the *British Journal of Educational Psychology*. Fifty-two students were asked to find the answers to two questions for each of eight abstracts presented in one format, followed by two questions for each of eight abstracts set in the other format. In a complementary test, 56 students were asked to find five abstracts that reported a particular kind of study, and then to find five more that reported another kind of study. Time and error data (which were recorded automatically) support the hypothesis that it is easier for users to use structured abstracts than unstructured ones.

Hartley, Sydes, and Blurton (1996) also studied the typographical aspects of structured abstracts and how they influence users' preferences. A series of studies was carried out in three stages with more than 400 students in total to determine readers' preferences for different typographic settings for subheadings in structured abstracts, and for overall positioning and layout of abstracts on a (European) standard page (which is almost identical to the 8.5-by-11-inch U.S. letter size format). The most preferred version was the one with subheadings in bold capital letters separated by a line space above each heading (introduction, objective, method, etc.). As for the layout, the preferred form was for the abstract to be centered over the top of the two-column article.

One of the possible reasons for the successful entry of RNdex Top 100 into a crowded market may have been the fact that it offers abstracts for every record, and that the abstracts created by the file producer follow the recommendation of the American College of Physicians Ad Hoc Working Group for the Critical Appraisal of the Medical Literature. It suggested that authors of articles with direct clinical implications prepare abstracts so that the key aspects of purpose, methodology, and results are consistently described in a standardized manner (Haynes 1987).

In an effort to gauge the quality of abstracts of *Referativnii Zhurnal Khimiya* (RZK), a Russian abstracting and indexing chemistry journal, Katritzky, Cato, and Deyrup (1993) consulted 923 abstracts from an experimental English version of RZK. Then—with the help of a native Russian chemist—they compared 102 randomly chosen abstracts of English language journal articles available in both Chemical Abstracts (CA) and RZK to determine if

1. a chemist could obtain information easily from the abstract,

2. the purpose of the research was made clear,

3. the major concepts in the article were presented in the abstract,

4. the abstract gave the most important conclusion,

5. chemical structures were present,

6. there were significant differences in the quantity of data in the abstract,

7.   there were obvious errors, and

8.   the quality of the abstract was a function of the geographical origin of the article.

The abstracts in the experimental English version set had some typos and errors, though not in the author name, journal title, pagination, or date fields, which were deemed of good quality. The in-depth comparison of the 102 abstracts found that the RZK abstracts were well written and longer, and gave more data about compounds and physical characteristics than those of CA. Their biggest weakness was in describing theoretical and general conclusions and the lack of graphic representation of the structure of compounds and intermediaries. There was no difference in the treatment of English versus Russian documents.

Milas-Bracovic and Zajec (1989) evaluated the quality of abstracts of research articles published in scholarly journals in Croatia, using a novel approach. The authors selected 1,372 research papers and their abstracts (53 percent in natural science, medicine, and technology; 47 percent in social sciences, humanities, and art) from 98 journals out of 160 published in Croatia.

The abstracts were analyzed by information specialists to determine the pattern of their macrostructure as for including the sections (introduction, methods, results, and discussion) expected from good abstracts, and the proportion of informative (62 percent), indicative (9 percent), and mixed (29 percent) abstracts. They found significant differences both in the macrostructure and in the proportion of the abstract types, in the two subsets.

The abstracts were then analyzed to determine to what extent they deviated from the abstracting standard in terms of grammar (22 percent), third-person form (6 percent), length (15 percent), self-containment (5 percent), and conciseness (17 percent). Again, there were significant differences between the two sample subsets.

As the acid test for quality, the abstracts were then compared with versions that made it to *Bulletin Scientifique*, the French abstracting and indexing publication, to determine what percentage was used without change (58 percent), revised (41 percent), and written anew (1 percent). In this category, the differences between the two subsets were minimal. Only abstracts of articles in social sciences, arts, and humanities needed rewriting.

Tenopir and Jacsó (1993) tested the most measurable criteria of abstracts using samples from three general interest periodical databases: Magazine Article Summaries (MAS) with 967 records; Resource One with 1,070 records; and Readers' Guide Abstracts (RGA) with 839 records. Abstracts for articles in the *Journal of Social Psychology* were also tested in two social science databases: PsycLIT (the CD-ROM version of PsycINFO—315 records) and Sociofile (379 records).

Quantitative scores for reading level; paragraph, sentence, and word length; percentage of passive voice; prepositions; and long, medium, and short sentences were determined using the Grammatik-IV style checker program. The raw scores were adjusted and interpreted from the perspective of readability and compatibility with the ANSI standard. Informativeness was evaluated by examining 300 randomly selected records for each database to determine the percentage of indicative, informative, and combined type of abstracts.

RGA was found to be the most informative because of its predominantly lengthy and substantial abstracts, with an almost identical reading ease and grade level score as MAS. Resource One was found to have the easiest to read abstracts, primarily because of the short sentences. As for the social science databases, the ease of reading score was better for PsycLIT than for Sociofile, but the latter had significantly longer abstracts.

THE PROCESS OF EVALUATING ABSTRACTS

Reading source documents and abstracts created for them by different file producers remains the best method of evaluating abstracts by the criteria discussed in the textbooks cited previously. However, the combination of the digital version of the abstracting and indexing journals and the search software offers possibilities to facilitate several phases of the process.

Selecting records that have abstracts is an easy process with software that offers this filtering criterion. This step must be executed on an existing set. Such a set may be created in the same way as any other set (i.e., by subject, journal name, author name, date, etc.). Limiting may be done either in command mode or in menu mode using a filter box. Figures 11.1 and 11.2 illustrate the two approaches.

Set	Term Searched	Items
S1	PAIN?/ENG,MAJ,HUMAN,ABS	21160

Fig. 11.1. Limiting in DIALOG command mode.

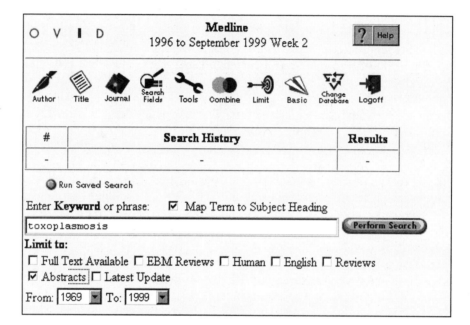

Fig. 11.2. Limiting in Ovid advanced menu mode.

Just because the name of a database includes the word *abstracts* does not mean that all records have abstracts. Samples taken for such databases show that a varying percentage of records in several databases don't have abstracts (figure 11.3). The documentation of some databases notes that abstracts are available only for records added since a given year or for certain document types, but many others don't give any warning about the absence of abstracts.

Unfortunately, many databases that have *Abstracts* in their name do not allow limiting a result set to records with abstracts, so they could not be tested. Not providing this limit feature may seem logical at first blush, assuming that a database such as LISA or ISA would have abstracts for all records, but this is unlikely to be a valid assumption. Finding many records in a set of abstracting databases without abstracts not only is frustrating, but can also be a waste of money, since it means choosing and paying for a more expensive display format that includes the abstract, only to find that several records in the output do not have abstracts.

Absence of abstracts in databases that don't use the word *Abstracts* in their name is more understandable and quite prevalent, as shown in figure 11.4. Some of them warn the users in the documentation that this important data element is not available in every record. (It is another question as to how many users read the documentation.)

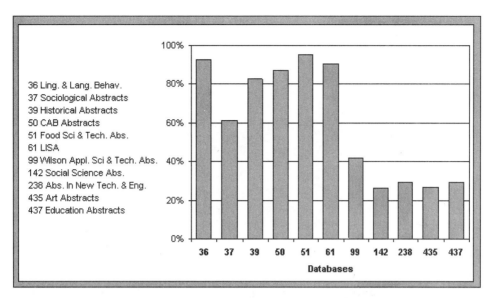

Fig. 11.3. Percentage of records with abstracts in databases with the word *Abstracts* in their name.

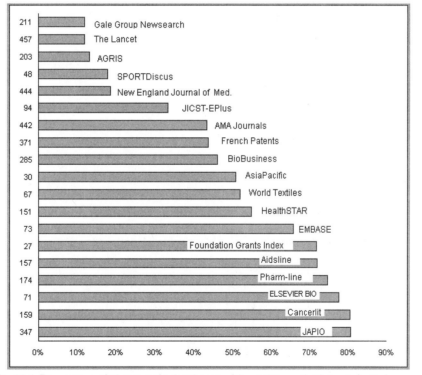

Fig. 11.4. Percentage of abstracts in databases without the word *Abstracts* in their name.

Many databases fall far short of the expected 150- to 250-word length suggested by ANSI for abstracts. It is fairly easy to test the average length of abstracts in a database by downloading a few hundred sample records and using the word count feature of a word processing software. This may be expensive in an online database that charges per record fees, but in a CD-ROM database, it is free. Figure 11.5 illustrates the average length of abstracts in LISA, ISA, PsycINFO, and Mental Health Abstracts. The same broad topical search was made in the abstract field of both database pairs, and then the first 500 records were downloaded from each and evaluated by Microsoft Word's word count utility. It may not be a statistically representative sample, but it works fine for those who want to get a feel for the length of abstracts in databases. PsycINFO and MHA are fairly close, while ISA has a definite advantage over LISA.

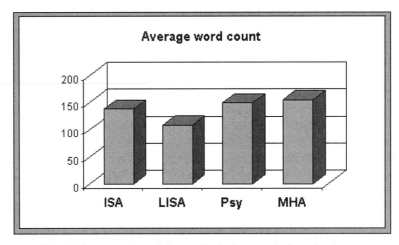

Fig. 11.5. Average length in words of abstracts in four databases.

The most notorious record types for the shortest and least informative abstracts are recipes and book and movie reviews. For example, there are records for two dozen reviews of the best-seller *Bridget Jones's Diary* in EBSCO's Academic Search Elite. The abstract is the same one-liner in all of them (figure 11.6), except for one that misspells *Bridget* as *Briget* (proving that these "abstracts" are not cut and pasted from one review to another).

Record: 4
    Title: The *marriage mystique*.
    Subject(s): BRIDGET Jones's Diary (Book)
    Source: New Yorker, 08/03/98, Vol. 74 Issue 22, p70, 6p, 1c
    Author(s): Merkin, Daphne
    Abstract: Reviews the book `Bridget Jones's Diary,' by Helen Fielding.
    AN: 916645
    ISSN: 0028-792X
    Database: Academic Search Elite

Record: 5
    Title: Book reviews: Fiction.
    Subject(s): BRIDGET Jones's Diary (Book)
    Source: Library Journal, 05/15/98, Vol. 123 Issue 9, p114, 1/6p
    Author(s): Blodgett, Jan; Hoffert, Barbara; et al
    Abstract: Reviews the book, `**Briget** Jones's Diary,' by Helen Fielding.
    AN: 622170
    ISSN: 0363-0277
    Database: Academic Search Elite

Fig. 11.6. Identical "abstracts" in book review records of Academic Search Elite.

Tests (to be discussed later) have shown that Bell & Howell typically creates very good informative abstracts for journal articles in the field of information technology. The same cannot be said of book review records. The same uninformative "abstracts" as seen in Academic Search Elite are characteristic also in the Periodical Abstracts PlusText database (figure 11.7). Interestingly, its sister database, Newspaper Abstracts Daily, has substantial abstracts for most book reviews, similar to the one about *Bridget Jones's Diary* (figure 11.8).

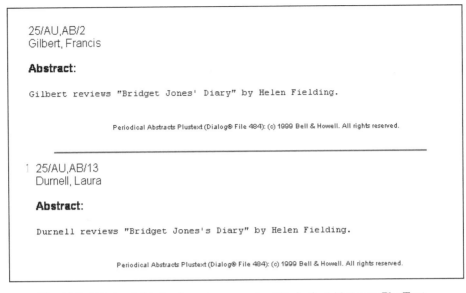

Fig. 11.7. "Abstracts" in book review records of Periodical Abstracts PlusText.

Fig. 11.8. Substantial abstract for a book review in Newspaper Abstracts Daily.

The average length of abstracts in a database is only a crude first approach to evaluating the abstracts. The length of abstracts does not guarantee informativeness. Longer is not necessarily better, although longer abstracts certainly have a better chance of accommodating the essential information of the primary document. Several of the classic works on abstracting and indexing provide guidelines for judging what makes a good abstract. This judgment, however, still remains subjective and requires reading the abstracts and the primary documents.

CASE STUDY FOR EVALUATING THE QUALITY OF ABSTRACTS

The easiest way to get started is to study the abstracts for the same article. It is relatively easy with databases of general interest periodicals, and more difficult with abstracts of scientific and technical documents. Figures 11.9, 11.10, and 11.11 represent abstracts for the same article in three databases.

The one from Readers' Guide Abstracts is by far the best. It answers the four *W*'s: who, what, when, and why. The abstract in Academic Search Elite does not provide some crucial detail. The abstract in Periodical Abstracts PlusText makes no mention of the key fact that the culprit was fired a few days before committing the crime. This piece of information would be needed to understand the title.

28/TI,JN,AB/1
Vengeance by 'virus'.

U.S. News & World Report (U S News World Rep)

Abstract: Donald Burleson, the former director of computer security at a Texas insurance firm, has become the world's first person to be convicted of sabotaging computer files. Three days after he was fired in 1985, USPA & IRA of Ft. Worth discovered that 168,000 sales records had been erased from its computer system. Burleson's crime involved what are now known as computer "viruses," self-replicating programs that destroy computer data. Viruses can wipe out records in seconds and continue to wreak havoc in system after system.

Fig. 11.9. Abstract for the "Vengeance" article in RGA.

Title:	***Vengeance*** by `***virus***.'
Subject(s):	COMPUTER security
Source:	U.S. News & World Report, 10/3/88, p10, 1/3p
Abstract:	Discusses codes planted in computer programs to destroy crucial data (viruses). Last week Donald Burleson became the first person convicted of such sabotage. Crime; Costs.
AN:	8800020150
ISSN:	0041-5537
Database:	Academic Search Elite

Fig. 11.10. Abstract for the "Vengeance" article in Academic Search Elite.

2/TI,AB/1
Vengeance by 'Virus'

Abstract:

Last week Donald Burleson, an insurance firm's director of computer security, became the first person ever convicted of destroying crucial data by implanting codes in computer programs. Burleson's crime involved an early form of what are now known as "viruses."

Fig. 11.11. Abstract for the "Vengeance" article in Periodical Abstracts PlusText.

The records for the "Crimson Copycat" editorial illustrate the different approaches of creating an abstract for the same article. The abstract in Academic Search Elite (figure 11.12) focuses on one specific event and gives the most details, whereas that of Periodical Abstracts PlusText (figure 11.13) does not even mention the actual case, but does summarize the thoughts of the author well. RGA combines the best of these two approaches, striking a perfect balance (fig. 11.14).

<table>
<tr><td>Title:</td><td>The crimson copycat.</td></tr>
<tr><td>Subject(s):</td><td>FRAZIER, Shervert</td></tr>
<tr><td>Source:</td><td>U.S. News & World Report, 12/12/88, p90, 1p</td></tr>
<tr><td>Author(s):</td><td>Leo, J.</td></tr>
<tr><td>Abstract:</td><td>Commentary on plagiarism. Report that Shervert Frazier, former director of the National Institute of Mental Health, former president of the American College of Psychiatrists, professor of psychiatry at Harvard Medical School and psychiatrist in chief at Boston's McLean Hospital admitted to plagiarism and resigned. Frazier's plagiarism was uncovered by graduate student Paul Scatena of the University of Rochester.</td></tr>
<tr><td>AN:</td><td>8800029690</td></tr>
<tr><td>ISSN:</td><td>0041-5537</td></tr>
<tr><td>Database:</td><td>Academic Search Elite</td></tr>
</table>

Fig. 11.12. Abstract for the "Crimson Copycat" article in Academic Search Elite.

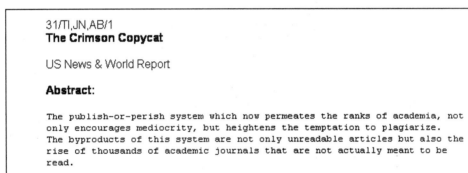

31/TI,JN,AB/1
The Crimson Copycat

US News & World Report

Abstract:

```
The publish-or-perish system which now permeates the ranks of academia, not
only encourages mediocrity, but heightens the temptation to plagiarize.
The byproducts of this system are not only unreadable articles but also the
rise of thousands of academic journals that are not actually meant to be
read.
```

Fig. 11.13. Abstract for the "Crimson Copycat" article in Periodical Abstracts PlusText.

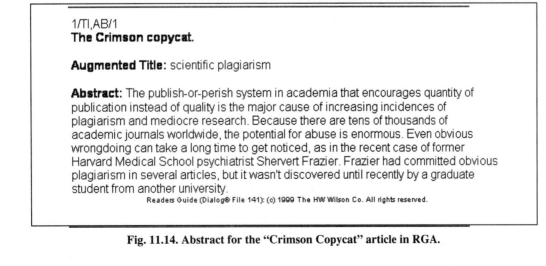

1/TI,AB/1
The Crimson copycat.

Augmented Title: scientific plagiarism

Abstract: The publish-or-perish system in academia that encourages quantity of publication instead of quality is the major cause of increasing incidences of plagiarism and mediocre research. Because there are tens of thousands of academic journals worldwide, the potential for abuse is enormous. Even obvious wrongdoing can take a long time to get noticed, as in the recent case of former Harvard Medical School psychiatrist Shervert Frazier. Frazier had committed obvious plagiarism in several articles, but it wasn't discovered until recently by a graduate student from another university.

Fig. 11.14. Abstract for the "Crimson Copycat" article in RGA.

The third example (brought to my attention by a former student, Marilyn Rappun, many years ago) still epitomizes some exceptionally valuable features of RGA. It is the only abstract that reports in the conclusion of the article that there is no proof that Lincoln had Marfan's syndrome (figure 11.15). It is a bonus that RGA includes the punch line as title augmentation, so it shows up even in the short display formats, and the word *Marfan* becomes searchable also in the title index. The other two abstracts leave out this important conclusion. The same informativeness applies also to the sentence that defines Marfan's syndrome. RGA concisely explains it. Periodical Abstracts PlusText (figure 11.16) merely indicates that it is a genetic disorder, and Academic Search Elite (figure 11.17) gives no hint about the implications of the disease.

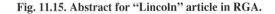

30/TI,JN,AB/6
The case of the president's feet.

Augmented Title: G. S. Boritt finds no evidence that A. Lincoln had elongated big toes
U.S. News & World Report (U S News World Rep)

Abstract: On the 125th anniversary of the Gettysburg Address, Professor Gabor Boritt, a leading expert on Abraham Lincoln, has reported the discovery of the only known outline of Lincoln's feet. Boritt contends that the outline partly answers the question of whether Lincoln had Marfan's syndrome, an uncommon genetic disorder characterized by long limbs, elongated big toes, and in many cases superior intelligence. Piqued by medical-journal arguments that Lincoln had the syndrome, Boritt found an original sketch of Lincoln's feet that had been made by the president's bootmaker. He notes that the sketch indicates that Lincoln did not have long toes.

Fig. 11.15. Abstract for "Lincoln" article in RGA.

33/TI,JN,AB/1
The Case of the President's Feet

US News & World Report

Abstract:

After spending ten years doing research, Gabor Boritt has discovered the only known outline of President Lincoln's feet. The drawing could help determine if Lincoln suffered from Marfan's syndrome.

Fig. 11.16. Abstract for "Lincoln" article in Periodical Abstracts PlusText.

The most practical approach for comparative evaluation purposes is to create the basic set by journal name, choosing journals that are known to have no abstracts. In library and information science, such journals include *Online*, *Database* (now *EContent*), *Searcher*, and *Computers in Libraries*. Otherwise, there will be many identical or at least very similar abstracts—taken from original articles in journals that do provide authors' abstracts, such as most of the academic journals. File producers happily take these abstracts, saving lots of time and money. However, there are high-quality journals in every discipline that include no abstracts written by the author or editor. These journals are the perfect candidates to compare and evaluate the abstracts created by the abstracting and indexing services.

Following this, finding duplicates in the different databases for the same articles will yield a set that is comparable. This set can then be evaluated by reading it and then running it through an inexpensive, comprehensive grammar checker program.

Title:	The **case** of the **President's feet**.
Subject(s):	LINCOLN, Abraham -- Health; BORITT, Gabor; PRESIDENTS -- United States -- Physiology; MARFAN syndrome
Source:	U.S. News & World Report, 11/28/88, p64, 2p
Author(s):	Lord, L.
Abstract:	Discusses efforts by Prof. Gabor Boritt, a leading expert on President Lincoln, to research the size of Lincoln's big toe. The professor has chosen this month, the 125th anniversary of Lincoln's Gettysburg Address, to report the discovery of the only known outline of the **President's feet**. Possibility of Marfan's syndrome a rare genetic disorder. INSETS: The rail splitter meets the rightWriter.
AN:	8800015512
ISSN:	0041-5537
Database:	Academic Search Elite

Fig. 11.17. Abstract for "Lincoln" article in Academic Search Elite.

To illustrate the typical strength and weakness of abstracts, articles of this author (one coauthored with the editor of this book) were selected. This took care of the requirement that the evaluator must be familiar with the original article. The articles selected were published in *CD-ROM Professional*, *Online*, and *Database*, none of which include abstracts; hence, substantial differences could be expected.

Some databases with excellent library and information science coverage don't appear in the samples. Library Literature of H. W. Wilson does not have abstracts at all. Social SciSearch of ISI has only original abstracts without any modification. The succinct, illustrative evaluations are presented next, article by article, for the following works:

"Quality of Abstracts"

"What Is in a(n) (Up)Date? Currency Test Searching of Databases"

"Data Transfer Capabilities of CD-ROM Software," parts 1 and 2

"Quality of Abstracts" Article

For the "Quality of Abstracts" article, ABI/INFORM has the most informative and best-structured abstract (figure 11.18). It covers most topics of the article except the substantial comparative analysis of the readability of abstracts of PsycLIT and Sociofile (which was also missed by all the other databases). It identifies the three general interest periodical databases, as well as the criteria and software tool used for the testing. It includes some important quantitative data from the article.

Interestingly, the Periodical Abstracts PlusText database (sister publication of ABI/INFORM) does not use the same abstract (figure 11.19), a common practice by producers who create several files. This approach certainly costs more for the file producer, but may be justified by the reason of a different target audience. The different target audience is likely to require different abstracts. The one in Periodical Abstracts PlusText is much shorter and does not have the quantitative details, but mentions the major evaluation criteria and identifies the general interest periodical databases. It is very comparable to the abstract of H. W. Wilson Business Abstracts (figure 11.20) and ISA (figure 11.21). The latter deserves credit for mentioning more details about the topics discussed in the article, and deserves a jeer for the grammatical error "the authors focuses."

```
DIALOG(R)File  15:(c) 2000 Bell & Howell. All rts. reserv.

 Quality of abstracts

ABSTRACT: Printed, online, and CD-ROM indexing and abstracting publications
are  familiar reference tools in libraries. The American National Standards
Institute  (ANSI)  recognizes  3  types  of  abstracts:  1.  indicative  or
descriptive,   2.   informative,   and   3.   combination  (indicative  and
informative).  The  quality  of  the  abstracts  in  3 major CD-ROM general
periodical  indexes  that  contain  abstracts  -  Reader's Guide Abstracts,
Resource-One,   and   Magazine   Article   Summaries  -  was  tested  using
quantitative  or  objective tests to provide a generalized view of quality.
The  abstracts  were examined for: 1. consistency of style and readability,
2.  the  extent  to  which  the  ANSI  standard  was  observed,  and  3.
informativeness.  Readability  was  determined using Grammatik-IV software.
The  results indicate that the abstracts of Resource-One are the easiest to
read,  but the Reader's Guide abstracts, with an average of 110 words, most
closely match the ANSI standards for recommended length (100 to 250 words).
The  Reader's  Guide  was also judged the most informative, with 81% of its
abstracts of the informative type.
```

Fig. 11.18. Abstract from ABI/INFORM.

```
DIALOG(R)File 484:(c) 2000 Bell & Howell. All rts. reserv.

 Quality of abstracts

ABSTRACT:  The quality of abstracts found in the three major CD-Rom general
periodical indexes is compared for consistency of style and readability,
the extent to which the American National Standards Institute (ANSI)
standard is observed and informativeness.  The three indexes studied were
H.  W.  Wilson Co's Readers' Guide Abstracts, UMI's Periodical Abstracts
Ondisc and EBSCO's Magazine Article Summaries.
```

Fig. 11.19. Abstract from Periodical Abstracts PlusText.

```
DIALOG(R)File 553:(c) 2000 The HW Wilson Co. All rts. reserv.

 Quality of abstracts.
AUGMENTED TITLE: H.W. Wilson's Readers' Guide Abstracts, UMI's Periodical
Abstracts Ondisc and EBSCO's Magazine Article Summaries

ABSTRACT:  The criteria for judging the quality of an abstract, including
the abstracting style used and the abstract's content and length, are
described and used to evaluate the quality of abstracts in three databases:
H.W. Wilson Company's Readers' Guide Abstracts, UMI's Periodical Abstracts
Ondisc, and EBSCO's Magazine Article Summaries..
```

Fig. 11.20. Abstract from H. W. Wilson's Business Abstracts.

```
DIALOG(R)File 202:(c)  Information Today, Inc. All rts. reserv.

    Quality of abstracts.
        The article examines those factors that contribute to high-quality
    abstracts contained in information databases, focusing on standards
    established in 1979 by the American National Standards Institute. The
    authors focuses on the benefits and drawbacks of abstracts contained in
    three general periodical indexes, including Readers' Guide Abstracts,
    Periodical Abstracts On Disc and Magazine Article Summaries. The
    authors explain what an abstract is, who writes abstracts, what goes
    into an abstract, length of abstract, measures of abstract readability
    and other variables.
```

Fig. 11.21. Abstract from ISA.

The abstract in the Trade & Industry Database (figure 11.22), created by Information Access Company (now part of the Gale Group), is unusually unbalanced, focusing on the first quarter of the article. It does not even mention the testing process and criteria, let alone the databases that were tested. A part of the second sentence ("to help focus a review of an on-line, printed or CD-ROM database") in the abstract does not make sense even to the authors of the original article. It also restricts the function of abstracts by claiming that "abstracts allow on-line searchers to view a short version of an original document." This has nothing to do with the medium; an abstract in a printed A/I publication has the same advantage.

```
DIALOG(R)File 148:(c)2000 The Gale Group. All rts. reserv.

 Quality of abstracts.

ABSTRACT:  Abstracts allow on-line searchers to view a short version of an
original document. Abstracts also provide additional search terms to help
focus a review of an on-line, printed or CD-ROM database. An abstract may
be written by the author of an original article; however, professional
services typically write their own abstracts. Abstracters may be hired for
writing skills, but in some cases abstracting and indexing tasks may be
combined. The quality of abstracts can be judged by readability and
informativeness.
```

Fig. 11.22. Abstract from the Trade & Industry Database.

The abstract in LISA (figure 11.23) adequately covers the topics and evaluation criteria and indicates the presence of statistical results, but does not identify the databases tested. Neither does the ERIC abstract (figure 11.24), which also remains mute about the presence of statistics but includes the number of references. The usually good abstracting of INSPEC certainly is not manifested for this article (figure 11.25). The abstract is a copy of two paragraphs from the background part of the article. It totally misses the essence of the article and misleads the reader as to what the article is about.

The exceptions referred to above indicate how important it is to evaluate dozens of abstracts to get a fair idea about the quality of abstracts, and not to judge the database by some uncharacteristically poor records.

```
DIALOG(R)File  61:(c) 2000 Reed Reference Publishing. All rts. reserv.

Quality of abstracts.

ABSTRACT: Abstracts enable users to judge the relevance of articles,
  provide a summary and may be a substitute for the original document.
  Defines abstracts and considers who they are written by according to the
  American National Standards Institute (ANSI) and other sources.
  Distinguishes between indicative and informative abstracts. Informative
  abstracts are preferred by ANSI and ERIC. Discusses the content and
  procedures for abstracting, writing style, tests of quality and
  readability and informativeness. Presents statistics analyzing abstracts
  from 3 general interest databases and on abstract length and type. GLC.
```

Fig. 11.23. Abstract from LISA.

```
DIALOG(R)File   1:(c) format only 2000 The Dialog Corporation. All rts.
reserv.

Quality of Abstracts.

  Reviews the factors to be considered in evaluating abstracts. Types of
abstracts, content, length, writing style, comprehensive criteria for
abstracts, readability, readability testing, compatibility with ANSI
(American National Standards Institute) standards, and informativeness are
among the topics covered. (12 references) (KRN)
```

Fig. 11.24. Abstract from ERIC.

```
DIALOG(R)File   2:(c) 2000 Institution of Electrical Engineers. All rts.
reserv.

  Title: Quality of abstracts
  Abstract:  One factor that differentiates between indexes and could be an
important consideration in evaluation is the quality of their abstracts. To
judge  the quality of abstracts, it is necessary to understand what makes a
good abstract. Judgments of 'good' are always dangerous, but, in the case
of  abstracts,  there  is  some  consensus  among the experts. The American
National  Standards  Institute  (ANSI) developed a standard for abstracts in
1979  (it  is currently being reviewed for reaffirmation) that in many ways
dictates  what  a  good abstract should be. ANSI defines an abstract as 'an
abbreviated, accurate representation of the contents of a document'.
```

Fig. 11.25. Abstract from INSPEC.

"What Is in an (Up)date?" Article

For the "What Is in an (Up)date?" article, ABI/INFORM has the most comprehensive (though not perfect) abstract again (figure 11.26). It sums up well the most important reasons for the time lag between the publication of the primary document and the appearance of its record in a database. It also clearly identifies the three currency testing techniques, but does not even allude to the large number of examples used as illustrations, and unnecessarily wastes space on a side comment of the original article ("End users are less interested . . .") .

```
DIALOG(R)File  15:(c) 2000 Bell & Howell. All rts. reserv.

What Is in a(n) (Up)Date? Currency Test Searching of Databases

ABSTRACT:  There can be a number of obstacles to delay the entry of current
citations in a database. Delays include source publications published late,
a backlog in the abstracting-indexing service, overcommitment by the CD-ROM
manufacturing  plant,  and  postal  service  problems.  End  users  are  less
interested  in  the  reasons than in the fact: the typical or average travel
time  between  the  date  of  publication and the date of availability of the
related  record  for  searching. The shorter the time gap, the more current
the  database.  Traditional  currency  indicators  measure  the currency of
publication  in  terms of months, comparing the date of issue of the source
document  and  the  date  of issue of the abstracting-indexing publication.
However,  these  dates may be ambiguous and may distort the results if used
without  reservation.  Techniques  for  currency  testing  include:  1. the
publication  date  versus  update date technique, 2. the update date versus
publication  date technique, and 3. the accession number versus publication
date  technique.  Online  databases  are  more  current  than  their CD-ROM
siblings.
```

Fig. 11.26. Abstract from ABI/INFORM.

The abstract in LISA (figure 11.27) deserves credit for pointing out a key aspect of the article—that the techniques offer the possibility of testing thousands of records or even the entire database. On the negative side, the two sentences in the middle of the abstract are annoyingly redundant ("Describes techniques that can be used for currency measurement. 3 basic currency measurement techniques are described.").

```
DIALOG(R)File  61:(c) 2000 Reed Reference Publishing. All rts. reserv.

What is in a (n) (up) date? Currency test searching of databases.

ABSTRACT: The on-line and CD-ROM search software offers excellent
  capabilities for performing measurements of a data base's currency and
  the time-gaps between publication of the sources and appearance in the
  data base, involving thousands of records or even the entire content of
  the data base. Describes techniques that can be used for currency
  measurement. 3 basic currency measurement techniques are described.
  Publication Date versus Update Date; Update Date versus Publication Date;
  and Accession Number versus Publication Date. Shows how currency test
  searches accross a few years time span can yield a historic perspective
  of how the currency profile of a data base has changed. Notes that
  measured currency of a data base can be affected by the pattern and
  regularity of the updating schedule for that file. N.L.M.
```

Fig. 11.27. Abstract from LISA.

The positive aspect of the abstract in ISA (figure 11.28) is that it makes it clear that currency profile evaluations are presented. The Trade & Industry Database (figure 11.29) gives a good summary of the techniques of currency testing but does not provide context. The abstract in Periodical Abstracts PlusText (figure 11.30) is just two sentences, and the second one merely paraphrases a side comment of the article. The abstract in H. W. Wilson's Business Abstracts database (figure 11.31) is deeply disappointing from this file producer, which usually creates the best abstracts. Not only is the abstract very short, but the single sentence does not add anything new to what we know from the title and the title enhancement fields.

```
DIALOG(R)File 202:(c)  Information Today, Inc. All rts. reserv.

 What is a(n) (up)date? Currency test searching of databases.
      This article examines the issue of currency test searching of
 databases. It argues that online and CD-ROM search software may offer
 excellent capabilities for doing wide-scale currency test searches.
 Specific comparisons of techniques include: publication date versus
 update date technique; update versus publication date technique;
 accession number versus publication date technique. Currency profile
 evaluations are also presented.
```

Fig. 11.28. Abstract from ISA.

```
DIALOG(R)File 148:(c)2000 The Gale Group. All rts. reserv.

 What is in a(n) (up)date? Currency test searching of databases.

ABSTRACT:  The currency of bibliographic databases can be tested using a
number of methods. Comparison of the publication date for a given set of
records with the update date for those records gives some indication of the
processing timelag. The converse method of comparing update date with
publication date offers some indication of the distribution of records of
different ages within a given update. Comparison of record accession
numbers with publication date allows for currency checking where update
dates are not available.
```

Fig. 11.29. Abstract from Trade & Industry Database.

```
DIALOG(R)File 484:(c) 2000 Bell & Howell. All rts. reserv.

 What Is in a(n) (Up)date?--Currency Test Searching of Databases

ABSTRACT:  The findings of a study to determine widescale currency test
searches of online databases are presented and discussed.  End-users are
more interested in the typical or average travel time between the date of
publication and the date of searching availability.
```

Fig. 11.30. Abstract from Periodical Abstracts PlusText.

```
DIALOG(R)File 553:(c) 2000 The HW Wilson Co. All rts. reserv.

 What is in a(n) (up)date? Currency test searching of databases.
AUGMENTED TITLE: online and CD-ROM

ABSTRACT:  Techniques for evaluating the currency of publications in online
and CD-ROM databases are presented.
```

Fig. 11.31. Abstract from H. W. Wilson's Business Abstracts.

"Data Transfer Capabilities" Article

The "Data Transfer Capabilities" article has the best abstract in ABI/INFORM (figure 11.32). It is the most informative of all and the only one that clearly identifies the seven output and downloading requirements. It also wraps up very well the essence of the article.

```
DIALOG(R)File  15:(c) 2000 Bell & Howell. All rts. reserv.

Data Transfer Capabilities of CD-ROM Software: Part I

ABSTRACT: Most  CD-ROM software offers sophisticated search techniques but
falls  short  when it comes to offering extensive output capabilities. This
may be typical of the online databanks, which also emphasize search
capabilities   instead   of   data   transfer.   A  study  of  data  transfer
capabilities  reviews  the  scope  of  output and downloading requirements.
Storing  results  on  a  hard  disk  or a floppy diskette is referred to as
downloading.  The transferring of this file into the host program is called
uploading.  Output  and  downloading  requirements  can  be  grouped into 7
categories:  1.  specification of output destination, 2. marking of records
to   be   transferred,   3.   predefined   and   display   print  formats,  4.
user-specified  display and print formats, 5. sorting of output records, 6.
page  formatting,  and  7. choice of transfer formats. CD-ROM products show
significant  differences within these categories. As a result, the specific
downloading features may be an important factor in the purchasing decisions
of  CD-ROM  buyers. Transfer options depend on the structural format of the
output downloaded from a CD-ROM database.
```

Fig. 11.32. Abstract from ABI/INFORM.

ISA has the second best abstract (figure 11.33), taking segments from the original text, a very common practice, and threading them together. The only minor modification made to the original text is in the first sentence: "but suffers from limited ability to offer extensive output capabilities." It replaces the text in the article "but falls short when it comes to offering extensive output capabilities"—without apparent reason.

```
DIALOG(R)File 202:(c)  Information Today, Inc. All rts. reserv.

Data transfer capabilities of CD-ROM software. Part I.
     Most CD-ROM software offers sophisticated search techniques, but
suffers from limited ability to offer extensive output capabilities. In
CD-ROM databases and other local systems, there are no direct
associated costs to sorting, formatting, displaying or printing
records. For such products, it would be reasonable to expect more
powerful output options, yet very few CD-ROM products offer appropriate
facilities for formatting the output of a search. The least one should
expect from any CD-ROM product is that the output of a search be
available in data exchange formats that are appropriate for importing
into word processors, text management, spreadsheet, database
management, and graphics software. This would allow the transfer of the
search output to an appropriate host program for further processing.
The scope of output and downloading requirements is examined, focusing
on the technical aspects of downloading from CD-ROM databases, a
process also known as saving, transferring, keeping, exporting, or
copying.
```

Fig. 11.33. Abstract from ISA.

INSPEC's abstract (figure 11.34) is close to that of ISA and uses a similar threading technique, but from different paragraphs of the original text. LISA's abstract of two sentences is rather poor, hardly adding anything to the information already included in the title (figure 11.35). Strangely, it devotes more words to what part 2 of the article discusses than to part 1.

```
DIALOG(R)File   2:(c) 2000 Institution of Electrical Engineers. All rts.
reserv.

  Title: Data transfer capabilities of CD-ROM software. I
   Abstract: The least one should expect from any CD-ROM product is that the
output of  a  search  be  available  in  data  exchange  formats which are
appropriate   for   importing   into   word  processors,  text  management,
spreadsheet,  database  management  and graphics software. This would allow
the  transfer  of  the  search  output  to  an appropriate host program for
further  processing. This study reviews the scope of output and downloading
requirements.  All  of  the  output restrictions discussed can be overcome if
you  are  able to upload the records of the search into an appropriate host
program. The transfer options depend on the structural format of the output
downloaded from a CD-ROM database.
```

Fig. 11.34. Abstract from INSPEC.

```
DIALOG(R)File   61:(c) 2000 Reed Reference Publishing. All rts. reserv.

 Data transfer capabilities of CD-ROM software. Part 1.

ABSTRACT: Reviews the scope of output and downloading requirements of
  CD-ROM data base software. Part 2 (March 91 issue) will discuss and
  illustrate the exchange formats most commonly used by potential host
  programs for importing data. N.L.M.
```

Fig. 11.35. Abstract from LISA.

Part 2 of the article was best abstracted once again in ABI/INFORM, providing enough details and good structure (figure 11.36). INSPEC's abstract (figure 11.37) does not mention the specific formats and does not clarify that both text and graphic exchange formats are discussed. The four exchange formats—left unidentified in the abstract—apply only to the text files, and the article discusses specific graphic formats.

```
    DIALOG(R)File   15:(c) 2000 Bell & Howell. All rts. reserv.

    Data Transfer Capabilities of CD-ROM Software, Part II

    ABSTRACT:  The  limitations  in output capabilities of many CD-ROM programs
    make  it  difficult  to  transfer  the  results of the search from a CD-ROM
    directly  into  the software or host program. Although it would be ideal to
    have  better  downloading  and  data  transfer capabilities inherent in the
    CD-ROM  retrieval  software,  one can use the transfer capabilities of other
    software  programs  to  edit  and further process the results of the CD-ROM
    search.  There  are  a  few standard formats that are understood by all the
    mainstream  programs  and thus provide a bridge among these programs. The 4
    most  common  formats  are:  1. unstructured or plain ASCII, 2. fixed field
    format,  3.  delimited  ASCII  format,  and  4.  MARC (machine readable
    cataloging)  communications  format.  The  best  graphic file conversion
    program,  Hijaak,  lists 30 formats. Fortunately, there are some widely used
    formats,  and most of the CD-ROM products that offer graphics are capable of
    transferring  the  images, drawings, clip-art, and line-art in one of these
    de  facto  standard formats. The simplest and most commonly accepted format
    is the PCX format made popular by the PC Paintbrush package.
```

Fig. 11.36. Abstract from ABI/INFORM.

```
DIALOG(R)File   2:(c) 2000 Institution of Electrical Engineers. All rts.
reserv.

  Title: Data transfer capabilities of CD-ROM software. II
   Abstract: For  pt.I  see  ibid., vol.4, no.1, p63-9 (1991). In the first
part, the output and downloading options of CD-ROM software were discussed.
Here the author illustrates what exchange/transfer format structures may be
used  to   upload  records into potential software host programs. The author
looks  at  moving  numbers,  text  and images from CD-ROMs. There are a few
standard  formats  which  are understood by all the mainstream programs and
thus   provide a bridge among these programs. The author focuses on the four
most  common  formats  and  the  capability of the major CD-ROM products to
produce outputs in these formats.
```

Fig. 11.37. Abstract from INSPEC.

ISA has two abstracts: the first one is acceptable (figure 11.38) but is inferior to the second one (figure 11.39), which was imported from the ERIC database. Although it is shorter than that of ABI/INFORM, it provides the specifics in a good layout.

```
DIALOG(R)File 202:(c)  Information Today, Inc. All rts. reserv.

  Data transfer capabilities of CD-ROM software, Part II.
     Limitations in output capabilities of CD-ROM programs are
  discussed. Moving numbers, text and images from CD-ROM, e.g., word
  processing, database management, and spreadsheets is described. The
  advantages of using basic ASCII are discussed. Programs that enable the
  transfer of graphics are explored.
```

Fig. 11.38. The first abstract from ISA.

```
DIALOG(R)File 202:(c)  Information Today, Inc. All rts. reserv.

  Data transfer capabilities of CD-ROM software, part II.
     Describes and compares several exchange/transfer formats used to
  upload records into software host programs, including: (1) unstructured
  or plain ASCII; (2) fixed field; (3) delimited ASCII; (4) tagged; (5)
  MARC (Machine Readable Cataloging); and (6) graphic. It is concluded
  that CD-ROM producers should strengthen the built-in output management
  of programs and offer download options in more than one exchange
  format.   (Abstract Source: ERIC)
```

Fig. 11.39. The second abstract from ISA, imported from ERIC.

LISA's two-sentence abstract (figure 11.40) is again rather uninformative and has a typo ("ooptions") . Strangely, the Trade & Industry Database did not have abstracts for either part of the "Data Transfer Capabilities" article. Oddly, ERIC had a record (shown in figure 11.39) only for part 2 of the article—a problem that has to do with consistency in selecting articles from source documents, not an issue of abstracting quality.

```
DIALOG(R)File  61:(c) 2000 Reed Reference Publishing. All rts. reserv.

 Data transfer capabilities of CD-ROM software Part 2.

ABSTRACT: Part 1 considered the output and downloading ooptions of CD-ROM
  software. Part 2 illustrates what exchange and transfer format structures
  may be used to upload records into potential software host programs.
  N.L.M.
```

Fig. 11.40. Abstract from LISA.

Abstracting policies change over time. Van Camp (1993) reported that CINAHL included abstracts only for articles in core nursing journals, and if the abstract was also available in the article; thus, merely 17 percent of the records had abstracts. This ratio, however, increased drastically as CINAHL started to include author abstracts for all the articles that had them.

This should remind you that quality of the abstracts may significantly improve also, but abstracts are never upgraded retrospectively as other data elements may be. Evaluating the quality of abstracts is a very time-consuming process, so mini samplings are much more likely than large-scale evaluations. Using too small of samples may not do justice to a database that most of the time would provide substantial and informative abstracts.

Cost Considerations

The old adage, "You get what you pay for," often does not apply to databases. Often you may get the same content for less money or even for free. What you, corporations, or colleges pay depends on the contract made with the information service. Of course, charges and charging schemes keep changing over time, and even in the same time frame may not be the same for all customers. Corporate rates, educational rates, and individual rates may vary widely. Within the same category, rates may be different depending on the total number of employees or students, or the total number of simultaneous users who are allowed access to the database.

Charges may be based on transactions (search statements, or resources used by search statements, and the number and format of the records displayed, saved, or printed). These are known as go-as-you-pay services. Alternatively, the contract may be made for unlimited use—a flat fee arrangement. The same information service may have several charging schemes for several types of customers. Cost comparison can be a complex task.

Beyond exploring and comparing the various charging schemes offered by different vendors, the content and the power, ease, and convenience of access from a software point of view must also be evaluated. Even if the content of the database is the same on two services, if one service has a mediocre software, it may incur more costs for end-users who spend more time struggling with the software, or are simply unable to perform certain types of searches that are readily available with the software of the somewhat more expensive other service.

No one doubts the overall superiority of the DIALOG software over most of the search programs available with the free Web versions of many government databases. No one questions that information professionals who make a living of searching databases benefit from the power features. But do you or your users really need the most advanced software features of DIALOG offered by the Explode, Rank, or Map commands? Would the employees of a corporation use the multiple database search possibilities of DIALOG? Is it worth the extra cost? Simplicity, natural language search capability, spell checking of queries, and guiding users to controlled vocabulary terms may be more important features than the ones that super searchers use in their sleep, and demand.

Similar factors apply to the content of databases in comparing alternatives and their cost implications. Often, you get access to a database for a lower price, or even for free, although possibly to a limited subset. The limit may apply to time period, document type(s) or language, or a combination of those.

Content Differences

Librarians could hardly imagine living without one of the serials directories in print, CD-ROM, or online format. Now that PubList is available free of charge on the Web, it is time to rethink the options. PubList is a subset of the Ulrich's International Periodicals Directory. It does not have records about the ceased titles, and it does not have all the data elements that the Ulrich's records include, but it does provide the most needed information (figure 12.1) along with errors from the original file.

How important is it to know about dead journals in your library's practice? The CODEN? The Dewey classification number? The document suppliers? The British Library shelfmark? These are not available in the PubList version, but only in the fee-based versions (figure 12.2). Neither are the LC call number and the indexing and abstracting services that cover the journal. But the LC call number is available for less than 20 percent of the records even in the fee-based versions of Ulrich's, which also have very incomplete (and appallingly outdated) information about the indexing and abstracting services coverage (figure 12.3).

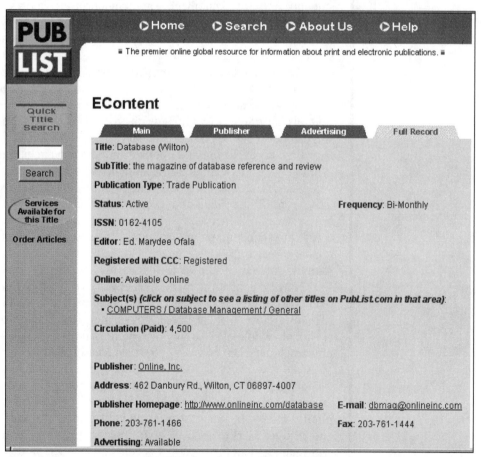

Fig. 12.1. Sample record from PubList.

EContent

Formerly (until June 1999): Database: ISSN 0162-4105

Status:	Active
Publisher:	Online, Inc.
	213 Danbury Rd
	Wilton
	CT 06897-4006
	Telephone: 203-761-1466, 800-248-8466
	E-mail: dbmag@onlineinc.com
	URL: http://www.onlineinc.com/database/;
	http://www.ecmag.net/
	FAX: 203-761-1444
Editor:	Pub. Jeffrey K Pemberton; Ed. Marydee Ofala
Country of Publication:	United States (US)
First Published:	1978; Online - full text edition: 1978
Frequency:	bi-monthly
Circulation:	4,500 (paid)
Special Features:	Index
Document Type:	Trade
Price:	$55 domestic ; $90 elsewhere; $65 CANADA (effective 2000)
ISSN:	1525-2531
CODEN:	ECONF4
Dewey Decimal Call Number:	025.04
LC Call Number:	Z699.A1

Fig. 12.2. Sample record from Ulrich's (part 1).

LC Call Number:	Z699.A1
British Library Shelf Mark:	BLDSC Shelfmark. 3659.530425
Document Suppliers:	IDS; Ei; CISTI; CINDOC; CASDDS; AskIEEE
Availability Online:	Also available online
Online Vendors:	Bell & Howell Information & Learning; Gale Group
Abstracting and Indexing Services:	Applied Science & Technology Index; Business Periodicals Index; Library Literature; Social Science Citation Index; INSPEC: Computers & Control Abstracts; A B I - INFORM; Current Index to Journals in Education; Computer Contents; Compumath Citation Index; Cumulative Index to Nursing and Allied Health Literature; Current Contents; Consumers Index; Key to Economic Science; Legal Information Management Index; Library Hi Tech News; Microcomputer Index; Trade & Industry Index; Library & Information Science Abstracts; Legal Resource Index; SoftBase; WPM
Listed in:	Ulrich's International Periodicals Directory Scientific & Technical Books & Serials in Print
Subject Headings:	COMPUTERS (0000621X); DATA BASE MANAGEMENT (0000621X)

Notes:
Features articles on a variety of topics of interest to online database users, and electronic content providers and users. Includes database search aids.
  back issues avail.
  Text in English
  Copyright Clearance Center
  Rights & Permissions: Jenny Pemberton

Fig. 12.3. Sample record from Ulrich's (part 2).

It does not mention, for example, the following databases that gave good coverage of *EContent*: Business & Industry, Business & Management Practices, H. W. Wilson's Applied Science & Technology, PASCAL, Information Science Abstracts, PIRA, Periodical Abstracts PlusText, or H. W. Wilson's Business Abstracts (figure 12.4). It mentions Microcomputer Index, which changed its name many years ago to Microcomputer Abstracts (and indeed, includes very informative abstracts) and in early 2000 changed to Internet & Personal Computing Abstracts.

Set	Term Searched	Items	File
S1	JN=ECONTENT?	889	
S1	JN=ECONTENT?	89	553
S1	JN=ECONTENT?	107	484
S1	JN=ECONTENT?	203	440
S1	JN=ECONTENT?	14	248
S1	JN=ECONTENT?	132	202
S1	JN=ECONTENT?	28	144
S1	JN=ECONTENT?	43	211
S1	JN=ECONTENT?	109	99
S1	JN=ECONTENT?	77	13
S1	JN=ECONTENT?	87	9

Show Database Details for:

9: Business & Industry(TM)

Fig. 12.4. Sample search for coverage of *EContent*.

Are the extra and often very incomplete and inaccurate data elements worth the nearly $1,000 subscription fee for the CD-ROM version, which is available only while the library is open or while the reference desk is open, which is likely to be an even more restricted period for picking up the CD-ROM in exchange for your library card? What is wrong in PubList is wrong in the fee-based Ulrich's versions, such as the name of the editor, who is Ojala, not Ofala.

The PubList software does not have all the features that Ovid, DIALOG, or Lexis-Nexis could offer, but it has better content layout and more efficient result list format, and it hotlinks from the subject, e-mail, and URL fields of the records, which, for example, DIALOG still can't do.

Software Differences

There is an increasing number of government databases available free of charge on the Web. They challenge the viability of subscribing to the version offered by commercial vendors, especially when the content is the same and the software is far better than the software of one or more of the commercial versions.

Take, for example, the ERIC database. It is available on a dozen commercial systems, and there are several free versions on the Web. Two of them have both the journal subset (known also as the EJ subset) and the report subset (known also as the ED subset). Now that both free versions were enhanced in mid-1999 to include all the records back to 1966, their content matches those available on the commercial information services. Actually, the best free version, available at the ERIC Assessment and Evaluation Clearinghouse (*http://www.ericae.org*), also includes the full text of many important sources relevant for educators. Beyond these extras of ERIC/AE, the only differences are in the software features—and the price.

Possibly the poorest commercial implementation of ERIC is offered by the CARL system for a yearly subscription fee of thousands of dollars—depending on the number of end-users. Possibly one of the best implementations of ERIC among all the versions is by the ERIC Assessment and Evaluation Clearinghouse (ERIC/AE) just mentioned. Interestingly, it was developed without taxpayers' money and is offered at no charge.

Both of these versions offer the ERIC Thesaurus, but CARL has it only as a separate database, whereas in ERIC/AE it is beautifully integrated with the bibliographic files. Moreover, it is automatically activated to match the words in the user's query. If the user enters a term that is not a preferred term in ERIC (such as *managers*), the search wizard will suggest the preferred term (*administrators*), and in a visually pleasing way, broader, narrower, and related terms, scope note, and non-preferred terms (figure 12.5).

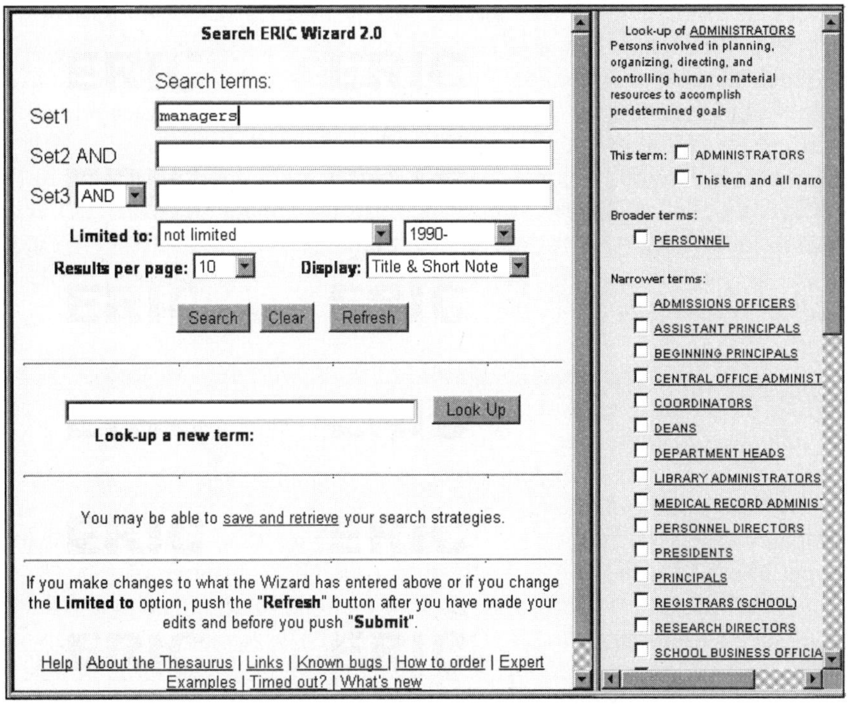

Fig. 12. 5. Term mapping and thesaurus display in ERIC/AE.

Users can choose from three options to match words. The simplest is the exact match (*manager*). The second option will find the regular plural and possessive format of the word (*managers, manager's*). The third one will find additional variant derivative words (*management, managerial, managed, managing*).

The search can be limited to the author, title, or descriptor field, and to one of several document types (book, conference paper, literature reviews, etc.) through a pull-down menu. There are three predefined output formats, and the "Find Similar" option automatically searches for documents with the same group of descriptor terms that the original document has. It is a nice feature that users can add additional descriptors and eliminate others, and may even bypass the whole process of looking up thesaurus terms for words in the query.

It is icing on the cake that the record can be displayed instantly in French, Italian, Spanish, Portuguese, and German. This feature is not perfect, and the computer translation produces funny things such as "The Errors of the Commission" instead of "Errors of Commission," but it is understandable, and the Spanish descriptors are far better than in PASCAL. The abstracts are sufficient for someone who does not read English really well to understand what the article or report is about, and the translation is lightning fast. The short result list is presented redundantly, and you cannot search the entire database at once. It is split into two segments: pre-1990 and from 1990, but for most users, the last decade is likely to be sufficient. It runs circles around the version offered by CARL and is better than the other commercial systems except for the ones from Ovid and the National Information Services Corporation (NISC).

In the CARL version, users first have to select the ERIC Thesaurus database, navigate it, jot down the term(s) selected, and then change to the ERIC bibliographic file and enter the search terms. The search and output capabilities are not superior, and only ERIC/AE has direct access to a plethora of other teaching-related materials (many of them full text).

Price Anomalies

It is more time-consuming to compare the value of two different databases covering similar disciplines, but it is often worthwhile. This is especially true for DIALOG, which has changed its pricing scheme from connect time rate to DialUnit rate, which is obscure and hard to estimate for a search. DIALOG promised that it would revert back to the former charging scheme in 2000, but this did not happen until early 2001.

DialUnit prices may still be used in comparing two or more DIALOG alternatives. For example, the price definitely is not proportional to value in the case of PsycINFO and Mental Health Abstracts. The DialUnit rate of the high-quality, very comprehensive PsycINFO database of 1.6 million records is $3.25, while MHA charges $4.00 for access to 513,000 records, 90 percent of which are more than 15 years old.

MHA adds fewer records to its database in a year than PsycINFO in a month. After the last update in December 1999, there were 26,563 records for items with a 1999 publication year in PsycINFO versus 1,473 in MHA. MHA's journal base is not simply incomparable to that of PsycINFO, but also ignores absolutely key journals in its purportedly prime subject domains. For 1997 MHA covered 4 of the 50 psychiatry and psychology journals with the highest impact factor. PsycINFO covered 49 of them. Even in light of the DialUnit price, there may still be users willing to pay the absurd price for a grossly inferior product like MHA.

The updating of the MHA database hit bottom in 2000 with the last update in June. It took nine months for DIALOG to announce in March 2001 that the database is to be closed with no more updating. It is likely to be on its way to extinction, as predicted by this author (Jacsó, 2000b).

The DialUnit rates for the library and information science database group are not really proportional to value either, and neither are the output prices. LibLit's $1.00 per full record price for an indexing record is expensive compared to the $1.10 price of LISA and $1.20 for ISA, which have abstracts. The output price difference between LISA and ISA is realistic, but the DialUnit price of ISA ($6.00) is unrealistic compared to the $3.75 DialUnit price of LISA. Both of them represent a bad deal when one searches for articles in journals such as *Searcher*, *Online*, *Database*, *E Media Professional*, *Computers in Libraries*, *Information Today*, and *Multimedia Schools,* which are all covered in Microcomputer Abstracts (now Internet & Personal Computing Abstracts), which charges only $2.50 and is much more current than either LISA or ISA.

Are its abstracts better than those of LISA? Definitely. Better than that of ISA? They are almost equal. Why? Because since mid-1999, ISA has borrowed the records for most articles published in the previously listed journals from Microcomputer Abstracts—a few months later and with a few data elements, such as the URLs and abstractor's code, removed. Microcomputer Abstracts (Internet & Personal Computing Abstracts) and ISA are now owned by the same company, Information Today, but are managed by different people. ISA certainly benefits from the quality and competent work that has been the trademark of Microcomputer Abstracts for a long time, but the price difference between the two databases remains absurd.

There are fee-based databases that are in a hopeless situation. The Magill's Survey of Cinema database often has good plot lines, but even its low $1.50 DialUnit price and $1.30 full record print price would be a deterrent compared to the free, information-rich, and magnificently implemented Internet Movie Database (IMDb), even if the Magill's database had not been left without updates since February 1997. It will probably be removed from the DIALOG stable, as there is not much chance to have income from this product.

Then again, one might wonder why college and public libraries spend $520 for Bowker's Complete Video Directory, which offers so far less in content, currency, and ease of use than either IMDb or the All-Movie Guide, both free Web databases. The Complete Video Directory may have some vocational movies and religious educational movies that the latter two don't have, but it is no reason to spend money on a CD-ROM that is accessible only during the opening hours of the library (and at that price) from only one workstation, and with dishearteningly inaccurate, inconsistent, incomplete, and outdated information.

Competing Online Information Services

Cost comparison among different implementations of the same datafile is an important factor in evaluation. Shopping around for the best deals certainly pays off for the heavy users. Again, the adage that "You get what you pay for" does not apply in the following examples, which are taken from Jacsó (1996). Using an earlier pricing example is justified because DIALOG now has a pricing scheme, the infamous DialUnit, that not even DIALOG insiders can explain and which makes it incomparable with other services.

Relatively minor cost differences may not be worth jumping ship. Dissertation Abstracts was $60 per hour on DIALOG and $50 per hour on OCLC. For a casual user familiar with DIALOG, this difference may not be sufficient. On the other hand, in the case of Economic Literature Index (EconLit), the price difference was remarkable. DIALOG charged $60 per hour for connect time, while OCLC charged only $30.

The output charges must also be considered in the comparison. For Dissertation Abstracts, OCLC charged $0.75 per record and DIALOG charged $1.00. For EconLit, OCLC had a higher per record cost than DIALOG ($0.75 versus $0.50), but this would not offset OCLC's half-price deal on database connect time charges. The pattern that Service A is always cheaper than Service B is not consistent. OCLC charged $50 per hour for Microcomputer Abstracts, but DIALOG charged only $30, and the per record charges were identical. PAIS was $60 on EPIC and $30 on DIALOG, and the per record charge was $0.75 versus $0.60, respectively.

The software features offered with particular databases could also be important and may justify higher charges. Still, this was not the case with EconLit, where neither service offered thesaurus features online. Ironically, DIALOG offers the thesaurus feature with its implementation of GeoRef, and it was still less expensive than OCLC's implementation without the thesaurus ($60 versus $70 for connect time and $0.85 versus $0.75 for full record).

Just because Service A is better than Service B does not mean that you should not look for even better deals, such as lower prices or more functionality (or both). DIALOG was less expensive for Sociofile than OCLC, in terms of both connect hour and print charges, even though DIALOG had the thesaurus capability for this database. But Ovid had an even better deal: $24 per hour and $0.75 per full record—and it had the best software features, including the best thesaurus handling options.

Even more poignant is the difference for ABI/INFORM, which does not have its thesaurus implemented in either OCLC or DIALOG. Ovid beats them hands down, with a thesaurus (although with some errors) (Johnson, 2000) and with the lowest hourly rate of $60 versus OCLC's $80 and DIALOG's $90 price tag. For full-text records, OCLC had the lowest charge of $1.50, but Ovid's $2.00 charge was better than DIALOG's $2.20.

Very often, the versions of databases on the Web by file producers offer the best deal. It is also to be considered that a file producer's version allows transaction pricing for each item, while third-party database publishers' versions are limited to fixed subscription-based pricing, offering transaction pricing only to members who pay a yearly membership fee in addition to the transaction pricing.

The Web has revolutionized pricing alternatives. Those who have been using fee-based databases of full-text general interest periodicals will find many of the same articles at far better prices at sites of Web entrepreneurs. For example, for a $9.99 monthly charge, individual users have unlimited search and print capabilities from the collection of the Electric Library, which in turn is based to a large extent on files produced by some of the largest content providers of general interest periodical databases.

Until very recently, no one has taken price reduction to the extent of Northern Light, which has a large collection of high-impact and prestigious journals. Until 1999 it often charged $1.00 for an article that would have cost three to five times as much through traditional online services, in addition to connect time or search charges, which Northern Light does not have (figure 12.6). Although Northern Light increased its prices in 1999, it still compares very favorably and its software capabilities are excellent.

However, in 2000, new players appeared on the scene with hard-to-resist offers. Contentville has free searching and abstracts, and its full-text prices are competitive with those of Northern Light. Providing free abstracts (figure 12.7) for 1.6 million dissertations from the Bell & Howell collection makes Contentville a formidable competitor to many of the online information services that charge for both searching and the display of dissertation abstracts. (Note that Contentville displays only the first 130 words of the abstracts, but it is likely to show the full abstracts in the future.) The FindArticles service is based on a subset of the Gale Group databases. Both searching and the full-text articles are free with no strings attached.

The XanEdu service, introduced in September 2000 by Bell & Howell, represents a breakthrough in the value per price battle. Although it is not free, it seems as if it were, considering the content, the form of delivery, and the subscription price. It has 1.3 million records from a variety of Bell & Howell databases. For a fixed monthly rate of $7.50 (a four-month minimum commitment is required), users have unlimited search and display/print capability to the content of about 1,600 journals, magazines, and newspapers. Although this is a much smaller journal base than the Northern Light special collection, it represents the cream of the crop.

The best scholarly journals, professional and general interest magazines, and highly respected newspapers from the United States and the United Kingdom are available in XanEdu in full-text, text-plus-graphics, and page-image formats just like in the full-blown ProQuest service. The service is aimed at college students and faculty, but anyone can sign up. The introductory price in September 2000 was $9.99 for four months.

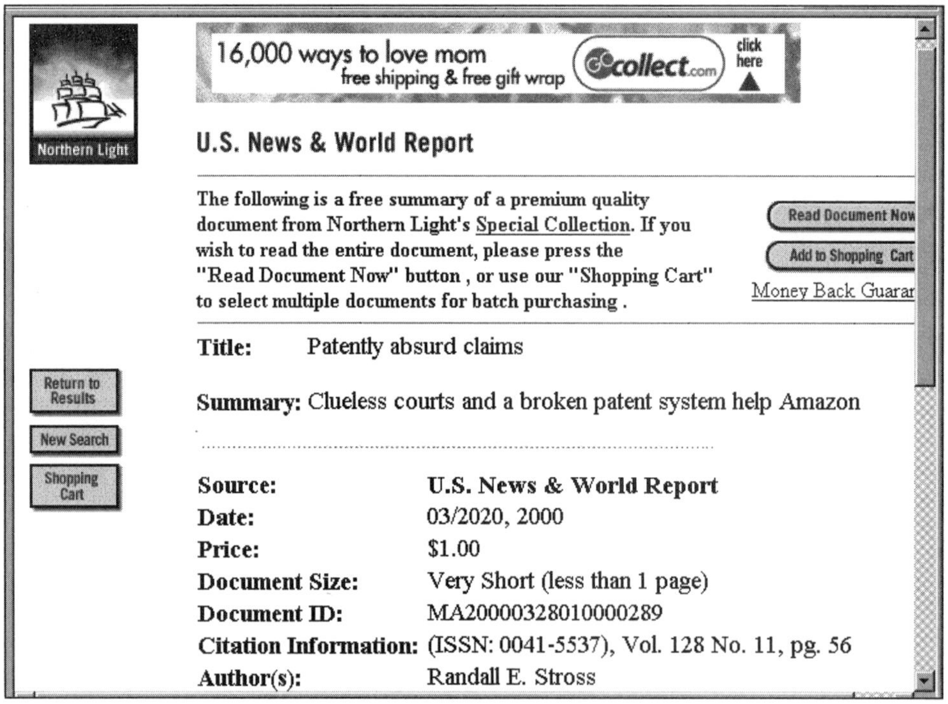

Fig. 12.6. Northern Light's $1 price for a long article.

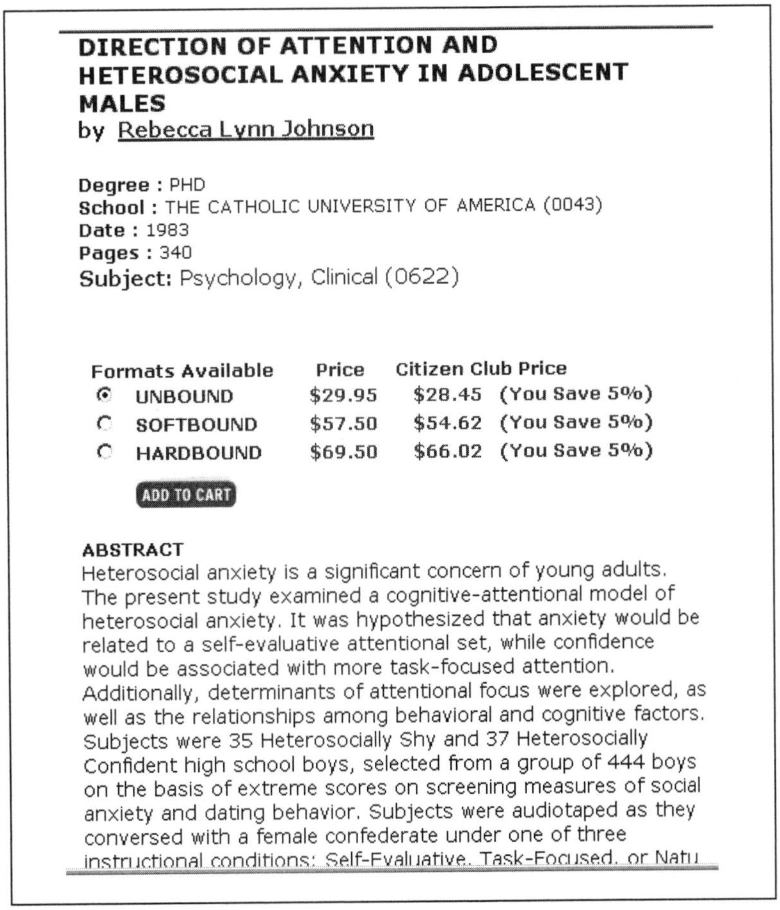

DIRECTION OF ATTENTION AND HETEROSOCIAL ANXIETY IN ADOLESCENT MALES
by Rebecca Lynn Johnson

Degree : PHD
School : THE CATHOLIC UNIVERSITY OF AMERICA (0043)
Date : 1983
Pages : 340
Subject: Psychology, Clinical (0622)

Formats Available	Price	Citizen Club Price
UNBOUND	$29.95	$28.45 (You Save 5%)
SOFTBOUND	$57.50	$54.62 (You Save 5%)
HARDBOUND	$69.50	$66.02 (You Save 5%)

ADD TO CART

ABSTRACT
Heterosocial anxiety is a significant concern of young adults. The present study examined a cognitive-attentional model of heterosocial anxiety. It was hypothesized that anxiety would be related to a self-evaluative attentional set, while confidence would be associated with more task-focused attention. Additionally, determinants of attentional focus were explored, as well as the relationships among behavioral and cognitive factors. Subjects were 35 Heterosocially Shy and 37 Heterosocially Confident high school boys, selected from a group of 444 boys on the basis of extreme scores on screening measures of social anxiety and dating behavior. Subjects were audiotaped as they conversed with a female confederate under one of three instructional conditions: Self-Evaluative, Task-Focused, or Natu

Fig. 12.7. Free abstracts of dissertations in Contentville.

It is not always directly the money that justifies the evaluation of a database. It could be the

more comprehensive subject coverage,

availability of more important journals,

presence of more value added information,

better quality of indexing or abstracting (or both),

timeliness of the information, or

convenience or more powerful functionality (or both) of software

that make one database better than another. Mary Ellen Bates (2000) provides excellent models and examples in comparing business information sources and services in her white paper available at *http://www.ask.djintractive.com/archive/story1oct899.htm.*

The actual figures in Bates's study may change over time, of course, and you must set up your own scenario for the comparison, but the examples are informative and make it clear that not all is gold that glitters, and some free services may cost more in the searcher's time than the well-organized, fee-based sources. But as was demonstrated in this book, many of the expensive, traditional databases used by professionals are much overpriced and have very serious deficiencies.

It is likely that the Darwinian principle of survival of the fittest will prevail (Jacsó 2000b), that the lowest quality commercial databases will disappear and will be replaced by reasonably priced alternatives that deliver what they promise. In another insightful article, Bates (2000) explains that "There ain't no such thing as a free lunch," but concedes that "you have a pretty hefty selection of reasonably priced options, particularly if you're willing to give up some search functionality." In this author's opinion (Jacsó 2000a), there *is* such a thing as a free lunch that is healthier to your diet and wallet than the expensive, stale, and nutritionally poor lunch (offered on some traditional systems) that doesn't even deserve plastic utensils and a paper cup.

The important thing is to always shop around to find better databases and to have good criteria by which to make comparisons. That is the purpose of this book: to alert you of the possibilities to quickly determine which database may be better for licensing or even for satisfying an important ad hoc search request. The criteria are changing from users to users; even for a single user depending on his or her particular preferences for meeting an information need. Knowing these criteria will, I hope, help you to do formal, in-depth evaluations, as well as informal, in the heat of the moment mini evaluations to make an educated decision, instead of taking at face value the often overly hyped and misleading claims of some datafile procedures and database publishers.

Bibliography

Ahmad, Nazir. 1991. Newspaper Indexing: An International Overview. *The Indexer* 17(4): 257–65.

Ajiferuke, Isola, and Clara M. Chu. 1988. Quality of Indexing in Online Databases: An Alternative Measure for a Term Discriminating Index. *Information Processing & Management* 24(5): 599–601.

Allcock, Harry M. 1997. IFI/Plenum Takes Jacso to Task. *Database* 20(3): 6.

Amba, S., and M. D. Naresh. 1994. Coverage of Leather Literature in CD-ROM Databases. *Online & CD-ROM Review* 18(6): 341–46.

American Libraries. 1986. News Brief: Just Doing Her Job. 17(2): 115.

———. 1996. News Fronts USA. Chicago PL Takes Heat for Calendar's Errors. 27(1): 25–26.

Atherton, Pauline Cochrane, and Stella Keenan. 1965. Review of AIP/Documentation Research Project Studies. Prepared for the American Institute of Physics, New York. Report No. AIFPDRP-65-2, March 1965. URL: *http://www.libsci.sc.edu/bob/ISP/cochrane2.htm.* Accessed July 15, 2001.

Ballard, Terry, and Arthur Lifshin. 1992. Prediction of OPAC Spelling Errors through a Keyword Inventory. *Information Technology and Libraries* 11(2): 139–45.

Basch, Reva. 1990a. May I Help You? Customer Service and Beyond. *Database Searcher* 6(6): 14–18.

———. 1990b. Measuring the Quality of the Data: Report on the Fourth Annual SCOUG [Southern California Online User Group] Retreat; Developing a Framework for Judging the Quality and Reliability of Databases. *Database Searcher* 6 (October): 18–23.

Bates, Mary Ellen. 2000. TANSTAAFL: In Search of the Free Lunch and No-Cost/Low-Cost Full Text Archives. *Searcher* 8(6): 55–59.

Beaubien, Denise M. 1992. Wilson vs. IAC on Tape: A Comparison. *Database* 15(1): 52–56.

Benning, Susan P., and Susan C. Speer. 1993. Incorrect Citations: A Comparison of Library Literature with Medical Literature. *Bulletin of the Medical Library Association* 81(1): 56–68.

Boissonnas, Christian M. 1979. The Quality of OCLC Bibliographic Records. *Law Library Journal* 72(1): 80–85.

Borko, Harold, and Charles L. Bernier. 1975. *Abstracting Concepts and Methods.* New York: Academic Press.

Bottle, Robert T., and Efthimis Efthimiadis. 1984. Library and Information Science Literature: Authorship and Growth Patterns. *Journal of Information Science: Principles & Practice* 9(3): 107–16.

Bourne, Charles P. 1977. Frequency and Impact of Spelling Errors in Bibliographic Data Bases. *Information Processing & Management* 13(1): 1–12.

251

Boykikeva, I. 1994. Online Access to Japanese Information in Engineering: Comparative Analysis of the JICST-E, INSPEC, and COMPENDEX Databases. *Information Services & Use* 14(1): 25–35.

Braam, Robert R., and Jeanet Bruil. 1992. Quality of Indexing Information: Author's Views on Indexing of Their Articles in Chemical Abstracts Online CA-File. *Journal of Information Science* 18(5): 339–408.

Brenner, Everett H. 1989. Should Abstractors Index? *Newsletter of the American Society of Indexers* (91): 1.

Brenner, Saundra H., and Emma Jean McKinin. 1989. CINAHL and MEDLINE: A Comparison of Indexing Practices. *Bulletin of the Medical Library Association* 77(4): 366–71.

Briggs, Kim, and Ian Crowlesmith. 1995. EMBASE—The Excerpta Medica Database: Quick and Comprehensive Drug Information. *Publishing Research Quarterly* 11(3): 51–60.

Brooks, Terrence A. 1993. All the Right Descriptors: A Test of the Strategy of Unlimited Aliasing. *Journal of the American Society for Information Science* 44(3): 137–47.

Buntrock, Robert. 1994. Chemical Compound Registration — Algorithmic or Otherwise (Use of Chemical Abstract Registry Numbers in Database Indexes). *Database* 17(1): 108–110.

———. 1995. GOLD [CASRN=7440-57-5] Is Where You Find It, or Caveats on Finding Chemical Substance Using CASRN. *Database* 18(3): 50–52, 54–55.

Byrne, Alex. 1983. How to Lose a Nation's Literature: Database Coverage of Australian Research Database. *Database* 6(3): 10–17.

Cahn, Pamela. 1994. Testing Database Quality. *Database* 17(1): 23–26, 28–30.

Chall, Miriam, and Terry M. Owen. 1995. Documenting the World's Sociological Literature: Sociological Abstracts. *Publishing Research Quarterly* 11(3): 83–95.

Chan, Lois Mai. 1989. Inter-Indexer Consistency in Subject Cataloging. *Information Technology and Libraries* 8(4): 349–58.

Cheeseman, Elanine N. 1995. Patents Preview and Patent Fast-Alert. *Database* 18(4): 65–71.

Cleveland, Donald B., and Ana D. Cleveland. 2001. *Introduction to Indexing and Abstracting*. Englewood, CO: Libraries Unlimited.

Cooper, William S. 1969. Is Interindexer Consistency a Hobgoblin? *American Documentation* 20(3): 268–78.

Dansey, P. 1973. A Bibliometric Survey of Primary and Secondary Information Science Literatures. *ASLIB Proceedings* 25(7): 252–63.

Dixon, Bernard. 1988. Science and Information Society. *Scholarly Publishing* 20(1): 3–12.

Dueltgen, Ronald R. 1991. Access to Japanese Technical Information. *Database* 14(2): 105–7.

Dwyer, Jim. 1991. Invisible College at Work: The Case of Dirty Database Test. *Cataloging & Classification Quarterly* 14(1): 75–82.

Edwards, Tom. 1976. A Comparative Analysis of the Major Abstracting and Indexing Services for Library and Information Services. *Unesco Bulletin for Libraries* 30(1): 18–25.

Eldredge, Jonathan D. 1993. Accuracy of Indexing Coverage Information as Reported by Serials Sources; Ulrich's International Periodicals Directory; SERLINE; The Serials Directory. *Bulletin of the Medical Library Association (Bull Med Libr Assoc)*. 81 (October): 364–70.

———. 1997. Identifying Peer-reviewed Journals in Clinical Medicine. In the Serials Directory and Ulrich's International Periodicals Directory. *Bulletin of the Medical Library Association (Bull Med Libr Assoc.).* 85(4): 418–22.

Ernest, Douglas J., Holley R. Lange, and Della Herring. 1988. An Online Comparison of Three Library Science Databases. *RQ* 28(2): 185–94.

Esteibar, Belen Altuna, and F. Wilfrid Lancaster. 1992. Ranking of Journals in Library and Information Science by Research and Teaching Relatedness. *The Serials Librarian* 23(1/2): 1–10.

Ewbank, Bruce W. 1982. Comparison Guide to Selection of Databases and Database Services. *Drexel Library Quarterly* 18(3/4): 189–204.

Freedman, Bernadette. 1995. Growth and Change in the World's Biological Literature as Reflected in BIOSIS Publications. *Publishing Research Quarterly* 11(3): 61–79.

Froehlich, Thomas. 1994. User Assumptions about Information Retrieval Systems: Ethical Concerns. In *Ethics in the Computer Age Conference Proceedings,* edited by Joseph M. Kizza, November 11–13, 1994, Gatlinburg, TN. New York: ACM, 146–50.

Froom, Paul, and Jack Froom. 1993. Deficiencies in Structured Medical Abstracts. *Journal of Clinical Epidemiology* 46(7): 591–94.

Fry, Sally A., and Kathy A. Parsons. 1994. Comparative Analysis of IAC, UMI, and Wilson Database Tape Products. *The Serials Librarian* 25(1/2): 133–44.

Fugmann, Robert. 1992. Predictability versus Consistency. *International Classification* 19(1): 20–22.

Funk, M. E., C. A. Reid, and L. S. McGoogan. 1983. Indexing Consistency in MEDLINE. *Bulletin of the Medical Library Association* 71(2): 176–83.

Gibson, Robert W., and Barbara K. Kunkel. 1980. Japanese Information Network and Bibliographic Control: Scientific and Technical Literature. *Special Libraries* 71(3): 154–62.

Gilchrist, Alan. 1966. Documentation of Documentation: A Survey of Leading Abstracts Services in Documentation and an Identification of Key Journals. *ASLIB Proceedings* 18(3): 62–80.

Gilchrist, Alan, and Alexandra Presanis. 1971. Library and Information Science Abstracts: The First Two Years. *ASLIB Proceedings* 23(5): 251–56.

Giral, Angela, and Arlene G. Taylor. 1993. Indexing Overlap and Consistency Between the Avery Index to Architectural Periodicals and the Architectural Periodicals Index. *Library Resource & Technical Services* 37(11): 19–44.

Goldberg, Martin. 1992. CD-ROM Periodical Indexes: Better Evaluation Necessary. *The Indexer* 18(1): 11–15.

Goldstein, Samuel. 1973. Statistical Bibliography and Library Periodical Literature. 1972 Abstracting, Indexing, and Coverage of Library and Information Science Periodicals, Part 4. *Current Awareness—Library Literature* 2(4): 3–13.

Griffith, Belver C., Howard D. White, Carl M. Drott, and Jerry D. Saye. 1986. Test of Methods for Evaluating Bibliographic Databases: An Analysis of the National Library of Medicine's Handling of Literatures in the Medical Behavioral Sciences. *Journal of the American Society for Information Science* 37(4): 261–70.

Grzeszkiewicz, Anna, and Craig A. Hawbaker. 1996. Investigating a Full-Text Journal Database: A Case of Detection. *Database* 19(6): 59–62.

Harbourt, Anna M., Lou Knecht, and Betsy L. Humphreys. 1995. Structured Abstracts in MEDLINE, 1989–1991. *Bulletin of the Medical Library Association* 83(2): 190–95.

Harter, Stephen P., Thomas E. Nisonger, and Aiwei Weng. 1993. Semantic Relationships Between Cited and Citing Articles in Library and Information Science Journals. *Journal of the American Society for Information Science* 44(9): 543–52.

Hartley, James, and Matthew Sydes. 1996. Which Layout Do You Prefer? An Analysis of Readers' Preference for Different Typographic Layouts of Structured Abstracts. *Journal of Information Science* 22(1): 27–37.

Hartley, James, Matthew Sydes, and Anthony Blurton. 1996. Obtaining Information Accurately and Quickly: Are Structured Abstracts More Efficient? *Journal of Information Science* 22(5): 349–56.

Hawkins, Donald T. 1999. What is Credible Information? *Online* 23(5): 86-89.

_____. 2001a. Information Science Abstracts: Tracking the Literature of information Science. Part 1: Definition and Map. *Journal of the American Society for Information Science and Technology.* 52(1): 44-53.

_____. 2001b. Setting the Database Record Straight. *Information World Review* No.166: 12-13.

Hawkins, Donald T., and Lynn A. Murray. 1998a. New Publishers for ISA. *Information Today, Inc. Home Page - ISA Editorials.* URL: *http://www.infotoday.com/isa/ed9807.htm.* Accessed July 15, 2001.

_____. 1998b. Synergy, New Journals. *Information Today, Inc. Home Page - ISA Editorials.* URL: *http://www.infotoday.com/isa/ed9808.htm.* Accessed July 15, 2001.

_____. 1998c. Currency. *Information Today, Inc. Home Page - ISA Editorials.* URL: *http://www.infotoday.com/isa/ed9810.htm.* Accessed July 15, 2001.

_____. 1998d. Core Journals. *Information Today, Inc. Home Page - ISA Editorials.* URL: *http://www.infotoday.com/isa/ed9812.htm.* Accessed July 15, 2001.

_____. 1999a. Looking Back, Looking Ahead. *Information Today, Inc. Home Page - ISA Editorials.* URL: *http://www.infotoday.com/isa/ed9901.htm.* Accessed July 15, 2001.

_____. 1999b. Currency, Relevance and Quality. *Information Today, Inc. Home Page - ISA Editorials.* URL: *http://www.infotoday.com/isa/ed9904.htm.* Accessed July 15, 2001.

_____. 2000a. ISA for the New Century! *Information Today, Inc. Home Page - ISA Editorials* 35(1). URL: *http://www.infotoday.com/isa/ed0001.htm.* Accessed July 15, 2001.

_____. 2000b. New features Added. *Information Today, Inc. Home Page - ISA Editorials* 35(7). URL: *http://www.infotoday.com/isa/edv35n7.htm.* Accessed July 15, 2001.

_____. 2000c. Special E-Journals Issue! *Information Today, Inc. Home Page - ISA Editorials* 35(8). URL: *http://www.infotoday.com/isa/edv35n8.htm.* Accessed July 15, 2001.

_____. 2000d. Letter to the Editor. *Online Information Review* 24(1): 93-95.

Haynes, R. Brian. 1987. A Proposal for More Informative Abstracts of Clinical Articles. *Annals of Internal Medicine* (106): 598–604.

————. 1993. More Informative Abstracts: Current Status and Evaluation. *Journal of Clinical Epidemiology* 46(7): 595–97.

Haynes, R. Brian, Cynthia D. Mulrow, Edward J. Hutn, Douglas G. Altman, and Martin J. Gardner. 1996. More Informative Abstracts Revisited. *The Cleft Palate–Craniofacial Journal* 33(1): 1–9.

Heller, M. B. 1990. Structured Abstracts. *Annals of Internal Medicine* 113(9): 722.

Hern, Elizabeth. 2001. Strong Belief. *Information World Review*. June, No. 110, p. 10.

Hernon, Peter, and Cheryl Metoyer-Duran. 1992. Literature Reviews and Inaccurate Referencing: An Exploratory Study of Academic Librarians. *College & Research Libraries* 53(5): 499–512.

Hightower, Christy, and Robert Schwarzwalder. 1991. A Comprehensive Look at Materials Science Databases. *Database* 14(2): 42–53.

Hitti, Angela. 1995. Secondary Publishing in Changing Times: Profile of Cambridge Scientific Abstracts. *Publishing Research Quarterly* 11(3): 80–82.

Holt, Janifer, and Karen A. Schmidt. 1995. CARL UnCover2 or Faxon Finder? A Comparison of Articles and Journals in CARL UnCover2 and Faxon Finder. *Library Resources & Technical Services* 39(3): 221–28.

Hood, William, and Conception S. Wilson. 1994. Indexing Terms in the LISA Database on CD-ROM. *Information Processing & Management* 30(3): 327–42.

Hurst, Jill Ann. 1999. *DIALOGWeb/FT*. Woodstock, GA: Hermograph Press.

———. 2000. DIALOGWeb Under the Microscope. *EContent*, 23(3): 35–38.

Jacsó, Péter. 1989. Directory of Library and Information Professionals on CD-ROM. *Laserdisk Professional* 2(4): 63–73.

———. 1991a. Coverage and Accessibility in Ulrich's Plus and EBSCO-CD. *The Serials Librarian* 18(1/2): 1–35.

———. 1991b. Data Transfer Capabilities of CD-ROM Software–Part 1. *CD-ROM Professional* 4(2): 63–66.

———. 1991c. Data Transfer Capabilities of CD-ROM Software–Part 2. *CD-ROM Professional* 4(3): 61–66.

———. 1992a. *CD-ROM Software, Dataware, and Hardware: Evaluation, Selection, and Installation*. Englewood, CO: Libraries Unlimited.

———. 1992b. What Is in a(n) (Up)date? Currency Test Searching of Databases. *Database* 15(3): 28–33.

———. 1993a. A Proposal for Database "Nutrition and Ingredient" Labeling. *Database* 16(1): 7–9.

———. 1993b. Searching for Skeletons in the Database Cupboard: Part 1. Errors of Omission. *Database* 16(1): 38–49.

———. 1993c. Searching for Skeletons in the Database Cupboard: Part 2. Errors of Commission. *Database* 16(2): 30, 32–36.

———. 1995. Testing the Quality of CD-ROM Databases. In *Electronic Information Delivery: Ensuring Quality and Value,* edited by Reva Basch. Brookfield, VT: Gower, 141–68.

———. 1996. Watching Your Online Bottom Line. *Online* 20(4): 50–51.

———. 1997a. Content Evaluation of Databases. In *Annual Review of Information Science and Technology,* vol. 32, chap. 5, edited by Martha E Williams. Chicago: American Society for Information Science, 231–67.

———. 1997b. Information Science Abstracts. *Link-Up* 14(3): 3, 11.

———. 1997c. Jacsó Drops the Bruno Magli Shoes. *Database* 20(3): 6.

————. 1997d. Péter's Picks and Pans. ASCE's Civil Engineering Database. *Database* 20(5): 80–81, 84–85.

————. 1997e. Péter's Picks and Pans: Information Science Abstracts. *Database* 20(1): 86–87.

————. 1998a. Analyzing the Journal Coverage of Abstracting/Indexing Databases at Variable Aggregate and Analytic Levels. *Library & Information Research* 20(2): 133–51.

————. 1998b. Péter's Picks and Pans: EconLit Index. *Database* 21(6): 70–72.

————. 1998c. Péter's Picks and Pans: Mental Health Abstracts on CD-ROM and Online. *Database* 21(1): 79–82.

————. 1998d. Publishing Textual Databases on the Web. *Information Today* 15(9): 47–48.

————. 1998e. Péter's Picks and Pans: World Databases. *Database* 21(5): 80–82.

————. 1999a. Savvy Searching: Database Currency. *Online Information Review* 23(6): 345–48.

————. 1999b. Savvy Searching Starts with Browsing. *Online & CD-ROM Review* 23(3): 169–72.

————. 1999c. Péter's Picks and Pans: PASCAL. *Database* 22(2): 70.

————. 2000a. Be Savvy! Sometimes the Free Resources Are Better. *Computers in Libraries* 20(5): 56–58.

————. 2000b. Endangered Database Species—December 2000. *Information World Review*. No. 166 (December), p. 72–73.

————. 2000c. Savvy Searching: Accuracy. *Online Information Review* 24(1): 90-93.

————. 2000d. Savvy Searching: Database Source Coverage: Myth and Reality. *Online Information Review* 24(6): 450-453.

————. 2000e Savvy Searching: Digital Journal Lists. *Online Information Review* 24(4): 337-339.

————. 2000f. Encyclopedia of the Orient. *Gale Group Home-Page - Péter's Digital Reference Shelf.* URL:*http://www.galegroup.com/servlet/HTMLFileServlet?imprint=9999&region=7&fileName= reference /archive/200007/orient.html.* Accessed July 15, 2001.

————. 2000g. Bowker's Complete Video Directory. *Gale Group Home-Page - Péter's Digital Reference Shelf.* URL:*http://ww.galegroup.com/servlet/HTMLFileServlet?imprint=9999&region= 7&fileName=reference/archive/200007/bowker.html.* Accessed July 15, 2001.

————.2000h. Péter's Picks and Pans: Davis Free Internet Encyclopedia. *EContent* 23(3): 82-85. See also URL: *http://www2.hawaii.edu/~jacso/extra/picks-pans/davis/davis.html.* Accessed July 15, 2001.

————. 2000i. Péter's Picks and Pans: Population Demographics Database. *EContent* 23(4): 83-86. See also URL: *http://www2.hawaii.edu/~jacso/extra/picks-pans/demographics\demographics.htm.* Accessed July 15, 2001.

————. 2001a. Awesome Library. *Gale Group Home-Page - Péter's Digital Reference Shelf.* URL:*http://www.galegroup.com/servlet/HTMLFileServlet?imprint=9999&region=7& fileName=reference/archive/200103/awesome.html.* Accessed July 15, 2001.

————. 2001b. Péter's Picks and Pans: TheReference. *EContent* 25(3): 89-92. See also URL: *http://www2.hawaii.edu/~jacso/extra/picks-ans/thereference\thereference_files\frame.htm.* Accessed July 15, 2001.

_____. 2001c. Scirus Biz 'R Us - Elsevier's Science Search Engine. 18(6): 34-35. *Information Today* 18(6): 34-35. See also URL: *http://www2.hawaii.edu/~jacso/ extra/infotoday/scirus/scirus.html.* Accessed July 15, 2001.

Jacsó, Péter, and F. Wilfrid Lancaster. 1999. *Build Your Own Database.* Chicago, IL: American Library Association.

Jacsó, Péter, and Judit Tiszai. 1995. Now Featuring ... Movie Databases. *Database* 18(1): 22–24, 26–28, 30–32.

Jaguszewski, Janice M., and Jody L. Kempf. 1995. Four Current Awareness Databases: Coverage and Currency Compared. *Database* 18(1): 33–44.

Johnson, David H., and David R. Bevan. 1996. Structured Abstracts. *Canadian Journal of Anesthesia* 43(1): 1–3.

Johnson, Susan. 1999. Using Information Technology to Improve Collection Management. *Library Computing* 18(2): 98–104.

———. 2000. Personal communication about the thesaurus implementation in ABI/INFORM.

Katritzky, Alan R., Stephen J. Cato, and James A. Deyrup. 1993. Comparison of the Scope, Timeliness, and Quality of Chemical Abstracts from VINITI and CAS. *Journal of Information Science* 19(3): 199–210.

Katz, William A. 1987. *Introduction to Reference Work.* New York: McGraw-Hill.

Killion, Vicki J. 1995. RNdex Top 100: A Quality-filtered Database for Nursing Research. *Medical Reference Services Quarterly* 14(3): 1–11.

Kister, Kenneth F. 1986. *Best Encyclopedias: Guide to General and Specialized Encyclopedias.* Phoenix, AZ: Oryx Press.

Klemmer, E. T., and Gregory. R. Lockhead. 1962. Productivity and Errors in Two Keying Tasks: A Field Study. *Journal of Applied Psychology* 46(6): 401–8.

Koehler, Wallace et al. 2000. A Profile in Statistics of Journal Articles: Fifty Years of American Documentation and the Journal of the American Society for Information Science. Cybermetrics 4(1). URL: *http://www.cindoc.csic.es/cybermetrics/articles/v4i1p3.html.* Accessed July 15, 2001.

Kohl, David F., and Charles H. Davis. 1985. Ratings of Journals by ARL Library Directors and Deans of Library and Information Science Schools. *College & Research Libraries* 46(1): 41–47.

Kulkarni, M., V. K. Gupta, and T. Viswanathan. 1996. An Automatic Index Generation Retrieval System for Bibliographic Databases Developed at the Indian National Scientific Documentation Center. *Program* 30 (January): 65–72.

LaBorie, Tim, Michael Halperin, and Howard D. White. 1985. Library and Information Science Abstracting and Indexing Services: Coverage, Overlap, and Context. *Library & Information Science Research* 7(2): 183–95.

LaGuardia, Cheryl. 1991. Philosopher's Index OnDisc. *CD-ROM Professional* 4(6): 119–20.

Lancaster, F. Wilfrid. 1971. The Evaluation of Published Indexes and Abstract Journals. *Bulletin of Medical Library Association* 59(3): 479–94.

———. 1979. *Information Retrieval Systems: Characteristics, Testing, and Evaluation.* New York: John Wiley.

———. 1991. *Indexing and Abstracting in Theory and Practice.* Champaign, IL: University of Illinois, Graduate School of Library and Information Science.

———. 1998. *Indexing and Abstracting in Theory and Practice.* 2d ed. Champaign, IL: University of Illinois at Urbana–Champaign.

Lavin, M. R. 1998. A Clash of Titans—Comparing America's Most Comprehensive Business Directories. *Database* 21(3): 44–48.

Lawrence, Barbara, and Tony Lenti. 1995. Application of TQM to the Continuous Improvement of Database Production. In *Electronic Information Delivery: Ensuring Quality and Value,* edited by Reva Basch. Brookfield, VT: Gower, 69–87.

Layne, Sara Shatford. 1994. Some Issues in the Indexing of Images. *Journal of the American Society for Information Science* 45(8): 583–88.

Leininger, Kurt. 2000. Interindexer Consistency in PsycINFO. *Journal of Librarianship and Information Science* 32(1): 4–8.

Leonard, Lawrence E. 1977. Inter-Indexer Consistency Studies, 1954–1975: A Review of the Literature and Summary of Study Results. *University of Illinois Graduate School of Library Science Occasional Papers,* no.131.

Markey, Karen. 1984. Interindexer Consistency Tests: A Literature Review and Report of a Test of Consistency in Indexing Visual Materials. *Library & Information Science Research* 6(2): 155–77.

Martin, Sabine, and Günter Bergerhoff. 1991. Chemical Abstracts Online: A Study of the Quality of Controlled Terms. *Journal of Chemical Information and Computer Science* 31(1): 147–52.

Martyn, John, and Margaret Slater. 1964. Test on Abstracts Journals. *Journal of Documentation* 20(4): 212–35.

McCain, Katherine W., Howard White, and Belver C. Griffith. 1987. Comparing Retrieval Performance in Online Data Bases. *Information Processing & Management* 23(6): 539–53.

McCormick, Edith. 1991. Al Aside-Ideas: The Dirty Database Test (Jeffrey Beall). *American Libraries* 22(3): 197.

Milas-Bracovic, Milica, and Jasenka Zajec. 1989. Author Abstracts of Research Articles Published in Scholarly Journals in Croatia (Yugoslavia): An Evaluation. *Libri* 39(4): 303–18.

Miller, Uri. 1996. The Sport Database: Some Comments. *Online & CD-ROM Review* 20(2): 67–74.

Milstead, Jessica L. 1994a. Needs for Research in Indexing. *Journal of the American Society for Information Science* 45(8): 577–582.

———. 1994b. *ASIS Thesaurus of Information Science and Librarianship.* Medford, NJ: Learned Information.

Mintz, Anne P. 1990. Quality Control and the Zen of Database Production. *Online* 14(6): 15–23.

———. 1995. Quality Issues in Information Retrieval: A Publisher Perspective. In *Electronic Information Delivery: Ensuring Quality and Value,* edited by Reva Basch. Brookfield, VT: Gower, 47–58.

Moed, H. F., and M. Vriens. 1989. Possible Inaccuracies Occurring in Citation Analysis. *Journal of Information Science: Principles & Practice* 15(2): 95–107.

Narine, L., D. S. Yee, T. R. Einarson, and A. L. Ilersich. 1991. Quality of Abstracts of Original Research Articles in CMAJ in 1989. *CMAJ* 144(4): 449–53.

Nicholls, Paul. 1998. Great Expectations: A Tale of Two or Three Directories. *Searcher* 6(8): 66–75.

Norton, Nancy Prothro. 1981. Dirty Data: A Call for Quality Control. *Online* 5(1): 40–41.

Ojala, MaryDee. 1992. The Prestige Factor in Electronic Business Journals. *Database* 15(5): 89–92.

O'Neill, Edward T., and Diane Vizine-Goetz. 1988. Quality Control in Online Databases. In *Annual Review of Information Science and Technology*, vol. 23, edited by Martha E. Williams. Amsterdam, the Netherlands: Elsevier Science Publishers for the American Society for Information Science, 125–56.

Orenstein, Ruth M. 1989. The Fullness of Full Text: Survey of Coverage, Currency, and Enhancement of 13 Services. *Database Searcher* 5 (September): 21–27.

———. 1993. "How Full Is Full" Revisited: A Status Report on Searching Full-Text Periodicals. *Database* 16(5): 14–23.

Pagell, Ruth A. 1987. Searching Full-Text Periodicals: How Full Is Full? *Database* 10(5): 33–36.

Pandit, Idrisa. 1993. Citation Errors in Library Literature: A Study of Five Library Science Journals. *Library & Information Science Research* 15(2): 185–98.

Pao, Miranda Lee. 1989. Importance of Quality Data for Bibliometric Research. In: Williams, Martha E. ed. *Proceedings of the 10ᵗʰ National Online Meeting,* edited by Martha E. Williams, May 9–11, 1989. Medford, NJ: Learned Information, 321–27.

Pedersen, Martin. 1992. Texas Schoolbook Massacre: 5,200 Errors Found in 10 History Books. *Publishers Weekly* 239 (March 2): 11.

Pemberton, Jeff. 1983. The Linear File: The Dark Side of Online Information—Dirty Data. *Database* 6(4): 6–8.

Perry, Stephen, and Lutishoor Salisbury. 1995. Access to Information in Both CitaDel and FirstSearch: A Comparative Study of Dissertation Coverage. *Information Technology and Libraries* 14(1): 17–29.

Pollock, J. J., and A. Zamora. 1975. Automatic Abstracting Research at Chemical Abstracts Service. *Journal of Chemical Information and Computer Sciences* 15(4): 226–32.

Quint, Barbara. 1989. Caveat Searcher: Liars, Damned Liars, and Statisticians. *Database Searcher* 5(9): 36–37.

———. 1995. Better Searching Through Better Searcher. In *Electronic Information Delivery: Ensuring Quality and Value,* edited by Reva Basch. Brookfield, VT: Gower, 99–116.

Reich, Phyllis, and Erik J. Biever. 1991. Indexing Consistency: The Input/Output Function of Thesauri. *College & Research Libraries* 52(4): 336–42.

Salager-Meyer, Francoise. 1991. Medical English Abstracts: How Well Are They Structured? *Journal of the American Society for Information Science* 42(7): 528–31.

Sievert, MaryEllen C., and Donald E. Sievert. 1991. Online Searching in Philosophy: A Comparison of Philosopher's Index and FRANCIS. *Online Review* 15(2): 63–76.

Sievert, MaryEllen C., and Mark J. Andrews. 1991. Indexing Consistency in Information Science Abstracts. *Journal of the American Society for Information Science* 42(1): 1–6.

Smith, Linda C. 1981. Citation Analysis. *Library Trends* 30(1): 83–106.

Snow, Bonnie. 1998. Alternative Medicine Information Sources. *Database* 21(3): 18–19.

Sodha, R. J. 1993. Trends in Biomedical Publications: US and Japanese Authors in US Journals and European Journals. *Journal of Information Science* 19(1): 71–73.

Soergel, Dagobert. 1994. Indexing and Retrieval Performance: The Logical Evidence. *Journal of the American Society for Information Science* 45(8): 589–99.

Soremark, Gun. 1990. MEDLINE Versus EMBASE: Comparing Search Quality. *Database* 13(6): 66–67.

Sparck Jones, Karen. 1973. Does Indexing Exhaustivity Matter? *Journal of the American Society for Information Science* 24(6): 313–16.

Sparck Jones, Karen, and C. J. Van Rijsbergen. 1976. Information Retrieval Test Collections. *Journal of Documentation* 32(1): 59–75.

Stieg, Margaret, and Joan L. Atkinson. 1988. Librarianship Online: Old Problems, No New Solutions. *Library Journal* 113(16): 48–59.

Svenonius, Elaine, and Dorothy McGarry. 1993. Objectivity in Evaluating Subject Heading Assignment. *Cataloging & Classification Quarterly* 16(2): 5–40.

Sweetland, James H. 1989. Errors in Bibliographic Citations: A Continuing Problem. *The Library Quarterly* 59(4): 291–304.

Taddio, Anna, Tapas Pain, Frank F. Fassos, Heater Boon, A. Lane Ilersich, and Thomas R. Einarson. 1994. Quality of Non-structured and Structured Abstracts of Original Research Articles in the *British Medical Journal*, the *Canadian Medical Association Journal,* and the *Journal of the American Medical Association. Canadian Medical Association Journal* 150(10): 1,611–15.

Tenopir, Carol. 1982. Evaluation of Database Coverage: A Comparison of Two Methodologies. *Online Review* 6(5): 423–41.

———. 1992. Evaluation Criteria for Online, CD-ROM. *Library Journal* 117(4): 66–67.

———. 1995. Priorities of Quality. In *Electronic Information Delivery: Ensuring Quality and Value,* edited by Reva Basch. Brookfield, VT: Gower, 119–39.

———. 1997. Reading Vendor Literature. *Library Journal* 122 (June 1): 35–36.

Tenopir, Carol, and Gerald Lundeen. 1988. *Managing Your Information.* New York: Neal-Schuman.

Tenopir, Carol, and Péter Jacsó. 1993. Quality of Abstracts. *Online* 17(3): 44, 46–48.

Tenopir, Carol, and Ralf Neufang. 1995. Electronic Reference Options: Tracking the Changes. *Online* 19(4): 67–73.

Thomas, Sarah E. 1990. Bibliographic Control and Agriculture. *Library Trends* 38(3): 542–61.

Tjoumas, Renee, and Virgil L. P. Blake. 1992. Faculty Perceptions of the Professional Journal Literature: Quo Vadis? *Journal of Education for Library and Information Science* 33(3): 173–94.

Tonta, Yasar. 1991. A Study of Indexing Consistency Between Library of Congress and British Library Catalogers. *Library Resources & Technical Services* 35(2): 177–85.

Turner, James M. 1995. Comparing User-Assigned Terms with Indexer-Assigned Terms for Storage and Retrieval of Moving Images: Research Result. In *Proceedings of the 58th Annual Meeting of the American Society for Information Science,* vol. 32, edited by Tom Kimney. Medford, NJ: Information Today, 9–12.

Turtle, Mary R., and William Robinson. 1974. The Relationship Between Time Lag and Place of Publication in Library and Information Science Abstracts and Library Literature. *RQ* 14(1): 28–31.

Ubico, Rafael E., John A. Baily, and Pamela J. Weaver. 1995. Statistical Analysis of the TULSA Database, 1965–1994. *Publishing Research Quarterly* 11(3): 138–44.

Van Camp, Anne J. 1993. Online Sources for Alternative Medicine Information. *Database* 16(5): 100–103.

Watson, Maureen Martin, and Richard Perrin. 1994. A Comparison of CINAHL and MEDLINE CD-ROM in Four Allied Health Areas. *Bulletin of the Medical Library Association* 82(2): 214–16.

Way, Harold E. 1988. The BRS 1988 Annual Meeting. *Database Searcher* 4(5): 15–22.

Weston, E. Paige, and Diane S. Lauderdale. 1988. How Do We Learn What a Database Includes? A Case Study Using Psychology Dissertation. *RQ* 28(1): 35–41.

Whitney, Gretchen. 1990. *Language Distribution in Databases: An Analysis and Evaluation.* Metuchen, NJ: Scarecrow Press, 379.

———. 1992. Access to Third World Science in International Scientific and Technical Bibliographic Databases. *Scientometrics* 23(1): 201–19.

———. 1993. Patterns of Authorship in Major Bibliographic Databases: The European Region. *Scientometrics* 26(2): 275–92.

Williams, Martha E. 1990. Highlights of the Online Database Industry and the Quality of Information and Data. In *Proceedings of the 11th National Online Meeting,* edited by Martha E. Williams, May 1–3, 1990. Medford, NJ: Learned Information, 1–4.

Williams, Martha E., and Laurence Lannom. 1981. Lack of Standardization of the Journal Title Data Element in Databases. *Journal of the American Society for Information Science* 32(3): 229–33.

Yannakoudakis, E. J., and D. Fawthrop. 1983. The Rules of Spelling Errors. *Information Processing & Management* 19(2): 87–99.

Index

About the Author

Péter Jacsó is the chair of the Library and Information Science Program of the Information and Computer Sciences Department of the University of Hawaii. He was selected as the winner of the American Society for Information Science (ASIS) Outstanding Information Science Teacher Award, 2000. In 1998 he was the recipient of the Louis Shores—Oryx Press Award from ALA's Reference and User Services Association (RUSA) for excellence in reviewing databases, and also received the Pratt–Severn Award from Pratt Institute School of Information and Library Science and the Association of Library and Information Science Educators (ALISE). He won UMI's Excellence in Writing Award previously.

Péter Jacsó has been writing his columns for *Information Today*, *Computers in Libraries*, *Online*, *DATABASE, EContent*, and *Online Information*, and has a digital column, "Péter's Digital Reference Shelf," hosted by the Gale Group. He is a regular speaker at national and international conferences.